Illuminate
Publishing

Pearson BTEC National

Applied Psychology

Book 1

Certificate Units

Cara Flanagan ▪ Rob Liddle
Advisor: Mark Walsh

Acknowledgements

The team who manage and produce this book are simply the best.

Illuminate Publishing, with the psychology list headed by the unique Rick Jackman, and assisted by Clare Jackman, Peter Burton, Saskia Burton and Vikki Mann, represent the best in educational publishing – always looking out for their authors and also for the people who buy the books.

Nic Watson, our editor, puts nothing short of love into ensuring our final product is as perfect as can be. We couldn't do it without her.

The third part of our team is design, fitting the text and pictures on each page. The initial ideas came from the gloriously talented Nigel Harriss and then Sarah Clifford of Kamae Design had the job of implementing this and has done a fabulous job of it.

Finally Cara, the lead author, owes much to Rob for the huge amount of work he has done (and always with such grace) and to the invaluable advice from Mark.

A very special thank you to all of you.

Endorsement Statement

In order to ensure that this resource offers high-quality support for the associated Pearson qualification, it has been through a review process by the awarding body. This process confirms that this resource fully covers the teaching and learning content of the specification or part of a specification at which it is aimed. It also confirms that it demonstrates an appropriate balance between the development of subject skills, knowledge and understanding, in addition to preparation for assessment.

Endorsement does not cover any guidance on assessment activities or processes (e.g. practice questions or advice on how to answer assessment questions), included in the resource nor does it prescribe any particular approach to the teaching or delivery of a related course.

While the publishers have made every attempt to ensure that advice on the qualification and its assessment is accurate, the official specification and associated assessment guidance materials are the only authoritative source of information and should always be referred to for definitive guidance.

Pearson examiners have not contributed to any sections in this resource relevant to examination papers for which they have responsibility.

Examiners will not use endorsed resources as a source of material for any assessment set by Pearson. Endorsement of a resource does not mean that the resource is required to achieve this Pearson qualification, nor does it mean that it is the only suitable material available to support the qualification, and any resource lists produced by the awarding body shall include this and other appropriate resources.

The authors

Cara has written many books for A Level Psychology, and she speaks at and organises student conferences. In addition to books, she is senior editor of *Psychology Review*. In a previous life she was a teacher probably for more years than you have been alive and also an examiner for an equally long time. Her spare time (what there is of it) involves travelling with her husband and/or children (all now 25+). She lives in the Highlands of Scotland (despite being American by birth) and loves a long walk in the mountains and night in a bothy.

Rob was an A Level Psychology teacher for more than 20 years, before turning to writing. He ventured back into teaching again recently and would like to give a big shout out to his ex-colleagues at Winstanley College. In his spare moments, Rob likes nothing better than to pluck away skill-lessly at his guitar. He is enthusiastically looking forward to *Frozen 2* coming out, even though his granddaughters couldn't care less.

Mark is a teacher, writer and mental health worker when he's not baking bread or playing football. He currently works with students in further and higher education teaching sociological psychology and providing mental health support. He has written many textbooks, course specifications and exam papers over the last 25 years, usually whilst listening to long, slow albums of electronic music.

Published in 2019 by Illuminate Publishing Ltd, P.O. Box 1160, Cheltenham, Gloucestershire GL50 9RW

Orders: Please visit www.illuminatepublishing.com or email sales@illuminatepublishing.com

© Cara Flanagan, Rob Liddle, Mark Walsh

The moral rights of the authors have been asserted.

British Library Cataloguing in Publication Data

A catalogue record for this book is available from the British Library

ISBN 978-1-912820-04-7

Printed by Cambrian Printers, Aberystwyth

06.19

The publisher's policy is to use papers that are natural, renewable and recyclable products made from wood grown in sustainable forests. The logging and manufacturing processes are expected to conform to the environmental regulations of the country of origin.

Every effort has been made to contact copyright holders of material produced in this book. Great care has been taken by the authors and publisher to ensure that either formal permission has been granted for the use of copyright material reproduced, or that copyright material has been used under the provision of fairdealing guidelines in the UK – specifically that it has been used sparingly, solely for the purpose of criticism and review, and has been properly acknowledged. If notified, the publisher will be pleased to rectify any errors or omissions at the earliest opportunity.

Editor: Nic Watson

Design: Nigel Harriss

Layout: Kamae Design

Contents

References

A full set of references are available for download from the Illuminate Publishing website.
Please visit www.illuminatepublishing.com/btecpsychreferences1

National certificate in Applied Psychology BTEC Level 3

Structure of the qualification

Unit	Unit title	Type	How assessed	GLH Guided learning hours	TQT Total qualification time (an estimate of the total amount of time to complete and show achievement for the unit)
1	Psychological approaches and applications	Mandatory	External exam 1.5 hours 72 marks	90	270 hours This means 90 hours should be spent across both units: Unit 1: Revising and taking the exam.
2	Conducting psychological research	Mandatory and synoptic	Internal	90	Unit 2: Writing three reports and conducting the pilot study.

How to use this book

Unit 1 and Unit 2 both open with a spread which has:

- A set of questions to start you thinking about the content to come.
- A detailed table of contents.

Content areas or learning aims

Unit 1 is divided into content areas A, B and C (because it is externally assessed).

Unit 2 is divided into learning aims A, B, C and D (because it is internally assessed).

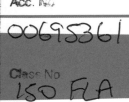

Acc. No
00695361

Class No
150 FLA

Main spreads

The specification content is covered on spreads such as the one on the facing page.

They all contain a similar pattern of boxes.

Extra material

Unit 1

Content areas A+B and C end with:

Summaries to revise from.

Multiple-choice questions to test yourself.

Assessment guidance to help supply the right material in your exam answers.

Revision guidance.

Practice questions, answers and feedback to see how student answers are marked.

Unit 2

Learning aims A, B and C+D end with:

Assessment guidance to guide you in writing your internally assessed report.

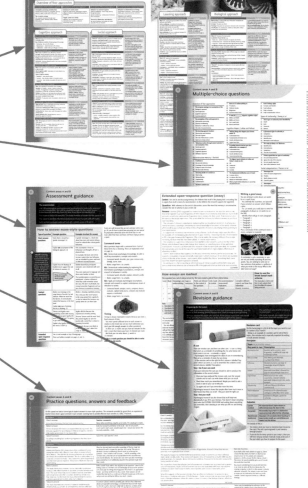

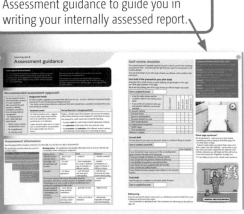

Description

Assessment objective 1 (AO1) is concerned with your ability to report ***detailed*** descriptions of psychological knowledge and demonstrate your ***understanding*** of this knowledge.

We have generally presented the AO1 material just on the left-hand side of each spread, though sometimes it is on both sides.

Evaluation

Assessment objective 3 (AO3) is concerned with your ability to ***evaluate*** (***assess***, ***analyse***) the concepts and studies you have learned about.

On most spreads in this book we have presented some AO3 material on the right-hand side. Some topics don't require evaluation so there isn't any on the spread.

Special note

Each evaluation point is divided into three **PET** paragraphs because this is a great way to ensure you explain your point well:

1. **POINT** State the point simply.
2. **ELABORATION** The point is now Explained, using Evidence and/or Examples.
3. **THIS** shows that ... Finish with a conclusion often beginning 'This suggests' or 'This shows' or 'Therefore ...'.

That's your PET evaluation.

A beginning

Each spread begins with something we hope will grab your interest – it represents the nub of the topic to be studied on the spread.

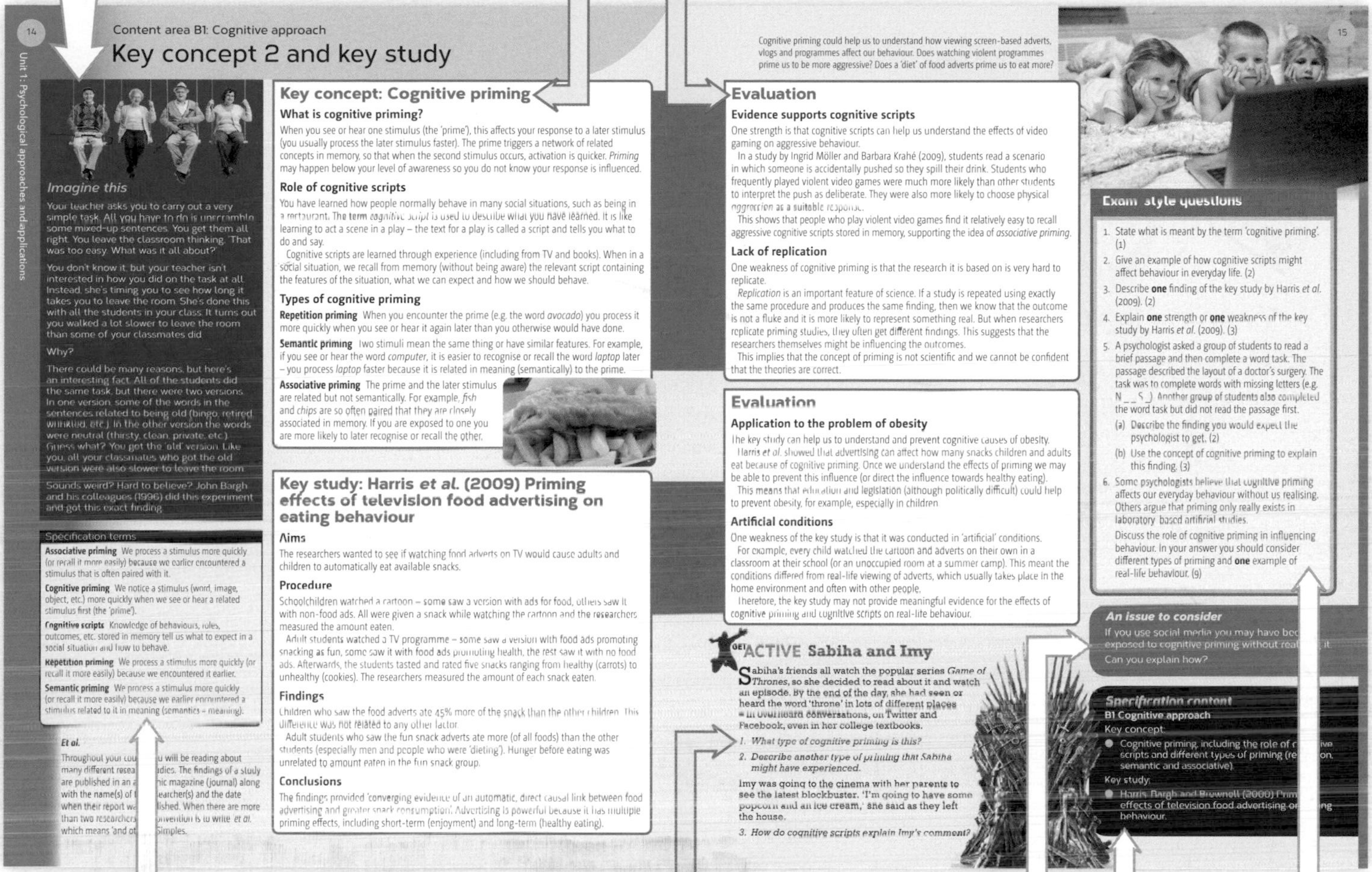

14

Unit 1: Psychological approaches and applications

Content area B1: Cognitive approach

Key concept 2 and key study

Imagine this

Your teacher asks you to carry out a very simple task. All you have to do is unscramble some mixed-up sentences. You get them all right. You leave the classroom thinking, 'That was too easy. What was it all about?'

You don't know it, but your teacher isn't interested in how you did on the task at all. Instead, she's timing you to see how long it takes you to leave the room. She's done this with all the students in your class. It turns out you walked a lot slower to leave the room than some of your classmates did.

Why?

There could be many reasons, but here's an interesting fact. All of the students did the same task, but there were two versions. In one version, some of the words in the sentences related to being old (bingo, retired, wrinkled, etc.). In the other version the words were neutral (thirsty, clean, private, etc.). Guess what? You got the 'old' version. Like you, all your classmates who got the old version were also slower to leave the room.

Sounds weird? Hard to believe? John Bargh and his colleagues (1996) did this experiment and got this exact finding.

Specification terms

Associative priming We process a stimulus more quickly (or recall it more easily) because we earlier encountered a stimulus that is often paired with it.

Cognitive priming We notice a stimulus (word, image, object, etc.) more quickly when we see or hear a related stimulus first (the 'prime').

Cognitive scripts Knowledge of behaviours, roles, outcomes, etc. stored in memory tell us what to expect in a social situation and how to behave.

Repetition priming We process a stimulus more quickly (or recall it more easily) because we encountered it earlier.

Semantic priming We process a stimulus more quickly (or recall it more easily) because we earlier encountered a stimulus related to it in meaning (semantics = meaning).

Et al.

Throughout your cou… u will be reading about many different resea… dies. The findings of a study are published in an a… ic magazine (journal) along with the name(s) of t… earcher(s) and the date when their report wa… lished. When there are more than two researchers… nvention is to write *et al.* which means 'and ot… Simples.

Key concept: Cognitive priming

What is cognitive priming?

When you see or hear one stimulus (the 'prime'), this affects your response to a later stimulus (you usually process the later stimulus faster). The prime triggers a network of related concepts in memory, so that when the second stimulus occurs, activation is quicker. *Priming* may happen below your level of awareness so you do not know your response is influenced.

Role of cognitive scripts

You have learned how people normally behave in many social situations, such as being in a restaurant. The term *cognitive script* is used to describe what you have learned. It is like learning to act a scene in a play – the text for a play is called a script and tells you what to do and say.

Cognitive scripts are learned through experience (including from TV and books). When in a social situation, we recall from memory (without being aware) the relevant script containing the features of the situation, what we can expect and how we should behave.

Types of cognitive priming

Repetition priming When you encounter the prime (e.g. the word *avocado*) you process it more quickly when you see or hear it again later than you otherwise would have done.

Semantic priming Two stimuli mean the same thing or have similar features. For example, if you see or hear the word *computer*, it is easier to recognise or recall the word *laptop* later – you process *laptop* faster because it is related in meaning (semantically) to the prime.

Associative priming The prime and the later stimulus are related but not semantically. For example, *fish* and *chips* are so often paired that they are closely associated in memory. If you are exposed to one you are more likely to later recognise or recall the other.

Key study: Harris *et al.* (2009) Priming effects of television food advertising on eating behaviour

Aims

The researchers wanted to see if watching food adverts on TV would cause adults and children to automatically eat available snacks.

Procedure

Schoolchildren watched a cartoon – some saw a version with ads for food, others saw it with non-food ads. All were given a snack while watching the cartoon and the researchers measured the amount eaten.

Adult students watched a TV programme – some saw a version with food ads promoting snacking as fun, some saw it with food ads promoting health, the rest saw it with no food ads. Afterwards, the students tasted and rated five snacks ranging from healthy (carrots) to unhealthy (cookies). The researchers measured the amount of each snack eaten.

Findings

Children who saw the food adverts ate 45% more of the snack than the other children. This difference was not related to any other factor.

Adult students who saw the fun snack adverts ate more (of all foods) than the other students (especially men and people who were 'dieting'). Hunger before eating was unrelated to amount eaten in the fun snack group.

Conclusions

The findings provided 'converging evidence of an automatic, direct causal link between food advertising and greater snack consumption'. Advertising is powerful because it has multiple priming effects, including short-term (enjoyment) and long-term (healthy eating).

15

Cognitive priming could help us to understand how viewing screen-based adverts, vlogs and programmes affect our behaviour. Does watching violent programmes prime us to be more aggressive? Does a 'diet' of food adverts prime us to eat more?

Evaluation

Evidence supports cognitive scripts

One strength is that cognitive scripts can help us understand the effects of video gaming on aggressive behaviour.

In a study by Ingrid Möller and Barbara Krahé (2009), students read a scenario in which someone is accidentally pushed so they spill their drink. Students who frequently played violent video games were much more likely than other students to interpret the push as deliberate. They were also more likely to choose physical aggression as a suitable response.

This shows that people who play violent video games find it relatively easy to recall aggressive cognitive scripts stored in memory, supporting the idea of *associative priming*.

Lack of replication

One weakness of cognitive priming is that the research it is based on is very hard to replicate.

Replication is an important feature of science. If a study is repeated using exactly the same procedure and produces the same finding, then we know that the outcome is not a fluke and it is more likely to represent something real. But when researchers replicate priming studies, they often get different findings. This suggests that the researchers themselves might be influencing the outcomes.

This implies that the concept of priming is not scientific and we cannot be confident that the theories are correct.

Evaluation

Application to the problem of obesity

The key study can help us to understand and prevent cognitive causes of obesity.

Harris *et al.* showed that advertising can affect how many snacks children and adults eat because of cognitive priming. Once we understand the effects of priming we may be able to prevent this influence (or direct the influence towards healthy eating).

This means that education and legislation (although politically difficult) could help to prevent obesity, for example, especially in children.

Artificial conditions

One weakness of the key study is that it was conducted in 'artificial' conditions.

For example, every child watched the cartoon and adverts on their own in a classroom at their school (or an unoccupied room at a summer camp). This meant the conditions differed from real-life viewing of adverts, which usually takes place in the home environment and often with other people.

Therefore, the key study may not provide meaningful evidence for the effects of cognitive priming and cognitive scripts on real-life behaviour.

GET ACTIVE **Sabiha and Imy**

Sabiha's friends all watch the popular series *Game of Thrones*, so she decided to read about it and watch an episode. By the end of the day, she had seen or heard the word 'throne' in lots of different places – in overheard conversations, on Twitter and Facebook, even in her college textbooks.

1. *What type of cognitive priming is this?*
2. *Describe another type of priming that Sabiha might have experienced.*

Imy was going to the cinema with her parents to see the latest blockbuster. 'I'm going to have some popcorn and an ice cream,' she said as they left the house.

3. *How do cognitive scripts explain Imy's comment?*

Exam-style questions

1. State what is meant by the term 'cognitive priming'. (1)
2. Give an example of how cognitive scripts might affect behaviour in everyday life. (2)
3. Describe **one** finding of the key study by Harris *et al.* (2009). (2)
4. Explain **one** strength or **one** weakness of the key study by Harris *et al.* (2009). (3)
5. A psychologist asked a group of students to read a brief passage and then complete a word task. The passage described the layout of a doctor's surgery. The task was to complete words with missing letters (e.g. N _ _ S _). Another group of students also completed the word task but did not read the passage first.
   (a) Describe the finding you would expect the psychologist to get. (2)
   (b) Use the concept of cognitive priming to explain this finding. (3)
6. Some psychologists believe that cognitive priming affects our everyday behaviour without us realising. Others argue that priming only really exists in laboratory based artificial studies.
   Discuss the role of cognitive priming in influencing behaviour. In your answer you should consider different types of priming and **one** example of real-life behaviour. (9)

An issue to consider

If you use social media you may have bee… exposed to cognitive priming without real… it. Can you explain how?

Specification content

B1 Cognitive approach

Key concept:

- Cognitive priming, including the role of c… scripts and different types of priming (re… semantic and associative).

Key study:

- Harris, Bargh and Brownell (2009) Prim… effects of television food advertising o… behaviour.

Specification terms

We have defined the terms in the specification box for this spread. Other terms are defined in the index/glossary starting on page 130.

Application

Assessment objective 2 (AO2) is concerned with being able to ***apply*** your psychological knowledge and evaluation.

On each spread there is at least one '***Get active***' which gives you a chance to practise this AO2 skill of application.

In addition many of the topics you study are applied and therefore involve AO2.

An issue to consider

An opportunity to reflect on the issues discussed on the spread.

Specification content

Tells you what you are required to study on this topic.

Exam-style questions

Questions similar to those in the exam provide some exam practice.

In Unit 2 these boxes are called **Assessment practice**, and aim to help you practise skills for writing your internally-assessed reports.

What are assessment objectives?

At the end of your studies you hope to have gained a qualification – this means someone has to assess your work.

To assist this process there are three assessment objectives (AOs): AO1, AO2 and AO3.

The course is designed so you can include all these AOs in what you learn. Each involves slightly different skills:

- AO1 involves reporting the knowledge coherently and including key terminology (details).
- AO2 involves PET skills (see top right).
- AO3 requires you to use what you have learned to explain a real-world situation.

What is psychology?

Psychologists study everything about people – and what could be more interesting than people? Just look in any newspaper or on Facebook – full of stories about people's behaviour.

These stories tell us about what people are doing and try to explain why they do the things they do – for example, reporting that someone had been married for 60 years, and offering an explanation about why their marriage was so successful. Or reporting that a person had committed a terrorist act and trying to explain that.

But psychology is more than just everyday interest in people...

Studying people (and animals).

Health psychology

Criminal and forensic psychology

Child psychology

Sport psychology

... Psychology is a science

This means it is a systematic investigation of what people do and why. This systematic investigation involves two things:

1. Developing theories to explain why people do things. In Unit 1 you will be studying the main approaches (theories) in psychology.

2. Conducting research studies to collect evidence of what people actually do. In Unit 2 you will be studying the research process.

Science is not perfect. Science takes small steps towards gradually getting at the 'truth'. This is where evaluation comes in – at all times scientists must question and retest their ideas.

But science is more than knowledge and evaluation...

... Science is applied

We depend on science to govern our world. Without science we could not develop safe and effective methods to treat disease, build bridges or buildings that don't fall down, try to forecast dangerous weather conditions, develop successful methods to deal with criminal behaviour and so on.

Psychological theory and research have a very large number of applications.

→ **Physical health** – advising the medical profession about, for example, how to best explain treatments to patients so they will remember what to do.

If you go on to study BTEC Level 3 Extended certificate in Psychology, you will study **Health psychology**.

→ **Mental health** – developing treatments for depression or anorexia and so on. This involves testing both psychological therapies and physical treatments such as the use of drugs.

If you go on to study BTEC Level 3 Extended certificate in Psychology, you have the option to study **Psychopathology** which is concerned with mental health.

The following three branches of psychology are also options for the extended certificate.

→ **Criminal and forensic psychology** Theories and approaches in psychology are applied to explain why some people become criminals. Psychological approaches are also used to develop successful methods to reduce reoffending and to research strategies to help the police solve crimes.

→ **Child psychology** is concerned with explaining how and why people change as they develop from birth through to adolescence.

→ **Sport psychology** Any sportsperson will tell you that winning is all in the mind. Yes, you do have to have certain skills but in the end it is the winning mindset that makes the difference between success and failure.

Professions using psychology

The BTEC course is a vocational one – which means it is concerned with the world of work. Therefore, a focus of the course is how the academic study of psychology is applied to the world of work. Someone who is a professional psychologist is likely to have a degree in psychology and then has gone on to do a postgraduate degree.

On the left we have mentioned some of these vocational areas, such as **criminal and forensic psychology** and **sport psychology** but there are jobs in these fields (and the ones further down this page) that don't require a degree in psychology or even a degree, but do benefit from knowledge of psychology, such as the ones below:

- Healthcare practitioner (nurse, radiographer, dietician, paramedic, physiotherapist, social care worker).
- Social worker.
- Teacher (understanding cognitive development).
- Counsellor (bereavement, drugs).
- Chaplain.
- Town planner.
- Police (dealing with people, not just crime).
- Crime scene investigator.
- Working with animals (zoo keeper, veterinarian, trainer).
- Law (solicitor, judge, court clerk).
- Military psychologist.
- Sports coach.
- Advertising and marketing.

Specialist branches of psychology

Clinical psychology

Psychologists are often confused with psychiatrists – a psychiatrist is first of all qualified as a medical doctor and then specialises in psychiatry. Psychiatrists study psychological disorders, diagnose patients and provide treatments.

Clinical psychologists, counselling psychologists and other therapists are concerned with health issues – both physical and mental (psychopathology). Like psychiatrists, they may research, diagnose and treat clients. However, only a psychiatrist can prescribe medicine.

Educational psychology

Educational psychologists may be involved in designing, implementing and evaluating educational programmes for children with autism or dyslexia. They may also advise on how to deal with problem behaviour and may work directly with children who challenge the educational system. They are often involved in using psychological tests, such as intelligence tests, to help diagnose educational or behavioural problems.

Organisational psychology

Also sometimes called industrial psychology, occupational psychology or business psychology – using psychological theory and research in the world of commerce, addressing the needs of employers, employees and consumers. An organisational psychologist might help human resources departments to interview applicants and find the best person–organisation fit. An organisational psychologist might also advise on strategies to improve sales by addressing customer needs or how to assess consumer satisfaction. The 'organisation' does not have to be commercial – the focus of the organisational psychologist is on how any organisation functions.

Environmental psychology

Environmental psychology studies the interaction between people and their environment, i.e. their surroundings. The physical and human environment affects our behaviour, feelings, health and performance. Environmental psychologists might advise on the design of cities or buildings or office work spaces, including schools and hospitals as well as businesses. They are also concerned with ways to encourage people to care more for the environment.

Research psychology

Many psychologists work in universities, teaching students but also pursuing their own research interests.

Any job involving people involves psychology – even **mind reading**. But psychology does not teach you to actually read minds, it teaches you about what people are likely to think and do.

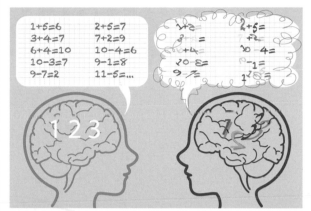

Dyscalculia – trouble with numbers. Perhaps a psychologist can help.

What's the ethics of using psychology to boost sales or win more votes? All practising psychologists must be registered with the British Psychological Society (BPS) and must show respect, competence, responsibility and integrity. So they can use psychology to make more money as long as they behave ethically in doing so.

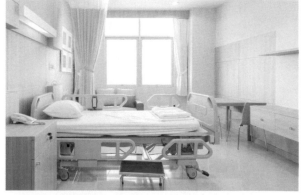

Designed by a psychologist? Research shows people recover more quickly if they have a nice view from their hospital room (Ulrich 1984).

Unit 1

Psychological approaches and applications

What is happening in these people's heads?

What is going on in their bodies?

How is their behaviour affecting each other?

How have their past experiences affected them?

There are so many different ways of explaining the same behaviour – what is the best approach to take?

Contents

Read important advice on assessment and revision before you begin!

Overview of four approaches

Some people call this addiction

Why do people become addicted? This is a question that psychologists would very much like to answer. There are lots of theories and lots of disagreement. Addiction is a behaviour and like all behaviours it can be explained from different points of view (or approaches, as we call them in this unit).

The people in the image above may well be addicted to their phones (are you?). Think about these questions:

- Is it possible to *think* in an 'addicted' way? How?

- Is there a *social* aspect to being addicted? What is it?

- Can you *learn* to be addicted? How?

- Is addiction *biological*? Is there something happening in the brain?

Specification terms

Central nervous system Consists of the brain and spinal cord, where complex decisions are made.

Computer analogy The human mind can be compared to a computer with input, processing and output stages.

Culture Refers to the norms and values that exist within any group of people.

Evolution The changes in inherited characteristics in a biological population over successive generations.

Genes Inherited DNA with instructions for building physical characteristics that influence behaviour. (See also page 30.)

Imitation Copying behaviour of others (called 'models'). (See also page 28.)

Information processing Behaviour can be understood in terms of information flowing through the cognitive (mental) system in a series of stages.

Learned response A behaviour acquired through conditioning, either association (classical) or rewards/punishments (operant).

Neurochemistry Relating to chemicals in the brain that regulate psychological functioning. (See also page 34.)

Observation Actively attending to and watching (or listening to) the behaviour of others (models).

Social context Influences from other people, either individually or in groups.

Assumptions of the cognitive approach

Information processing and behaviour

The word *cognitive* means mental processes. The cognitive approach views humans as processors of information – they take information in and blend it together to come up with new thoughts. Our minds use internal mental processes such as reasoning and remembering, which work together to enable us to make sense of the world and respond to it.

Psychologists in the 1950s created a model (like a theory) to explain what happens to information from the environment. At each stage 'something happens' to the information (i.e. it is processed). These processes occur together and work cooperatively. For example, when you see a dog you notice it (perception), you focus on it to the exclusion of other things (attention), you recognise it (memory) and you can even name it (language).

The computer analogy

Computers are also information processors, so it is natural for cognitive psychologists to compare the mind to a computer. Computers and humans process information through three basic stages. Information goes into the system (input), it is changed and/or stored (processed) and then it is used to respond to the environment (output).

Cognitive psychology uses several concepts borrowed from computing. The brain is our central processing unit (the 'hardware') and it codes information to change it from one format to another (the 'software'). This approach to understanding the mind and behaviour has helped to develop artificial intelligence (AI).

Assumptions of the social approach

Behaviour in a social context

The word 'social' means other members of your species. Humans are 'social animals', so social psychologists believe behaviour is best understood by considering the influence of other people. For example, have you ever 'gone along' with a group of friends just because you didn't want to be the odd one out? Perhaps you had a different view from everyone else, but still outwardly agreed with them. *Conforming* is one way in which *social context* affects our behaviour.

This pressure can be so powerful other people do not even have to be physically present – we just have to think about how others behave. Many social psychologists believe that social situations are the biggest influence on behaviour rather than an individual's disposition (their personality).

People, culture and society

Behaviour can also be understood and explained in terms of wider society or *culture*. Some psychologists believe there are two broad types of culture: *individualist* and *collectivist*.

In individualist cultures (e.g. UK and USA) the main priority is the needs of the individual person. So what really matters is that we can achieve our potential and goals in life. For example, two people who want to share their lives together are expected to be 'in love' – the important thing is their individual happiness.

In collectivist cultures (e.g. China and India), people prefer to prioritise their family and community before their own needs and wants. In such cultures, people tend to seek partners approved by their family, so being 'in love' is less important.

GET ACTIVE Cycling

Norman Triplett (1898) found that children would wind fishing reels much faster when competing against each other than when they did it alone (even when they were told to wind as quickly as they could). However, interestingly some of the children consistently performed worse against a partner than when alone.

*Choose **one** assumption from the cognitive approach and **one** from the social approach. Explain how these assumptions relate to this scenario.*

Assumptions of the learning approach

Behaviour is a learned response to environmental stimuli

Things in the environment bring about learning – if you touch a frying pan that has just been on the hob, you get hurt and you learn not to do that again. If you smile when you ask a favour you may find you are more likely to get what you want, so you learn to do that again.

Classical conditioning The word *conditioning* means 'learning'. Ivan Pavlov (1927) noticed that his laboratory dogs salivated when they heard a door opening because they learned to associate that noise with the arrival of food. *Classical conditioning* is learning through association.

Operant conditioning Burrhus Frederic Skinner (1938) demonstrated that when a behaviour produces a pleasurable consequence from the environment (e.g. a reward) it is likely to be repeated in future. The environment reinforces (strengthens) the behaviour, so this is called *reinforcement*.

The roles of observation and imitation

Albert Bandura (1977) argued that learning occurs through *observation* and *imitation* of other people's behaviour in a social context. As children, we observe the behaviour of other people (e.g. parents) who may become *role models*. We are likely to imitate role models if we observe their behaviour being rewarded (e.g. with praise, fame, money). This is *vicarious reinforcement*. It is not the child's behaviour that is reinforced, but the behaviour of the *model* they are observing.

Assumptions of the biological approach

Behaviour is influenced by our biology

This approach believes that everything that is psychological is firstly biological – our behaviours, thoughts and feelings have a physical basis.

The central nervous system (CNS) is your brain and spinal cord. This is the control centre of your body. Different areas and regions of the brain perform different functions (e.g. language, aggression, vision, emotions). Damage to the brain/CNS can seriously affect these functions.

Genes are biological 'units' of DNA inherited from our parents. These interact with environmental influences. Many behaviours are in part passed on from one generation to the next.

Neurochemistry refers to chemicals called *neurotransmitters* (e.g. *serotonin, dopamine*) that are active in the brain and affect behaviour. For example, a low level of serotonin is thought to be involved in depression.

Behaviour and evolution

According to Charles Darwin (1859), genetically-determined behaviours continue into future generations (i.e. they are inherited). The behaviours that continue are those that are *naturally selected* because they enhance the individual's chances of survival and particularly reproduction.

For example, an individual who has good hunting skills is more likely to survive because they have food to eat. If they are well fed they are more likely to reproduce successfully and then their hunting skills (e.g. fast reactions) are passed on to their offspring.

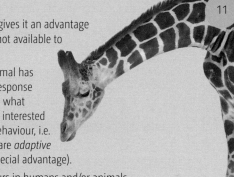

The giraffe's long neck gives it an advantage in getting food that is not available to shorter-necked rivals.

This shows how an animal has adapted physically in response to its environment. But what psychologists are really interested in is the *evolution* of behaviour, i.e. how some *behaviours* are *adaptive* (give an individual a special advantage).

Identify some behaviours in humans and/or animals and suggest what their adaptive advantages might be.

Exam-style questions

1. Describe what is meant by 'information processing' in relation to the cognitive approach. (2)
2. Outline the information processing assumption of the cognitive approach. (2)
3. Explain what is meant by 'social context' in relation to the social approach. (2)
4. Describe the assumption that other people, culture and society influence behaviour. Illustrate your answer with **one** example from the social approach. (3)
5. With reference to the learning approach, explain the assumption that behaviour is a learned response from environmental stimuli. (2)
6. Explain the roles of observation and imitation in the learning approach. (2)
7. In relation to the biological approach, briefly explain what is meant by the 'evolution and behaviour' assumption. (2)
8. Describe the assumption that behaviour is influenced by the central nervous system, genes and neurochemistry. Illustrate your answer with **one** example from the biological approach. (3)

Specification content

Know the key assumptions of the following different approaches to psychology: cognitive, social, learning (including behaviourism) and biological

Cognitive assumptions:
- Behaviour is a product of information processing.
- Computer analogy – input, processing and output.

Social assumptions:
- Behaviour occurs in a social context.
- Other people, culture and society influence people's behaviour.

Learning assumptions:
- Behaviour is a learned response from environmental stimuli.
- Behaviour can be learned from observation and imitation.

Biological assumptions:
- Behaviour is influenced by central nervous system (CNS), genes and neurochemistry.
- Behaviour is a product of evolution.

GET ACTIVE Growing up

Wilma's three teenage sons have all bullied other children at school. They grew up in a violent household and witnessed their father physically abuse Wilma several times. Wilma herself once served a prison sentence for assaulting someone. When she asked one of her sons why he bullied, he replied, 'Because I get what I want'. Last year one of her sons had a serious head injury (causing brain damage) in an accident and is now a very placid and calm person.

How can the assumptions of the learning approach and the biological approach help us to understand this scenario?

Content area B1: Cognitive approach
Key concept 1 and key study

The War of the Ghosts

The following story was told to participants in Bartlett's key study:

One night two young men from Egulac went down the river to hunt seals, and while they were there it became foggy and calm. Then they heard war-cries, and they thought: 'Maybe this is a war-party'. They escaped to the shore and hid behind a log. Now canoes came up, and they heard the noise of paddles, and saw one canoe coming up to them. There were five men in the canoe, and they said:

'What do you think? We wish to take you along. We are going up the river to make war on the people.'

One of the young men said: 'I have no arrows.'

'Arrows are in the canoe,' they said.

'I will not go along. I might get killed. My relatives do not know where I have gone. But you,' he said, turning to the other, 'may go with them.'

So one of the young men went, but the other returned home.

And the warriors went up on the river to a town on the other side of Kalama. The people came down to the water, and they began to fight, and many were killed. But presently the young man heard one of the warriors say: 'Quick, let us go home: that Indian has been hit.' Now he thought: 'Oh, they are ghosts.' He did not feel sick, but they said he had been shot.

So the canoes went back to Egulac, and the young man went ashore to his house, and made a fire. And he told everybody and said: 'Behold I accompanied the ghosts, and we went to fight. Many of our fellows were killed, and many of those who attacked us were killed. They said I was hit and I did not feel sick.'

He told it all and then became quiet. When the sun rose he fell down. Something black came out of his mouth. His face became contorted. The people jumped up and cried.

He was dead.

Specification terms

Confabulation When details are added to a memory to fill in the 'gaps', to make recall meaningful.

Rationalisation When parts of a memory are distorted to fit your schema, to make the memory meaningful.

Reconstructive memory Pieces of stored information are reassembled during recall. The process is guided by our schemas so that we produce a 'memory' that makes sense (even if it is inaccurate).

Schema A mental package of beliefs and expectations that influence memory. They change (reconstruct) memories through shortening, rationalisation and confabulation.

Shortening When part of a memory is left out, so what remains is shorter.

Key concept: Reconstructive memory

What is reconstructive memory?

Sir Frederic Charles Bartlett (1932) argued that memories are not reproductions but *reconstructions* (constructing the memory again). We don't record events in memory like a video recorder would. Instead we store fragments of information and when we recall something, we build (reconstruct) these fragments into a meaningful whole. The result is that memory is not a totally accurate record of what happened.

Role of schema in memory

A *schema* is a mental structure or 'package' containing our stored knowledge of an aspect of the world. So we have schema for a mother, teacher, fire engine, birthday party, firework, etc. – for people, objects, events. Bartlett believed our schemas affect memory by influencing what we store and what we recall (see the key study below). Therefore, some parts of a memory are missing, some are distorted and some are added:

Shortening Parts of a memory that don't fit in with your schemas are left out (e.g. unfamiliar or unexpected details) so what you remember is shorter.

Rationalisation Parts of a memory are recalled but in a distorted way that fits your schemas. So your memory of an event changed because it didn't match relevant schemas (but now it does). This happens so that strange or unfamiliar memories make more sense.

Confabulation Parts of a memory are invented to fill in 'gaps'. This isn't deliberate (it's not 'lying') and it doesn't happen randomly. It is guided by schemas to (again) make better sense of the memory.

Key study: Bartlett (1932) War of the Ghosts

Aims

Bartlett wanted to see if recall from memory is reconstructive. Would British participants' recall of unfamiliar material be affected by schemas so that their errors followed a pattern?

Procedure

Bartlett showed 20 British participants an Inuit (Native American) folk tale (*War of the Ghosts*, see left). Each person read the story twice and 15 minutes later told it (from memory) to someone who had not read it. This person told it to someone else and so on (like Chinese whispers). This method of testing memory is called *serial reproduction*. Bartlett kept a record of what each person remembered.

Findings

The story was transformed in several ways:

1. *Shortening* – it was shortened significantly (because details were left out). The story is 326 words long, but after six or seven reproductions it became about 180 on average.

2. *Rationalisation* – Bartlett noticed that the supernatural element (at the heart of this ghost story) vanished altogether.

3. *Confabulation* – phrases were changed to language and concepts from the participants' own *culture* (e.g. 'boats' instead of 'canoes').

Conclusions

The transformations occurred because participants' schemas influenced what they could remember about the story. The material became more meaningful and easier to understand and remember.

Evaluation

Application to EWT

One strength is that reconstructive memory can help explain problems with eyewitness testimony (EWT).

EWT is often used in court trials to give a picture of what happened when a crime was committed. For example, an eyewitness might swear on oath that they had seen a certain person at the crime scene, only for their testimony to be challenged by evidence presented later. Memory can be affected by schemas (including expectations of what 'should' happen), so people do not always recall events accurately.

Consequently, convictions in court are less likely to be based on EWT alone as it can be unreliable – a very important application of research.

Some memories are accurate

One weakness is that not all memories are affected by schemas.

Recall can be very accurate. For example, in situations that are personally important or distinctive we can remember a lot of accurate detail. In Bartlett's study, participants often recalled the phrase 'Something black came out of his mouth' because it was quite unusual.

This shows that people may not always actively reconstruct memories, and memory can be highly accurate and relatively unaffected by schemas.

Evaluation

Realistic theory and research

One strength is that Bartlett used realistic methods to study memory.

Before Bartlett's work, psychologists used artificial materials (e.g. 'nonsense syllables' such as RIZ and KUY). These are artificial because we rarely use memory to learn such meaningless things. Instead, Bartlett used an everyday kind of task (recalling a story) to show what happens when we try to recall an unfamiliar story.

Therefore, he was able to draw conclusions more relevant to real-life memory.

Unscientific research

One weakness of Bartlett's study is that its procedures lacked consistency, which is a key requirement for scientific research.

In scientific research, procedures are 'standardised' so the experience of the study is the same for every participant. This was not true of Bartlett's study. For example, some of his participants only reproduced the *War of the Ghosts* story when he happened to 'bump into' them.

This means we cannot be confident that reconstructive memory theory is correct, as it is based on unscientific research.

GET ACTIVE Wedding memories

Prince Harry and Meghan Markle were married in May 2018. The wedding was 'witnessed' by millions of people on TV. Were you one of them?

1. What do you remember about it?
2. Looking back, do you think that your memory of the wedding is accurate?
3. Choose a well-known event in the news that you 'witnessed' (e.g. on TV).

Try to recall as much detail about it as you can, and jot down some notes about what you remember.

Now, find an account in the media of the event and compare it with your recall. Look for evidence of how your schemas may have influenced your memory. Are there any important details you missed out or recalled inaccurately? Is there anything you were convinced must have happened but hasn't been reported?

Exam-style questions

1. State what is meant by the term 'reconstructive memory'. (1)
2. Using an example, explain what is meant by the term 'schema'. (3)
3. Explain **one** feature of schemas that can influence reconstructive memory. (2)
4. Explain how a cognitive psychologist would account for reconstructive memory. Use the concept of schema in your answer. (3)
5. Bob and Sue are friends who together witnessed a street robbery and gave statements to the police. They discussed afterwards what they had said. Bob's statement was much longer than Sue's. Sue included some details that Bob did not remember happening. Both realised that they included the same events but described them very differently.

   Outline how a cognitive psychologist might explain the differences between the two statements. (3)
6. Explain how the findings of Bartlett (1932) support the view that schemas influence memory. (3)
7. Dev and Suni are discussing memory. Dev believes that recall is like playing back a recording. But Suni argues that recall is more of a reconstruction. Suni also believes that studies support her argument.

   Discuss the view that memory is reconstructive. In your answer you should consider the role of schemas, including shortening, rationalisation and confabulation. (9)

Witnesses very rarely lie. But they do sometimes get it wrong. They take an oath to tell 'the truth, the whole truth and nothing but the truth', so they try their hardest to remember things accurately. But memory is often reconstructive, so piecing together memories of what they saw is likely to be affected by schemas. This is why witnesses to the same crime can often have different memories of it.

An issue to consider

Can we rely on memory if it is reconstructive? Can you think of any real-life examples where inaccurate recall could have serious consequences?

Specification content

B1 Cognitive approach

Key concepts:
- Reconstructive memory, including the role of schema (shortening, rationalisation and confabulation).

Key study:
- Bartlett (1932) War of the Ghosts.

Key concept 2 and key study

Imagine this

Your teacher asks you to carry out a very simple task. All you have to do is unscramble some mixed-up sentences. You get them all right. You leave the classroom thinking, 'That was too easy. What was it all about?'

You don't know it, but your teacher isn't interested in how you did on the task at all. Instead, she's timing you to see how long it takes you to leave the room. She's done this with all the students in your class. It turns out you walked a lot slower to leave the room than some of your classmates did.

Why?

There could be many reasons, but here's an interesting fact. All of the students did the same task, but there were two versions. In one version, some of the words in the sentences related to being old (bingo, retired, wrinkled, etc.). In the other version the words were neutral (thirsty, clean, private, etc.). Guess what? You got the 'old' version. Like you, all your classmates who got the old version were also slower to leave the room.

Sounds weird? Hard to believe? John Bargh and his colleagues (1996) did this experiment and got this exact finding.

Specification terms

Associative priming We process a stimulus more quickly (or recall it more easily) because we earlier encountered a stimulus that is often paired with it.

Cognitive priming We notice a stimulus (word, image, object, etc.) more quickly when we see or hear a related stimulus first (the 'prime').

Cognitive scripts Knowledge of behaviours, roles, outcomes, etc. stored in memory tell us what to expect in a social situation and how to behave.

Repetition priming We process a stimulus more quickly (or recall it more easily) because we encountered it earlier.

Semantic priming We process a stimulus more quickly (or recall it more easily) because we earlier encountered a stimulus related to it in meaning (semantics = meaning).

Et al.

Throughout your course you will be reading about many different research studies. The findings of a study are published in an academic magazine (journal) along with the name(s) of the researcher(s) and the date when their report was published. When there are more than two researchers the convention is to write 'et al.' which means 'and others'. Simples.

Key concept: Cognitive priming

What is cognitive priming?

When you see or hear one stimulus (the 'prime'), this affects your response to a later stimulus (you usually process the later stimulus faster). The prime triggers a network of related concepts in memory, so that when the second stimulus occurs, activation is quicker. *Priming* may happen below your level of awareness so you do not know your response is influenced.

Role of cognitive scripts

You have learned how people normally behave in many social situations, such as being in a restaurant. The term *cognitive script* is used to describe what you have learned. It is like learning to act a scene in a play – the text for a play is called a script and tells you what to do and say.

Cognitive scripts are learned through experience (including from TV and books). When in a social situation, we recall from memory (without being aware) the relevant script containing the features of the situation, what we can expect and how we should behave.

Types of cognitive priming

Repetition priming When you encounter the prime (e.g. the word *avocado*) you process it more quickly when you see or hear it again later than you otherwise would have done.

Semantic priming Two stimuli mean the same thing or have similar features. For example, if you see or hear the word *computer*, it is easier to recognise or recall the word *laptop* later – you process *laptop* faster because it is related in meaning (semantically) to the prime.

Associative priming The prime and the later stimulus are related but not semantically. For example, *fish* and *chips* are so often paired that they are closely associated in memory. If you are exposed to one you are more likely to later recognise or recall the other.

Key study: Harris *et al.* (2009) Priming effects of television food advertising on eating behaviour

Aims

The researchers wanted to see if watching food adverts on TV would cause adults and children to automatically eat available snacks.

Procedure

Schoolchildren watched a cartoon – some saw a version with ads for food, others saw it with non-food ads. All were given a snack while watching the cartoon and the researchers measured the amount eaten.

Adult students watched a TV programme – some saw a version with food ads promoting snacking as fun, some saw it with food ads promoting health, the rest saw it with no food ads. Afterwards, the students tasted and rated five snacks ranging from healthy (carrots) to unhealthy (cookies). The researchers measured the amount of each snack eaten.

Findings

Children who saw the food adverts ate 45% more of the snack than the other children. This difference was not related to any other factor.

Adult students who saw the fun snack adverts ate more (of all foods) than the other students (especially men and people who were 'dieting'). Hunger before eating was unrelated to amount eaten in the fun snack group.

Conclusions

The findings provided 'converging evidence of an automatic, direct causal link between food advertising and greater snack consumption'. Advertising is powerful because it has multiple priming effects, including short-term (enjoyment) and long-term (healthy eating).

Cognitive priming could help us to understand how viewing screen-based adverts, vlogs and programmes affect our behaviour. Does watching violent programmes prime us to be more aggressive? Does a 'diet' of food adverts prime us to eat more?

Evaluation

Evidence supports cognitive scripts

One strength is that cognitive scripts can help us understand the effects of video gaming on aggressive behaviour.

In a study by Ingrid Möller and Barbara Krahé (2009), students read a scenario in which someone is accidentally pushed so they spill their drink. Students who frequently played violent video games were much more likely than other students to interpret the push as deliberate. They were also more likely to choose physical *aggression* as a suitable response.

This shows that people who play violent video games find it relatively easy to recall aggressive cognitive scripts stored in memory, supporting the idea of *associative priming*.

Lack of replication

One weakness of cognitive priming is that the research it is based on is very hard to replicate.

Replication is an important feature of science. If a study is repeated using exactly the same procedure and produces the same finding, then we know that the outcome is not a fluke and it is more likely to represent something real. But when researchers replicate priming studies, they often get different findings. This suggests that the researchers themselves might be influencing the outcomes.

This implies that the concept of priming is not scientific and we cannot be confident that the theories are correct.

Evaluation

Application to the problem of obesity

The key study can help us to understand and prevent cognitive causes of obesity.

Harris *et al.* showed that advertising can affect how many snacks children and adults eat because of cognitive priming. Once we understand the effects of priming we may be able to prevent this influence (or direct the influence towards healthy eating).

This means that education and legislation (although politically difficult) could help to prevent obesity, for example, especially in children.

Artificial conditions

One weakness of the key study is that it was conducted in 'artificial' conditions.

For example, every child watched the cartoon and adverts on their own in a classroom at their school (or an unoccupied room at a summer camp). This meant the conditions differed from real-life viewing of adverts, which usually takes place in the home environment and often with other people.

Therefore, the key study may not provide meaningful evidence for the effects of cognitive priming and cognitive scripts on real-life behaviour.

GET ACTIVE Sabiha and Imy

Sabiha's friends all watch the popular series *Game of Thrones*, so she decided to read about it and watch an episode. By the end of the day, she had seen or heard the word 'throne' in lots of different places – in overheard conversations, on Twitter and Facebook, even in her college textbooks.

1. *What type of cognitive priming is this?*

2. *Describe another type of priming that Sabiha might have experienced.*

Imy was going to the cinema with her parents to see the latest blockbuster. 'I'm going to have some popcorn and an ice cream,' she said as they left the house.

3. *How do cognitive scripts explain Imy's comment?*

Exam-style questions

1. State what is meant by the term 'cognitive priming'. (1)

2. Give an example of how cognitive scripts might affect behaviour in everyday life. (2)

3. Describe **one** finding of the key study by Harris *et al.* (2009). (2)

4. Explain **one** strength or **one** weakness of the key study by Harris *et al.* (2009). (3)

5. A psychologist asked a group of students to read a brief passage and then complete a word task. The passage described the layout of a doctor's surgery. The task was to complete words with missing letters (e.g. N _ _ S _). Another group of students also completed the word task but did not read the passage first.

   (a) Describe the finding you would expect the psychologist to get. (2)

   (b) Use the concept of cognitive priming to explain this finding. (3)

6. Some psychologists believe that cognitive priming affects our everyday behaviour without us realising. Others argue that priming only really exists in laboratory-based artificial studies.

   Discuss the role of cognitive priming in influencing behaviour. In your answer you should consider different types of priming and **one** example of real-life behaviour. (9)

An issue to consider

If you use social media you may have been exposed to cognitive priming without realising it.

Can you explain how?

Specification content

B1 Cognitive approach

Key concept:

● Cognitive priming, including the role of cognitive scripts and different types of priming (repetition, semantic and associative).

Key study:

● Harris, Bargh and Brownell (2009) Priming effects of television food advertising on eating behaviour.

Key concept 3 and key study

Do you live in a filter bubble?

You might well do if you get your news from social media such as Facebook. Algorithms detect your preferences and tailor what the news feeds serve up to you. You see only items that match your preferences and these reinforce your current opinions. You rarely get to see information that contradicts or challenges what you already believe.

Such 'filter bubbles' are sometimes called an echo chamber because all you ever read or hear are your own views reflected back at you.

Some people argue that filter bubbles are a threat to democracy because other viewpoints and opinions are excluded from social media feeds. If you want to read other views you have to work harder to find them. Most of us can't be bothered to spend the time or effort doing that extra work.

Specification terms

Cognitive biases Errors in how we process information that affect our attention, memory and decision-making.

Confirmation bias We pay more attention to (and recall more easily) information that supports our existing beliefs. We may seek it out and ignore contradictory information.

Fundamental attribution error In explaining the reasons for other people's behaviour, we focus on their personal characteristics and overlook the role of the situation.

Hostile attribution bias A tendency to assume that someone else's behaviour has an aggressive or antagonistic motive when it is actually neutral.

'The strongest bias in American politics is not a liberal bias or a conservative bias; it is a confirmation bias' (Roller 2016).

Key concept: Cognitive biases

What are cognitive biases?

These are errors in how we process information. They affect ('bias') what we notice, what we remember and how we make decisions. *Cognitive biases* are risky because they undermine our ability to make rational choices and logical decisions. But on the plus side they simplify social interactions and allow us to make decisions quickly (they are 'shortcuts' that help us process incoming information).

Fundamental attribution error (FAE)

Attribution is the process of trying to explain other people's behaviour, for example explaining why someone was late or aggressive. Generally our explanations are either in terms of personal characteristics (maybe he is late because he doesn't think it is important to be on time) or situation (maybe he is late because he missed his bus).

We naturally tend to overemphasise personal characteristics and downplay the role of the situation. For example, if a student fails to hand in an essay on time, their teacher might believe it's because the student is lazy (a personal characteristic). But in fact there could be many situational causes of the behaviour (e.g. the dog ate it).

Confirmation bias

We tend to favour information that supports a belief we already hold. For example, if you support a particular football team you are more sensitive to information that confirms your view of the team. We notice confirmatory information more quickly and we store and recall it more readily. But we ignore, downplay or reject examples that challenge our beliefs, and stop looking for contradictory information.

Hostile attribution bias

We may wrongly interpret other people's behaviour as threatening (hostile) when in fact it is neutral. Someone with this bias may respond aggressively to what they see as a deliberate intention to cause them harm but is really an innocent act (e.g. an accidental jostle in a crowded pub).

Key study: Loftus and Palmer (1974) Reconstruction of automobile destruction

Aims

The researchers wanted to see how changing one word in a question would affect (bias) people's estimate of the speed of a car in an accident.

Procedure

University students watched film clips of car accidents and then answered written questions. One of the questions (the critical question) was: 'About how fast were the cars going when they _____ (into) each other?'.

The students were divided into five groups. Each group was asked the same critical question but with a different verb (in the space). One group was asked the question with *contacted* in it, another with *bumped* in it, and the other groups with *hit*, *collided* or *smashed* instead.

Findings

The students' speed estimates were influenced by the verb in the critical question. The average (mean) estimated speed was highest for smashed (40.5 mph) and lowest for contacted (31.8). The other mean estimates were 39.3 for collided, 38.1 for bumped and 34.0 for hit.

Conclusions

Changing just one word in a question can bias responses (because the participants' estimates matched the 'strength' of the verb). Loftus and Palmer later showed that changing the verb did more than just bias responses; it changed the participants' memories of the accidents.

Evaluation

Applications to real-life behaviour

One strength of cognitive biases is that they can be applied to behaviour in real life.

For example, the *hostile attribution bias* helps us understand why some people are aggressive. Their thinking is biased towards an aggressive interpretation of other people's behaviour. *Confirmation bias* explains why behaviour can be 'tribal' (e.g. politics, sport). We only seek information that supports our current preferences (e.g. for one political party) and ignore everything else.

This is useful because understanding cognitive biases is the first step in preventing them affecting behaviour, reducing *aggression* and conflict.

The FAE is not universal

One weakness is evidence that the *fundamental attribution error* (FAE) only exists in some *cultures*.

Some cultures (e.g. USA) are described as *individualist* because people value individual needs above the needs of the wider community. So behaviour tends to be attributed to individual characteristics because that is how behaviour is understood in such cultures. However, in *collectivist* cultures (e.g. China) the group/community is prioritised over individual needs, so people tend to attribute behaviour to situational factors and not to personality.

This suggests that the FAE is likely to be culturally-specific and not a feature of all human behaviour (this may also be true of other biases).

Evaluation

Experimental control

One strength of the key study is that it was highly controlled.

As it was carried out in lab conditions, irrelevant variables could be controlled. For example, each participant witnessed the (filmed) accidents from the same viewpoint. In a real-life situation participants' estimates of speed might have been affected by where they were standing.

This means we can be more confident that the critical word changed the speed estimates because *extraneous variables* were controlled.

Biased sample of participants

One weakness of the key study is that the participants were relatively young (university students).

Some studies (e.g. Anastasi and Rhodes 2006) have shown that younger people (18–25 years) are more accurate in their eyewitness reports than older people (55–78 years).

This means estimates in this study are unlikely to represent the responses of older people, making it hard to generalise findings to the wider population (where estimates may be even less accurate).

'Did you spill my pint?' Some aggression can be explained by the hostile attribution bias. Spilling someone's drink is not usually deliberate but someone with this cognitive bias might think it is.

Exam-style questions

1. State what is meant by the term 'cognitive biases'. (1)
2. Choose **one** type of cognitive bias and explain how it might affect behaviour in everyday life. (2)
3. Jessie and Keira were trying to persuade Lennie to join them on a night out in town. Lennie didn't want to go, so Jessie said to Keira, 'He doesn't want to go because he's just a grumpy old misery guts.'

   Describe **one** type of cognitive bias Jessie is showing. (2)
4. Describe **one** example of the hostile attribution bias in everyday life. (2)
5. Describe **one** finding of the key study by Loftus and Palmer (1974). (2)
6. Explain how **one** finding by Loftus and Palmer (1974) demonstrates the role of cognitive biases. (3)
7. Explain **one** strength or **one** weakness of the key study by Loftus and Palmer (1974). (3)
8. Charlie was convinced he had cancer because he had a dull aching pain in his lower abdomen. So he went on the internet and found out that a dull aching pain in the lower abdomen is a symptom of cancer. 'You see,' he said to his best friend, 'I told you I had cancer.'

   Explain Charlie's behaviour using your knowledge of cognitive biases. (3)
9. Evaluate the role of cognitive biases in real-life behaviour. In your answer you should consider **two** or more different types of cognitive bias and **one** example of real-life behaviour. (9)

GET ACTIVE A wrong diagnosis

This real case was described by Caroline Wellbery (2011). A woman visited her doctor with two major symptoms – a rash under her arms and pain in her joints. The patient was obese and had Type 2 diabetes. The doctor diagnosed *intertrigo*, which is inflammation caused by folds of skin rubbing together. He prescribed ointment for the rash and ibuprofen for the pain.

Unhappy with this outcome, the patient sought a second opinion. The second doctor ordered a blood test and diagnosed Lyme disease. This is a bacterial infection usually caused by a bite from a tick (for example when walking in the countryside).

1. *How did confirmation bias contribute to the wrong diagnosis and treatment? Identify at least **two** specific examples from the case to support your explanation.*
2. *Do you think the fundamental attribution error might also have played a role? Explain how.*

An issue to consider

Think back over what you were doing in the last 30 minutes. What attributions have you made about the people around you (i.e. what explanations have you given for someone's behaviour)? List some of them.

Now tick the ones which might be biased.

Specification content

B1 Cognitive approach

Key concept:
- Cognitive biases, including fundamental attribution error, confirmation bias and hostile attribution bias.

Key study:
- Loftus and Palmer (1974) Reconstruction of automobile destruction.

Content area B2: Social approach

Key concept 1 and key study

Cavewoman speaks

A woman is visiting a museum and has to pass through a metal detector on the way in. There is a queue. While she queues she watches as someone dressed as a 'cavewoman' is encouraged by the tour guide to grunt very loudly at the visitors, as if trying to communicate with them. The tour guide (who is 'fluent in Neanderthal, Caveman and Geordie') asks the visitors to join in.

Without questioning what is going on, the woman begins grunting along with the others, with the tour guide 'interpreting' for her. All the other visitors behave as if this is the most natural thing in the world.

Of course the whole situation was a set-up, for the BBC programme *Michael McIntyre's Big Show*. But have you ever 'gone along' with what everyone else was doing, even if you thought it a bit strange?

Specification terms

Conformity 'A change in a person's behaviour or opinions as a result of real or imagined pressure from a person or group of people' (Aronson 2011).

Informational social influence (ISI) We agree with the behaviour of others because we believe it is correct. We accept it because we want to be correct.

Normative social influence (NSI) We agree with the behaviour of others because we want to be accepted and liked, and to avoid rejection.

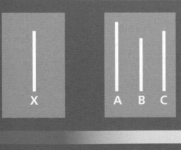

Asch's study

The line X on the left-hand card is the standard line. The lines A, B and C are the three comparison lines. The participants had to say which of the comparison lines was the same length as the standard line (the answer was always obvious – here it is C).

The naïve (genuine) participant was always seated around a table either last or (as here) next to last in the group. Participants gave their answers out loud, one at a time, beginning with the first person.

Key concept: Conformity

What is conformity?

When we are part of a group, we may choose to 'go along' with other people by agreeing with their opinions or behaving as they do. This is *conformity*. The other people do not *tell* us how to behave or what opinions to have. But conformity is the result of 'invisible' pressure from others.

Social psychologists Morton Deutsch and Harold Gerard (1955) devised the two-process theory, suggesting there are two main processes that explain why people conform.

Process 1: Normative social influence (NSI)

NSI is about group norms. In any group of people there are behaviours and beliefs that are considered to be 'normal' or typical. Norms guide the behaviour of the individuals in the group and are part of what glues the group together, which is why we pay attention to them. We accept the norms of a group (i.e. we conform) because we want to be liked by the other group members and we want to avoid being rejected by them. This means NSI is an emotional process because it is about how you *feel*. It may be stronger in stressful situations where people have a greater need for social support.

Process 2: Informational social influence (ISI)

ISI is about who has the better information, you or someone else. Often we are unsure about what behaviours/beliefs are right or wrong. For example, you may not know the answer to a question in class. But if most students agree on one answer, you accept it because you feel they are probably right. So we may conform to the views of others because we want to be right. This means ISI is a *cognitive* process because it is about what you *think*.

ISI is most likely to happen in situations that are new to you (so you don't know what is right) or situations where it isn't clear what is right (ambiguous). It also occurs when one person is regarded as being more of an expert.

Key study: Asch (1951) Effects of group pressure upon the modification and distortion of judgements

Aims

Solomon Asch wanted to see if individuals would agree with answers given by a group when the answers were obviously wrong (i.e. would they conform to the majority?).

Procedure

Asch arranged for groups of about seven students to take part in a line judgement task. Each person in turn was asked to identify which line (A, B or C) matched the standard line X (see left). However, only one student was a genuine participant ('naïve') who did not know what the procedure was really about. The others (*confederates*) were instructed by Asch to sometimes give the wrong answer. In total there were 16 sets of cards and on 12 of these the confederates gave the wrong answer. The naïve participant always answered last or second to last.

Findings

The naïve participants gave wrong answers (conformed with the group) on 36.8% of the trials. Overall 25% of the participants did not conform on any trials, which means that 75% conformed at least once.

Conclusions

A proportion of people conform to the majority even when the situation is unambiguous (the answer is clear). Most conform to avoid rejection by the group (NSI).

However, we should also note that most of the time the participants' responses were correct. So the study can also be interpreted as showing that people usually behave independently of the group in unambiguous situations (i.e. we are usually able to *resist* conformity).

Evaluation

Research supports NSI

One strength is that Asch provided evidence of NSI.

He discovered that many of his participants went along with a clearly wrong answer just because other people did. When he asked them why, some said they felt self-conscious giving the correct answer and were afraid of disapproval. So Asch repeated his study but asked the naïve participants to write down their answers instead of saying them out loud. The conformity rate fell to just 12.5%.

This suggests that we sometimes conform to avoid rejection by the majority. When this pressure is removed because you don't have to disagree publicly, then conformity is less likely.

NSI and ISI work together in real life

One weakness is that the two processes (NSI or ISI) are interdependent.

You are less likely to conform if there is another person present ('dissenter') who disagrees with the group. Asch found this in some versions of his study. The dissenter may reduce the power of NSI (because he or she provides social support). They may also reduce the power of ISI (because there is an alternative source of information).

This shows that we can't always be sure whether NSI or ISI is at work. It is most likely that both are operating, especially in real-life conformity.

Evaluation

Level of control

One strength of the key study is that it was carried out in lab conditions.

Therefore, Asch was able to control several variables. He standardised the study so that every participant experienced the same procedure (e.g. the same behaviour by the confederates, the same materials).

This level of control meant that these variables could be ruled out as explanations for the conformity seen in the study.

Limited application of findings

One weakness of the study is that Asch used only male and American participants.

This matters because other studies indicate that some women may be more conformist, at least in some contexts. This might be because women are more concerned about maintaining social relationships than men are. Also, the USA is an *individualist* culture which values individual needs above those of the wider social group. Studies in *collectivist* societies (e.g. China, where group needs are prioritised) show that conformity is more common.

This means that Asch's findings may generally underestimate the true level of conformity.

Sometimes giving up your independence and pulling in the same direction makes us feel part of a group. Then we can achieve things we wouldn't be able to on our own.

A man is lying on the pavement in a busy street. People are walking round him and ignoring him. No one stops to see if there is anything wrong. One woman finally kneels on the ground to speak to the man. She looks like she's knows what she is doing. Several other people stop to help now as well.

Twelve members of a jury are discussing the trial they have been involved in. Most of the jury members have been convinced by the evidence and the comments of other jurors, so they believe the defendant is guilty. One jury member is sure the defendant is not guilty. But as he has a carpet being delivered that afternoon he is keen to get home, so he changes his verdict to guilty.

1. Why did the people in these cases conform – NSI or ISI? Explain your answer.
2. Are there any real-life examples of conformity that you have been involved in (remember, in conformity, no one tells you to agree)? Why do you think the conformity happened?

Exam-style questions

1. State what is meant by the term 'conformity'. (1)
2. Briefly explain **one** example of normative social influence from everyday life. (2)
3. Using an example, explain what is meant by the term 'informational social influence'. (3)
4. Miriam is part of a book club and hated the latest book that was chosen for the group to read. However, at the next meeting she said she loved it along with everyone else.

   Did Miriam conform because of normative social influence or informational social influence? Explain your answer with reference to her behaviour. (3)
5. Describe **one** finding of the key study by Asch (1951). (2)
6. Explain what the findings of Asch's (1951) study tell us about the concept of conformity. (3)
7. Explain **one** strength and **one** weakness of the key study by Asch (1951). (4)
8. A team of nurses is meeting to discuss a patient's treatment plan. All are agreed that the plan should continue. However, Amos disagrees but is afraid to say so publicly. So he goes along with the plan even though he thinks it is not the best option.

   Analyse the concept of conformity. In your answer you should consider: (a) the roles of normative and informational social influence, and (b) Amos' experience as outlined above. (9)

An issue to consider

Conformity is often seen as bad in Western cultures because it undermines an individual's independence.

Is conformity a good or bad thing?

Specification content

B2 Social approach

Key concept:
● Conformity (normative social influence and informational social influence).

Key study:
● Asch (1951) Effects of group pressure upon the modification and distortion of judgements.

Key concept 2 and key study

Are brown eyes better?

Did you know that people with brown eyes are superior to their blue-eyed minions? They are more intelligent, they have greater capacity to learn, are cleaner and better behaved.

This is what Jane Elliott, a teacher, told her class of primary-aged children. With their agreement, she divided them into 'brownies' and 'blueys'. She gave the brownies privileges and helped them with their work. She gave the blue-eyed children collars to wear round their necks to mark them out as inferior.

According to Elliott, within an hour the children began to behave in ways that matched their status. The brownies became more confident and worked harder, but also acted with contempt towards their blue-eyed classmates. The blueys became demotivated and their work suffered.

But there's a twist in this tale. On the next school day, the roles were reversed, and the blueys were deemed superior. Everyone's behaviour changed with the new situation.

The children all conformed to the roles they were given in a process called *identification*.

Specification terms

Compliance The individual does not privately agree with the majority but goes along with it anyway, usually because they do not want to be rejected.

Identification The individual temporarily goes along with the norms and roles of the group because they see membership as part of their identity.

Internalisation The individual goes along with the group opinion because they genuinely believe it is correct, so private views are changed.

Guards and prisoners in the SPS had their own 'uniforms' which were constant reminders of their different social roles.

Key concept: Types of conformity

We looked at explanations of *conformity* on the previous spread. We saw how social psychologists have tried to explain why we conform to the views and behaviours of others. But psychologists also believe that there are different types of conformity. For example, Herbert Kelman (1958) argued there are three main ways we conform.

1. Internalisation

Sometimes we genuinely come to agree with the view of the group. The group's opinion becomes part of how we think (we internalise it). We privately as well as publicly change our view or behave to follow other group members. We continue to conform even when other group members are not present, so this is a permanent type of conformity. *Internalisation* is most likely to occur because of *informational social influence* (ISI) – we think the group view is right.

2. Compliance

Sometimes we just 'go along' with the majority, but privately we do not change our opinion/behaviour. This is a temporary type of conformity because agreement with the majority ends as soon as the group is no longer present (and there is no group pressure felt). *Compliance* is most likely to occur because of *normative social influence* (NSI) – we want the group to accept us.

3. Identification

Identification combines elements of the other two types of conformity. It is stronger than compliance because we privately change some of our views (as well as publicly). It is weaker than internalisation because we conform only as long as we are part of the group. We conform because we *identify* with the other members of the group.

In the study below group membership led to identification – the participants took on the social roles required by being a member of either the guards' group or the prisoners' group.

Key study: Haney *et al.* (1973) A study of prisoners and guards in a simulated prison

Aims

Philip Zimbardo was the lead researcher in this Stanford Prison Study (SPS), though Craig Haney's name comes first. The aim of the study was to investigate whether prison guards behave brutally because they have sadistic *personalities*, or is it the *situation* that creates such behaviour?

Procedure

The researchers set up a mock prison. They recruited 22 'emotionally stable' volunteer students and randomly gave them the role of either prison guard or prisoner. Prisoners were given a uniform and were addressed by number. They had to follow 16 rules which were enforced by the guards. The guards had their own uniform plus wooden club, handcuffs, keys and mirror shades. They were told they had power over the prisoners, even deciding when they could go to the toilet.

Findings

The guards identified very closely with their role, quickly becoming brutal and aggressive. The prisoners also identified with their own role. They initially rebelled against their treatment. But the guards put down the rebellion and the prisoners became subdued, depressed and anxious. Three prisoners had to be 'released' early. The guards' behaviour threatened the prisoners' psychological and physical health, so the study was stopped after six days instead of the intended 14.

Conclusions

Guards, prisoners and researchers all conformed to their roles within the prison (because they identified with them). Even volunteers who came in to perform certain roles found themselves behaving as if they were in a prison rather than in a psychological study.

The SPS showed that situations influence people's behaviour very powerfully.

Evaluation

Support for Kelman's three types

One strength is that research studies have found evidence for all three types of conformity.

Many of Asch's participants gave answers they knew were wrong, to avoid disapproval (compliance). Participants in the SPS conformed strongly to their roles in the mock prison (identification). In a study by Muzafer Sherif (1935), participants conformed with the answers of people they believed had more expertise than they did (internalisation).

These supporting studies show that Kelman was right to suggest there is more than one type of conformity.

Conformity types lack influence

One weakness is that, even if the three types exist, they may not influence behaviour much.

For example, Erich Fromm (1973) said that the SPS exaggerated the power of the situation and minimised the role of personality. About one third of the guards sympathised with the prisoners and actively tried to help them (e.g. offering cigarettes and reinstating privileges).

Therefore, identifying with social roles may not be a strong influence on behaviour, as the guards were able to exercise choice despite situational pressures to conform.

Evaluation

The study was controlled

One strength of the SPS is that the researchers had control over some key variables.

For example, emotionally stable students were selected and randomly assigned to the roles of guard and prisoner. The group of guards and group of prisoners behaved very differently from each other, but were in their roles only by chance, so their behaviour must have been due to the situation.

This means that we can be confident in drawing conclusions about one type of conformity (identification) in this study.

The SPS lacked realism

One weakness is that some psychologists (e.g. Banuazizi and Movahedi 1975) have argued that participants in the SPS were just play-acting.

Instead of genuinely conforming to a role, their performances were based on beliefs about how prisoners and guards are *supposed* to behave. For example, one guard claimed he based his role on a brutal character from the film *Cool Hand Luke*. This also explains why the prisoners rioted – they thought that was what real prisoners did.

This means that the participants' behaviour may not tell us much about conformity in real-life situations.

GET ACTIVE Abu Ghraib

The Iraq war began in March 2003. During the following year, personnel from the United States Army Military Police and the CIA committed serious human rights violations against Iraqi prisoners. These occurred at Abu Ghraib prison in Baghdad. The prisoners were tortured, physically and sexually abused, routinely humiliated and some were murdered. Photographs of the abuse were published by an American news channel in April 2004. Several of the personnel involved were eventually prosecuted and imprisoned and/or discharged from the military.

Zimbardo noticed some remarkable similarities between the behaviour of the personnel at Abu Ghraib and the guards in the Stanford prison study. One key factor was identification.

How do you think identification explains what happened at Abu Ghraib prison?

Although the 'prison' in the key study wasn't a real one, the researchers tried to make the experience as realistic as possible. For example, the students who played the role of prisoner were 'arrested' by the local police and taken to the police station. They then went through a genuine imprisonment procedure, including fingerprinting, a strip search and delousing.

Exam-style questions

1. State what is meant by the term 'compliance'. (1)
2. Briefly explain an example of internalisation from everyday life. (2)
3. Eve's friends decide to go to Club Phantom for a night out. Eve prefers Club Crystal but she tags along with the group anyway. Vik became a vegan after his friends persuaded him it is wrong to kill animals for food.

   Identify the types of conformity operating in each of these situations. (2)
4. Sol is a carer in a nursing home. He wears a uniform and has to carry out certain tasks every day. He is very helpful and cheerful towards the residents because he believes that is part of his role.

   (a) What type of conformity is Sol showing? Explain your answer. (3)

   (b) Use the findings from the study by Haney *et al.* (1973) to explain Sol's behaviour at work. (2)
5. Explain what the findings of Haney *et al.*'s (1973) study tell us about types of conformity. (3)
6. Explain **one** strength and **one** weakness of the key study by Haney *et al.* (1973). (6)
7. Discuss different types of conformity. In your answer you should consider: (a) internalisation, identification and compliance, and (b) the key study by Haney *et al.* (1973). (9)

An issue to consider

Psychologists disagree over whether unthinking conformity is due to the pressure of the situation or to the personalities of individuals.

What do you think? When people conform (at work, with friends or strangers, etc.), is it because they are the 'conforming type' or is the situation responsible? How would you know?

Specification content

B2 Social approach

Key concept:

● Types of conformity, including internalisation, identification, compliance.

Key study:

● Haney *et al.* (1973) A study of prisoners and guards in a simulated prison.

Key concept 3 and key study

PSYCHO, RETARD, NUTTER, MENTAL

These are all words that are used to describe people with mental health problems. A recent survey found that two thirds of young people have heard these words (and worse) used in reference to people with mental health issues – these words have become almost normal, especially on social media (YMCA 2017).

Why is this bad news?

It's because words like these reflect widespread stereotypes of people with mental health issues, stereotypes that are completely negative. These words are harmful because their use makes it harder for people with difficulties to seek help.

Imagine how hard it must be to admit to your friends that you are depressed, when you know that they think a depressed person is a 'psycho' or a 'nutter'. The reaction you might get could be enough to put you off.

The musician and activist Professor Green has faced such language himself on Twitter after speaking about his own mental health issues. That's one reason he joined the YMCA's #IAMWHOLE campaign to encourage young people to challenge this language.

Specification terms

Social categorisation Putting people into social groupings based on their shared characteristics (e.g. ethnicity).

Stereotypes Fixed views of other people based on their perceived membership of a social category.

Gender stereotypes are still widespread, especially in childhood. Certain clothes, behaviours, language, toys and even colours are considered appropriate for one gender but not another.

Key concept: Social categorisation

What is social categorisation?

We place individuals into social groups depending on their shared characteristics, often based merely on appearance (e.g. gender, ethnicity, age). We perceive people in a category to be similar, for example we think all young people are the same.

At the same time, we perceive the people in one category to be very different from the people in another, for example all girls are different from boys.

What is a stereotype?

A *stereotype* is a fixed view we hold of a person based on the fact that we have placed them into a social category (e.g. 'old people', 'students', 'feminists', etc.). We assume the person represents the social category. The obvious danger of this is that our assumptions may be wrong and unfair.

How are stereotypes formed?

Social learning theory (page 28) argues that we learn stereotypes from sources of social information (parents, peers, the media). We *observe* and *imitate* these sources. For example, if a child hears a parent telling a racist joke, he or she may enjoy the laughter the parent receives. This makes it more likely the child will repeat the stereotype (imitate the behaviour).

Many stereotypes reflect norms of appropriate behaviour that are rooted in *culture*. This is why they are so powerful – we learn them in the course of becoming a member of a culture.

What are the effects of stereotypes?

A positive effect is that stereotypes simplify our interactions with other people in a complex social world. We assume the individuals we meet have certain characteristics and this saves time and *cognitive* processing effort.

However, stereotypes can lead to prejudice (e.g. racism, sexism). We assume each person shares the stereotyped characteristics of their social group(s). So stereotypes distort and bias our social judgements. Stereotypes also affect our behaviour because they are self-fulfilling. We end up behaving towards other people in line with our stereotypes. The individuals may respond by behaving in ways that confirm the stereotype.

Key study: Chatard *et al.* (2007) 'How good are you in math?'

Armand Chatard *et al.* carried out two studies – we are concentrating here on the second one.

Aims

Can gender stereotypes affect memory? If students are reminded of a gender stereotype (boys are better at maths and girls are better at arts subjects), do they recall their maths and arts test results incorrectly?

Procedure

French high school students rated their agreement (on a 7-point scale) with statements about the maths and arts abilities of males and females *in general* (e.g. 'Women are gifted in the arts'). This gave them a strong reminder of relevant gender stereotypes. They then rated *their own abilities* (e.g. 'I am gifted in the arts'). Another group rated their own abilities first, so the gender stereotype could not affect their ratings. All participants finished by recalling their last school marks in maths and the arts.

Findings

Boys and girls who were given the gender stereotype reminder overestimated their arts performance (boys much less so than girls).

Girls who were given the gender stereotype reminder underestimated their maths performance (while boys overestimated theirs).

Conclusions

When boys and girls accept a gender stereotype about maths ability, their recall of their past maths performance is biased in the direction of the stereotype. Accepting this gender stereotype could have consequences for career choices. Female students who believe the stereotype may avoid careers in science and maths, even though they show ability in the subjects (and the same is true of male students and careers in the arts).

Evaluation

Research supporting stereotyping

One strength is there is other psychological research that confirms how stereotypes can distort memory.

Gordon Allport and Leo Postman (1947) showed participants a drawing that reversed a well-known stereotype (see right). The image was viewed by a participant, who described it to another, and so on for six or seven participants. This procedure was carried out many times. In 50% of these sequences, the black man was described as holding the razor.

This shows that a racist stereotype (black men are more likely to be violent than white men) can bias memory in a way that supports the stereotype (at least in a substantial proportion of people).

Effects of stereotypes

One weakness is that stereotypes do not always result in prejudice.

For instance, many people are aware of stereotypes of ethnic groups within a culture and may even hold them themselves. But they do not necessarily agree with them, and in fact may strongly oppose them and ensure that they do not affect their feelings or behaviour towards others.

This suggests that stereotypes should not always been seen as 'bad' and inevitably resulting in prejudice.

Evaluation

Tackling stereotypes

One strength of the key study is that it helps us become aware of the effects of stereotypes so we can take steps to overcome them.

Chatard et al. noted that women may be less likely to choose careers in science and maths because they underestimate their abilities in these areas. Because many of these women actually have high ability and achievement, this is depriving maths- and science-related fields of talented women.

This suggests that training can raise teachers' awareness of how their stereotyped expectations of male and female students can have negative impacts on students.

Role of participants' expectations

One weakness is that the findings of the key study might have been affected by participants trying to work out what the study was about.

The participants completed two questionnaires, one immediately after the other. They then wrote down what they recalled of their test results. Some participants would probably have wondered what the connection was between these two things. They may have realised that their responses to the questionnaires were supposed to influence what they wrote down for their test results.

Therefore, some of the participants might have written down grades they thought the researchers wanted instead of what they could really remember.

In this drawing based on the one from Allport and Postman's (1947) study, a white man is holding a razor and is confronting a black man with it. This reverses a commonly-held stereotype of the time (still held by some people today) that black men are dangerous and more likely than white men to commit violent crimes.

Exam-style questions

1. State what is meant by the term 'social categorisation'. (1)

2. Using an example, explain what is meant by the term 'stereotype'. (3)

3. Sam hears his mum and dad having a conversation in which they use racist terms to refer to members of an ethnic group. The next day at school, Sam shouts the same words in the playground at a boy from that ethnic group and tries to pick a fight with him.

   (a) Explain Sam's behaviour using the concept of stereotypes. (3)

   (b) Referring to Sam's behaviour, explain the formation of stereotypes. (3)

4. Describe **one** finding of the key study by Chatard et al. (2007). (2)

5. Explain what the findings of Chatard et al's (2007) study tell us about the effects of stereotypes. (3)

6. Explain **one** strength of the key study by Chatard et al. (2007). (3)

7. Tim has cerebral palsy and learning difficulties. He is bullied in and out of school by a boy who calls him hurtful names usually focusing on his disability. Other students are more supportive. But although their language is less harsh, they still often assume that Tim cannot do anything for himself.

   Evaluate social categorisation using the above scenario. In your answer you should consider both the formation and effects of stereotypes. (9)

An issue to consider

TV programmes used to cast white men in the roles of doctors, judges etc. But now great efforts are made to use counterstereotypes to change attitudes.

Do you think this works?

GET ACTIVE Our stereotypes

Social groups that are often stereotyped include: old people, teenagers, fat people, skinny people, students, nurses, politicians.

Write down some words you associate with each of these groups (please avoid extreme insults or slurs). Bear in mind that thinking about these stereotypes does not mean you accept them.

1. Compare your list with someone else's. What are the similarities and differences? Are any of the words you have used positive?

2. Why do you think some stereotypes are positive and some (most?) are negative?

3. You probably know individual people who are members of these groups. Would you apply your words to them? Why or why not?

Specification content

B2 Social approach

Key concept:

● Social categorisation (formation and effect of stereotypes).

Key study:

● Chatard et al. (2007) 'How good are you in math?' The effect of gender stereotypes on students' recollection of their school marks.

Key concept 1 and key study

BOGOF

Buy One Get One Free! 50% off! Two for the Price of One! Big Discounts Today Only!

Everyone likes a special offer – but why do shops and brands do them? Surely such offers reduce profits?

The answer is that special offers are good in the longer term because they encourage loyalty and repeat business. They do this by making us feel good about the brand.

When a chocolate bar or bottle of wine is 30% cheaper in a shop it makes you feel good to think you've grabbed yourself a bargain. You associate this good feeling with the product, so that next time you see it you'll feel good about it again even if it is full price. You might even feel good about the shop as well and decide to shop there again.

Retailers use lots of ways to make us learn to love their products. This spread will help you to understand the psychological principles behind this.

Specification terms

Classical conditioning A form of learning where a neutral stimulus is associated with an unconditioned stimulus, taking on its properties so that a new stimulus–response is learned.

Conditioned response (CR) The response produced by the CS on its own. A new association has been formed so that the NS now produces the UCR (which is now called the CR).

Conditioned stimulus (CS) A stimulus that only produces the desired response after pairing with the UCS.

Neutral stimulus (NS) Any stimulus that does not produce the desired response. It becomes a conditioned stimulus after being paired with the UCS.

Unconditioned response (UCR) An unlearned response to an unconditioned stimulus.

Unconditioned stimulus (UCS) Any stimulus that produces a response without learning taking place.

Before conditioning	During conditioning	After conditioning
Food (UCS) → Salivation (UCR)	Bell (NS) → No response	Bell (NS) paired with food (UCS) → Salivation (UCR)	Bell (CS) → Salivation (CR)

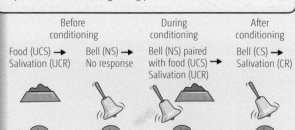

Pavlov's dogs formed a new association between food and the sound of a bell. They were quickly classically conditioned to salivate to the sound of the bell on its own.

Key concept: Classical conditioning

Classical conditioning is a form of learning first scientifically studied by Ivan Pavlov (see diagram below left). It is learning through *association*. It takes place when we associate two stimuli with each other. An *unconditioned (unlearned) stimulus* (UCS) is repeatedly paired with a *neutral stimulus* (NS). Initially, the NS produces no response but eventually produces the same response as the one produced by the UCS.

Before conditioning

The UCS triggers an unlearned response. The smell of food is a good example of a UCS because it makes us salivate automatically. We do not have to learn this response so it is an *unconditioned response* (UCR). Any other stimulus that does not produce the target response (salivation in this example) is an NS. For example, the sound of a bell or of your name being spoken, a tap on the wrist, none of these will produce salivation.

During conditioning

The individual repeatedly experiences the UCS and NS close together in time ('pairing'). The NS is no longer 'neutral' when the person eventually learns to associate it with the UCS. Pairing has the strongest effect on conditioning when the NS occurs just before the UCS. It usually has to happen several times for conditioning to take place.

After conditioning

After enough pairings, the NS (on its own) produces the same response as the UCS. The NS is now a *conditioned stimulus* (CS) and the response it produces is called a *conditioned response* (CR).

Key study: Watson and Rayner (1920) Conditioned emotional reaction – 'Little Albert'

Aims

John Watson and Rosalie Rayner wanted to show that emotional responses such as fear can be learned through classical conditioning.

Procedure

The participant was a baby boy called Albert. He was shown several objects one at a time (e.g. white rat, rabbit, masks, wooden blocks). A metal bar was struck with a hammer to test his response to a loud noise. Classical conditioning began two months later over several sessions. Albert was shown the white rat several times and the metal bar was struck (loud noise) whenever he reached out for the animal.

Findings

In the first session Albert showed no fear responses to any of the stimuli. However, he showed an unconditioned response (UCR) of fear to the loud noise (UCS) – he cried.

In the second session, Albert showed clear avoidance of the rat, pulling away when it came towards him. He eventually cried as the rat approached and tried to crawl away.

In the third session he showed a conditioned fear response (CR) to each white furry object (and no response to other objects).

Albert continued to show a fear response to white furry objects in later sessions but these became less extreme over time and when experienced in a different environment.

Conclusions

Classically conditioning a fear response to a neutral stimulus is relatively straightforward, at least in very young children. Watson and Rayner also concluded that a fear response conditioned to one stimulus will generalise to other similar stimuli without further conditioning (*stimulus generalisation*).

A useful application of classical conditioning is for treating gambling addiction. It works on the basis that if a behaviour can be conditioned, then it can be reduced or eliminated through counterconditioning. For example, each time a person reads a gambling-related phrase they are given an electric shock so that they learn to associate gambling with pain rather than pleasure.

Evaluation

Application to aversion therapy

One strength is that classical conditioning is the basis of a therapy used to treat some psychological disorders, including gambling addiction.

In *aversion therapy*, a gambling addict is given a painful electric shock (UCS) when they read gambling-related phrases on cards (NS). The shock produces an unconditioned response (UCR) of discomfort/anxiety. After several pairings, the NS becomes a CS and produces the same discomfort (now a CR).

This shows that classical conditioning has useful applications that can reduce psychological suffering and improve quality of life.

Incomplete explanation of learning

One weakness is that classical conditioning only explains how a limited range of behaviours is learned (e.g. simple reflex behaviours).

More complex behaviours involve other learning processes (see the next two spreads). For example, classical conditioning can explain how a phobia of dogs is acquired. But on its own it cannot account for how that phobia is then maintained over time (e.g. how we learn to avoid dogs).

This means classical conditioning is just a partial explanation of learning.

Evaluation

Some good experimental controls

One strength of the study is that it was well-designed to control potentially *extraneous variables*.

For instance, conditioning took place in a controlled environment to prevent irrelevant stimuli (temperature, lighting, etc.) from influencing the procedure.

This meant Watson and Rayner knew that the changes in Albert's responses were due to classical conditioning and not to other factors.

Poor generalisability

One weakness is that Little Albert was the only participant in the study, which limits the applicability of the findings.

Albert was an emotionally stable baby who rarely cried or was afraid. This in itself is quite unusual, so indicates that Albert was unlike most babies. In other words, he was not representative of the population of babies.

Therefore, the findings of the study are not generalisable and tell us little about classical conditioning of fear responses in other children.

GET ACTIVE Say cheese!

Laila is a professional photographer. She often takes photos of people indoors using a flash. The camera also makes a 'whirring' noise when the picture is taken. Laila has noticed that most people blink the first couple of times the flash goes off. If she then takes a picture without the flash, they still blink.

1. *Draw a diagram of the classical conditioning process in this scenario. Include 'before', 'during' and 'after' stages. Identify the UCS, UCR, NS, CS and CR at the various stages.*

Laila has also noticed that if she continues to take pictures without the flash, the blinking eventually stops.

2. *Describe a similar finding from the Little Albert study.*

Exam-style questions

1. State what is meant by the term 'classical conditioning'. (1)
2. Describe **one** example of classical conditioning from everyday life. (2)
3. Marcus is a smoker. The first time he had a cigarette he enjoyed the pleasurable sensations of the first draw. Now every time Marcus looks at his lighter he gets a bit of a buzz.

   Identify the UCR, the CS and the CR in this scenario. (3)
4. Freya is a solicitor who works in a big law firm. Every time Freya's boss asks her to come into her office, Freya feels anxious. Her heart rate increases, she sweats and her hands shake.

   Use your knowledge of classical conditioning to explain Freya's reaction. (3)
5. Describe **one** finding of the key study by Watson and Rayner (1920). (2)
6. Explain what the findings of Watson and Rayner's (1920) study tell us about classical conditioning. (3)
7. Explain **one** weakness of the key study by Watson and Rayner (1920). (3)
8. Marina is explaining to her friends how she developed a phobia of dogs. 'It's because I was bitten by a dog when I was a kid. It hurt a lot and made me cry.' One of her friends says, 'OK, but I was bitten by a dog and it hurt but I didn't get a phobia.'

   Evaluate the concept of classical conditioning. In your answer you should consider: (a) Marina's and her friend's experiences, and (b) Watson and Rayner's (1920) key study. (9)

An issue to consider

Recent research has found that plants can be classically conditioned.

How would that work and why would this be an advantage for plants?

Specification content

B3 Learning approach

Key concepts:

● Classical conditioning – learning by association, to include the role of the unconditioned stimulus, unconditioned response, neutral stimulus, conditioned stimulus and conditioned response.

Key study:

● Watson and Rayner (1920) Conditioned emotional reactions – 'Little Albert'.

Key concept 2 and key study

Put down your guns

Up until 2010 the city of Richmond in California had a serious problem with gun violence. It was the ninth most dangerous city in the whole of the US. The police knew that 17 young men were responsible for 70% of shootings.

DeVone Boggan was the head of Richmond's Office of Neighborhood Safety and he had a plan to tackle the violence. Prison, fines and other punishments had failed to make a difference. So Boggan began in 2007 by employing streetwise people to build relationships with these young men. In 2010 Boggan invited the men to a meeting and made them an offer – he would pay them not to fire their guns. They could earn up to $1000 every month for nine months as long as they stuck to a mentoring programme and didn't use their guns.

In other words, instead of punishing bad behaviour, Boggan was going to reward (reinforce) good behaviour.

Did it work? In the first year, gun crime in the city reduced by half. By 2014 the reduction was 76%. Drug use also declined, and school and job attendance went up. For most, the positive results continued even after the cash stopped.

Specification terms

Negative reinforcement The reinforcer is the removal of an unpleasant stimulus, which makes the behaviour more likely to be repeated.

Operant conditioning A form of learning in which behaviour is shaped and maintained by its consequences: reinforcement (positive or negative) or punishment (positive or negative).

Positive reinforcement The reinforcer is a pleasant consequence of the behaviour, making the behaviour more likely to happen again.

Punishment The consequence of a behaviour is unpleasant, making the behaviour less likely to be repeated.

Reinforcement A behaviour is followed by a consequence that increases the probability of the behaviour being repeated.

A Skinner box

In this very controlled environment, the food dispenser provides reinforcers (food pellets) for the rat's behaviour (e.g. pressing the lever). The electrified grid can provide a positive punisher (electric shock) or a negative reinforcer (when the shock is turned off).

Loudspeaker Response lever Lights Electrified grid Food dispenser

Key concept: Operant conditioning

What is operant conditioning?

We form a link between a behaviour (the operant) and its consequence (the result that follows it), therefore it is learning by consequences rather than by association (classical conditioning).

Depending on the consequence, the probability of the behaviour being repeated increases or decreases. There are two consequences.

Consequence 1 – Reinforcement

This is the consequence that *increases* the probability of a behaviour being repeated. Any consequence that does this is said to *reinforce* the behaviour (it is reinforcing, it is a reinforcer). There are two main types:

- **Positive reinforcement** occurs when a behaviour is followed by a pleasant consequence. The consequence could be something tangible (e.g. food, money) or intangible (e.g. a smile or nice comment). Either way, the consequence reinforces the behaviour and makes it more likely to happen.
- **Negative reinforcement** occurs when a behaviour is followed by the removal of an unpleasant stimulus. For example, the removal of pain negatively reinforces the behaviour it follows and makes it more likely the behaviour will be repeated.

Consequence 2 – Punishment

This is the consequence that *reduces* the probability of a behaviour being repeated. Any such consequence is said to *punish* the behaviour (it is punishing, it is a punisher). Again, there are two main types:

- **Positive punishment** is when a behaviour is followed by an unpleasant consequence (e.g. a slap or harsh words).
- **Negative punishment** occurs when a behaviour is followed by the removal of something pleasant (e.g. being fined or grounded, because there has been *removal* of money or freedom).

Key study: Skinner (1932) On the rate of formation of a conditioned reflex

Aims

B.F. Skinner wanted to measure the rate at which rats would press a lever when a food pellet was delivered after each lever-press. Would the food act as a reinforcer of lever-pressing?

Procedure

Four rats individually spent time in a Skinner box (left). To begin with the lever could not be pressed but food pellets were dispensed at various time intervals. The rats ignored these for a while, but then would eat one as soon as it appeared. This was done so the rats 'knew' the pellet was food. Skinner then released the lever so that it could be pressed and now food was dispensed every time the rat pressed the lever.

Findings

For two of the rats, it took just one press of the lever (and delivery of food) for them to immediately start pressing the lever at a high rate, i.e. they had learned that pressing the lever brought food.

Another rat pressed the lever once (receiving food), but it took over an hour for it to press a second time (and get food). Only then did it start pressing at a high rate.

The fourth rat pressed the lever five times (receiving food each time) before starting to press at a high rate (with over two hours between the first and fifth presses).

Conclusions

The behaviour of animals is not free, it is determined by 'natural laws'.

Skinner claimed he had discovered a new form of learning, different from Pavlov's classical conditioning. He argued that operant conditioning was more like learning in everyday life (because it was faster).

Skinner also concluded that just one reinforcement was all it took to change the rats' behaviour immediately.

Evaluation

Supporting research evidence

One strength is that operant conditioning is supported by both human and animal studies.

Many lab studies (by Skinner and others) have shown how operant conditioning works in various animal species. The findings reliably demonstrate how behaviour is influenced by reinforcement and punishment. Human studies (e.g. Chase *et al.* 2015) have even discovered brain areas and structures that are linked with reinforcement of behaviour.

This research supports the view that operant conditioning is a key form of learning in many animal and human behaviours.

Not a complete explanation of learning

One weakness is that operant conditioning can only explain how existing behaviours are strengthened or weakened.

Operant conditioning can explain some complex behaviours where classical conditioning cannot. For example, it can explain how a phobia is maintained over time (through avoidance that is negatively reinforcing). But it cannot explain how the phobia first appears.

This means operant conditioning is an incomplete theory that does not account for all behaviours.

Evaluation

Operant conditioning in education and childcare

One strength is that there are numerous practical applications of Skinner's research and operant conditioning.

Reinforcement is often used in educational and childcare settings such as schools and nurseries. For example, good work and behaviour can be reinforced by praise or gold stars. Punishment is often used in schools and by parents to eliminate undesirable behaviour (e.g. isolation, 'naughty step').

This shows Skinner was right to say that operant conditioning has uses in the real world as well as theoretical importance.

Problems with generalisation

One weakness is that Skinner made some sweeping conclusions about behaviour based on the rats in his study.

He argued that all animals (including humans) learn in the same ways, but this is debatable. In the key study, Skinner was not at all interested in any mental processing that may have come between the stimulus (food) and the response (lever-pressing). But humans probably have more conscious insight into their behaviour than rats. To understand human behaviour we have to consider mental processes.

Therefore, it is inappropriate to generalise the behaviour of the rats in Skinner's study to more complex human behaviour.

A person's obsession with their mobile phone can be explained by operant conditioning. There are lots of features of phones that most people find very rewarding.

GET ACTIVE Conditioning weight loss

Max joined a slimming club because he wanted to lose 20 kilos. The programme worked by allocating points to different foods. But he was allowed to use some points on treats that he liked such as chocolate. He was set targets and each time he achieved one he was given a badge. Max also joined the club's online community where members helped each other with encouraging messages.

1. *How could operant conditioning help Max lose weight?*
2. *Can you think of any other ways operant conditioning can be used to encourage healthy behaviours?*

Exam-style questions

1. State what is meant by the term 'operant conditioning'. (1)
2. Describe an example of operant conditioning from everyday life. (2)
3. When five-year-old Larry helped tidy the living room, his mum gave him a sweet. But when he bit his sister he had to go and sit on the naughty step. He was allowed off when he apologised.

   Using the scenario above, give **one** example of each of the following: positive reinforcement, negative reinforcement and punishment. (3)
4. Ellie works in a call centre selling insurance policies to customers. Every time someone sells a policy, the manager plays a fanfare and praises them. When this happened to Ellie, she worked even harder and made more calls.

   Use **one** aspect of operant conditioning to explain Ellie's behaviour. (3)
5. Explain how the findings of the key study by Skinner (1932) support the view that learning can take place through operant conditioning. (3)
6. Explain **one** strength or **one** weakness of the key study by Skinner (1932). (3)
7. Russ is addicted to playing on fruit machines. He gets a thrill from all the flashing lights and loud noises and occasionally the money he wins. His partner is violent towards him, so he likes to escape his real life sometimes.

   Discuss the view that learning takes place through operant conditioning. In your answer you should consider: (a) different kinds of reinforcement and punishment, and (b) Russ' behaviour in the scenario outlined above. (9)

An issue to consider

Do you think that operant conditioning is a realistic way of changing other people's behaviour (as described in the box on the facing page (Put down your guns)?

Do you think there are ethical issues with controlling people's behaviour like this?

Specification content

B3 Learning approach

Key concept:
- Operant conditioning – learning by consequences, to include the role of positive reinforcement, negative reinforcement and punishment.

Key study:
- Skinner (1932) On the rate of formation of a conditioned reflex.

Key concept 3 and key study

Are criminals born or made?

The idea that some people are 'born bad' is a popular one. But even bad people have to learn how to behave like criminals. Take Pablo Escobar for instance. He rose from obscurity to control the trade in cocaine between Colombia and the USA, and in the process became one of the wealthiest and most feared people in the world.

But he started his criminal career selling stolen gravestones before moving on to selling stolen cigarettes. He learned his trade from other more experienced criminals. He accompanied them on 'jobs' and observed what was involved in criminal activity.

Escobar was highly motivated. He aimed to be a millionaire before he was 22, so he wanted to learn. He was a bodyguard for a local drug kingpin which gave him the opportunity to observe at first-hand exactly what was involved in successful drug smuggling. He was surrounded by people with greater status than him, who were well-off and respected in their world.

This was Escobar's 'training ground'. He used it as the foundation of a criminal career that brought him unimaginable wealth and cost thousands of people their lives before he was killed in a shootout in 1993, aged 44.

Specification terms

Imitation Occurs when a learner reproduces the behaviour they observed being demonstrated by a model. It is more likely to occur when the observer identifies with the model.

Modelling Either an observer imitates the behaviour of a model or a model demonstrates a behaviour that may be imitated by an observer.

Observation Actively attending to and watching (or listening to) the behaviour of others (models).

Social learning A form of learning in which behaviours are acquired through observation, modelling, imitation and vicarious reinforcement. Cognitive factors play a key role.

Vicarious reinforcement Occurs when a learner observes a model's behaviour being reinforced.

Key concept: Social learning theory (SLT)

Albert Bandura (1962) proposed SLT to explain how learning often occurs without *direct* reinforcement. Instead, a behaviour can be learned *indirectly* just by *observing* and *imitating* another individual whose behaviour has been reinforced.

Modelling

Modelling a behaviour means demonstrating it to another person (usually not deliberately). The person who performs the behaviour is the *model*.

The term 'modelling' is also used when a person imitates a model's behaviour.

Learning through observation

The observer actively focuses their attention on the model's behaviour and watches how it is performed. The model's actions have to be retained in the observer's memory before they can be repeated.

Imitation

The observer may imitate the model. This is more likely if the observer identifies with the model. This happens for two main reasons – either the observer perceives the model to be similar to themselves (e.g. same age or gender) or they value and/or admire the model (e.g. because they have social status).

Vicarious reinforcement

A behaviour is imitated if the learner is motivated to do so – and this depends on observing positive consequences. If the observer sees a model performing an action and being reinforced, this makes it more likely that the observer will repeat the action. This is *vicarious* (seeing someone else do it) and reinforcing. This could explain the influence of media celebrities. For example, a young girl who sees a very thin celebrity having her behaviour rewarded with fame, status and attention might be more inclined to imitate the celebrity's 'look'.

Vicarious reinforcement is *indirect* reinforcement.

Key study: Bandura *et al.* (1961) Transmission of aggression through imitation of aggressive models

Aims

Bandura *et al.* wanted to see if children were more likely to behave aggressively after observing an *aggressive* model, and if they were more likely to imitate same-sex models.

Procedure

Male and female children were randomly placed into one of three groups. The aggression group observed an adult model behaving aggressively towards an inflatable 'Bobo doll' (punching, kicking, shouting, etc.). The non-aggression group observed an adult constructing mechanical toys. The control group played with no model present.

The children were then allowed to play with some toys (including the Bobo doll) and their behaviour was observed and rated (see page 108).

Findings

The children who observed the model behaving aggressively were more likely to behave aggressively (both imitating the model and acts of non-imitative aggression) than the other two groups of children.

Boys imitated the aggressive behaviours of a male model more often than they imitated a female model.

Conclusions

Aggression is a social behaviour that can be imitated by children through observing models.

Imitation is more likely when the model is the same sex as the observer, which supports the role of *identification*.

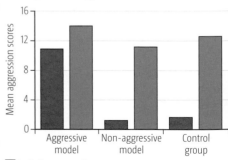

Bar chart showing overall comparison of aggression following modelled aggression and control conditions.

■ Imitative aggression
■ Non-imitative aggression

The graph above shows that all the groups showed fairly similar levels of general aggression – it was just the specific imitation of the model's behaviour towards Bobo that was different.

The word 'bobo' is Spanish for 'clown'.

The word 'doll' is English for 'doll'.

Evaluation

Evidence supporting SLT

One strength is support for SLT from studies of humans and animals.

The key study by Bandura *et al.* shows that children will imitate an aggressive adult model, especially if the child identifies with the model. Bandura's later research (e.g. 1965) confirmed that children are more likely to imitate an adult model when the model's behaviour is reinforced (i.e. rewarded). Christine Nicol and Stuart Pope (1999) showed that even chickens imitated a same-sex model with high status (in pecking for food).

This supports the SLT view that behaviours are learned through observation and imitation, and that vicarious reinforcement and identification play important roles in imitation.

Not a complete explanation

One weakness of SLT is that it cannot explain the role of genetic factors in learning.

Ken Kendler *et al.* (2015) found that levels of aggression are more similar in identical twins than they are in non-identical twins. As identical twins are more closely genetically related than non-identical twins, this strongly suggests aggressive behaviour is partly genetic and not just due to *social learning*.

This suggests that SLT is not a complete explanation of learning, and a full account can only be produced by considering other factors.

Evaluation

Learning aggressive behaviours

One strength is that the findings of the key study can help us understand how children acquire aggressive behaviours and how they can be reduced.

Thanks to Bandura's research, psychologists appreciate how the family environment can create aggression in children, through observation and imitation of aggressive adult models. The findings are especially relevant to how boys learn to be physically aggressive, through identification with their fathers.

This has important implications for social *policy*, for example on custody of children and parental contact after divorce.

Artificial environment

One weakness of the key study is that it was carried out in controlled lab conditions.

This means that the situation in which the researchers measured aggression was very different from the real-life situations in which children typically behave aggressively towards other people (rather than towards a doll).

Therefore, the findings of the study are difficult to generalise and may tell us little about children's aggressive behaviour in real-life situations such as playgrounds and the home.

GET ACTIVE Guitar lessons

Hari is learning to play the guitar. He is getting lessons from Nisha. She shows him how to play the chords, where to place his fingers and how to strum. Hari copies and Nisha praises him when he gets it right. Hari likes the way Nisha really seems to enjoy playing the guitar as well.

How can Hari's learning be explained in terms of classical conditioning, operant conditioning and social learning?

Exam-style questions

1. State what is meant by the term 'vicarious reinforcement'. (1)

2. Describe an example of social learning from everyday life. (2)

3. Ava and Livvy are playing football when Ava flicks the ball up and volleys it into the back of the net. Livvy is impressed and Ava explains that she watched her brother doing the trick. When he got it right he ran around the garden shouting with joy.

   Use your knowledge of social learning theory to explain Ava's behaviour. (3)

4. Barney is eight years old and has started bullying other children. Several times he has seen an older boy bullying children in the playground to get money or sweets or just to show who's the boss.

   (a) Describe **one** type of social learning Barney is showing. (2)

   (b) Use **one** finding of the key study by Bandura *et al.* (1961) to explain Barney's experience. (2)

5. Explain how **one** finding of the key study by Bandura *et al.* (1961) demonstrated the influence of social learning. (2)

6. Explain **one** strength and **one** weakness of the key study by Bandura *et al.* (1961). (4)

7. Most students learn in a social environment made up of many people.

   Analyse how social learning might contribute to student learning in a school/college context. In your answer you should consider observation, modelling, imitation and vicarious reinforcement. (9)

An issue to consider

Can you think of any things you do which could not be explained by direct or indirect conditioning?

Specification content

B3 Learning approach

Key concept:

● Social learning theory – learning through observation, to include the role of observation, imitation, modelling and vicarious reinforcement.

Key study:

● Bandura *et al.* (1961) Transmission of aggression through imitation of aggressive models.

Introduction and key concept 1

How identical is identical?

Psychologists call twins identical because they have exactly the same genes. Most people use the word in everyday language to mean that twins look identical. But do they really? Look more closely and you will see that even the most 'identical' of twins look a bit different.

Things get even more interesting when you consider behaviour. Even identical twins who have been brought up together in the same home do not behave identically. For instance one might be gay and the other straight. One becomes a scientist, the other an artist.

What this tells us is that, even if you had an identical twin, there will never be someone exactly like you. Your experiences and your environment will affect you in different ways to make you the person you are. It's not 'all in the genes'.

Specification terms

Genes A unit of inheritance. They consist of chemical instructions (DNA) which tell your body what proteins to manufacture – and basically that is what you are, a huge number of proteins. Genes are inherited from parents and contribute to the development of an individual's characteristics.

Genotype An individual's total set of genes.

Phenotype The observable characteristics which result from the interaction between a person's genotype and environmental factors.

SRY gene Sex-determining region Y gene which triggers the appearance of testes in an embryo and the development of that individual into a biological male.

The chromosome on the left is an X chromosome and on the right is a Y chromosome. They are called X and Y because they resemble the shape of these letters. This photograph was taken using a very high-powered microscope.

Influence of biology on behaviour

Biology and behaviour

Biological structures and processes within the body have a profound effect on our psychological functioning and behaviour. Biological psychologists argue that, as the mind basically 'lives' in the brain, our thoughts, feelings and behaviour have a physical basis (everything psychological is first biological).

There are several biological influences we look at on the next few spreads. They all vary slightly between males and females, leading to some *sex differences* in behaviour.

- **Genes** are described below.
- **Neuroanatomy** refers to the *structure* of the nervous system, including the brain. Different parts of the structure have different functions such as one area controls what we see (the visual area) and another area controls movement (the motor area).
- **Neurochemistry** concerns the chemical processes that occur within the brain and nervous system. Messages are sent around the brain and body via nerves (also called *neurons*) but also via chemical messengers (*neurotransmitters*).
- **Evolution** concerns the way animals change over millions of years. At one time the only life on Planet Earth was small one-celled organisms. Over time these life forms have evolved into all the species you see around us today. The process of *evolution* explains how this happened.

Key concept: Genes

What are genes?

Genes are located on chromosomes and humans have 46 chromosomes (23 pairs). Each gene is made up of strands of DNA (deoxyribonucleic acid). Genes carry 'instructions' relating to the physical and non-physical characteristics of living organisms, such as the colour of your hair and whether you have a calm temperament. Typically each individual inherits two copies (called *alleles*) of every gene, one from each parent.

Genotype and phenotype

Genotype refers to an individual's actual genetic make-up. It is what you inherit from your parents.

However, your genotype doesn't determine your physical and non-physical characteristics directly because the genes have to be expressed through an interaction with your 'environment'. Even within your body the environment has an influence, for example the food you eat affects your body's internal environment.

A person's *phenotype* is how their genes are actually expressed. A phenotype is therefore an interaction of genotype and environmental influences.

Identical twins have the same genotype because they have inherited exactly the same genes. But the expression of their genes (phenotype) differs. They may look physically different because, for example one twin goes to the gym and the other doesn't and therefore one twin has developed bigger muscles. The other twin might develop bigger muscles too – but only if their environment changed.

The distinction between genotype and phenotype strongly suggests that most human behaviours are due to an interaction of inherited (nature) and environmental (nurture) factors.

The *SRY* gene

One pair of chromosomes determines biological sex – XX for female, XY for male. The so-called Y-chromosome is in reality just a stunted X-chromosome, missing some of the genetic material.

Located on the Y chromosome is a gene called the sex-determining region Y gene (*SRY* gene). In typical development before birth, the *SRY* gene switches on other genes causing an XY embryo to develop testes. In adult males the testes produce sperm but during development the testes produce male *sex hormones* and these hormones cause the embryo to become biologically male. Without the *SRY* gene, other genes remain switched off so the embryo develops into a female.

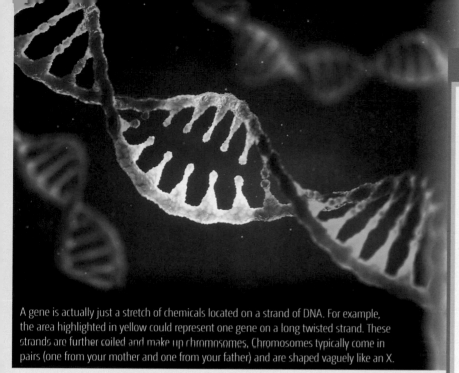

A gene is actually just a stretch of chemicals located on a strand of DNA. For example, the area highlighted in yellow could represent one gene on a long twisted strand. These strands are further coiled and make up chromosomes. Chromosomes typically come in pairs (one from your mother and one from your father) and are shaped vaguely like an X.

Evaluation

An interactionist approach

One strength of understanding genotype and phenotype is that these concepts support interactionism in psychology.

For example, one version of the *BRCA1* gene has been linked to breast cancer risk in women. But not every woman who has this version of the *BRCA1* gene develops breast cancer, so clearly other factors (e.g. stress) interact with the genotype to produce the observable outcome (phenotype).

Taking into account the interactions between nature and nurture provides a much fuller and richer explanation of human behaviour.

Risk of oversimplification

One weakness is that some research oversimplifies the influence of genes.

It is very rare that only one gene determines a behaviour. We talk about one version of the *BRCA1* gene causing cancer but what it causes is an increased risk. Not everyone with the abnormal version develops cancer. The same is true for 'a gene for depression' or 'a gene for blue eyes'. This is not an accurate view of how genes operate. No human behaviours are caused by single genes. Instead, many genes (sometimes hundreds or thousands) make small but important contributions in complex interactions with each other. Also genes do not produce effects in isolation. They interact with environmental influences to produce a phenotype.

The danger is that oversimplified explanations of how genes work exaggerate the role of nature and present a misleading view of the causes of behaviour.

GET ACTIVE

We have seen that genetically identical twins are not identical in their behaviour or even their appearance (even their fingerprints are different). This is why we make a very important distinction between genotype and phenotype.

For example, the ability to taste phenylthiocarbamide (PTC), a bitter-tasting chemical) in food is genetically controlled by a single gene. But even people in whom the gene is 'switched on' will not always taste it.

1. *How can the concepts of genotype and phenotype explain this?*
2. *What environmental factors could influence the genotype?*

ct it in newborn babies. A baby with PKU placed on a low-protein diet is very likely to develop normally and never experience symptoms.

Evaluate the influence of genes on behaviour with reference to this scenario. In your answer you should consider the roles of genotype and phenotype, and relate this to PKU. (9)

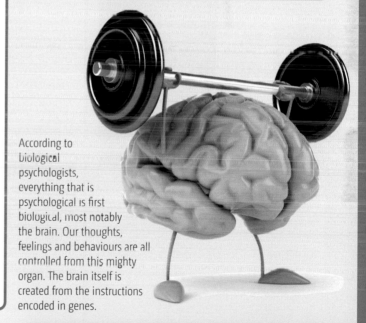

According to biological psychologists, everything that is psychological is first biological, most notably the brain. Our thoughts, feelings and behaviours are all controlled from this mighty organ. The brain itself is created from the instructions encoded in genes.

An issue to consider

Given what you have read on this spread, how do you think psychologists use genes in their explanations of behaviour?

Specification content
B4 Biological approach
Key concepts:
● The influence of biology on behaviour.
● Genes, including the role of genotype, phenotype and the SRY gene.

Key concept 2 and key study

Poking around in the brain

If you open up a person's skull you can poke different areas of a person's brain – it doesn't hurt as there aren't pain receptors in the brain. The interesting thing is that if you poke some areas (well, electrically stimulate them), the person being poked may suddenly experience a particular memory. If you poke a different area the person might experience a different memory, hear music, report sensations on their skin or they might move a part of their body.

The brain surgeon who famously did this for the first time in the 1950s was Wilder Penfield. He was treating people with epilepsy and tried to relieve their seizures by destroying small areas of their brains.

But to do this (and because every patient's brain is different) he first of all had to work out which areas to destroy and which to avoid.

This poking around enabled Penfield and others to draw a map of the brain. Some of the brain areas Penfield stimulated are described on this spread.

Specification terms

Localisation of function Specific brain areas control and regulate specific physical and psychological activities.

Neuroanatomy Structure of the brain and other parts of the nervous system.

Sex differences The ways in which males and females are not the same.

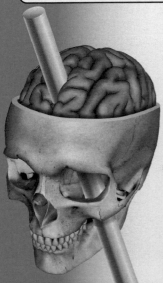

This drawing shows the path the tamping iron took through Gage's skull. Harlow described the iron as 'passing completely through his head...picked up afterwards by his men, smeared with blood and brain'.

Key concept: Neuroanatomy

What is neuroanatomy?

Neuroanatomy refers to the structure of the brain and nervous system. The most basic neuroanatomical feature of the brain is that it is divided into two halves, called *hemispheres* (left and right).

Localisation of brain function

Psychologists generally accept the view that different brain areas perform certain specific functions. This is *localisation*. If a specific brain area is damaged, the function associated with that area is affected (impaired). The brain's outer layer is called the *cortex*. It is a very thin and highly folder layer that covers the inner structures of the brain (like an orange peel). This part of the brain is highly developed in humans. Some major areas of it are:

Motor area Each hemisphere has a motor area which controls the voluntary movements of the opposite side of the body. Damage can cause a loss of control over fine movements.

Somatosensory area This is again in both hemispheres. Sensory information from the skin is represented here (e.g. touch, heat, etc.) in proportion to the sensitivity of the body part (e.g. the regions for the face and hands account for over half of the somatosensory area).

Visual area This is at the back of the brain in both hemispheres. Each eye sends information from the right 'half' of the visual field to the left visual area, and from the left 'half' of the visual field to the right visual area. This is why damage to one visual area can cause partial blindness in both eyes.

Sex differences in brain structure

The 'average' brains of women and men are not identical. Total brain volume is greater (on average) in males, even when body size is accounted for.

More importantly there are also volume differences in specific parts of the brain. For example, the *thalamus* is bigger (on average) in females (Ruigrok *et al.* 2014). The thalamus controls signals from the sense organs (eyes, ears, etc.) to other parts of the brain. Women also have stronger nerve connections between the brain hemispheres (see facing page).

One other consistent sex difference is in the thickness of the cortex. According to Stuart Ritchie *et al.* (2018), brains scans show that the cortex is thicker (on average) in females across almost the whole brain. They also found that cortical thickness varies much more between men than it does between women.

Key study: Harlow (1868) Recovery from the passage of an iron bar through the head

Aims and procedure

To report the unusual case of Phineas P. Gage and the implications for understanding how the brain works. Harlow recorded the details of the case.

Findings

Gage was a foreman working on the railroad in the USA. He was filling holes with gunpowder and pressing down on it with a 'tamping iron', a long iron bar. The powder exploded prematurely, forcing the tamping iron all the way through Gage's skull, fracturing bones and removing parts of his brain (see image on the left). Gage had a seizure but eventually regained consciousness and was able to walk to a cart that took him back to his hotel.

Gage recovered physically, but after seven months the change in his personality was so great that his previous employers would not give him his job back. Gage had been a hard-working and conscientious employee, but now he was often very obstinate. He swore a lot but was 'a child in his intellectual capacity'. He would often make grand plans but then immediately change his mind. His friends said he was 'no longer Gage'. He suffered from epileptic seizures and died at the age of 36, twelve-and-a-half years after the accident.

Conclusions

Harlow believed that Gage's intellectual ability had been severely impaired by the accident but not lost. The accident damaged part of the left side of his brain, affecting its function. The corresponding area on the right side was unaffected but could not completely make up for damage to the left side.

Harlow recognised that some functions and behaviours must be localised in the brain.

Some of the main structures of the brain are shown on the right. The most obvious neuroanatomical feature of the brain is that it is divided into two halves (left and right hemispheres). This image shows the left hemisphere.

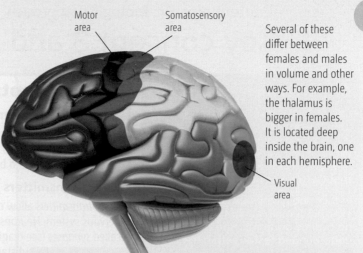

Motor area — Somatosensory area — Visual area

Several of these differ between females and males in volume and other ways. For example, the thalamus is bigger in females. It is located deep inside the brain, one in each hemisphere.

Evaluation

Support for sex differences

One strength is evidence that women's and men's brains are structured differently.

Madhura Ingalhalikar *et al.* (2014) used a brain scanning method called *MRI* (*magnetic resonance imaging*). They found that women's brains had stronger connections *between* the brain hemispheres, but men's brains had stronger connections *within* the hemispheres.

Combined with other studies, this means there may be some truth in the *stereotype* that women are more able than men to cope with several tasks at once.

Structure not function

One weakness is that, just because the brains of females and males differ in structure, it does not mean they function differently.

Some *sex differences* in *brain structure* definitely exist, but research has to then show that these are linked to differences in brain functioning (and also behaviour). Research is ongoing and very few conclusions have been reached.

This means that there has been a lot of unjustified speculation about differences between women and men, unsupported by evidence.

Evaluation

Ahead of his time

One strength is that Harlow made careful *observations* of Gage's recovery

These are not up to modern standards for a thorough *case study* (he wrote just 200 words about the effects on Gage's behaviour). But he did try to link the area of Gage's brain injury to the changes in his personality and intellectual functioning.

This suggests that Harlow was ahead of his time in providing support for localisation as a theory of brain function.

Unjustified conclusions

One weakness is that there is not enough information from the study to draw firm conclusions about localisation.

Harlow insisted that Gage's behaviour and personality had changed out of all recognition so that he was 'no longer Gage'. But little is known about Gage before the accident, so it is hard to judge how much he changed afterwards. He may not have changed that much because he was able to hold down a demanding job later in Chile for at least nine years.

This means it is hard to link brain functions to changes in Gage's behaviour and these changes may have been exaggerated.

GET ACTIVE Read all about it

Here are two headlines from different newspaper websites:

- Men take a fact-based approach to the work environment, while women take a more intuitive approach.
- Can we finally stop talking about 'male' and 'female' brains?

There is a huge gender pay gap in workplaces in the UK. Men consistently earn more than women, often when doing the same job. Some people think it's because men's and women's brains are different. What do you think?

Which of the two headlines best matches your own view? Explain your answer based on your knowledge of sex differences in brain structure.

Exam-style questions

1. State what is meant by the term 'neuroanatomy'. (1)

2. Reg had a stroke which affected his speech. He found it hard to find the right words and was very slow in speaking. A brain scan showed damage to a small area in the left side of Reg's brain.

   Explain what Reg's experience tells us about localisation of function. (3)

3. Jerry and Ruby are arguing about the differences between women and men. 'Our brains are bigger,' says Jerry. 'Yes well, size isn't everything,' replies Ruby.

   Outline sex differences in brain structure with reference to this argument. (3)

4. Give **one** finding from the key study by Harlow (1868). (2)

5. Explain what the key study by Harlow (1868) can tell us about localisation of function. (3)

6. Explain **one** strength or **one** weakness of the key study by Harlow (1868). (3)

7. Sam was stabbed with a knife through the front of his brain's left hemisphere. He survived the attack and recovered, but his friends noticed that his personality had changed and his college work was nowhere near as good as before.

   Evaluate neuroanatomy with reference to this scenario. In your answer you should consider: (a) basic localisation of function, and (b) the key study by Harlow (1868). (9)

An issue to consider

Does it matter if men's and women's brains are different?

In your experience, how different are men and women anyway?

Do you think difference can be traced back to the brain, or are other factors more important?

Specification content

B4 Biological approach

Key concept:

● Neuroanatomy, including basic localisation of function and sex differences in brain structure.

Key study:

● Harlow (1868) Recovery from the passage of an iron bar through the head.

Key concept 4 and key study

Stressed out

Modern life can be stressful. So many things to do, so little time. Homework, part-time job, Instagram updates... Today you may have to cope with any or all of these. But I can (almost) guarantee that running away from an attacking lion will not be something you have to worry about.

It wasn't always like this. Our evolutionary ancestors were much more concerned about attacking lions than they were about dealing with their overdrafts. The problem is, the body's stress response is still stuck in those days (referred to as the *environment of evolutionary adaptation*).

Our body is great at helping us cope with short-term emergency situations that are over (one way or another) almost as soon as they've begun. But long-term drawn-out stress, of the type so common in modern life, is much more damaging. We have not evolved to deal with that kind of stress.

Specification terms

Environment of evolutionary adaptation (EEA) The habitat in which a species evolved its most recent adaptations. In humans this ended about 10,000 years ago.

Genome lag Changes to the environment occur much more rapidly than changes to our genes.

Sexual selection Attributes or behaviours that increase reproductive success are more likely to be passed on and may become exaggerated over succeeding generations of offspring.

Survival of the fittest Natural selection selects the genes giving rise to characteristics that promote survival and reproduction so they are retained in the population.

Key concept: Evolutionary psychology

Survival of the fittest

The word *evolution* means change. The form and behaviour of all living things change over time through the process of *natural selection*. When life is hard those individuals who possess characteristics that help them to stay alive (and reproduce) are the ones who pass their *genes* on to the next generation. In this way they are 'selected'. This idea, proposed by Charles Darwin (1859), is often called the *survival of the fittest*. Fittest in this context refers to the characteristics that best match ('fit') the demands of the environment.

Environment of evolutionary adaptation (EEA)

When we look at the living things around us today we see the outcome of natural selection – all plants and animals are what they are because their traits enabled them to survive in a particular environment.

In the case of humans, the environment during 99% of our evolutionary history was during the Pleistocene era which ended about 10,000 years ago. At that time humans lived on the African savannah (warm grasslands) as hunter-gatherers. During this time we changed from apes moving around on four legs to upright hairless animals who could use tools and language. Our behaviour and minds have changed to ensure we could survive in that habitat. Therefore, what we are today is largely based on the evolutionary pressures in that environment.

Genome lag

Our minds are still adapted to the EEA. It takes thousands of years for evolutionary pressures to change the human genome (collection of genes). But the world around us changes much more quickly than that. Most of the population no longer lives in small groups but in vast cities alongside countless others – but we still have a 'small group' mentality.

Sexual selection

Evolutionary pressures also act on reproductive success. Darwin noted that some characteristics continued to exist even when they threaten an organism's survival. He realised that such characteristics must confer an advantage, and suggested that the advantage was that they make the individual attractive to potential mates.

An example is the peacock's tail. It is hard for the male bird to carry around (and a big target for predators), but it is attractive to females. So possessing a burdensome tail actually increases the male bird's chances of reproducing and passing on the genes that led to his success.

Key study: Buss *et al.* (1992) Sex differences in jealousy: Evolution, physiology and psychology

Aims

David Buss *et al.* wanted to see if males and females experience different forms of jealousy (sexual or emotional) in response to thoughts of infidelity.

Procedure

Male and female participants (American students) were asked to think of a current or former partner becoming involved with someone else (person X). Which would be more upsetting – their partner forming a deep emotional attachment with X or having passionate sexual intercourse with X? Some participants imagined the two scenarios while their physiological responses were measured (e.g. pulse rate).

Findings

60% of men (17% of women) were more distressed by the sexual infidelity scenario than the emotional infidelity one. 83% of women (40% of men) were more distressed by the emotional infidelity scenario than the sexual one. Men showed more physiological activity in the sexual infidelity scenario compared with the emotional one. Women showed the opposite but the differences were not as strong as they were for men.

Conclusions

The findings support an evolutionary explanation of jealousy.

Male sexual jealousy defends against raising another man's child which would not enhance their own reproductive success. Therefore, sensitivity to sexual infidelity is a trait that would be selected in men.

Female emotional jealousy defends losing a male partner to another woman, and the loss of support raising a child. Emotional infidelity would reduce successful reproduction and thus would be selected in women.

Evaluation

Support for genome lag

One strength is support for the concept of *genome lag* from research into partner preferences.

Our preferences have changed hugely over the last 100 years. Women have a greater role in the workplace that has made many less dependent on men to provide for them (despite ongoing inequalities in earning power). So women's partner preferences are now less dictated by resource considerations.

This shows that a behaviour important to survival – choosing a mate – has been influenced by cultural changes while the genome has changed hardly at all.

Problems with the EEA concept

One weakness is that the concept of the EEA implies that significant evolution of human characteristics halted about 10,000 years ago.

However, there are some evolved changes that suggest this is not the case. For example, most humans are lactose intolerant but some are not. The gene that allows us to digest milk was selected and passed on because it conferred a survival advantage. But this happened less than 10,000 years ago. Other changes are occurring now.

Therefore, some human characteristics may be the outcomes of evolutionary pressures operating much more recently than the EEA. This undermines the significance of the EEA as a main plank of evolutionary psychology.

Evaluation

Physiological and psychological methods

One strength is that Buss *et al.* measured physiological activity as well as feelings of distress.

The question that was posed required a *subjective* answer and assessed the psychological component of jealousy. The physiological measures were *objective* and showed the sex difference in jealousy has a biological basis. This is what we would expect to find if the evolutionary explanation is correct.

Therefore, the findings are more convincing because they are supported by two lines of evidence rather than just one.

Limited sample of participants

One weakness is that the participants were from a single *culture*.

Evolutionary psychology deals in universals – it claims that all humans must show the same behaviours because they are all exposed to the same selective pressures. But the key study investigated jealousy in American students only and their behaviour may have been determined by shared *social norms*.

This means that, as the study focused on only one culture, it could not fully support an evolutionary explanation of jealousy.

We evolved to function in a very different environment from the ones most of us live in today. Perhaps we overeat, become anxious and depressed because we are trying to cope using a mind better-suited to a much earlier time.

GET ACTIVE Phobias

As we have seen on this spread, evolutionary psychologists argue that we try to cope with the stresses of the modern world with a mind that is better-suited (or adapted) to the pressures of the EEA.

Perhaps this explains the existence of some psychological disorders. An example is phobia, usually defined as an extreme or irrational fear of an object, situation or event. Many people from all sorts of cultures are afraid of snakes and spiders. A lot of these people are afraid of such creatures even though they have never personally encountered one.

How do you think evolutionary psychology explains the existence of such fears?

Exam-style questions

1. State what is meant by the term 'survival of the fittest'. (1)

2. A group of schoolchildren are visiting the zoo. They see a peacock unfurl his magnificent tail. One child says, 'I don't know how he manages to get around carrying that.'

   With reference to the child's comment, explain how the peacock's tail supports the concept of sexual selection. (3)

3. Josef is feeling very stressed because he has so much work to do on top of his part-time job. 'I don't think we're cut out for this kind of lifestyle,' he says to his friend.

   Explain the concept of genome lag with reference to Josef's comment. (3)

4. Give **two** conclusions from the key study by Buss *et al.* (1992). (2)

5. Explain what the key study by Buss *et al.* (1992) can tell us about evolutionary psychology. (3)

6. Explain **one** strength or **one** weakness of the key study by Buss *et al.* (1992). (3)

7. Humans have adapted to live in a very different environment from the ones we live in now. Many behaviours that evolved a long time ago are still helping us to survive today.

   Discuss the view that evolutionary psychology can explain human behaviour. In your answer you should consider at least **two** of the following: (a) the environment of evolutionary adaptation, (b) genome lag, (c) survival of the fittest, and (d) sexual selection. (9)

An issue to consider

Evolutionary medicine is an application of evolutionary principles to the treatment of modern health and disease. It suggests that genetically-based physical and psychological disorders actually must have some selective advantages otherwise they would not continue in the gene pool.

If depression is inherited, what might be the selective advantage?

Specification content
B4 Biological approach

Key concept:
- Evolutionary psychology, including the environment of evolutionary adaptation, survival of the fittest, sexual selection and genome lag.

Key study:
- Buss *et al.* (1992) Sex differences in jealousy: Evolution, physiology and psychology.

Revision summary

Overview of four approaches

Assumptions of the cognitive approach	Assumptions of the social approach	Assumptions of the learning approach	Assumptions of the biological approach
Information processing and behaviour Internal mental processes (e.g. perception, memory) operate in stages to make sense of the world.	**Behaviour in social context** People are social animals, psychologists study the influence of others to understand behaviour (e.g. in conformity).	**Behaviour is a learned response** Classical conditioning – Pavlov's dogs, learning through association. Operant conditioning – reinforcement of behaviour from environment.	**Behaviour is influenced by our biology** Physical basis to behaviour – central nervous system (brain), genes, neurochemistry (e.g. serotonin).
The computer analogy Like computers we process through input-processing-output. Hardware (brain), software (information).	**People, culture and society** Differences can be understood in terms of individualist (own needs) vs. collectivist (community's needs).	**The roles of observation and imitation** We observe behaviour and imitate role models, especially if they are rewarded.	**Behaviour and evolution** Natural selection of survival-promoting behaviours, genes passed on (Darwin 1859).

Cognitive approach

Key concept 1: Reconstructive memory

What is it? Memories reconstructed from fragments into meaningful whole.

Role of schema in memory Mental package of knowledge.
- Shortening – bits cut to fit schemas.
- Rationalisation – details distorted to fit schemas.
- Confabulation – details made up to fill gaps in memory.

Evaluation
Application to EWT Eyewitnesses not accurate, due to schemas.

Some memories are accurate Personally important or distinctive details are remembered.

Key study: Bartlett (1932)

Aims Recall of unfamiliar story affected by schemas?

Procedure British participants read *War of the Ghosts* story and then told to another person and so on (serial reproduction).

Findings Recall transformed story – it was shortened, left out supernatural bits, phrases changed to be familiar.

Conclusions Schemas influence recall so story more meaningful, memory is reconstructive.

Evaluation
Realistic theory and research Everyday task, not artificial materials, conclusions relevant to real life.

Unscientific research Procedures not standardised or consistent, different experiences, conclusions may be wrong.

Key concept 2: Cognitive priming

What is it? Experience of one stimulus (prime) affects response to later stimulus.

Role of cognitive scripts Expectations of social situation (e.g. restaurant script).

Types of cognitive priming
- Repetition – same stimulus again.
- Semantic – later stimulus related in meaning to prime.
- Associative – later stimulus associated with prime but not in meaning.

Evaluation
Evidence supports cognitive scripts Playing violent video games, easier recall of aggressive scripts (Möller and Krahé 2009).

Lack of replication Repeating priming studies produces different findings. Therefore, findings are flukes, concept may not be scientific.

Key study: Harris et al. (2009)

Aims Does watching TV food adverts cause snacking?

Procedure (1) Children – cartoon + food or no-food ads. (2) Adults – TV programme + food (fun-snacking or health-promoting) or no-food ads. (3) Measured snacks eaten.

Findings (1) Children who saw food ads ate 45% more snacks than no-food ad group. (2) Adults who saw 'fun' ads ate more than others, unrelated to prior hunger.

Conclusions TV ads prime snack consumption, short-term and long-term.

Evaluation
Application to the problem of obesity Prevent priming influence of TV snack adverts, promote healthy eating and prevent obesity.

Artificial conditions Watching adverts alone in classroom not real-life environment, therefore not meaningful findings.

Key concept 3: Cognitive biases

What are they? Errors in information processing, undermine rational decision-making but speed it up.

Fundamental attribution error (FAE) Explaining other people's behaviour as a result of their personality not situation.

Confirmation bias Notice, store, recall information that confirms existing beliefs.

Hostile attribution bias Neutral behaviour seen as a threatening, aggressive response.

Evaluation
Applications to real-life behaviour Hostile attribution bias explains aggression, confirmation bias explains tribal politics, understanding it can help reduce conflict.

The FAE is not universal Only in individualist cultures e.g. USA (not collectivist e.g. China).

Key study: Loftus and Palmer (1974)

Aims Will changing one word in a sentence affect memory of car speed?

Procedure Films of car accidents, 'About how fast were the cars going when they _____ (into) each other?'

Findings Verb influenced estimates, *smashed* 40.5 mph, *collided* 39.3, *bumped* 38.1, *hit* 34.0, *contacted* 31.8.

Conclusions Changing one word biased responses (later research found memory of event actually changes).

Evaluation
Experimental control Lab setting, e.g. control witness viewpoint, so change of word affected estimates.

Biased sample of participants Young students, more accurate eyewitnesses than older people, hard to generalise findings.

Social approach

Key concept 1: Conformity

What is it? Going along with a group due to invisible 'pressure'.

Normative social influence (NSI) Accept norms of group (conform) to be liked and avoid rejection. Emotional process, stronger in stressful situations.

Informational social influence (ISI) Change behaviour/opinions when we believe others are right/have better information. Cognitive process, especially new or unclear situations.

Evaluation
Research supports NSI Asch's participants went along with group to avoid disapproval. No public pressure, no conformity.

NSI and ISI work together in real life Lower conformity with dissenter, who gives social support (NSI), and is source of information (ISI).

Key study: Asch (1951)

Aims Would people conform with obviously wrong answers given by a group?

Procedure Group of students matched line lengths. Only one participant was genuine, others deliberately gave wrong answers.

Findings Participants conformed on 36.8% of trials, 25% never conformed.

Conclusions People conform mostly to avoid rejection (NSI). But people usually act independently.

Evaluation
Level of control Lab, standardised procedure, so irrelevant variables cannot explain conformity.

Limited application of findings Male US participants, so findings hard to generalise to women and other cultures, may underestimate true conformity level.

Key concept 2: Types of conformity

Internalisation We agree privately and publicly with others, permanent, due to ISI.

Compliance We agree publicly but not privately, temporary conformity, due to NSI.

Identification Combination of other types, agree publicly and privately because we identify with group, only lasts while we are members (Kelman 1958).

Evaluation
Support for Kelman's three types Compliance (Asch 1951), identification (Haney et al. 1973), internalisation (Sherif 1935).

Conformity types lack influence SPS minimises personality and effect of identification (Fromm 1973).

Key study: Haney et al. (1973)

Aims Is guard behaviour due to sadistic personality or brutal situation?

Procedure Stanford Prison Study (SPS), volunteer students played guard or prisoner, uniforms for both roles, guards had power.

Findings Both identified with roles, guards aggressive, prisoners rebellious but then subdued, study ended early.

Conclusions Everyone conformed to roles (identification), including visitors and researchers, power of situations.

Evaluation
The study was controlled e.g. emotionally stable students selected and randomly given roles, so findings due to identification.

The SPS lacked realism Participants play-acted based on belief about how guards and prisoners should behave, so not real-life conformity.

Key concept 3: Social categorisation

What is it? Group membership based on shared characteristics, assume members all the same and different from other groups.

What is a stereotype? Fixed view of a person's behaviour/character based on social category.

How are stereotypes formed? Observe and imitate social information (SLT).

What are the effects of stereotypes?
- Positive – simplifies interactions, reduces cognitive effort.
- Negative – can lead to prejudice, distort and bias social judgements.

Evaluation
Research supporting stereotyping Half of white participants thought black man was holding razor, racist stereotype biased memory (Allport and Postman 1947).

Effects of stereotypes Don't inevitably lead to prejudice. Can hold a stereotype but not agree.

Key study: Chatard et al. (2007)

Aims Does gender stereotype affect recall of maths test results?

Procedure Students rate agreement with general gender stereotype, then rate own abilities, recall last maths/arts results.

Findings Both boys and girls given stereotype reminder overestimated arts results, girls underestimated maths results.

Conclusions Recall of previous maths performance biased in direction of gender stereotype, may affect female career choice.

Evaluation
Tackling stereotypes Awareness of gender stereotype encourages women into science and maths careers.

Role of participants' expectations Some students may have realised stereotypes linked to recall of results, so wrote down what they thought researchers wanted.

Learning approach

Key concept 1: Classical conditioning (CC)

What is it? Learning through association of two stimuli with each other (Pavlov).

Before conditioning Unconditioned stimulus (UCS e.g. food) produces unconditioned response (UCR e.g. salivation), other stimuli are neutral (NS).

During conditioning UCS + NS (e.g. bell) repeatedly paired, associate NS + UCS.

After conditioning NS now a conditioned stimulus (CS) producing response (CR) on its own.

Evaluation

Application to aversion therapy Electric shock (UCS) given when reading gambling phrases (NS), become CS producing discomfort (CR).

Incomplete explanation of learning Can't explain complex learning, e.g. phobias not maintained over time through CC.

Key study: Watson and Rayner (1920)

Aims Emotional responses (fear) can be learned through classical conditioning.

Procedure Little Albert shown white rat and loud noise made (hammer on metal bar) when he reached out for it.

Findings Showed fear and avoidance of rat by second session, cried when it approached. Showed CR of fear to other white furry objects, lessened over time.

Conclusions Easy to condition fear response in children which generalises.

Evaluation

Some good experimental controls Controlled environment with no irrelevant stimuli, findings due to CC not other variables.

Poor generalisability Just Little Albert studied, emotionally stable, unlike most babies, findings not applicable to others.

Key concept 2: Operant conditioning (OC)

What is it? Learning from consequences.

Consequence 1 – reinforcement Increases probability of behaviour repeating.
- Positive – pleasant consequence.
- Negative – remove unpleasant stimulus.

Consequence 2 – punishment Reduces probability of behaviour repeating.
- Positive – unpleasant consequence.
- Negative – remove pleasant stimulus.

Evaluation

Supporting research evidence Animal and human lab studies show OC, also brain basis of reinforcement (Chase et al. 2015).

Not a complete explanation of learning Explains how phobias maintained over time but not how acquired in first place.

Key study: Skinner (1932)

Aims Is food a reinforcer in rats?

Procedure Food pellets dispensed in a Skinner box every time rats pressed a lever.

Findings Rats varied in time it took for them to press at a high rate (after either first, second or fifth presses).

Conclusions Behaviour caused by natural laws, OC is relevant to everyday life, just one reinforcement can change behaviour.

Evaluation

OC in education and childcare Schools use rewards and punishers to change behaviour.

Problems with generalisation Sweeping conclusions about humans based on rats, ignoring mental processes, humans have conscious insight.

Key concept 3: Social learning theory (SLT)

What is it? Indirect learning, observation, vicarious reinforcement and imitation.

Modelling (1) demonstrating a behaviour to another, (2) person imitates the behaviour.

Observation Observer watches model's behaviour, retains in memory.

Imitation Act of copying the model's behaviour, more likely if observer identifies with model (same gender, high status, etc.).

Vicarious reinforcement Observing the model receive reinforcement of behaviour makes observer more likely to imitate.

Evaluation

Evidence supporting SLT Imitation more likely when model is rewarded (Bandura 1965), also in chickens when high status (Nicol and Pope 1999).

Not a complete explanation Aggression more similar in identical than non-identical twins (Kendler et al 2015), SLT cannot explain role of genetics.

Key study: Bandura et al. (1961)

Aims Would children imitate an aggressive, same-sex model?

Procedure Children observed adult hit Bobo doll, controls saw adult play with toy or no model. All children frustrated and then played with toys.

Findings Children who observed aggression towards Bobo most likely to imitate, boys imitated male model most.

Conclusions Aggression imitated by children, especially same sex (identification).

Evaluation

Learning aggressive behaviours Children observe and imitate aggression within family, implications for social policy.

Artificial environment In real-life situations children would have to be aggressive towards people not dolls, low generalisability.

Biological approach

Key concept 1: Genes

What are they? Strands of DNA carry 'instructions' for physical and non-physical characteristics.

Genotype The genes you inherit.

Phenotype How genes are expressed in interaction with environment.

The SRY gene On Y chromosome, switches on other genes, embryo develops testes and testosterone.

Evaluation

An interactionist approach e.g. version of BRCA1 gene linked to breast cancer but not all with the gene get cancer.

Risk of oversimplification No one gene for a behaviour. Small contributions of many genes, interactions with environment.

Key concept 2: Neuroanatomy

What is it? Structure of nervous system.

Localisation of brain function e.g.
- Motor area – controls movements on opposite side of body.
- Somatosensory area – represents skin sensitivity of body (e.g. hands).
- Visual area – receives information from right and left visual fields.

Sex differences in brain Males greater total brain volume. Females bigger thalamus, stronger connections, thicker cortex.

Evaluation

Support for sex differences MRI found women have stronger connections between hemispheres, may explain better multitasking (Ingalhalikar et al. 2014).

Structure not function Sex differences in structure do not mean differences in functioning, very few conclusions but much speculation.

Key study: Harlow (1868)

Aims and procedure Recorded details of Phineas Gage case, indicated aspects of how brain works.

Findings Iron bar through Gage's skull and front part of brain, changed personality, 'no longer Gage'.

Conclusions Intellect impaired but not lost, damage to left hemisphere so some brain functions localised.

Evaluation

Ahead of his time Careful observations linking brain area (localisation) to behaviour.

Unjustified conclusions Can't make before-and-after comparisons, amplifies effects.

Key concept 3: Neurochemistry

What is it? How activity of substances in nervous system affect brain and behaviour.

Neurotransmitters Communication between neurons across synapses, e.g. serotonin (low levels linked to depression, activity changed by drugs).

Sex hormones
- Ovaries (females) produce oestrogen – affects female reproductive organs and menstrual cycle.
- Testes (males) produce testosterone – affects male organs, linked to aggression.

Evaluation

Support for sex hormones Transgender women (female hormones) decreased aggression (Van Goozen et al. 1995).

Contradictory research No consistent effect of sex hormones on visuo-spatial skills, effects are real but limited (Slabbekoorn et al. 1999).

Key study: Deady et al. (2006)

Aims Is there a link between testosterone and maternal personality in females?

Procedure Females completed BSRI plus questionnaire, salivary testosterone measured.

Findings High testosterone linked to masculinity, lower maternal personality/reproductive ambition.

Conclusions Women's maternal tendencies due to testosterone, biological basis to maternal personality.

Evaluation

Support from other research Aggressive female prisoners had higher testosterone (Dabbs and Hargrove 1997).

Correlation not causation Variables correlate with each other but doesn't mean one causes other, need more data.

Key concept 4: Evolutionary psychology

What is it? Darwin (1859) explained natural selection – when resources are scarce, genes that produce characteristics helping survival (and reproduction) are selected and passed on.

Environment of evolutionary adaptation (EEA) Human minds and behaviour evolved to adapt to life on the African savannah.

Genome lag The gap between changes in our environment and adaptive changes to genome.

Sexual selection Characteristics that threaten survival continue because attractive to potential mates.

Evaluation

Support for genome lag Partner preferences changed in last 100 years (e.g. women less dependent), changes in culture but not genome.

Problems with the EEA concept Human evolution didn't stop in EEA (e.g. ability to digest lactose), some characteristics evolved much more recently.

Key study: Buss et al. (1992)

Aims Is male/female jealousy different?

Procedure Asked students which is more upsetting – partner falling in love with another (emotional infidelity) or having sex with another (sexual infidelity). Physiological measures, e.g. pulse rate.

Findings 60% men (17% women) chose sexual infidelity, 83% women (40% men) chose emotional infidelity, correlated with physiological measures.

Conclusions Male sexual jealousy prevents raising another man's child, female emotional jealousy prevents losing partner's resources.

Evaluation

Physiological and psychological measures Study used objective and subjective measures, showed biological basis of jealousy.

Limited sample of participants From one culture only, so could not show that jealousy is universal, does not fully support evolutionary explanation.

Content areas A and B

Revision guidance

A cue

There are snooker cues and there are other cues – a cue is a thing that serves as a reminder of something else. An actor knows she must come in on cue – a reminder or signal.

Psychologists have investigated the value of cues in remembering. They act as a reminder of what else you know.

In the revision card on the right the first column is labelled 'Key point' which can serve as a cue to remember the contents in the second column, labelled 'Description'.

Step 1 See if your cues work

If you just memorise the cues you should be able to produce the information in the second column:

- Once you have produced the revision card, cover the second column and for each cue write down what you can recall.
- Check how much you remembered. Maybe you need to add a word or date to your cue to help you.
- Try again and see if you remember more this time.

Psychological research shows that people often have much more in their heads than they can recall – they just need the right cue.

Step 2 Test your recall

Psychological research has also shown that recall improves dramatically if you TEST your memory. That doesn't mean rereading your notes but CLOSING YOUR BOOK and writing down everything you remember, then checking to see what you left out and testing it again.

Believe in the power of psychology

Revision card

On the facing page is a list of all the topics you need to cover for content areas A and B.

Below is an example of a revision card for one of these topics. This revision card is especially important for writing 9-mark answers (essays).

Description

Topic Reconstructive memory	
Key point (a cue)	**Description**
Reconstructive	Bartlett: active process, store fragments, recall builds it up into meaningful whole.
Not accurate	Bits missing and distorted, e.g. *War of the Ghosts*.
Schemas	Mental structures, package of knowledge of world (objects, events).
Innate	Born with some basic schemas but acquire more through experience.
Experience	When a person has a new experience, relevant schema activated, helps process info, make guesses.
Shortening	Left out if doesn't fit schema (unexpected).
Rationalisation	Distorted to fit schema because strange or unfamiliar, more sense.
Confabulation	Invented to fill gaps, guided by schemas.

Evaluation

Lacks control	No standardised instructions so differences may be due to this.
Accurate	Personally important or distinctive memories less affected by schemas.
Eyewitness testimony	Example of reconstruction leading to inaccurate recall, so convictions not based on this alone.

The beauty of this is:

- You reduce what you have to memorise (just memorise the cues). The rest is just engraved in your memory through practice.
- If you do this for every spread as you study it, then you will have all your revision materials ready at the end of the year when you have to prepare for the exam.

This picture is described as a man 'revising' an excavation tyre.

Revise = reconsider or alter.

Revise = reread work previously done. Which means you need to read your notes first and then reread them.

Question 4:

Chen's answ...

Neurochemis...
that pass 'me...
neurons whe...

Sex hormone...
females and...
testosterone...
small amoun...

Oestrogen c...
development...
of breasts, a...
emotional, e...

Testosterone...
development...
Testosterone...
generally mo...

The study by...
maternal per...
asked questi...
taking sampl...

The research...
sense of mas...
ambition and...
orientation.

What this su...
there was a c...
levels of fem...
way people t...

Saturn's ans...

One example...
related to ge...
would relate...

Testosterone...
Testosterone...
shows that w...
Tess says abo...
testosterone...

On the other...
which predis...
issue with De...
(women with...
the other.

One strength...
Van Goozen e...
to decreases...
because, if sh...
interested in...

One weaknes...
people who d...
there may be...
be that Tess'...
attitudes and...

Revision checklist for content areas A and B

Below are the key topics for content areas A and B. For each topic you should:

1. Construct a revision card and/or use our summaries (pages 38–39 and 72–73).
2. Test your recall using your cues. Check afterwards to see what you have forgotten.
3. Test your recall again using the cues.
4. Now test your memory of the cue words.

		1. Construct revision card	2. First test of recall	3. Second test of recall	4. Test memory using cues
Cognitive	Cognitive assumptions				
	Reconstructive memory				
	Bartlett (1932)				
	Cognitive priming				
	Harris *et al.* (2009)				
	Cognitive biases				
	Loftus and Palmer (1974)				
Social	Social assumptions				
	Conformity				
	Asch (1951)				
	Types of conformity				
	Haney *et al.* (1973)				
	Social categorisation				
	Chatard *et al.* (2007)				
Learning	Learning assumptions				
	Classical conditioning				
	Watson and Rayner (1920)				
	Operant conditioning				
	Skinner (1932)				
	Social learning theory (SLT)				
	Bandura *et al.* (1961)				
Biological	Biological assumptions				
	Influence of biology on behaviour				
	Genes				
	Neuroanatomy				
	Harlow (1868)				
	Neurochemistry				
	Deady *et al.* (2006)				
	Evolutionary psychology				
	Buss *et al.* (1992)				

Specification terms are important

We have highlighted 'specification terms' on each spread in a definition box but there are others too. These are examples of specialist psychological knowledge.

Make sure you include these on your revision cards.

The specialist terms turn an impressionist answer ...

... into a detailed one.

Practice

No athlete would dream of running a race without doing many practice runs of the right distance and within a set time. Always write exam answers in the allotted time – allow yourself about 12–15 minutes for a 9-mark essay (it is precisely 11¼ minutes but it pays to spend a bit of extra time on the essays). You should plan for the essay beforehand and maybe even write a few notes but then write the answer with the clock ticking. Afterwards, check your revision card and textbook and note any really important things you forgot to mention.

46
48
Unit 1: Psychological approaches and applications
Unit 1: Psychological approaches and applications
Content area C1: Use of psychology to explain contemporary issues of aggression in society

Cognitive approach to explaining aggression in society

Road rage

If you wanted to carry a gun, you wouldn't be able to in the UK because the law prevents you. It's different in the USA. People who are allowed to own guns sometimes keep them in their cars. Does this make them kinder, more considerate drivers? No, it does not.

According to Brad Bushman and his colleagues (2017), people drive more aggressively and are more abusive to other road users when there is a gun in the car (as opposed to a tennis racket). The gun doesn't even have to do anything – it just has to be there.

This is called the *weapons effect* and is nicely summarised by a quote from Leonard Berkowitz (1967), 'The finger pulls the trigger, but the trigger may also be pulling the finger'.

Specification terms

Aggression Behaviour that is intended to cause psychological or physical injury.

Hostile aggression Angry and impulsive aggression usually accompanied by physiological arousal.

Hostile attribution bias A tendency to assume that someone else's behaviour has an aggressive or antagonistic motive when it is actually neutral.

Instrumental aggression Goal-directed and planned aggression usually not accompanied by physiological arousal.

Priming We notice a stimulus (word, image, object, etc.) more quickly when we see or hear a related stimulus first (the 'prime').

Instrumental aggression. Not that kind of instrument.

Types of aggression

Psychologists define *aggression* in terms of three main types of behaviour.

Hostile aggression is sometimes called reactive or 'hot-blooded', this is angry and impulsive aggressive behaviour. It is accompanied by physiological arousal, e.g. increased heart rate and blood pressure. It is often physical but sometimes verbal or relational (see below).

Instrumental aggression is proactive or 'cold-blooded' because it involves using aggression (as an 'instrument') to get what you want. Therefore, it is goal-directed, planned and usually *not* accompanied by physiological arousal. This would be typical, for example, of bullying. It can be physical, verbal or relational, usually intended to provoke a response.

Relational aggression involves damaging relationships by, for example, spreading gossip or withdrawing friendships. This is instrumental when used as part of a plan or campaign of aggression to undermine an individual. But it can also be hostile, for example firing off an angry text or social media post in the 'heat of the moment'.

The cognitive approach

Priming for aggression

Leonard Berkowitz and Anthony LePage (1967) noted that the presence of a weapon in a *laboratory* was associated with stronger electric shocks being selected by participants. They argued that the weapon was a cue that triggered (or primed) aggressive *schemas* in the minds of participants.

Berkowitz (1984) and many others have used this theory to explain how violent media (e.g. films, games) can cause aggressive behaviour. Repeatedly viewing such media provides us with a *cognitive script* (see page 14) which indicates what violent situations involve and how they can develop. The script is stored in memory until environmental cues (e.g. an accidental nudge) prime it, making it easier to recall.

Researchers have expanded this account to incorporate modern social media sources such as Instagram and Facebook (e.g. constant exposure to angry and aggressive social media posts may prime aggressive thoughts in users).

Priming occurs without us even being aware of it. We might observe someone's hostile and aggressive behaviour in one social situation, for example, watching a TV programme. And then later, we would make a wrong interpretation of someone else's behaviour in a completely unrelated situation, for example when out shopping we might believe that someone who 'jumped the queue' in a shop was being hostile when it was really an accident. This partly accounts for the automatic nature of much hostile aggression.

Hostile attribution bias (HAB)

We looked at this briefly on page 16.

People with a *hostile attribution bias* (HAB) tend to interpret other people's behaviour as threatening or aggressive (hostile) even if it is in fact neutral or ambiguous (unclear). For most of us, if someone accidentally stumbles into you, you understand it wasn't their 'fault' and they meant nothing by it (you might even apologise to them!). But someone with a HAB is more likely to see this as a deliberate act directed personally at them.

This is a self-fulfilling process. Someone with a HAB may feel provoked and become verbally or physically aggressive. If the people around them respond with their own aggressive behaviour, then this confirms to the person with a HAB that their belief was correct and they were justified in being aggressive.

According to Nicki Crick and Ken Dodge (1996), a HAB is the result of abnormal processing of social information. A person with a HAB pays special attention to cues in a social situation that might be aggression-related (even if other people interpret them as neutral). If that person has a schema for supermarkets that includes the information 'there is intense competition for a place at the checkout', this predisposes the person to behave aggressively in supermarkets. Thus a HAB is created.

 GET ACTIVE Tomos and Sheena

Tomos regularly uses social media. He contributes angry posts to fierce arguments often in the evenings, sometimes during the night and in the morning. Tomos is a teacher and by the time he gets to school he is usually in a bad mood. He shouts at students and is very 'short' and offhand with other teachers.

Sheena is a firefighter who has a reputation for being 'spiky'. She often misinterprets her colleagues' behaviour. For example, once during training the person she was working with accidentally dropped a hose reel on her foot. He apologised but Sheena squared up to him and they almost came to blows.

1. Identify and explain the types of aggression in these scenarios.
2. Explain how the cognitive approach accounts for the behaviour of Tomos and Sheena.

Social media can have priming effects by exposing us to angry and aggressive interactions that we may carry over into the face-to-face world.

Evaluation

Research support for priming

One strength is that several forms of media have been found to prime aggressive attitudes and behaviours.

Peter Fischer and Tobias Greitemeyer (2006) investigated how song lyrics can prime aggressive cognitive scripts. Male participants listened to songs featuring aggressively derogatory lyrics about women. Compared with when they listened to neutral lyrics, participants later recalled more negative qualities about women. They also behaved more aggressively towards a female confederate (someone instructed by the researchers about how to behave). Similar findings were obtained with female participants listening to 'men-hating' lyrics.

This provides experimental support for the role of cognitive factors in aggression.

Research support for hostile attribution bias

Another strength is that many studies have found a link between HAB and aggression.

Bram Orobio de Castro et al. (2002) reviewed 41 studies of HAB in children. They found that 37 of the studies agreed there was a significant association between hostile attributions and aggressive behaviour. Sarah Healy et al. (2015) found that mothers with a HAB tended to have more aggressive children who also showed a HAB at the age of five years. Possibly a HAB is the result of social learning (see page 28).

This research shows the importance of HAB in aggression and suggests one way in which it could develop in children.

Correlation not causation

One weakness is that most of the research shows a correlation between cognitive factors and aggression.

For instance, studies show that a strong HAB is associated with more aggression. But correlational research does not show that HAB (or priming) causes aggressive behaviour. This is because no variables are manipulated or controlled. Instead of people with a strong HAB being more aggressive, it may be that being more aggressive produces a strong HAB. Or perhaps a third factor is responsible for both the strong HAB and aggressive behaviour such as lack of money.

This means the conclusions are limited because correlational research does not allow us to identify the direction of causality.

Applications of the cognitive approach

One strength is that aggressive behaviour could be reduced using the cognitive approach.

Explanations for any behaviour are useful because they help us to understand the behaviour – but also because they can be developed into methods to reduce problematic behaviours. In this case, we can apply the cognitive understanding of aggression to a means of reducing aggression. Cognitive therapy, for example, tries to change HABs and thoughts that prime aggressive behaviour. Nancy Guerra and Ronald Slaby (1990) helped male and female adolescent prison inmates to replace hostile attributions with positive ones. Compared with a control group, they showed a much reduced HAB and less aggression (as rated by staff).

This means that real practical benefits are possible using the cognitive approach, reducing aggression and the social costs that go with it.

Exam-style questions

1. Explain what is meant by the term 'instrumental aggression'. (2)
2. Explain how the cognitive approach accounts for aggression. Use the concept of cognitive bias in your answer. (3)
3. Give **three** features of the cognitive approach that can explain aggression. (3)
4. Harris et al.'s (2009) study showed how cognitive priming can influence behaviour. Explain how cognitive priming can affect aggressive behaviour. (3)
5. Freida was in a pub when a man accidentally trod on her foot. Even though he apologised, Freida still got angry and hit him in the face.
   (a) Describe the type of aggression shown by Freida. (2)
   (b) Use **one** aspect of the cognitive approach to explain Freida's behaviour. (2)
   (c) Evaluate the view that aggression is mainly the result of cognitive factors. In your answer you should consider: (i) the concept of cognitive biases, and (ii) reference to Freida. (9)

Link it

How can Bartlett's (1932) study of schemas help to explain aggressive behaviour?

Explain the link between the findings of Harris et al.'s (2009) study and priming of aggressive behaviour

How do different types of cognitive bias explain aggression?

In this section of the unit we have changed 'An issue to consider' to 'Link it' because you may be asked to link topics in content area C to the studies in content area B.

Specification content

C1 Use of psychology to explain contemporary issues of aggression in society

Learners should be able to demonstrate knowledge of different types of aggression, including:
● Hostile and instrumental.

Learners should understand and apply knowledge of how psychological concepts and research can be used to explain aggression in society:
● Cognitive, including priming for aggression, hostile attribution bias.

Social approach to explaining aggression in society

Can stereotypes have fatal consequences?

In 2014 Michael Brown, an 18-year-old African American man, was shot 12 times and killed by a white police officer. Brown was unarmed. Other incidents in which young black men are killed by police officers have continued since.

In these cases, it has been argued that the police officers involved held strong racist stereotypes of young black men and this influenced their behaviour. Because the police officers associate young black men with aggression, violence, threat and gun crime, they have expectations about what the young men will do (e.g. they expect them to pull out a gun). Therefore, the police get their defence in first and are more likely to resort to armed force than they would do in similar cases involving white men.

It was Michael Brown's killing that led to the #BlackLivesMatter movement becoming nationally recognised in the US and around the world.

Specification terms

Conformity 'A change in a person's behaviour or opinions as a result of real or imagined pressure from a person or group of people' (Aronson 2011).

Social norm Something that is standard, usual or typical of a social group.

Stereotypes Fixed views of other people based on their perceived membership of a social category.

There is a strong perception, mostly amongst white people, of Serena Williams as an 'angry black woman' because she brings an aggressive attitude to her tennis playing.

Social explanations

Conformity to social/group norms

As we saw on page 18, a *norm* is an unstated 'rule' about what behaviours are considered appropriate and inappropriate. Such rules are shared by members of a group (which could be a whole society or *culture*). Group membership, and the benefits stemming from that membership, depend upon accepting the group's norms (i.e. *conforming* to them). *Aggression* is closely associated with conformity to two sets of norms – gender and cultural.

Gender-role norms Alice Eagly and Wendy Wood (1991) argue that norms dictate that men should be independent and assertive and use aggression to achieve status, money or other social rewards.

Gender-role norms dictate that women, on the other hand, should generally not be aggressive, but there are exceptions. It is acceptable for women to be verbally aggressive as long as it releases anger (part of the gender-role norm that states women should be emotionally expressive).

Conformity to gender-role expectations varies depending on how much a person identifies with their gender. For example, women who identify with masculine traits are more likely to be physically aggressive (Reidy et al. 2009).

Cultural norms Cultures differ drastically in levels of aggressive and violent crimes. For instance recorded cases of 'intentional homicide' (including murder) are 18.1 per hundred thousand population in Mexico, 5.0 in the USA, 2.9 in Korea, 1.1 in England and Wales and 0.3 in Iceland (OECD 2015). This implies that there are different cultural norms about aggression.

Even within cultures there are different norms about aggression. For example, in the United States, the southern states share a 'culture of honour', a cultural norm that condones aggressive responses to perceived insults. It is entangled with gender-role norms of masculinity – it is only men who are expected to respond with violence. Disputes escalate very swiftly so that dangerous and sometimes fatal violence arises from relatively minor threats to a man's social status.

Stereotypes and aggression

Stereotypes are *cognitive* 'shortcuts' that allow us to interact in the social world (see page 22). When we meet an individual we can label them (e.g. woman, old person, teenager) and then we think we know what they are like and how they will behave just because our stereotypes tell us they fit into a certain social category. Aggression is one example and it commonly features as part of gender and racial/ethnic stereotypes.

Gender stereotypes Men are often stereotyped as physically aggressive and women as verbally aggressive. Aggression is very strongly associated with stereotyped masculinity. Although the situation has improved, gender stereotypes are still frequent in TV programmes aimed at children. One of the most common is male cartoon characters presented as more aggressive than female characters (Hentges and Case 2013).

According to Melinda Burgess (2017), gender stereotypes of aggression are dangerous because they can lead to acceptance and tolerance of sexual harassment and intimate partner violence (IPV) perpetrated by men against women (i.e. because it is expected).

Racial and ethnic stereotypes Black people are often stereotyped as aggressive, more so than any other ethnic group. Tall black men are particularly stereotyped as threatening whereas tall white men are perceived as competent (Hester and Gray 2018).

Other ethnic stereotypes are also linked with aggression. An Ofcom report from 2018 showed that Scottish people are more often portrayed as aggressive than English, Welsh and Northern Irish people in British TV programmes.

Again, ethnic and racial stereotypes are potentially dangerous because they may lead to tolerance of racist opinions and aggressive behaviour towards young black men (e.g. by the police, a concern highlighted by the #BlackLivesMatter movement, see top left).

Evaluation

Support for conformity to norms

One strength is that research shows aggression is linked to a culture of honour.

Dov Cohen *et al.* (1996) told a *confederate* to collide (individually) with male participants in a corridor and insult them. Participants from southern states (where the culture of honour operates) were more likely (than northern participants) to judge that their masculinity was threatened. They also showed higher levels of *testosterone* and were more aggressive towards another confederate later.

These findings support the view that conformity to cultural norms can partly determine aggressive behaviour in a society.

Role of biological sex

One weakness is that there is much debate in psychology about the influences of norms and biological factors.

Although norms are important in determining aggression, some psychologists argue that biological sex is at least equally influential. For example, as we saw earlier in the biological approach (page 34), the male *sex hormone* testosterone is linked in many studies to aggression in males and females. Castrating a male animal (removing its testes) is accompanied by a reduction in both testosterone and aggression (Giammanco *et al.* 2005).

This suggests that conformity to gender-role norms is only part of the explanation for male aggressive behaviour.

Research support for the role of stereotypes

Another strength of social explanations is research showing aggression is associated with stereotypes of African Americans in reality TV programmes.

Jack Glascock and Catherine Preston-Schreck (2018) analysed one week's worth of the most popular American reality TV programmes from 2013. Black contestants, especially women, were depicted as more verbally aggressive than contestants from any other ethnic group. This is real-world evidence that racial stereotypes are associated with aggressive behaviour.

Contradictory evidence on gender stereotypes

Another weakness is that not all research supports the view that gender stereotypes are linked with aggression.

Steve Stewart-Williams (2002) asked students to read a description of an aggressive act. There were eight acts in total, read by different participants. They varied in combinations of male and female perpetrators and victims. The participants (including males) did not perceive more aggression in the acts when they were carried out by a man than a woman.

These findings appear to contradict the usually-held gender stereotype and suggest that the power of gender stereotypes to influence perceptions of aggression may be overestimated.

Do you find this image surprising? Is this woman failing to conform to gender-role or cultural norms? Does her behaviour violate commonly-accepted stereotypes about older people, especially women?

GET ACTIVE Images of stereotyping

Go to shutterstock.com or fotolia.com. These websites hold thousands of what are called 'microstock' images that can be used in media as illustrations (there are some in this book). Search for images using terms such as *professional*, *criminal*, *terrorist*.

1. *Do you think the images are based on stereotypes?*
2. *Are any of the stereotypes linked to aggression?*
3. *Do the representations of black and white people in the media reflect the stereotypes we already hold or do they help to form them?*

Exam-style questions

1. In the context of aggression, explain what is meant by the term 'social norms'. (2)
2. Explain how the social approach accounts for aggression in society. (3)
3. Give **two** features of the social approach that can explain aggression. (2)
4. Phil and Ryan were walking along the street when a man bumped into them and said something threatening. Phil immediately punched the man. After they had run away, Ryan asked Phil why he had been so aggressive. Phil replied, 'I had to because he insulted my family.'

   Use **one** aspect of the social approach to explain Phil's behaviour. (3)
5. Serena Williams played in the US Open tennis final in 2018. During the match, she deliberately broke her racket and was involved in a dispute with the umpire which led to her shouting at him. There was much discussion about Williams' behaviour. Some people thought she was very aggressive, others believed she was being stereotyped as an 'angry black woman'.

   Analyse the view that aggression in society is linked to social factors. In your answer you should consider: (a) conformity to social/group norms and stereotypes, and (b) reference to Serena Williams. (9)

Link it

This spread discusses conformity to social or group norms. Explain how this relates to the key study by Asch (1951).

Haney *et al.* (1973) investigated conformity to social roles in the context of a mock prison. How do their findings relate to the examples of conformity on this spread?

Chatard *et al.* (2007) concluded that stereotyping may limit career choices. Is there any evidence on this spread to support that view?

Specification content

C1 Use of psychology to explain contemporary issues of aggression in society

Learners should understand and apply knowledge of how psychological concepts and research can be used to explain aggression in society:

- Social, including conformity to social/group norms, stereotypes.

Learning approach to explaining aggression in society

'Mobbing' at work

Bullying is a daily reality in many workplaces. One bully can have a huge effect on the working lives of large numbers of people, but they rarely operate successfully without support. They often have accomplices who assist them in bullying their victims.

Sometimes the bullying is an organised campaign of harassment by several people to get rid of an employee. Ken Westhues (2002) calls this 'mobbing' and it can be explained by the concepts on this spread.

Accomplices learn how to bully by observing their 'leader'. They interact with victims by copying the bully's methods. The bully is often in a senior position, so accomplices look up to them because of their status. It also means the bully is in a position to reward his or her accomplices for their support. Because the bully often achieves their goals, accomplices are motivated to imitate the bully.

The conditions for imitation to occur in a workplace are almost perfect and are explained on this spread.

Specification terms

Operant conditioning A form of learning in which behaviour is shaped and maintained by its consequences: reinforcement (positive or negative) or punishment (positive or negative).

Social learning A form of learning in which behaviours are acquired through observation, modelling, imitation and vicarious reinforcement. Cognitive factors play a key role.

Unplanned, impulsive, uncontrolled. An angry outburst is an example of hostile aggression – not explained well by learning theories.

Learning explanations

Operant conditioning

Aggression can be learned directly (see page 26 for a reminder of the basic processes of *operant conditioning*).

Positive reinforcement According to B.F. Skinner (1932), behaviour is shaped by its consequences – a behaviour that is reinforced is more likely to reoccur, a behaviour that is punished is less likely to reoccur. Aggressive behaviours are mostly acquired and maintained through *positive reinforcement* because aggression is an effective way of gaining rewards.

Furthermore, Skinner argued that behaviours that are *positively* reinforced only *occasionally* (and at irregular intervals) are especially strong. This is called *variable interval reinforcement* (it is how fruit machines and social media notifications work, for instance). Reinforcement is much more 'hit and miss' in everyday life than it is in a lab. A person who behaves aggressively may be reinforced only a proportion of the time (because there is no one else around to approve, for example). If there is no pattern to when the aggression is reinforced (i.e. it is unpredictable), then that is even more powerful.

Types of reward Aggression brings two main types of rewards. One type is tangible rewards such as money, sex and food. Tangible rewards (e.g. getting a toy off another child) positively reinforce up to 80% of children's aggressive behaviours (Patterson *et al.* 1967).

Another type of reward is social status. Bullying is reinforced not just by tangible rewards (e.g. money) but also by increased status in the school playground (or workplace, etc.) through fear. Other examples include gang members who gain status through fighting, and whole societies that provide social status rewards (e.g. medals) for aggressive behaviour in wartime.

Social learning theory (SLT)

Albert Bandura (1973) realised that aggressive behaviour in humans cannot be fully explained by direct forms of learning such as operant conditioning. As we saw on page 28, he argued that most learning of aggression is indirect and occurs through *observation*, *modelling*, *vicarious reinforcement* and *imitation*.

Observational learning and modelling Children (and to a lesser extent adults) learn specific aggressive behaviours through observing aggressive *models* (e.g. parents, siblings, peers, media figures). A person observes how an aggressive behaviour is performed, but this does not guarantee they will behave aggressively – another social learning mechanism is required.

Vicarious reinforcement As well as observing the aggressive behaviour of models, people also observe the consequences of that behaviour. If the behaviour is rewarded (or at least not punished) then the observer learns it can be a successful means of getting a reward the aggressor wants.

This is vicarious reinforcement – the observer experiences the model's reward 'second-hand', but this is enough to increase the likelihood that the observer will imitate the model's behaviour.

Self-efficacy Unlike Skinner, Bandura emphasised the role of *cognitive* processes in social learning. As humans, we not only experience the consequences of behaviour, we anticipate them too. We have expectations about whether an aggressive behaviour will bring rewards or not.

Self-efficacy in this context is a person's confidence in their ability to achieve rewards through behaving aggressively. This increases as the individual uses aggression successfully. For example, the aggressor learns he or she has the motor skills to force someone to hand over money and the belief that this behaviour will continue to bring successful outcomes in the future.

Cognitive control of aggression The likelihood that an observed behaviour is imitated depends on four cognitive processes:

- The observer must firstly pay *attention* to the model's aggressive actions.

- Then the observer needs to remember the model's actions. This is *retention*, a mental representation of how the behaviour is performed.

- The observer must have the ability to transform the retained memory into a physical action. This is *reproduction*.

- The observer must want to reproduce the aggressive behaviour because they expect it to bring a reward. This is *motivation*.

Evaluation

Research support for the learning approach

One strength is strong evidence that children learn aggressive behaviours.

François Poulin and Michel Boivin (2000) found that the most aggressive boys between nine and 12 years old became friends with each other. These relationships were 'training grounds' for antisocial behaviour because the boys were exposed to models of physical aggression (i.e. each other). They gained direct reinforcement through tangible (money, goods) and intangible (approval, praise) rewards. They experienced vicarious reinforcement through observing the rewarding consequences of each other's aggression.

This study showed that aggressive behaviour readily develops in conditions predicted by learning theories (especially SLT).

SLT explains the effects of media

One strength of the SLT explanation is that models do not have to be 'real life'.

Aggressive characters in media such as TV (soap operas), film and video games may provide models. SLT predicts the conditions under which modelling is most likely to happen. For instance, an aggressive individual may have attractive characteristics. They may be charismatic or physically attractive or have superior status. If their aggressive behaviour is rewarded, an observing child may experience vicarious reinforcement.

This shows that SLT is useful because it helps to explain how aggressive behaviour in the media may be imitated by children.

Applications to social policy

Another strength is that the learning approach has important implications for social *policy*.

The approach suggests that the aggressive behaviours that underlie some serious crimes are learned through exposure to models in the family and in peer networks. Policymakers (e.g. government) could focus their efforts to reduce aggression on developing programmes based on social learning. One example is mentoring, providing 'at risk' children and young adults with non-aggressive *role models* to imitate.

This means the learning approach could significantly reduce the costs to individuals and societies of human aggression in its various forms.

Learning does not account for all aggression

One weakness is that learning theories have trouble explaining *hostile aggression* (see explanation on page 48).

A hostile violent outburst may easily escalate an aggressive encounter so that the individual receives *punishment* in return. Operant conditioning and SLT predict that punishment (experienced directly or vicariously) makes future aggressive behaviour less likely.

This means that alternative explanations for hostile aggression (e.g. biological or social) may be more useful.

Social learning theory explains how TV characters might influence children to behave aggressively.

Exam-style questions

1. Explain how the learning approach accounts for aggression. Use the concept of operant conditioning in your answer. (3)

2. Give **three** features of social learning theory that can explain aggression. (3)

3. Bandura *et al*'s (1961) study showed how aggressive behaviour can be imitated by children. Explain how the findings of Bandura *et al*. support the view that aggression is learned. (3)

4. Oscar has been arrested again for physically assaulting his partner. During the police interview Oscar said that whenever he got angry he just 'blew up' and couldn't control himself. He described how he had grown up in a violent household, where his father had frequently assaulted his mother. Oscar also explained how he used to bully other children at school to get money. Some of the younger children used to look up to him.

   (a) Describe the type of aggression shown by Oscar. (2)

   (b) Use **one** aspect of social learning theory to explain Oscar's behaviour. (2)

   (c) Analyse the view that aggressive behaviour is learned. In your answer you should consider: (i) the concept of operant conditioning and social learning, and (ii) reference to Oscar and his experiences. (9)

⚡GET ACTIVE **Bullied out of a job**

Gregor is a senior manager of a supermarket and has to make cutbacks in his department. He has been making negative comments about one employee, Hadley. More than once he has shouted loudly at Hadley in his office. Adi has many times seen how badly Gregor treats Hadley. Adi held a meeting with other employees and didn't invite Hadley, even though it was about her area of work. Adi has also spoken very negatively about Hadley in meetings and around the office. Gregor approved of Adi's behaviour, praised him in front of other staff and privately promised him promotion. The bullying continued for several weeks until Hadley was signed off with stress.

1. Identify and explain **three** types of aggressive behaviour in this scenario.

2. Use the learning approach to explain the aggressive behaviour of Gregor and Adi. Using examples in your explanation, refer to the concepts of: operant conditioning, observational learning, modelling/imitation, vicarious reinforcement and self-efficacy.

Link it

How can classical conditioning studied by Watson and Rayner (1920) explain the development of aggressive behaviour?

How can reinforcement studied by Skinner (1932) explain aggression?

How does Bandura *et al*.'s study (1961) explain aggression?

Specification content

C1 Use of psychology to explain contemporary issues of aggression in society

Learners should understand and apply knowledge of how psychological concepts and research can be used to explain aggression in society:

● Learning, including operant conditioning, social learning.

Biological approach to explaining aggression in society

Violence in the genes?

In 1978, a group of women from the same family attended appointments at a hospital in the Netherlands. They were planning to have children, but there was something about the male side of their family that worried them – they were thinking of 14 of their brothers, sons, and nephews.

These 14 had two things in common – they were intellectually impaired and also extremely aggressive. One had attempted to rape his sister, another tried to mow down his boss with his car, two had set fire to houses more than once. They were all prone to aggressive outbursts, threatening people and constantly getting into fights.

15 years later, Han Brunner took blood samples from these 14 men and another 14 of their male relatives. He identified a defect in one gene. All the violent men had it, but the non-violent men did not.

The gene, described on this spread, became known in the media as the 'Warrior Gene'.

Specification terms

Brain structures Physical components that make up the neuroanatomy of the brain, including the amygdala and the orbitofrontal cortex (OFC).

Evolution The changes in inherited characteristics in a biological population over successive generations.

Genes A unit of inheritance. They consist of chemical instructions (DNA) which tell your body what proteins to manufacture – and basically that is what you are, a huge number of proteins. Genes are inherited from parents and contribute to the development of an individual's characteristics.

Neurochemistry Relating to substances in the brain and other parts of the nervous system that regulate psychological functioning.

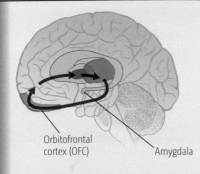

Orbitofrontal cortex (OFC)   Amygdala

A slice through the midline of the brain showing two of the key brain structures related to aggression.

Biological explanations

Evolution of aggression

As we saw on page 36, the origins of sexual jealousy are *evolutionary*, i.e. this behaviour is *naturally selected* because it confers reproductive advantages for males (Buss *et al.* 1992). Men are sexually jealous because, unlike women, they cannot be sure they have truly parented a particular child. They risk using their resources to raise another man's offspring. This would assist the survival of a rival's *genes*, leaving the man with fewer resources to invest in his own offspring (and hence genes).

Sexual jealousy helps to defend against this possibility by promoting aggressive countermeasures. Margo Wilson and Martin Daly (1996) called these *mate retention strategies*. Such strategies often involve *instrumental aggression* because they are intended to achieve a goal – men use them to prevent their partners from 'straying'.

These are two such sexually selected mate retention strategies:

Direct guarding A man may monitor his partner's behaviour and actively prevent her from meeting other men. This could involve him using physical violence.

Negative inducements A man may issue threats of violence or other consequences for infidelity ('I'll kill you if you leave me').

Brain structures in aggression

The amygdala has a central role in how an organism assesses and responds to environmental threats. Amygdala reactivity is a key predictor of human *aggression*. People with *intermittent explosive disorder* (IED) experience outbursts of extreme aggression. Brain scans reveal high levels of amygdala activity when individuals view images of angry faces (Coccaro *et al.* 2007). This links amygdala activity, aggression and a real-life sign of threat.

The orbitofrontal cortex (OFC) is a region of the brain which plays an important role in higher *cognitive* functions such as rational thinking. It regulates impulse control and its activity is reduced in people with psychiatric disorders that feature aggression (Coccaro *et al.* 2007). The OFC's reduced activity disrupts its impulse control function, so the individual cannot inhibit their aggressive behaviours.

Neurochemistry of aggression

Serotonin levels in the OFC are normally associated with a reasonable degree of behavioural self-control. But decreased *serotonin* disrupts this link – self-control is reduced and impulsive behaviours (including aggression) become more frequent. For example, 5-HIAA (a serotonin-related chemical) was found in significantly lower amounts in violent impulsive offenders compared with violent non-impulsive offenders (Virkkunen *et al.* 1994).

Dopamine helps to regulate motivational behaviours and our experience of reward. It interacts with serotonin to influence aggression. Dongju Seo *et al.* (2008) argue that serotonin underactivity stimulates *dopamine* overactivity to cause impulsivity and aggression. So serotonin underactivity is the main cause of *hostile aggression* and dopamine overactivity also contributes.

Genes and aggression

The key gene linked to the inheritance of aggression is the MAOA gene. It controls the production of an enzyme called *monoamine oxidase A* (which is written as MAO-A). MAO-A 'mops up' *neurotransmitters* in the brain after a nerve impulse has been transmitted from one *neuron* to another. It breaks down the neurotransmitters into constituent chemicals to be recycled or excreted. A dysfunction in the operation of the MAOA gene leads to abnormal activity of the MAO-A enzyme, which in turns affects neurotransmitter levels in the brain.

One variant of the MAOA gene leads to low MAO-A activity in some areas of the brain and is associated with aggressive behaviour. This low-activity MAOA variant was found in the men of the Dutch family studied by Brunner *et al.* (1993, see top left) and is also implicated in intimate partner violence (IPV, Stuart *et al.* 2014).

Evaluation

Support for the evolutionary explanation

One strength of evolutionary explanations is support from studies of intimate partner violence (IPV).

Todd Shackelford *et al.* (2005) found that men who used mate retention behaviours (e.g. direct guarding) in heterosexual relationships were more likely to be physically violent towards their partners (a strong positive *correlation*). Retention behaviour was a reliable predictor of aggression.

These findings support the evolutionary view that predicts a link between risk of infidelity, sexual jealousy and aggression.

Role of the amygdala

A further strength of the biological approach is evidence supporting the amygdala's role in aggression.

Dustin Pardini *et al.* (2014) followed up 56 males who were part of a *sample* of 503 first recruited for a study when they were 6/7 years old. The 56 were selected 20 years later because they had been involved in violent crimes. Brain scans showed that smaller amygdala volumes in both childhood and adulthood were associated with greater aggression. These strong negative correlations continued into a further follow-up three years after the scans. The researchers controlled other factors (e.g. race, substance abuse, earlier aggression levels).

This is strong support for the role of the amygdala because amygdala volume predicted degree of aggressive behaviour.

Correlation not causation

One weakness is that many research studies into biological factors are correlational.

For example, the two studies described above found strong correlations between aggression and the other variables (mate retention, amygdala volume). Correlational research is helpful because it is unethical to conduct experiments on aggression in humans (it would mean actively manipulating biological influences so participants behaved aggressively). But correlation is not the same as causation.

This means we cannot know for sure if a biological factor (e.g. amygdala volume) is a *cause* of aggression, an *effect* of it, or if a third variable is involved.

Role of genes

Another weakness is that the influence of genes on aggression is very complex, with no simple answers.

Studies show that the role of the MAOA gene is important but probably exaggerated. For instance, in the study by Stuart *et al.* (facing page) IPV was associated not just with the MAOA gene but also with the serotonin transporter gene (the 5-HTT gene). Evangelos Vassos *et al.* (2014) reviewed 185 studies but found no single gene was associated with aggression.

The conclusion is that aggressive behaviour is the outcome of hundreds or thousands of genes (*genotype*) all interacting with each other and with environmental factors to produce the aggressive *phenotype*.

Sexual jealousy in men can be a powerful cause of aggressive behaviour.

Exam-style questions

1. Explain how the biological approach accounts for aggression. Use the concept of genes in your answer. (3)

2. Give **three** features of the biological approach that can explain aggression. (3)

3. Harlow's (1868) study of Phineas Gage showed how injury to the brain can change behaviour. Explain how the findings of Harlow (1868) support the view that aggression is linked to neuroanatomy. (3)

4. Explain **one** strength or **one** weakness of the biological approach to explaining aggression. (3)

5. Graham doesn't like his partner Pippa leaving the house. He asks her lots of questions when she returns, such as 'Where have you been?' and 'Who did you see?'. He is planning to install a tracking app on her mobile. Graham has also used physical force to keep Pippa under his control.

   (a) Describe the type of aggression shown by Graham. (2)

   (b) Use **one** aspect of the biological approach to explain Graham's behaviour. (2)

   (c) Discuss the view that aggressive people are born not made. In your answer you should consider: (i) the concept of evolution, and (ii) reference to Graham's behaviour. (9)

Link it

How does Harlow's (1868) study help us to understand the link between neuroanatomy and aggression?

What did Deady *et al.* (2006) investigate that could be relevant to the neurochemistry of aggression?

What is the possible link between Buss *et al.*'s (1992) study of jealousy and the evolution of aggressive behaviour?

Specification content

C1 Use of psychology to explain contemporary issues of aggression in society

Learners should understand and apply knowledge of how psychological concepts and research can be used to explain aggression in society:

● Biological, including evolution, brain structures, neurochemistry, genes.

GET ACTIVE A probation officer reflects

Erwin is a probation officer working with high-risk offenders who have been in prison for violent crimes. He has worked in this field for over 20 years and has a lot of experience of criminals and their families.

Erwin has noticed that a high proportion of the people he works with have a medical history that includes brain injury. Others come from families where violent behaviour goes back several generations. Many of the people on his current caseload are addicted to drugs. He has even dealt with cases of murder and attempted murder with a large element of jealousy.

Erwin wonders if there could be a biological basis to a lot of aggressive behaviour.

Write a brief outline of the biological causes of aggression that would address Erwin's question and that he could share with his probation officer colleagues.

Cognitive approach to consumer behaviour

Hidden messages?

In 1957 an advertising executive called James Vicary called a press conference to make a sensational claim.

He said that he had shown a film to cinema-goers in which he had repeatedly flashed the phrases 'Drink Coca-Cola' and 'Eat popcorn'. The twist was that the phrases were on the screen so briefly that the viewers were not even aware of seeing them.

But Vicary went further. He claimed that sales of Coca-Cola and popcorn had rocketed in the cinema. Ever since then, people have worried that their behaviour could be manipulated by advertising messages that they can't see or hear. This 'subliminal advertising' is one of the topics on this spread.

But the Coca-Cola effect is a myth. Vicary made it all up just to promote his advertising company.

Specification terms

Brainwashing techniques Methods used to alter or try to control what a person is thinking. In advertising it is used to entice consumers to accept an advert's message uncritically.

Consumer behaviour The study of all the activities associated with the purchase and use of goods and services.

Subliminal messages Stimuli that are not perceived consciously. In advertising such messages may be presented quickly or hidden so a consumer is not aware of them.

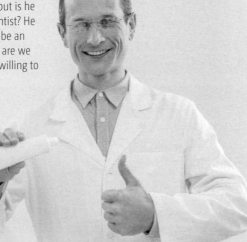

Nice man but is he really a dentist? He might just be an actor. Why are we always so willing to believe?

What is consumer behaviour?

Consumer behaviour refers to how people make decisions about what products or services to buy, and all the activities that influence those decisions, including advertising. There are two major types of advertising:

Product recognition Most advertising aims to make consumers more aware of a product (or brand or service). Similar products compete for the greatest share of the market, so making your product recognisable is crucial.

Campaigns to change public opinion Some advertising tries to change the views of the public about a product or brand. For example, cigarette advertising used to try to overcome negative attitudes towards smoking in order to increase sales.

Cognitive explanations

Schemas

A *schema* is a mental 'package' of knowledge relating to a concept, object, event, etc. (see page 12). Schemas help us to make sense of the world by making it more predictable, and this is true of commercial brands and products. However, predictability is the enemy of advertising. Schemas allow us to say, 'If you've seen one vodka advert, you've seen them all', and we will be less likely to recall the brand being advertised to us. Therefore, adverts are more likely to challenge our schemas rather than confirm them. This is *schema incongruity*, a deliberate conflict between our schemas and an advert's content (e.g. advertising an everyday product in a 'wacky' way).

Cognitive priming and advertising

We looked at *cognitive priming* on page 14. In advertising, Youjae Yi (1990) argued that a key form of *priming* is the context of an advert. Like any prime, context activates schemas in the minds of viewers, making a product more accessible. Car advertising is a good example. Very few car TV adverts begin with the brand or model name. They start with a context, a positive one such as 'roominess' or 'smooth ride'. This is then associated with the brand name. Then, at a later time when the context is encountered the viewer is primed to recall the brand.

Subliminal messages are a form of priming below the level of awareness. Often the message is 'hidden' within a stimulus that we can detect. For instance, in 1990 Absolut Vodka ran a TV advert with an image of their brand name hidden in ice cubes.

Another form of 'voluntary' *subliminal messaging* is self-help podcasts and videos. These claim to contain undetectable messages for you to see or hear, that will improve your memory or self-esteem, or help you give up smoking or lose weight, etc.

Brainwashing In the context of consumer behaviour, 'brainwashing' is intended to encourage uncritical acceptance of whatever messages the advertiser wishes to communicate.

A common technique is repetition, whereby the central message (a word, sentence or image) is repeated many times to create an association with a product. Sounds and colours are also used repetitively. Another important feature is an obvious appeal to emotions, to bypass critical thinking.

Biases and advertising

Confirmation bias Consumers prefer to hear information that confirms what they already believe, called a *confirmation bias*. This helps explain brand loyalty. Someone who has a good experience of a product will be receptive to its advertising and may even filter out competing brands. They seek to confirm that their decision was correct.

This is important in a retail market where customers upgrade their device every couple of years. However, because it is hard to overturn a negative opinion of a brand that a consumer has already formed, confirmation bias can work against a product.

Authority bias Consumers tend to assign more credibility to the opinion of an authority figure, who is likely to be an 'expert'. For example, adverts for toothpaste often use 'dentists' to explain the benefits of the product. Consumers are more persuaded by the authority even when they suspect the dentist is actually an actor.

GET ACTIVE 'A Mars a day...

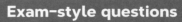

...helps you work, rest and play'. That sentence is part of my schema for Mars bars.

We have schemas for countless aspects of the world around us. This includes products that are advertised to us as consumers. To get an idea of how product schemas work, think about a product you are familiar with, such as a Mars bar.

1. *Make a list of the words you associate with a Mars bar. This list represents your product schema for Mars bars.*

2. *Compare your schema to those of others. How similar are they? If they are similar, why are they so similar?*

3. *Outline an advert for Mars bars based on your schema.*

4. *What would be the advantage of making an advert 'schema-incongruent'?*

Evaluation

Supporting research for cognitive priming

One strength is evidence for the effects of priming in different senses.

Adrian North (2012) asked four groups of people to taste and describe wine as background music was played. Each group heard a piece of music that had different characteristics: one heard a 'powerful and heavy' piece, another heard something that was 'subtle and refined', a third group's music was 'zingy and refreshing' and the fourth's was 'mellow and soft'. The descriptions given by the participants tended to match the characteristics of the music, even though they all tasted the same wine.

This supports priming as a key influence on memory.

Effects of subliminal messages are weak

One weakness is poor evidence for the effects of subliminal messages.

The popular view is that these messages can make us buy or do something against our will, but it is more likely that they have very weak influences on behaviour and only for very short periods of time. Laura Smarandescu and Terence Shimp's (2015) participants carried out a visual detection task on a computer screen. However, the participants were being subliminally primed with the word 'Powerade' flashing on their screens without their awareness. Later, the participants were asked to select a drink from a shelf. Compared with a control group, participants were more likely to select Powerade, but only if they were already thirsty. However, this effect disappeared altogether when a 15-minute delay between the prime and selection was introduced.

Similarly, self-help programmes continue to be popular even though, according to Anthony Pratkanis and Elliot Aronson (1992), there is no evidence at all that they work.

These findings suggest that priming effects through subliminal messages have little or no effect on behaviour even in very limited circumstances.

Problems of replication in research

Another weakness is that the findings of research into priming are often contradictory.

Most studies do not support the view that priming can significantly affect consumer behaviour. But some studies do show positive effects. This apparent contradiction illustrates a serious problem in research into *cognitive priming* and advertising – that of *replication*. For a study to be considered scientific, psychologists must be able to replicate it. That is, they should be able to repeat the study and get the same outcome. This was the issue that uncovered James Vicary's deception (see facing page) – no one could replicate the effect.

This undermines the claims about the value of priming in consumer behaviour.

Ethical issues

A final weakness is that there are ethical issues involved in advertising techniques based on the cognitive approach.

For instance the use of subliminal messages in advertising is unethical because consumers are by definition unaware they exist. The person therefore does not know the true nature of the advert and the product. This is one reason why direct subliminal advertising is banned in most countries. The use of cognitive priming is perhaps less obviously unethical but it could be interpreted as a form of deception.

This means that psychologists should think very carefully about their professional involvement with techniques deliberately designed to manipulate consumers' perceptions of a product.

Exam-style questions

1. Explain what is meant by the terms 'subliminal messages' and 'brainwashing'. (4)

2. Explain how the cognitive approach accounts for consumer behaviour. Use the concept of schema in your answer. (3)

3. Give **three** features of the cognitive approach that can explain consumer behaviour. (3)

4. Explain **one** strength of the cognitive approach to consumer behaviour. (3)

5. Edgar uses social media a lot and sees many adverts. His partner thinks he is too easily influenced by them because he sometimes buys products he has seen advertised. He booked a hotel through a website because he liked the look of the beaches in their advert. Edgar always buys things advertised by experts in white coats.

   (a) Explain **one** example of priming in this scenario. (2)

   (b) Outline how **one** information processing bias might influence Edgar's behaviour as a consumer. (3)

6. Discuss techniques based on the cognitive approach that are used to influence consumer behaviour. In your answer you should consider: (a) schemas and cognitive priming, and (b) advertising. (9)

Link it

Bartlett (1932) found that schemas influence recall. What might this tell us about the effects of advertising?

What can Harris *et al*'s (2009) study tell us about the influence of cognitive priming in advertising?

Loftus and Palmer (1974) found that the alteration of one word in a question influenced participants' responses. Explain the link with subliminal advertising.

Specification content

C2 Use of psychology in business to explain and influence consumer behaviour.

Learners should be able to demonstrate knowledge of the means used to influence behaviour, including types of advertising (product recognition, campaigns aimed at changing public opinion).

Learners should understand and apply knowledge of how psychological concepts and research can be used to understand and inform strategies aimed to change behaviour:

- Cognitive, including schema, cognitive priming (including subliminal messages and brainwashing techniques in advertising), biases in information processing.

Social approach to consumer behaviour

Make it stop, please!

'Baby Shark doo doo da-doo da-doo, Baby Shark doo doo da-doo da-doo, Baby Shark…' repeat until the end of time.

Quite possibly the catchiest song in history, *Baby Shark* has been around for a century and has cropped up occasionally on social media since the mid-2000s. But in 2018 it suddenly became massively popular with over three billion views on YouTube. Why?

Its success is a good illustration of how the concepts on this spread work to influence our behaviour as consumers. It appears to have 'gone viral' after a Twitter hashtag #BabySharkChallenge was created which instantly made the song something that had to be heard by everyone, even though it was originally aimed at toddlers. From there it spawned other hashtags, other videos and spread, until it took over the world…

Specification terms

Bandwagon effect Behaviour change or purchasing decisions can result from the perception that 'everyone else is doing it' (join the bandwagon).

Social proof In situations where we are not sure what to do or believe, we may look to other people for guidance because we think the others are better informed.

A bandwagon – a wagon with a band playing on top. P.T. Barnum (*The Greatest Showman*) invited people to jump on and join in!

Social explanations

In content area B2 we looked at social explanations such as *conformity to norms*, which we will use here to explain certain aspects of *consumer behaviour*.

Conformity to social norms

Social norms are beliefs, expectations and unwritten rules about the behaviours that any social group considers to be 'proper' behaviour. Most people have a strong desire to conform to these social norms and this is often exploited by advertising.

Behaviours that are publicly visible are ways we signal our group memberships, such as the clothes we wear, our smoking (or non-smoking) habits, the phone we use. Therefore, campaigns and adverts try to influence us by promoting the message that 'if you do X you are like these other people'.

Conformity to social norms is partly explained by *normative social influence* (NSI, first explained on page 18).

Normative social influence and behaviour change

According to Morton Deutsch and Harold Gerard (1955), acceptance by other people is a powerful reason for conforming to the norms of a group. It appeals to our natural desire to be liked and to avoid being rejected. It leads to *compliance*, that is changing behaviour publicly even if privately we still hold a different view.

Someone subjected to NSI may buy products (or specific brands) in order to 'fit in' with their friends because not doing so might risk being rejected or ousted. The same goes for behaviour – we may be willing to change our behaviour (e.g. give up smoking, take up smoking, lose weight, recycle, etc.) if a group's social norms dictate that as the (unspoken) 'price' of membership.

Social proof

People do not just conform in order to fit in and be accepted (NSI). *Social proof* is another term for *informational social influence* (ISI). Often, going along with other people is the result of believing that those others know more than you do about the current situation (i.e. they influence you because you believe they are better informed). The more people who agree on a course of action or a belief, the more influenced we are.

According to Robert Cialdini (1984) in a situation in which we don't know what to think or do, we look to others for social proof of what is happening and how we should behave. For example, in the context of public health, a campaign to change behaviour might imply that lots of people like you are doing something ('72% of people lost weight after following this tip'). This is social proof of what people are doing.

Social proof also explains why rating systems on websites such as Amazon are influential, and why we are more likely to read Facebook posts with lots of likes than those with very few.

The bandwagon effect

This is a social phenomenon similar to NSI. It refers to the tendency most people have of doing something because other people are doing it (a 'herd mentality'). The bandwagon was historically a vehicle used in political rallies in 19th century America. It would carry musicians and dancers and people would jump on it to have fun.

Bandwagon advertising operates on the basis that 'success breeds success'. Once a product or brand is adopted by a 'critical mass' of people, many more join in. This is the motivation behind using 'social media influencers' such as Kylie Jenner to promote products. The hope is that once a trend is adopted by influencers and their followers it will 'go viral' and potentially be taken up by millions.

Adverts (and campaigns) exploit the bandwagon effect by trying to create the illusion that a product (or behaviour) is already popular, perhaps by showing lots of people using it or talking about it. It is a manipulation of consumer behaviour because it stimulates demand for a product that was not previously there. For example, up to 2017 the cosmetics company Rimmel used the slogan 'Get the London Look', implying that huge numbers of people in London were using it.

Evaluation

Research support for conformity to social norms

One strength is that research shows that many people readily conform to norms once they are aware of them.

Jerry Burger and Martin Shelton (2011) placed signs next to lifts in university buildings. The notices said, 'Did you know? More than 90% of the time, people in this building use the stairs instead of the elevator. Why not you?' Compared to the week before, 46% more people used the stairs rather than the elevator [lift], a figure maintained for a week after the notices were removed.

This demonstrates the influence of social norms on health-related behaviours (it also supports the concept of social proof).

Research support for the bandwagon effect

Another strength of social explanations is research support for the bandwagon effect.

Małgorzata Niesiobędzka (2018) tested the bandwagon effect among a group of teenage Polish students. Some of the students saw an advert for a luxury product (a Ralph Lauren T-shirt) which was associated in the experiment with a famous person (e.g. Beyonce or Bill Gates). Compared with a control group of students who saw the advert without the famous person, the experimental group were willing to display a significantly bigger Ralph Lauren logo on their T-shirt.

This shows that the bandwagon effect can explain the sudden popularity of even expensive products in terms of conformity to social norms.

Cultural differences in social proof

One weakness is that social proof is not an equally effective influence technique in all *cultures*.

Robert Cialdini *et al.* (1999) compared social proof in an *individualist* culture (USA) and a *collectivist* culture (Poland). Participants in both cultures were more willing to agree with a request when told all their peers had agreed than when told none of them had agreed. This is evidence of social proof in both cultures. However, the level of agreement was much greater in Poland, suggesting that social proof is more effective in a collectivist culture. This confirms previous findings showing that conformity is more common in collectivist cultures.

This means that campaigners and advertisers who wish to use social proof must take cultural factors into account.

The boomerang effect

Another weakness is that attempts to use norms to positively change behaviour can backfire.

Carol Werner and colleagues (2008) used a group discussion to persuade students to replace environmentally-damaging (toxic) household products with non-toxic alternatives. When the students discussed their reasons for using the toxic products, none of them were persuaded to switch. Use of toxic products became the group norm and reminded the participants why they used them.

This shows that the social-psychological processes involved are 'neutral' and can have unintended consequences that undermine attempts to change behaviour.

Bandwagon marketing may have potentially dangerous consequences. The same bandwagon techniques that promote the benefits of vaccination can be used for the opposite purpose by so-called anti-vaxxers (see page 99).

Exam-style questions

1. Explain what is meant by the term 'social norms'. (2)
2. Explain how the social approach accounts for consumer behaviour. Use the concept of social proof in your answer. (3)
3. Explain **one** way in which the social approach can inform strategies to change behaviour. (3)
4. Give **three** features of the social approach that can explain consumer behaviour. (3)
5. Ranjana was staying in a hotel for three nights. When she used the bathroom, she noticed a sign saying, 'Please help us save water and protect the environment by reusing your towels. Most guests at the hotel reuse their towels at least once during their stay'. So Ranjana used the same towels through her whole stay.
   (a) Explain **one** example of the bandwagon effect in this scenario. (2)
   (b) Outline how social proof might have influenced Ranjana's behaviour. (3)
   (c) Evaluate techniques based on the social approach that are used to change behaviour. In your answer you should consider: (i) conformity to social norms, and (ii) reference to Ranjana. (9)

Link it

How could advertisers use the findings of Asch's (1951) key study?

Explain how Haney *et al.*'s (1973) study supports the link between conformity to social norms and consumer behaviour.

Chatard *et al.* (2007) researched gender stereotypes. How might this information be used by advertisers?

GET ACTIVE Getting students to drink less

The level of drinking on some student university campuses is a cause for concern. Psychologists have tried to use the techniques explained on this spread to reduce alcohol use. Some programmes have been more successful than others.

One issue is that most students have completely the wrong idea about how much other students drink. They think other students drink a lot more than the other students really do. Ironically, this means that individual students drink more because they think they need to 'keep pace' with everyone else.

1. *With reference to the concepts on this spread, what strategies could you use to reduce student drinking?*
2. *Are there any potential unintended consequences of trying to change drinking behaviour?*

Specification content

C2 Use of psychology in business to explain and influence consumer behaviour

Learners should understand and apply knowledge of how psychological concepts and research can be used to understand and inform strategies aimed to change behaviour:

● Social – conformity to social norms ('Bandwagon Effect', social proof).

Learning approach to consumer behaviour

What is Christmas to you?

Is it warmth, comfort, excitement, a welcome break from routine, nostalgia about childhood Christmases?

Or is it annoying relatives, useless presents, the same old same old, too many people forced to have a good time?

For many people (perhaps most?) it's the former – a time associated with good feelings, happiness and enjoyment. Also for many, Christmas is now a time for adverts by big companies such as John Lewis, M&S, McDonalds, Coca-Cola, and not forgetting Lidl.

Why do these companies spend so much money advertising their already well-known brands at this time of year?

The answer is on this spread. They want you to associate their products with the good feelings you have about Christmas. Does it work? Think about a Christmas advert you've seen – how does it make you feel?

Specification terms

See pages 24, 26 and 28.

Learning explanations

Classical conditioning

Classical conditioning involves learning through association (see page 24). It is the main learning process used in advertising because it does not require a response from the consumer in order for it to be effective (unlike *operant conditioning*).

The aim is to associate the topic of an advert (product, brand, logo, behaviour change) with positive feelings (e.g. happiness, humour). Advertisers and campaigners hope this will make the consumer more likely to change their behaviour (e.g. buy the product, reduce smoking). Even if this doesn't happen, other desirable outcomes are possible such as a more positive attitude towards the product, or greater awareness of it in the marketplace.

For example, an advert for a burger might present the product in a way that makes you associate it with being happy. Or it might show attractive people (or celebrities, see below) enjoying themselves as they visit the burger restaurant. Even in political campaign adverts that are intended to change behaviour, a voice-over will express warmth and friendliness, and posters and leaflets may be colourful and fun, etc.

Operant conditioning

Operant conditioning has become more frequently used for advertising following the growth of interactive media such as the internet. This is because the response from the consumer can then be reinforced or punished. Watching a TV advert or viewing a poster or flyer is a passive behaviour, but responding to a survey on Instagram is much more active.

Social media platforms exploit operant conditioning techniques to change behaviour. For instance the number of Facebook 'likes' and comments a post attracts is a powerful reinforcer of continued use and phone-checking. What is especially powerful is that the reinforcements are not predictable or constant. Sometimes when we check our status there are several likes, sometimes there are none. This is called *variable interval reinforcement* and Skinner found it created responses that are very hard to extinguish (remove).

Social learning

Modelling occurs when someone *observes* the behaviour of another person (a *model*) and *imitates* it. Many adverts show a 'model' using the product (e.g. a vacuum cleaner, a car, a phone) and enjoying it. The adverts may suggest that using the product will gain us popularity, success or status or make us admired. This is one reason why advertising for alcoholic drinks is not allowed to be associated with these things.

The consumer hopefully experiences *vicarious reinforcement* from the positive emotions of the model, imagining themselves imitating the behaviour and enjoying the same feelings.

Use of celebrities in advertising As we noted on page 28, imitation is more likely if the observer identifies with the model. Identification is a social learning process. The consumer identifies with a celebrity endorsing a product because he or she possesses something the consumer admires – status, wealth, fame, physical attractiveness, etc.

On the other hand, identification also occurs when the consumer believes the model is similar to themselves. This is why some adverts use 'down-to-earth' celebrities or at least places celebrities in everyday situations to 'humanise' them.

Celebrities also have a classical conditioning effect. For example, the chef Jamie Oliver was 'the face of Sainsbury's' for many years, presumably to associate his expertise and charm with the Sainsbury's brand in the minds of consumers.

The effects of celebrities are thought to be so powerful that they are not allowed to be used in UK TV advertising aimed at children.

Gary Lineker, still the face of Walker's crisps. Would his endorsement make you buy the product? Perhaps that depends on your feelings towards Gary.

o explaining gender

sociated with gender

lowing spreads, we look at the topic of *gender* – being a male or
ychological construct and a person's gender may not always be the
n's biological sex (XX or XY chromosomes).

y seen on a spectrum along which people vary from one another and
heir lives. It is a spectrum rather than a *binary* construct in which you
ne or feminine. *Non-binary* people – who do not identify as exclusively
nine – may be gender-neutral (neither masculine nor feminine) or
masculine and feminine).

der are changing but the gender binary is a *social norm* in most
r) *cultures*. Therefore, we refer to *gender identity* or behaviour that
as 'gender-typical'. Identity or behaviour that does not match is
his is intended to convey the fact that *gender-fluid* identity is not
ior, but is not common.

e explanations

chema is a mental structure containing stored knowledge of an aspect
e case of *gender schema* these are constructs that tell us how men
xpected to behave, and these influence our personal gender identities
. Gender schema theories try to explain how and when we acquire our

schema theory (GST)

arned about the *Bem sex-role inventory* (BSRI), a measure of how
nine a person perceives themselves to be. Sandra Bem's (1981) gender
scribes how we *cognitively* process gender-related information.
of two years, children start to learn about schema related to gender
Because some cultures make strong distinctions between men and
mbers grow up holding *stereotyped* views of gender. For example, we
frequently have a gender (ships are feminine). As for jobs and roles –
ing nurses, men are decisive doctors.

c/aschematic Gender-schematic people have a strong gender schema
her people's behaviour as 'masculine' or 'feminine', even when the
especially gender-relevant. They also behave in ways consistent with
na. Gender-schematic people are highly sensitive to deviations from
cal behaviour (e.g. a woman exhibiting masculine characteristics).
atic people attach very little significance to gender, hardly noticing it in
ctions.

designed the BSRI to measure *androgyny*, proposing that a person can
e and feminine. Traditionally people hold a binary view, that masculine
aviours are two separate clusters. Bem argued – that it is psychologically
void fixed gender identities. Instead men and women should feel free to
masculine- and feminine-type behaviours, i.e. be androgynous.

alverson's (1987) gender schema theory

Charles Halverson suggested that gender schema has an important
y and what we remember affects our gender schema and consequently

sistent with the child's schema is more likely to be stored in memory
inconsistent information. For instance, if a girl believes that dolls are 'for
is 'for boys' she will seek out information about dolls, adding it to her
But she will ignore information about football. She can recall more about
l.

r recall of gender-inconsistent information may be distorted to fit her
which at a young age is essentially made up of common stereotypes).
calling a story about a male nurse and a female doctor, she may get the
vay round and this misremembering confirms her previous schema.

Evaluation

Research support for classical conditioning

One strength is evidence that demonstrates how classical conditioning operates in advertising.

Elnora Stuart *et al.* (1987) arranged for participants to be shown images of a fictitious brand ('Brand L toothpaste') followed immediately by images designed to provoke positive responses (e.g. an ocean sunset). Other fictitious brands were also presented, followed by neutral images (e.g. a microscope). The participants expressed significantly more positive attitudes towards Brand L toothpaste than towards other brands. The degree of positivity increased with the number of presentations, highlighting the role of repetition.

This shows that, at least in lab conditions, it is plausible that classical conditioning can explain positive consumer attitudes towards a product.

Research support for social learning

Another strength of learning explanations is that support comes from research into the effects of celebrities.

Johannes Knoll and Jörg Matthes (2017) reviewed 46 studies of these effects. They found that consumers' attitudes towards products were significantly more positive when the products were endorsed by a celebrity than when they were not. Some of the reviewed studies concluded that consumers perceive the celebrities as 'someone they like'.

This shows that identification plays a key role in the influence of celebrities on attitudes towards products.

No underlying mechanism

One weakness is that *conditioning* is more of a description than an explanation.

Conditioning is both a process (what happens when it takes place) and an effect (the outcome). But it does not explain the mechanisms involved. For example, there must be *cognitive* factors involved in associating an advertised product with positive emotions, otherwise everyone would feel the same way about it (how positively you feel about a product advertised by Jamie Oliver depends on what you *think* about Jamie Oliver). But the learning approach has nothing to say about cognitive factors.

This means that conditioning is not a powerful explanation of how we learn to respond to advertising or behavioural change campaigns.

Real-world effects are unclear

A further weakness of this research into the conditioning effects of advertising has been mostly *laboratory* based.

The effects are clear in such highly controlled conditions. However, in the real world of TV viewing and social media use the influence of advertising is a lot 'messier'. For instance, lab research investigates the short-term effects of advertising on a narrowly-defined behaviour (e.g. choice of snacks 20 minutes after watching an advert for a fictitious brand). There is much less research into the longer-term effects of conditioning, and what there is suggests the effects are weaker (Schachtman *et al.* 2011).

Therefore, the research tells us little about the effects of advertising in the real world where conditions are less controlled.

GET ACTIVE The power of Pepsi (not)

In 2017 Pepsi ran an advert in the US that backfired so spectacularly the campaign was ended early.

A major celebrity, Kendall Jenner, was shown walking along a street when she saw a protest and decided to join in. She removed her wig first, as if to imply 'This is the real me', approached a police officer and gave him a can of Pepsi. At this point the protesters realised there was no need to demonstrate for social justice anymore so they stopped. Thanks to Pepsi and the power of Jenner's celebrity, the world was a much happier place.

To make the situation worse, when the backlash took hold, Pepsi apologised… to Kendall Jenner.

1. *Using your knowledge of the learning approach, explain why this advert failed.*

2. *Explain how you would present the advert to make it effective.*

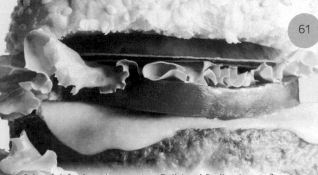

Colourful, fresh and vegetarian. Delicious! Feeling hungry? What else do you associate with this image? Get the point?

Exam-style questions

1. In the context of consumer behaviour, describe what is meant by the term 'operant conditioning'. (2)

2. Explain how the learning approach accounts for consumer behaviour. Use the concept of social learning in your answer. (3)

3. Explain **one** way in which the learning approach can inform strategies to change behaviour. (3)

4. Give **three** features of the learning approach that can explain consumer behaviour. (3)

5. Ieuan was watching a TV advert for a yoghurt. He liked the colourful backgrounds, the jolly music and the people dressed up in silly clothes. He noticed that the yoghurt was being eaten in the advert by one of his favourite singers, so he decided to buy this particular yoghurt when he went out shopping later.

   (a) Explain the use of celebrity in this scenario. (2)

   (b) Outline how classical conditioning might have influenced Ieuan's behaviour. (3)

6. Analyse techniques based on the learning approach that are used to change behaviour. In your answer you should consider: (a) classical and operant conditioning, and (b) social learning. (9)

Link it

How do Watson and Rayner's (1920) findings about classical conditioning apply to advertising?

Skinner (1932) studied operant conditioning in rats. Are we like his rats when we respond to adverts?

Bandura *et al.* (1961) investigated aggression, but what can the social learning concepts in that study tell us about advertising?

Specification content

C2 Use of psychology in business to explain and influence consumer behaviour

Learners should understand and apply knowledge of how psychological concepts and research can be used to understand and inform strategies aimed to change behaviour:

● Learning – classical and operant conditioning, social learning (the use of celebrity in advertising).

Biological approach to consumer behaviou

It's a virtual world

Imagine putting on a virtual reality headset and seeing, not a racing car circuit or a battle landscape, but the aisles of a supermarket. Retailers sometimes ask volunteers to do this as part of their neuromarketing, in what is called 'in-store simulation'.

The VR environment allows retailers to see where the virtual shoppers are looking. Which products get most of their attention? Is it something to do with location? It's well-known for instance that the products that become more popular are those placed at eye level because most people ignore the lower shelves. VR is highly interactive, so virtual shoppers can pick products up and put them in a virtual trolley.

VR can also be used in a similar way to assess the impact of adverts and packaging – what do viewers look at most? VR allows researchers to create a 'heat map' showing the most and least viewed areas of a shelf, label or advert (see facing page).

Specification terms

Neuromarketing The application of the scientific study of the brain (neuroscience) to marketing (e.g. advertising).

Scanning techniques Methods used to investigate the brain and other parts of the body. Images are taken of the living brain and sometimes regions of the brain are matched to behaviour by asking participants to engage in particular activities while the scan is done. Brain scans are also used to detect brain abnormalities such as tumours. Examples include CT scan, PET scan, fMRI scan.

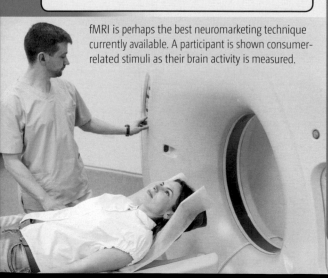

fMRI is perhaps the best neuromarketing technique currently available. A participant is shown consumer-related stimuli as their brain activity is measured.

Neuromarketing

What is neuromarketing?

Neuromarketing applies the study of the brain (neuroscience) to marketing (selling products or services), including advertising. Neuroscience is based on technologies measure brain activity, including *functional magnetic resonance imaging* (*fMRI*) an *electroencephalography* (*EEG*). Neuromarketing uses these to study people's respon aspects of marketing such as products, brands and adverts.

Neuromarketeers look for insights into consumers' motivations, feelings and dec making processes in relation to brands etc. The findings of neuroscience are incorp into campaigns to 'tap into' the brain activity associated with a positive attitude to brand or product, for example.

Functional magnetic resonance imaging (fMRI)

fMRI is a form of brain scanning which measures the activity (function) of the brai is 'working'. It detects changes in blood oxygenation and flow in specific parts of th An active brain area requires more oxygen so blood flow has to be directed to this

The participant lies in an fMRI scanner and sees an advert or other stimulus as th activity is measured continuously in 'real time'. The fMRI scan produces three-dime images showing which parts of the brain are active during a mental process (such deciding whether to buy a product).

In the language of neuromarketing, fMRI helps advertisers understand what feat an advert activate a brain area that 'pushes a consumer's buy button'. So they claim fMRI can show, for example, whether a person is bored or excited by an advert, or they like a product or not.

Electroencephalogram (EEG)

An EEG measures the brain's electrical activity via electrodes attached to the individ scalp using a geodesic net (skull cap). The EEG recording represents brainwave patt generated by millions of individual *neurons*, giving an overall picture of brain activi is presented on a screen.

It tracks changes in brain activity over fractions of a second and is much more co than fMRI. But it only measures activity at the surface of the brain (the *cortex*) and deep in the *subcortical* areas (where emotions are regulated for instance).

Just as with fMRI, the aim is to identify the effects of marketing and advertising va on brain activity. But because the EEG is portable this can be done in more 'natural' environments.

Eye tracking

Eye movements are intimately linked to brain activity and are therefore of interest i neuromarketing. Researchers use technology to track the consumer's eye movemen or she views a product or advert.

It helps us to understand the features of an advert that attract the most attention viewers spend the most time gazing at. This can be associated with brain activity to identify the most interesting, exciting or motivating aspects of the stimulus.

Like EEG, because the equipment is portable, eye tracking can be used in real-life situations such as restaurants, supermarkets or online. It can also be used in a virtu reality environment (e.g. a virtual supermarket).

Facial coding

People's facial expressions are thought to offer a window into their feelings, an idea goes back scientifically to Charles Darwin (1872).

In neuromarketing, electrodes attached to people's faces detect slight muscle move as they watch an advert. These movements are correlated with emotional expression (e.g. smiling) and feelings (e.g. happiness, surprise) to indicate which aspects of an the consumer finds appealing.

Because the meanings of facial expressions are to some extent open to interpretat Paul Ekman and Wallace Friesen (1978) developed a system of coding called FACS, the *facial action coding system*. This is a way of trying to provide some *objectivity* by categorising 'micro' facial expressions from the combined positions of 43 facial musc

---

Cognitive approach t

Unit 1: Psychological approaches and applications

Livvy James

Livvy was born Samuel and raised as a boy. But for as long as she could remember, she felt strongly that she was really a girl. She dressed and played as a girl, she behaved as a girl, she viewed herself as a girl. Livvy's sense of her own gender was being a girl. But when she went to school, she did so as a boy.

The conflict between her assigned and expressed gender was causing Livvy distress (which psychologists call *gender dysphoria*). So when she was 10, Livvy decided she wanted to be herself. With her family's support, after the summer holiday of 2011, she returned to school as a girl. Some of her schoolmates accepted her gender but others bullied her severely.

Livvy's experience shows the importance of being sensitive towards the wishes of people who are *transgender*. Language matters, and how we refer to people is part of that. Livvy still identifies and lives as female, and works to support transgender people.

John Anyon/Worcester News

Specification terms

Androgyny Displaying a balance of masculine and feminine characteristics in one's personality (ando = male and gyny = female).

Binary Describes a choice of two states, for example something can be either on or off, or a person can only be male or female.

Gender The label of being male or female, as distinct from biological sex (the sex chromosomes are either XX or XY, see page 30).

Gender dysphoria A person feels dysphoria (discomfort) with the gender assigned to them at birth.

Gender fluid Not having a fixed gender.

Gender schema An organised set of beliefs and expectations related to gender that are derived from experience. Such schemas guide a person's understanding of their own gender and gender-appropriate behaviour in general.

Non-binary A term that suggests gender (or any concept) cannot be divided into two distinct categories, e.g. gender is not a question of being one or the other (male or female).

Transgender Relating to a person whose gender does not correspond with their birth sex. (Discussed on next spread.)

Terms as

On this and the fo female. This is a p same as that pers

Gender is useful even throughout t are either masculi masculine or femi *androgynous* (bot

Views about ge Western (and oth matches this norm 'gender-atypical'. 'abnormal' or infe

Cognitiv

You know that a s of the world. In th and women are e and our behaviou gender schema.

Bem's gender

On page 34 you le masculine or fem schema theory de

Around the age from their culture women, most me learn that objects women are nurtu

Gender-schemat and categorise ot behaviour is not their gender sche gender-stereotyp

Gender-aschem their social intera

Androgyny Bem be both masculin and feminine bel more healthy to a adopt a variety o

Martin and H

Carol Martin and effect on memor our behaviour.

Information co and recalled than girls' but football gender schema. dolls than footba

Alternatively, h gender schema (For instance, in r roles the wrong

Social approach to explaining gender

Do you still watch Friends?

A survey in 2019 by the charity Childwise found that *Friends* was the most popular TV show amongst five- to 16-year-olds in Britain.

Two of the reasons children gave for enjoying it were: 'It teaches me a lot about life' and 'Most people can relate to one of the characters'. It seems that some children perceive the main characters as role models.

Friends' popularity 15 years after it ended its run is astonishing but the show has been criticised for its rigid portrayal of gender. Most of the characters have gender-stereotyped jobs. Women without a date on Valentine's Day are to be pitied. Weddings mean everything to women but men are commitment-phobic. The supporting characters who do not conform to a conventional gender role are treated as figures of fun – the male nanny, Chandler's drag queen dad, men who carry bags, anyone who might be gay.

Is this one of the reasons why young children like the show, because it reflects the gender stereotypes they are familiar with?

Specification terms

Conformity to gender roles The extent to which a person identifies with a gender-typical (i.e. masculine or feminine) role.

Peer influences Refers to the effect that other people of the same age (and/or those with shared interests) have on how we think and behave.

Felt pressure for gender conformity.

Social explanations

The social approach focuses on how other members of our species influence our thinking and behaviour. Two of the concepts introduced in content area B2 were *peer influences* (which is also explained by *social learning theory*, see the next spread) and *conformity*.

Peer influences on gender

Childhood According to Susan Egan and David Perry (2001) *gender identity* in young childhood has just one element – *self-identification of gender membership*. This means that children are the ones who select their gender.

By the age of three years most children can state whether they are a boy or a girl (Egan and Perry acknowledge that identification may not be binary but this is an under-researched area). This age also sees the beginning of gender segregation, a preference for playmates of the same sex. By the time children reach primary school age they spend very little time with opposite-gender peers.

According to Kristina Zosuls *et al.* (2008), more time spent with same-gender peers inevitably has a significant effect on a child's self-identity as a boy or a girl. During childhood, peers contribute to the development of gender identity by acting as *models* for gender-typical behaviour (e.g. 'We don't play with dolls, they're for girls') and as a source of sanctions for gender-atypical behaviour (e.g. 'You're a tomboy because you like football'). These influences contribute to the child's developing identity as a member of a gender category.

Adolescence Further elements of gender identity appear in adolescence. One of these is particularly sensitive to peer influence – *gender typicality*. This is the extent to which a person feels they are like other members of their gender category (i.e. typical).

This thinking means the individual has to reflect on their personal qualities and make a judgement about how closely they fit a gender category. Gender typicality is powerfully influenced by *social context*, including peer influence.

This is because the adolescent compares themselves with their peers in order to judge their typicality ('I am like my friends X and Y, but not like Z, so I am not a typical male').

Comparing themselves with their peers, some adolescents may become increasingly aware they are *transgender*, in that their expressed gender does not match their assigned (birth) sex.

Gender and conformity to gender roles

Felt pressure for gender conformity This is another aspect of adolescent gender identity according to Egan and Perry (above). It is an example of *normative social influence* (NSI, see page 18) because the person feels social pressure to conform to the norms associated with a gender role (e.g. how a male or female is 'meant' to behave or feel).

This includes pressure not to behave in gender-atypical ways (i.e. for boys *not* be feminine and for girls *not* to be masculine). The pressure comes from the individual themselves and their parents, but also from peers.

Peer pressure to conform increases with the amount of time spent with members of the same gender category. The more time girls spend playing with other girls, the more likely they are to identify as a girl and the more girl-like their behaviour becomes (the same for boys, Martin and Fabes 2001).

Gender non-conformity Peer pressure is a major cause of stress for adolescents who do not conform to gender role norms. This is because they are trying to cope with a role that many still feel is socially unacceptable. Peer groups tend to expect conformity and enforce this.

Some of the negative peer-related outcomes for non-conforming adolescents include teasing, bullying, and rejection by peers (Jewell and Brown 2014). The stress associated with a non-conforming identity (and not necessarily the identity itself) may explain the incidence of *gender dysphoria* and accompanying psychological ill health (Nagoshi *et al.* 2014).

Peer pressure to conform to gender-role norms is especially strong for boys in Western *cultures*. This is probably due to the differing values placed on masculine and feminine traits. Girls are allowed more flexibility in displaying masculine characteristics because male traits are valued more highly than feminine ones (e.g. independence, assertiveness, etc.). Therefore, boys who show feminine traits are particularly likely to be bullied and harassed by peers.

Barbie's house is nowadays overwhelmingly pink. The version sold in the 1950s and 1960s was red, yellow and white.

GET ACTIVE The pinkification of girls

If you take a walk along the aisles of any toy shop, you will notice it immediately. Girls' toys are overwhelmingly pink. So are girls' clothes, and shoes, make up, sports equipment, school equipment… There is even a range of pink Lego aimed at girls.

More broadly, products aimed at children are increasingly either pink or blue, with fewer in gender-neutral colours such as green and yellow.

There is a huge market for pink, because many girls appear to love it. This preference is unlikely to be innate. In the middle of the 19th century, the association was the other way round – pink was for boys and blue was for girls. Before then, it was white for both.

How might gender schema theory explain the apparent preference of young girls for the colour pink?

Evaluation

Explains rigidity of gender-related beliefs

One strength is that GST can account for how it is that children's attitudes and beliefs about gender are very fixed.

This is because children (and adults) tend to ignore information that conflicts with their gender schema. At the same time they pay greater attention to information that confirms their gender schema (e.g. a girl seeing a woman portrayed in a TV drama as a teacher rather than as a surgeon) because it is more consistent with their schema especially if it is related to their own gender.

This means that GST has explanatory power – it can explain a wide range of ways in which young children think about gender.

Neglects key non-cognitive factors

One weakness is that GST exaggerates the role of cognitive factors and underplays the importance of *social context*.

It is very likely that social factors are crucial in the early years during which a gender develops. For instance, the gender-related behaviour of parents and the rewards and punishments they hand out to children are key influences that are much better explained by *social learning theory* (see page 68). Bem (1981) did argue that the origins of the gender schema are cultural, but this is the least well-developed aspect of her theory.

This failure to address how social and cognitive factors interact means that GST is an incomplete explanation.

Narrow view of gender

Another weakness is that GST assumes that gender is binary.

This is clear from the theory's concepts of 'masculinity' and 'femininity'. It is true that Bem (1981) added the concept of androgyny but this is not a third gender. Instead, someone who is androgynous merely has a mixture of masculine and feminine characteristics (e.g. they are both assertive and nurturing). This is a narrow definition of 'non-binary' and not as flexible as it appears.

Therefore, GST is outdated and at odds with more recent views of gender as complex, fluid and non-binary.

Evidence for effects on memory

Another strength is that research supports the suggestion that memory is distorted by a person's gender schema.

Martin and Halverson (1983) showed 5/6-year-old children images of boys and girls behaving in ways that were either consistent or inconsistent with gender stereotypes (e.g. a boy playing with a truck, a girl chopping wood). When tested one week later, the children recalled the gender-consistent behaviour more accurately. When recalling gender-inconsistent images, the children tended to change the details to make their recall more consistent with their schema (e.g. it was the boy chopping wood, not the girl).

This finding is just one from many research studies that support predictions from GST, in this case that memories are distorted to fit with the existing gender schema.

Exam-style questions

1. Explain what is meant by the term 'gender'. (2)
2. Explain how the cognitive approach accounts for gender behaviours. Use the concept of gender schema in your answer. (3)
3. Give **three** features of the cognitive approach that can explain gender. (3)
4. Explain **one** strength or **one** weakness of the cognitive approach to explaining gender. (3)
5. Leo and Maria are siblings. Leo loves pretending to be a superhero, running around the house shouting and waving a sword which he uses to attack his sister. Maria enjoys playing quietly with dolls, changing their outfits, talking to them and helping them do household chores. She often has girlfriends round to join in.
   (a) Use **one** aspect of the cognitive approach to explain Leo's and/or Maria's behaviour. (2)
   (b) Discuss the view that gender is mainly the result of cognitive factors. In your answer you should consider: (i) gender schema theory, and (ii) reference to Leo and Maria. (9)

Link it

What is the link between Bartlett's (1932) concept of a schema and the cognitive approach to gender?

Harris *et al.* (2009) studied priming effects. Gender terms such as 'boy' prime people to think of associated characteristics. How does that influence expectations?

Cognitive biases (Loftus and Palmer 1974) influence what information we pay attention to and remember. How does this relate to our gender?

Specification content

C3 Application of psychology to explain gender

Learners should understand key terms associated with gender, including binary, non-binary, gender fluid, androgyny, transgender, masculinity, femininity, gender dysphoria.

Learners should understand and apply knowledge of how psychological concepts and research can be used to understand the typical and atypical gender of individuals in society.

The influence of the following on gender:

● Cognitive – role of biases and schema in gender (gender schema theory).

Boys and girls play together a lot in images like this one. In real life, not so much (see gender segregation, left).

Evaluation

Gender segregation explains gender-typical identity

One strength is that gender segregation offers a plausible explanation of gender identity development.

Gender segregation is a self-fulfilling process. When children spend more time with same-gender friends (e.g. at nursery and school), they share interests and activities. Because they find this fun, they want to spend even more time together, which means they interact less and less with children of other genders. Same-gender children have many opportunities to influence each other's identities and behaviours. This gender segregation cycle reinforces children's gender-typical interests, beliefs and biases (Martin *et al.* 2014).

This means that peer norms, and conformity with them, are likely to have a strong influence on developing gender identity in childhood.

Research into gender non-conformity

Another strength of social explanations is that research shows a strong link between gender non-conformity and being bullied.

Vicky Holt *et al.* (2016) found that half their sample of adolescents referred in the UK for gender dysphoria reported being bullied. Canadian research by Marc Shiffman *et al.* (2016) showed that gender-atypical young people were 4.5 times more likely to be bullied than gender-typical participants. The experience of gender-based bullying was also strongly associated with behavioural and psychological issues such as depression and self-harm.

This supports the view that peer influences on gender non-conforming adolescents are mostly negative.

Role of non-peer influences

One weakness is that being bullied and other negative outcomes of atypical gender may not be entirely explained by peer influences.

In a study of Finnish adolescents referred for gender dysphoria, Riittakerttu Kaltiala-Heino *et al.* (2015) found high levels of severe bullying at school. However, 75% of these participants reported the bullying began some time before they identified as gender-atypical. The bullying was also mostly not gender-related, but linked to other factors such as academic success.

This shows that many young people with gender dysphoria may have psychological and behavioural difficulties that are unrelated to the influence of their peers.

Recent research into direct effects of peer influences

Another weakness is that research on the direct effects does not fully support peer influence.

Most research into peer influences has been indirect. The research investigates the impact on gender-related beliefs or behaviours rather than identity. But recent research into direct effects has drawn different conclusions. For example, Olga Kornienko *et al.* (2016) looked at how peers directly influence aspects of gender identity in adolescence. As expected, they found that peers significantly influenced *felt pressure for gender conformity*. However, the researchers were surprised to find that peers were not a significant influence on *gender typicality*. It appears that some aspects of gender are influenced by peers and some are not.

The findings of this study highlight the fact that direct peer influences on gender are complex because gender identity itself is complex.

GET ACTIVE Tatiana

Whilst at primary school, Tatiana spent most of her time with other girls. She had two sisters but no brothers. When given the choice, she always preferred to play with other girls and with girls' toys. But by the time she was 13, Tatiana did not feel she was a 'real' girl and wanted to be a boy. But she felt a lot of pressure to behave like a girl. It made her so unhappy she saw a counsellor who suggested she might have gender dysphoria.

Use the social approach to explain Tatiana's gender identity as a child and as an adolescent.

Exam-style questions

1. In the context of gender, explain what is meant by the term 'peer influences'. (2)

2. Explain how the social approach accounts for gender. Use the concept of conformity to gender roles. (3)

3. Give **three** features of the social approach that can explain the gender a child identifies with. (3)

4. Explain how conformity to gender roles can explain atypical gender. (3)

5. Viola is a nine-year-old girl who loves pink, is happy but quiet and enjoys looking after her dolls and pet cat. Roly is a nine-year-old boy. He has a lot more female friends than male ones, and his parents have noticed how feminine he is.

   Use **one** aspect of the social approach to explain Viola's and Roly's gender preferences. (3)

6. Evaluate the view that gender is best explained by the social approach. In your answer you should consider: (a) peer influences and conformity to gender roles, and (b) typical and atypical gender. (9)

Link it

How do Asch's (1951) findings about conformity to group norms help to explain gender?

Haney *et al.* (1973) investigated conformity to social roles. Explain the link with gender.

How does gender identity relate to Chatard *et al.*'s (2007) findings about gender-role stereotypes?

Specification content

C3 Application of psychology to explain gender

Learners should understand and apply knowledge of how psychological concepts and research can be used to understand the typical and atypical gender of individuals in society.

The influence of the following on gender:

● Social – peer influences (normative and informational), conformity to gender roles.

Learning approach to explaining gender

The 'Beauty Boys' of Instagram

When American vlogger James Charles (left) visited Birmingham in January 2019, the city centre came to a standstill as thousands of young adults and children turned out to see him.

James is one of several 'beauty boys' who have been on YouTube and other social media sites. They offer tips about make-up to boys and men (as well as girls and women) and promote an image of masculinity which is to say the least at odds with the mainstream binary view.

The most prominent of the beauty boys are ambassadors for big cosmetics corporations such as Maybelline and CoverGirl.

We've been here before. In the 1970s, pop stars like David Bowie, Marc Bolan and Lou Reed presented a gender-fluid approach to the world, sparking outrage and adoration alike.

Specification terms

Conditioning Means 'learning'. Operant conditioning is a form of learning in which behaviour is shaped and maintained by its consequences, which include positive reinforcement, negative reinforcement and punishment.

Social learning A form of learning in which behaviours are acquired through observation, modelling, imitation and vicarious reinforcement. Cognitive factors play a key role.

Children learn the differences between masculine and feminine gender behaviours from an early age.

Learning explanations

Two of the common learning explanations for behaviour are *operant conditioning* and *social learning*, described earlier on pages 26 and 28.

Operant conditioning of gender

Rewards and punishments Operant conditioning of gender works through the application of rewards (*reinforcement*) and *punishments*.

When children behave in ways considered appropriate to their gender, parents (and grandparents, teachers, peers, etc.) tend to reward them with praise, encouragement and approval – this reinforces (strengthens) the behaviour. On the other hand, gender-inappropriate behaviour is punished (or at least ignored), weakening those behaviours.

For example, boys are encouraged to play football or with toy cars, to be active and 'rough' in their play ('Boys will be boys') and will be discouraged from girl-type activities. Girls are encouraged to play with dolls or engage in 'craft' activities, to be passive, gentle and considerate ('Girls should know better'). Tellingly, a girl who is active, who fights and gets into scrapes may well be labelled a 'tomboy' – she isn't seen as being a 'proper' girl.

Differential reinforcement The kind of reinforcement that is given is called *differential reinforcement* because boys are reinforced for one type of behaviour (masculine behaviours) and girls are reinforced for different, feminine ones.

According to Patricia Kerig *et al.* (1993) the driving force behind differential reinforcement is usually the father. He is more likely than the mother to apply differential rewards and punishments for gender-appropriate behaviours.

Differential reinforcement of gender-appropriate behaviours is a key process in learning *gender identity*, and one that continues throughout life and is not confined to childhood (Block 1978).

Social learning and gender

Gender is learned in a *social context*.

Direct reinforcement Parents reward and punish their children's behaviour directly, as outlined above. A child is likely to repeat gender-appropriate behaviours that have been reinforced (rewarded), but punished (or ignored) behaviours usually disappear.

Modelling Parents encourage gender-appropriate behaviours in their children by *modelling* them. For example, a mother may *model* feminine-typical behaviour whenever she cleans the house or cooks the tea or tends to the child's needs. Modelling also occurs from the child's perspective – the girl may *observe* her mother's behaviour and *imitate* it.

There are also many models of gender-appropriate behaviour available to children through the media, including increasingly online (e.g. YouTube, Snapchat).

Vicarious reinforcement Children also observe the consequences of a model's behaviour, not just the behaviour itself. The child experiences the consequences indirectly. If the consequence is rewarding, the child is likely to imitate the behaviour (e.g. a girl who sees her older sister praised for looking after her dolly may well imitate that behaviour when she can).

But if the consequence is punishment, then imitation is less likely (so if a boy observes a classmate being bullied for 'cissy' behaviour, that behaviour will probably not be imitated).

Identification The processes of social learning are more powerful when the child identifies with a model. *Identification* occurs when the child perceives the model as 'like me' and therefore as 'someone I want to be'. This happens because the model has qualities the child finds particularly rewarding.

The media is a key source of models, for example pop stars, sports stars and YouTube stars who are attractive, exciting and have high status. Crucially for the development of gender identity, children are more likely to imitate same-sex models because they identify with them more (they are more 'like me').

And today, as illustrated by vlogger James Charles, these high status figures may be providing a different kind of *role model*, changing gender concepts.

Contents

Contents

Section 6 Magnetism and electromagnetism

Section 7 Radioactivity and particles

Index

Getting the most from this book

At the start of each Section you will find the learning objectives for that section.

Welcome to the Edexcel International GCSE and Certificate Physics Student's Book. This book has been divided into seven Sections, following the structure and order of the Edexcel Specification, which you can find on the Edexcel website for reference. Section 1 has been divided into two parts to help you structure your learning.

Each Section has been divided into a number of smaller Chapters to help you manage your learning.

The following features have been included to help you get the most from this book.

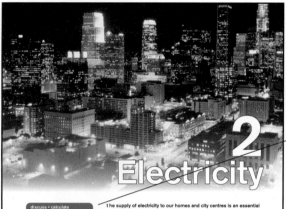

2 Electricity

discuss • calculate

1 How would your life have been different had you lived in the same country as you do now, in 1880?
2 How much does it cost to provide electricity to your home each year? How much does it cost to provide electricity to your school each year?
3 What impact does electricity generation have on our environment?
4 What hazards are associated with the use of electricity?

the supply of electricity to our homes and city centres is an essential part of twenty-first century life. lights in the streets, our homes and offices allow us to be active 24 hours a day. However, electricity comes at a price and care must be taken with how much we use it.

By the end of this section you should:
* know and use the electrical units
* recall the hazards of electricity
* understand the need for insulation, fuses and earthing
* understand that resistors transfer heat
* use the formula: power = current × voltage
* be able to work out the cost of electricity
* understand the difference between a.c. and d.c. supplies
* understand the uses of series and parallel circuits
* understand the factors that affect the current in a series circuit
* describe how the current varies with voltage in various devices
* recall and use the formula: voltage = current × resistance
* know that current is a flow of charge
* recall the definition of a volt
* explain the nature of static electricity
* recall some hazards and uses of static electricity

70

CALCULATE • PRESENT

Try the activity before you start, and then have a look at it again once you have completed the Section to see if your responses are different before and after learning more about the topics.

EXAM TIP

Exam tips throughout the book will guide you in your learning process.

PRACTICAL

Practical boxes highlight the practical work covered in the book. They provide hints on key things to remember, or alternative practical work that you can do to help you learn more about that topic.

Section 3 Waves

3.6 Reflection

Light is a transverse wave, which can be reflected in the same way that water waves are reflected. Studying the way in which water waves behave in a ripple tank will help you to understand the way in which light behaves when it is reflected.

Reflection

In Figure 6.2 you can see a representation of waves approaching a straight metal barrier in a ripple tank. In the diagram, a line is drawn at right angles to the surface of the barrier. This line is called the **normal**. The angle between the normal and the direction of travel before reflection is called the **angle of incidence**, i. The angle between the normal and the direction of travel after reflection is called the angle of reflection, r. When waves are reflected, i always equals r.

Figure 6.1 How does this trick work?

EXAM TIP
The rays are perpendicular to the wavefronts.

before reflection   after reflection

direction of travel   during reflection

metal plate

Figure 6.2 Reflection of waves off a plane surface; angle of incidence, i = angle of reflection, r.

Reflection of light rays

You may use a mirror every day for shaving or putting on make-up. Mirrors work because they reflect light. In Figure 6.4 you can see an arrangement for investigating how light is reflected from a mirror. A **ray box** is used to produce a thin beam of light. Inside the ray box is a light bulb; light is allowed to escape from the box through a thin slit.

Before the light ray strikes the mirror it is called the **incident ray**. The **angle of incidence**, i, is defined as the angle between the incident ray and the normal. The **normal** is a line at right angles to the surface of the mirror. After the ray has been reflected it is called the **reflected ray**. The angle between the normal and this ray is called the **angle of reflection**, r. Light waves reflect in the same way as waterwaves.

There are two important points about reflection of light rays, which can be summarised as follows:

The angle of incidence always equals the angle of reflection; $i = r$.
The incident ray, the reflected ray and the normal always lie in the same plane.

PRACTICAL
Make sure you understand how to investigate angles of incidence and reflections using ray boxes.

Figure 6.3 Light is reflected from a rough surface in all directions.

narrow sl

Figure 6

object   10cm

eye
Figure 6.5 Seeing

132

STUDY QUESTIONS

At the end of each Chapter you will find Study Questions. Work through these in class or on your own for homework. Answers are available on the CD.

Section 7 Radioactivity and particles

- Coal-fired power stations cause acid rain and produce radiation; they should be closed down as well.
- Nuclear power stations produce dangerous quantities of radioactive waste.
- It is irresponsible to store radioactive wastes with long half-lives; it pollutes the environment for our grandchildren.
- The fast reactor at a power station blew up in 1986, and the Fukushima plant was devastated in 2011. We also need to remember that a nuclear plant might be a target for terrorists.

EXAM TIP
Make sure you understand both the advantages and disadvantages of nuclear power.

Figure 9.5 A lot of people are worried by the dumping of radioactive waste.

Now go through the tutorial Nuclear fission and fusion.

STUDY QUESTIONS

1 a) State and explain three points in favour of the use of nuclear power in the France to produce electricity.
  b) State and explain three points against the use of nuclear power in the France.
  c) Evaluate the arguments and decide whether you are for or against the use of nuclear power to produce electricity.
2 a) Why does France export electricity to other countries?
  b) Explain how pumped storage power stations are used in France together with nuclear power stations.
3 a) Explain how a fast-breeder reactor could greatly increase the supply of fissionable nuclear fuel.
  b) Write nuclear equations to describe the three stages of producing plutonium from uranium, shown in Figure 3.4.
4 After the Fukushima disaster the Japanese Government decided to close all their nuclear power stations. In the UK, the Government plans to start

building new nuclear power station. Discuss the reasons for these differences in policy.
5 Uranium is the heaviest naturally occurring element, with an atomic number of 92. Elements with higher atomic numbers can be made artificially in nuclear reactors. These are called **transuranic elements**; they are all unstable and undergo radioactive decay. These elements are created by colliding (at high energies) and then fusing together smaller elements. The equation below shows an example of how rutherfordium (^{258}Rf) is made.

$$^{250}_{98}U + ^{26}_{12}Mg \rightarrow ^{258}_{104}Rf + ^2_0n$$

a) Balance the equation to find the number for x – to show how many neutrons are emitted in this reaction.
b) Rutherfordium-259 emits alpha particles to decay to the element nobelium (No) which emits a further alpha particle to decay to fermium (Fm). Write equations to show the atomic and mass numbers of these two isotopes.

Summary

Make sure you can answer all the questions in the *Interactive quiz.*

I am confident that:

✓ **I can describe the structure of the atom**
- The atom is electrically neutral: each proton in the nucleus carries a positive charge, which is balanced by the negative charge on an equal number of electrons.
- The mass of the atom is concentrated in the nucleus: a proton and a neutron have approximately the same mass – an electron has a very small mass by comparison.

✓ **I can recall definitions and use symbols correctly**
- Atomic (proton) number: the number of protons in the nucleus.
- Mass (nucleon) number: the number of protons and neutrons in the nucleus.
- An ion is formed by either adding or removing an electron from a neutral atom.
- An isotope of an atom is another atom that has the same number of protons, but a different number of neutrons.

✓ **I can explain radioactivity**
- An alpha particle is a helium nucleus ($^4_2$He)
- A beta particle is a fast-moving electron ($^0_{-1}$e).
- A gamma ray is a short-wavelength electromagnetic wave.
- An alpha particle travels 5 cm through air and is stopped by paper.
- Beta particles travel many metres through air and can be stopped by aluminium sheet a few millimetres thick.
- Gamma rays travel great distances through air and can only be absorbed effectively by very thick lead sheets - several centimetres thick.

✓ **I understand nuclear transformation**
- On ejecting an α- or β-particle a nucleus is transformed into another nucleus (a γ-ray makes no change to its nucleus). Two examples are:

  α-particle decay $^{238}_{92}U \rightarrow ^{234}_{90}Th + ^4_2He$

  β-particle decay $^{234}_{90}Th \rightarrow ^{234}_{91}Pa + ^0_{-1}e$

- β-decay causes the atomic number to increase by 1.

✓ **I can calculate radioactive decay**
- Radioactive decay is a random process – like throwing a lot of dice or tossing a lot of coins.
- In one half-life, half of the radioactive nuclei will decay. In a further half-life, a further half of what is left will decay.
  - after 1 half-life, ½ of the sample is left
  - after 2 half-lifes, ¼ of the sample is left
  - after 3 half-lifes, ⅛ of the sample is left, and so on.

✓ **I can discuss hazards of radiation**
- Alpha particles, beta particles and gamma rays are ionising radiations. These radiations knock electrons out of atoms thereby making ions.

✓ **I understand Rutherford scattering**
- When alpha particles are directed towards a thin metal foil (such as gold), most of them pass through with no or only a small deviation. However, a very small number bounce back. This is because the nucleus of the atom is very small, massive and positively charged.

✓ **I understand nuclear fission**
- A large nucleus can split into two; this is called nuclear fission. This process releases a lot of energy, which can be used to generate electricity in power stations.
- Unlike radioactive decay, fission can be controlled.
- Fission can be triggered by a neutron. The neutrons released in the fission reaction trigger further fissions in other nuclei. This is a chain reaction.

  $^1_0n + ^{235}_{92}U \rightarrow ^{137}_{52}Te + ^{97}_{40}Zr + 2^1_0n$

- The fission reaction can be controlled in a nuclear reactor by boron rods.

288

289

You will find Exam-style questions at the end of each Section covering the content of that Section and the different types of questions you will find in an examination.

Mark schemes are available on the CD.

At the end of each Section, you will find a Summary checklist, highlighting the key facts that you need to know and understand, and key skills that you learnt in the Section.

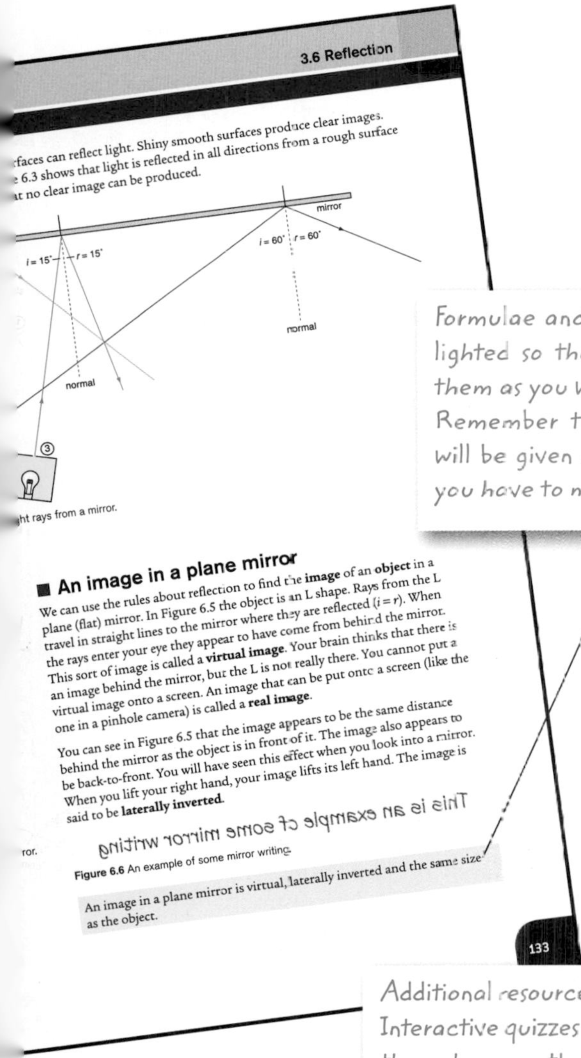

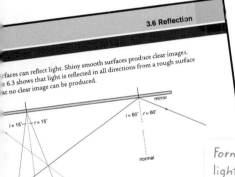

3.6 Reflection

...faces can reflect light. Shiny smooth surfaces produce clear images. ...e 6.3 shows that light is reflected in all directions from a rough surface ...at no clear image can be produced.

$i = 15°$ $r = 15°$ $i = 60°$ $r = 60°$

mirror

normal

normal

③

...ght rays from a mirror.

Formulae and laws have been highlighted so that you can easily find them as you work through the book. Remember that in your exam you will be given some formulae; others you have to memorise.

■ An image in a plane mirror
We can use the rules about reflection to find the **image** of an **object** in a plane (flat) mirror. In Figure 6.5 the object is an L shape. Rays from the L travel in straight lines to the mirror where they are reflected ($i = r$). When the rays enter your eye they appear to have come from behind the mirror. This sort of image is called a **virtual image**. Your brain thinks that there is an image behind the mirror, but the L is not really there. You cannot put a virtual image onto a screen. An image that can be put onto a screen (like the one in a pinhole camera) is called a **real image**.

You can see in Figure 6.5 that the image appears to be the same distance behind the mirror as the object is in front of it. The image also appears to be back-to-front. You will have seen this effect when you look into a mirror. When you lift your right hand, your image lifts its left hand. The image is said to be **laterally inverted**.

This is an example of some mirror writing

Figure 6.6 An example of some mirror writing

An image in a plane mirror is virtual, laterally inverted and the same size as the object.

133

EXTEND AND CHALLENGE

When you have completed all the Exam-style questions for the Section, try the Extend and Challenge questions.

EXTEND AND CHALLENGE

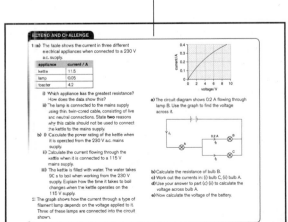

1 a) The table shows the current in three different electrical appliances when connected to a 230 V a.c. supply.

appliance	current / A
kettle	11.5
lamp	0.05
toaster	4.2

  i) Which appliance has the greatest resistance? How does the data show this?
  ii) The lamp is connected to the mains supply using thin, twin-cored cable, consisting of live and neutral connections. State **two** reasons why this cable should not be used to connect the kettle to the mains supply.
  b) i) Calculate the power rating of the kettle when it is operated from the 230 V a.c. mains supply.
    ii) Calculate the current flowing through the kettle when it is connected to a 115 V mains supply.
    iii) The kettle is filled with water. The water takes 90 s to boil when working from the 230 V supply. Explain how the time it takes to boil changes when the kettle operates on the 115 V supply.
2 The graph shows how the current through a type of filament lamp depends on the voltage applied to it. Three of these lamps are connected into the circuit shown.

a) The circuit diagram shows 0.2 A flowing through lamp B. Use the graph to find the voltage across it.

b) Calculate the resistance of bulb B.
c) Work out the currents in: (i) bulb C, (ii) bulb A.
d) Use your answer to part (c) (ii) to calculate the voltage across bulb A.
e) Now calculate the voltage of the battery.

Additional resources including Interactive quizzes for you to work through are on the CD.

The Publisher would like to thank the following for permission to reproduce photographs:

p. 1 © Philippe Devanne – Fotolia; p. 2 t © Jack.Q – Fotolia, b © OLIVIER MORIN/AFP/Getty Images; 5 t © Carolina K. Smith – Fotolia, c © jpmatz – Fotolia, b © PA/PA Archive/Press Association Images; p. 8 © Gustoimages/Science Photo Library; p. 10 © 2010 MIT. Courtesy of MIT Museum; p. 11 t © Daniel Vorley/LatinContent/Getty Images, b © Toutenphoton – Fotolia; p. 14 © luiggi33 – Fotolia; p. 17 © NASA; p. 18 © Richard Coombs / Alamy; p. 21 © Look and Learn / The Bridgeman Art Library; p. 22 © 2happy – Fotolia; p. 23 © Stephen Finn – Fotolia; p. 25 © bytesurfer – Fotolia; p. 26 © Volvo Car UK Ltd; p. 27 © Caspar Benson/fstop/Corbis; p. 28 © Sondra Paulson/ iStockphoto.com; p. 30 © Letizia – Fotolia; p. 32 © Paul Heasman – Fotolia; p. 33 © Steve Mann – Fotolia; p. 38 © Peter Ginter / Science Faction / SuperStock; p. 41 © neutronman – Fotolia; p. 42 © Bartłomiej Szewczyk – Fotolia; p. 44 b © Bob Thomas/Getty Images; p. 46 © Wolf/ Corbis; p. 49 © MSPhotographic – Fotolia; p. 52 © Mount Stromlo and Siding Spring Observatories/Science Photo Library; © Terrance Emerson – Fotolia; p. 53 © photomic – Fotolia; p. 54 tl © Digital Vision/Getty Images, tr © NASA/ Johns Hopkins University Applied Physics Laboratory/Carnegie Institution of Washington, br © NASA, bl © Digital Vision/Getty Images, b © Galaxy Picture Library / Alamy; p. 55 b © NASA/Science Photo Library; p. 57 © bhofack2 – Fotolia; p. 60 © ricknoll – Fotolia; p. 62 t © David Brewster/Minneapolis Star Tribune/ZumaPress/Corbis; p. 63 t © neutronman – Fotolia; p. 64 © Royal Observatory, Edinburgh/AATB/Science Photo Library; p. 70 © Photodisc/Getty Images; p. 71 t l © SeanPavonePhoto – Fotolia, t r © nastazia – Fotolia, b © nikkytok – Fotolia; p. 72 t © photobyjimshane – Fotolia, c © st-fotograf – Fotolia, b l © ermess – Fotolia, b r © Jason Yoder – Fotolia; p. 73 t l © Mario Beauregard – Fotolia, t r © gzmks – Fotolia, b © Aaron Kohr – Fotolia; p. 74 © Andy Rhodes – Fotolia; p. 76 t © Sanguis – Fotolia. c © Reidos – Fotolia, b © ia_64 – Fotolia; p. 79 © Dariusz Kopestynski – Fotolia; p. 82 © Leslie Garland Picture Library / Alamy; p. 85 © Calek – Fotolia; p. 89 l © ColdCoffee – Fotolia, r © xalanx – Fotolia; p. 96 © adisa – Fotolia; p. 100 © 2004 The Image Works / TopFoto; p. 103 t © Jean-Loup Charmet / Science Photo Library, b © Peter Menzel / Science Photo Library; p. 108 l © lucielang – Fotolia, r © Bondarau – Fotolia; p. 113 © Photodisc/Getty Images; p. 114 t © ikepict – Fotolia, b © Junjie – Fotolia; p. 118 l © Martin Dohrn / Science Photo Library, r © Dale Boyer / Science Photo Library; p. 120 © Airfotos Ltd; p. 121 © montego6 – Fotolia; p. 122 © Freefly – Fotolia; p. 123 © Jinx Photography Animals / Alamy; p. 124 t © Sipa Press / Rex Features, c © FRANCK FIFE/AFP/Getty Images, b © Csák István – Fotolia; p. 126 t © Georgios Kollidas – Fotolia, b © SSPL/Getty Images; p. 127 © Andrew Buckin – Fotolia; p. 129 © jcsmilly – Fotolia; p. 132 © Digital Vision/ Photolibrary Group Ltd; p. 135 © alexsalcedo – Fotolia; p. 138 © Nick England; p. 140 © Igor Kali – Fotolia; p. 142 l © Cosmic – Fotolia, r © BSIP SA / Alamy; p. 143 t © Dean Chalkley / PYMCA / Rex Features, b © BSIP SA / Alamy; p. 144 © Schweinepriester – Fotolia; p. 146 © Grafvision – Fotolia; p. 147 © Philip Harris; p. 156 © zagorskid – Fotolia; p. 157 t © Zoe – Fotolia, a © Glenn Frank/iStockphoto.com, b © Ingram Publishing Limited, c © Markus Bormann – Fotolia; p. 158 t © heysues23 – Fotolia, b © All Canada Photos / Alamy; p. 162 t © neil manuell – Fotolia, b © PiLensPhoto – Fotolia; p. 163 t © Alexander Erdbeer – Fotolia, b © yevgeniy11 – Fotolia; p. 165 Siegi – Fotolia; p. 168 t © Photodisc/Getty Images, b © Alex Hinds / Alamy; p. 171 © AVAVA – Fotolia; p. 174 t © Image Source IS2 – Fotolia, c © mgrushin – Fotolia, b © Stefan Scheer / http://en.wikipedia.org/wiki/File:Vampire_Chessington.jpg / http://creativecommons.org/licenses/by-sa/2.5/ deed.en; p. 176 © Lovrencg – Fotolia; p. 179 © Robert Clayton / Alamy; p. 180 © krsmanovic – Fotolia; p. 181 t © Artem Merzlenko – Fotolia, b © starush – Fotolia; p. 183 © Gary – Fotolia; p. 185 © Stockbyte/ Photolibrary Group Ltd; p. 186 © Radu Razvan – Fotolia; p. 187 © Eric Isselée – Fotolia; p. 188 t © China Photos/Getty Images, b © Laurence Gough – Fotolia; p. 196 © fotonanny – Fotolia; p. 197 © DigiMagic Editorial / Alamy; p. 198 © ISO400 – Fotolia; p. 200 t l © Bluestock – Fotolia, t r © Valuykin S. – Fotolia, c © minik – Fotolia, b l © Gina Sanders – Fotolia, b r © Nick England; p. 202 © frantisek hojdysz – Fotolia; p. 205 © popov48 – Fotolia; p. 207 t © Michael Luckett – Fotolia, c © Dr Mitsuo Ohtsuki/Science Photo Library, b © Science Source/Science Photo Library; p. 208 t © Elizabeth Warren, b © sciencephotos / Alamy; p. 209 t © Fedor Bolba – Fotolia, b l © Goinyk Volodymyr – Fotolia, b c © EpicStockMedia – Fotolia, b r © Olga Vasik – Fotolia; p. 211 © Ungor – Fotolia; p. 215 © The Natural History Museum / Alamy; p. 218 © wajan – Fotolia; p. 229 b © Jay Pasachoff/Science Faction/Corbis; p. 230 © Stockbyte/Getty Images; p. 232 © Pasieka / Science Photo Library; p. 233 © sciencephotos / Alamy; p. 234 © Leslie Garland Picture Library / Alamy; p. 235 l © Scott Camazine / Alamy, r © Martin Bond/Science Photo Library; p. 237 t © Gorchy / http://upload.wikimedia.org/wikipedia/commons/b/b4/NdFeB-Domains.jpg / http:// creativecommons.org/licenses/by-sa/3.0/deed.en b © SSPL/Getty Images; p. 238 © dvande – Fotolia; p. 239 t © eyewave – Fotolia, c © Reflekcija – Fotolia, b © Andrew Lambert Photography / Science Photo Library; p. 240 © Leslie Garland Picture Library / Alamy; p. 241 © Nick England; p. 242 © mario beauregard – Fotolia; p. 244 © Supertrooper – Fotolia; p. 247 © AP/Press Association Images; p. 251 © Artem Merzlenko – Fotolia; p. 254 © TebNad – Fotolia; p. 255 © David J. Green – technology / Alamy; p. 264 © Mark Clifford / Barcroft Media / Getty Images; p. 265 © Everett Collection Historical / Alamy; p. 267 © ullsteinbild / TopFoto; p. 270 © Science Photo Library; p. 272 © NASA / Harrison Schmitt; p. 274 © James King-Holmes/Science Photo Library; p. 275 © Ton Keone/Visuals Unlimited/Science Photo Library; p. 276 t © Centre Oscar Lambret / Phanie / Rex Features, b © Martyn F. Chillmaid/Science Photo Library; p. 278 © AP/Press Association Images; p. 279 © Hellen Sergeyeva – Fotolia; p. 280 © John Lund/Blend Images/Corbis; p. 281 © The Art Archive / Alamy; p. 283 © Tim Wright/Corbis; p. 286 © Stefan Kühn / http://upload.wikimedia.org/wikipedia/commons/4/4e/ Nuclear_Power_Plant_Cattenom.jpg / http://creativecommons.org/licenses/by-sa/2.5/deed.en; p. 288 © Yann / http:// upload.wikimedia.org/wikipedia/commons/e/e9/Antinuclear_Walk_Geneva-Brussels_2009_Geneva.jpg / http:// creativecommons.org/licenses/by-sa/2.5/deed.en

1 Forces and motion 1

1 Can you suggest how many forces are acting on the surfer in the photograph?
2 How do they balance to keep him upright and moving forwards?

When moving in a straight line at a constant speed, balanced forces must act on this surfer.

By the end of this section you should:
- be able to calculate average speed
- know the difference between speed and velocity
- be able to calculate acceleration
- understand how to measure acceleration
- know Newton's three laws of motion
- know what the acceleration due to gravity is, and understand the term 'terminal velocity'
- know about car safety
- be able to interpret distance–time and velocity–time graphs
- know that a force is a vector quantity
- be able to calculate changes in momentum, and know about the principle of conservation of momentum
- understand how rockets and jets work

1.1 How fast do things move?

Moving object	Speed / m/s
glacier (Rhonegletsher)	0.000001
snail	0.0005
human walking	2
human sprinter	10
express train	60
jet plane	200
Earth moving round the Sun	30000
light and radio waves	300000000

Figure 1.1 How long would this snail take to travel 1500 m?

■ Average speed

When you travel in a fast car you finish your journey in a short time. When you travel in a slow car your journey takes longer. If the speed of a car is 100 kilometres per hour (100 km/h) it will travel a distance of 100 kilometres in one hour. We can write a formula connecting distance, speed and time.

$$\text{average speed} = \frac{\text{distance travelled}}{\text{time taken}} = \frac{d}{t}$$

We write *average* speed because the speed of the car may change during the journey. When you travel along a motorway your speed does not remain exactly the same. You slow down when you get stuck behind a lorry and speed up when you pull out to overtake a car.

Figure 1.2 Hannah, Jenny and Natalia finish the 1500 m in 4 minutes and 5 seconds. What was their average speed?

Example. At top speed a guided-missile destroyer travels 170 km in 3 hours. What is its average speed in m/s?

$$\text{average speed} = \frac{d}{t}$$

$$= \frac{170 \times 1000 \text{ m}}{3 \times 3600 \text{ s}}$$

$$= 16 \text{ m/s}$$

EXAM TIP

Remember: 1 km = 1000 m;
1 hour = (60 × 60 s) = 3600 s

2

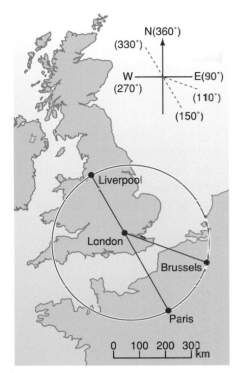

Figure 1.3 At the same speed, in 1 hour a helicopter from London can reach Liverpool, Brussels or Paris.

Velocity

It is not just the speed that is important when you go on a journey. The direction matters as well. Figure 1.3 shows three possible routes taken by a helicopter leaving London. The helicopter travels at 300 km/h. So in 1 hour the helicopter can reach Liverpool, Paris or Brussels, depending on which direction it travels in.

When we want to talk about a direction as well as a speed we use the word **velocity**. For example, when the helicopter flies towards Liverpool, we can say that its velocity is 300 km/h, on a compass bearing of 330°. Velocity is a vector; speed is a scalar (see page 14).

Timetabling railway trains

You have probably sat on a slow train in a railway station wondering why the train was taking so long to start. You might have been waiting for an express train to overtake. There is often only one line between railway stations. The trains must be timetabled so that the faster express trains can overtake a slower train that has stopped at a station.

A passenger train planning officer has to make sure that a slow train going from Reading to Chippenham does not get in the way of the London to Cardiff express train. The slow train travels at an average speed of 70 km/h and the express train at an average speed of 120 km/h.

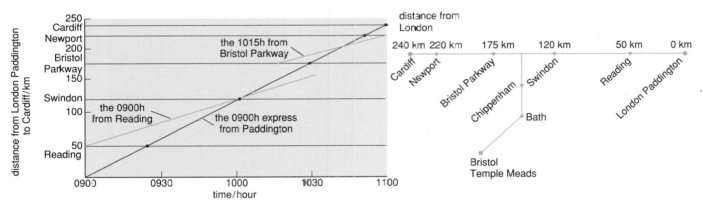

Figure 1.4 Graph of train journeys and route map showing distances from London.

Plotting a graph of the distance travelled by these trains against time helps to solve the problem. You can see from Figure 1.4 what happens if both trains leave their stations at 0900 h. The slow train travels the 70 km to Swindon, and the faster train travels from London to Swindon in the same time. So the express train can overtake at Swindon without waiting. You can also see from the graph that there is a slow train to Newport leaving Bristol Parkway at 1015 h which is going to get in the way of the express train.

STUDY QUESTIONS

1 The table below shows average speeds and times recorded by top male athletes in several track events. Copy and complete the table.

2 Sketch a graph of distance travelled (y-axis) against time (x-axis) for a train coming into a station. The train stops for a while at the station and then starts again.

3 This question refers to the train timetabling shown in Figure 1.4.
   a) How can you tell from the graph that the express train travels faster than the other two?
   b) At what time does the express train reach Bristol Parkway?
   c) At what time should the slow train from Bristol Parkway leave so that it arrives at Newport at the same time as the express train?

Event	Average speed / m/s	Time
100 m		9.6 s
200 m	10.3	
400 m	8.9	
	7.1	3 m 30 s
10 000 m		29 m 10 s
	5.5	2 h 7 m 52 s

4 Ravi, Paul and Tina enter a 30 km road race. The graph below shows Ravi's and Paul's progress through the race.
   a) Which runner ran at a constant speed? Explain your answer.
   b) What was Paul's average speed for the 30 km run?
   c) What happened to Paul's speed after 2 hours?
   Tina was one hour late starting the race. During the race she ran at a constant speed of 15 km/h.
   d) Copy the graph and add to it a line to show how Tina ran.
   e) How far had Tina run when she overtook Paul?

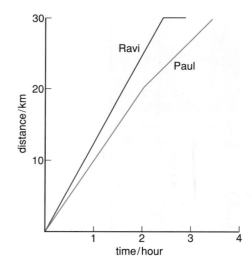

1.2 Acceleration

Which accelerates faster – the flea or the racing car? The F1 car reaches a speed of 10 m/s after 1 s. The flea reaches a speed of 1 m/s after 0.001 s.

Figure 2.1

■ Speeding up and slowing down

When a car is speeding up, we say it is *accelerating*. When it is slowing down we say it is *decelerating*. A deceleration can be thought of as a negative acceleration.

You may be interested in driving a sports car that can accelerate quickly away from traffic lights when they turn green. A car that accelerates rapidly reaches a high speed in a short time. For example, a sports car speeds up to 45 km/h in 5 seconds. A truck speeds up to 45 km/h in 10 seconds. We say the acceleration of the car is twice as big as the truck's acceleration.

You can work out the acceleration of the car or truck using the formula:

$$\text{acceleration} = \frac{\text{change of velocity}}{\text{time}}$$

Figure 2.2

$$\text{acceleration of sports car} = \frac{45 \text{ km/h}}{5 \text{ s}}$$
$$= 9 \text{ km/h per second}$$
$$\text{acceleration of truck} = \frac{45 \text{ km/h}}{10 \text{ s}}$$
$$= 4.5 \text{ km/h per second}$$

■ Units of acceleration

We usually measure velocity in metres per second. This means that acceleration is usually measured in **m/s per second**. What is the acceleration of our sports car in m/s per second?

$$45 \text{ km/h} = \frac{45\ 000 \text{ m}}{3600 \text{ s}} = 12.5 \text{ m/s}$$
$$\text{So acceleration} = \frac{\text{change of velocity}}{\text{time}}$$
$$= \frac{12.5 \text{ m/s}}{5 \text{ s}} = 2.5 \text{ m/s per second}$$

or

$$2.5 \text{ m/s}^2 \text{(metres per second squared)}$$

Figure 2.3 This car has been in a major accident. A fast moving, massive object like a car experiences a very large force when it decelerates rapidly. The force is large enough to crumple the roof.

EXAM TIP
Remember the unit of acceleration is m/s².

■ Acceleration formula

$$a = \frac{v - u}{t}$$

In this formula, a is the acceleration, v is the final velocity, u is the starting velocity and t is the time taken.

■ Velocity–time graphs

It can be helpful to plot graphs of velocity against time.

Figure 2.4 shows the velocity–time graph for cyclist as she goes on a short journey.

■ In the first 8 seconds, she accelerates up to a speed of 12 m/s (section AB of the graph).

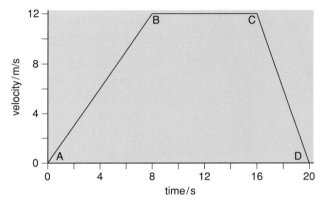

Figure 2.4

■ For the next 8 seconds she cycles at a constant speed (section BC of the graph).
■ Then for the last 4 seconds of the journey she decelerates to a stop (section CD of the graph).

The gradient of the graph gives us the acceleration. In section AB she increases her speed by 12 m/s in 8 seconds.

$$\text{acceleration} = \frac{\text{change of speed}}{\text{time}}$$
$$= \frac{12 \text{ m/s}}{8 \text{ s}}$$
$$= 1.5 \text{ m/s}^2$$

You can also work out the distance travelled by calculating the area under the velocity–time graph. The area under section AB gives the distance travelled because:

$$\text{distance} = \text{average speed} \times \text{time}$$
$$= 6 \text{ m/s} \times 8 \text{ s}$$
$$= 48 \text{ m}$$

The average speed is 6 m/s as this is half of the final speed 12 m/s. The area can also be calculated using the formula for the area of the triangle:

$$\text{area of triangle} = \frac{1}{2} \times \text{base} \times \text{height}$$
$$= \frac{1}{2} \times 8 \text{ s} \times 12 \text{ m/s}$$
$$= 48 \text{ m}$$

EXAM TIP

The area under a velocity–time graph is the distance travelled.

EXAM TIP

The gradient of a velocity–time graph is the acceleration.

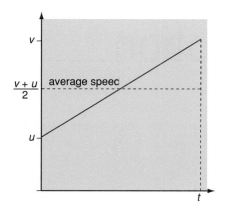

Figure 2.5

■ Equations for motion

Figure 2.5 shows a velocity-time graph for something that accelerates from an initial speed, u, reaching a final speed, v, in a time, t. Two useful equations can be derived from this graph:

$$\text{acceleration} = \frac{v - u}{t}$$

$$\text{average speed} = \frac{u + v}{2}$$

The average speed is halfway between the starting speed and the finishing speed. The change in speed is $v - u$.

STUDY QUESTIONS

1 This question refers to the journey shown in Figure 2.4.
   a) What was the cyclist's deceleration over region CD of the graph?
   b) Use the area under the graph to calculate the distance covered during the whole journey.
   c) What was the average speed over the whole journey?

2 Table 1 shows how the speed, in km/h, of Jenson Button's Formula 1 racing car changes as he accelerates away from the starting grid at the beginning of the Brazilian Grand Prix.
   a) Plot a graph of speed (y-axis) against time (x-axis).
   b) Use your graph to estimate the acceleration of the car in km/h per second at:
      i) 16 s
      ii) 1 s.

3 Copy Table 2 below and fill in the missing values.

4 Drag cars are designed to cover distances of 400 m in about 6 seconds. During this time the cars accelerate very rapidly from a standing start. At the end of 6 seconds, a drag car reaches a speed of 150 m/s.
   a) What is the drag car's average speed?
   b) What is its average acceleration?

5 Describe the motion shown in the following two graphs:

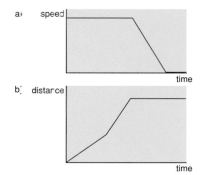

Table 1

Speed / km/h	0	35	70	130	175	205	230	250	260	260
Time / s	0	1	2	4	6	8	10	12	14	16

Table 2

	Starting speed / m/s	Final speed / m/s	Time taken / s	Acceleration / m/s²
Cheetah	0	30	5	6
Second stage of a rocket	450	750	100	
Aircraft taking off	0		30	2
Car crash	30	0		−150

1.3 Observing motion

Figure 3.1 This high-speed photograph of the athlete's long jump enables the coach to work on style, strength and distance, and helps the athlete to improve technique.

A trainer who wants to know how well one of his athletes is running stands at the side of the track with a stopwatch in his hand. By careful timing, the athlete's speed at each part of the race can be analysed. However, if the trainer wants to know more detail the measurements need to be taken with small intervals of time. One way to do this is by filming the athlete's movements.

■ Multiflash photography

Another way to look at motion is to use multiflash photography. In Figure 3.6 on page 10 you can see a photograph of a golfer hitting a ball. In this technique the golfer swings his club in a darkened room, while a lamp flashes on and off at regular intervals. When the images of the club are close together, the club is moving slowly. When the images are far apart, it is moving quickly.

■ Ticker timer

Changing speeds and accelerations of objects in the laboratory can be measured directly using light gates, data loggers and computers. However, motion is still studied using the ticker timer (Figure 3.2), because it collects data in a clear way, which can be usefully analysed. A ticker timer has a small

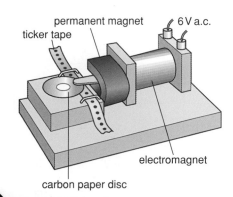

permanent magnet

ticker tape

6 V a.c.

electromagnet

carbon paper disc

Figure 3.2 Ticker timer.

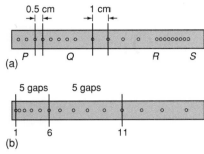

(a)

(b)

Figure 3.3

hammer that vibrates up and down 50 times per second. The hammer hits a piece of carbon paper, which leaves a mark on a length of tape.

Figure 3.3 shows you two tapes that have been pulled through the timer. In tape (a) you can see that the dots are close together over the region PQ. Then the dots get further apart, so the object moved faster over QR. The movement slowed down again over the last part of the tape, RS. Since the timer produces 50 dots per second, the time between dots is $1/50$ s or 0.02 s. So we can work out the speed:

$$speed = \frac{distance\ between\ dots}{time\ between\ dots}$$

$$Between\ P\ and\ Q,\ speed = \frac{0.5\ cm}{0.02\ s}$$

$$= 25\ cm/s\ or\ 0.25\ m/s$$

In tape (b) the dots get further and further apart, so the object attached to this tape was accelerating all the time.

■ Calculating acceleration

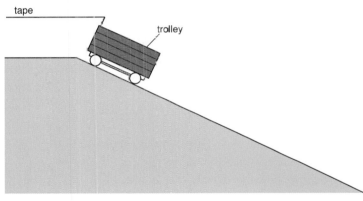

Figure 3.4

Figure 3.4 shows how you might calculate the acceleration of a trolley moving down a slope. When you have let the trolley go down the slope the tape attached to it will look a bit like tape (b) in Figure 3.3. It is helpful to cut up the tape into 5-tick lengths. You do this by cutting through the first dot, then the sixth, eleventh, and so on. Each length of tape is the distance travelled by the trolley in $1/10$ s (5 spaces between dots means $5 \times 1/50$ seconds). You can then use your pieces of tape to make a graph and see how the trolley moved. If your pieces of tape form a straight line then the acceleration was constant (see Figure 3.5).

Cutting up your tape like this is like plotting a graph of speed against time; the steeper the slope the greater the acceleration.

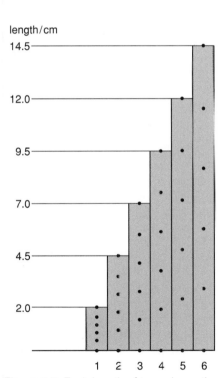

Figure 3.5 Each length of tape shows the movement of the trolley over 0.1 s.

■ Light gates

The speed of a moving object can also be measured using light gates. Figure 3.7 shows an experiment to determine the acceleration of a rolling ball as it passes between two light gates. When the ball passes through a light gate, it cuts a beam of light. This allows the computer to measure the time taken by the ball to pass through the gate. By knowing the diameter of the ball, the speed of the ball at each gate can be calculated. You can tell if the ball is accelerating if it speeds up between light gates A and B. Question 4 shows you how the gates can be used to calculate the ball's acceleration – although of course the computer can be programmed to do the work for you.

Figure 3.6 Multiflash image of a golfer's swing.

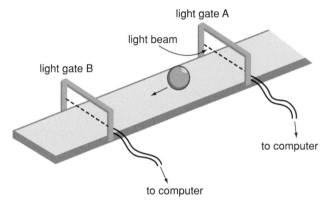

Figure 3.7 Light gates can be used to measure speeds and determine acceleration.

STUDY QUESTIONS

1 Work out the speed of the tape in Figure 3.3(a) in the region *QR*

2 a) How can you tell from Figure 3.5 that the trolley accelerated down the slope at a constant rate?
   b) Work out the average speed of the trolley in:
      (i) interval 4, (ii) interval 6.
   c) What is the time between the middle of interval 4 and the middle of interval 6?
   d) Now use your results from parts (b) and (c) to calculate the acceleration of the trolley.

3 The graph shows how the velocity of a jet aircraft increases as it takes off from the deck of an aircraft carrier.
   Calculate its acceleration (a) during the first second, (b) between 3 and 4 seconds.

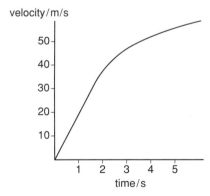

4 This question shows you how to use the apparatus in Figure 3.7 to determine the acceleration of the ball.

The measurements taken in an experiment are shown below.

diameter of the ball	6.2 cm
time for the ball to go through gate A	0.12 s
time for the ball to go through gate B	0.09 s
time taken for the ball to travel from gate A to gate B	0.23 s

   a) Explain why it is important to adjust the light gates to the correct height.
   b) Calculate the speed of the ball as it goes through:
      (i) gate A, (ii) gate B.
   c) Calculate the ball's acceleration as it moves from gate A to gate B.
   d) State and explain one improvement you would make to improve the reliability of the experiment.

5 a) Examine the photograph of the golfer, Figure 3.6 above. The swing is anti-clockwise. Where is the club moving fastest? Explain your answer.
   b) The time interval between each flash was about 0.03 s. Use this information and the scale below the photograph to calculate (i) the speed of the club on impact with the ball, and (ii) the initial speed of the ball.
   c) Use the increasing gap size between successive positions of the club to estimate the club's acceleration on its downward swing.

1.4 Forces near and far

A force is a push or a pull. The shot putter pushes the shot and the archer pulls the string on the bow. Forces are measured in newtons, N. Where does the name come from?

Figure 4.1

■ What is a force?

A force is a push or a pull. Whenever you push or pull something you are exerting a force on it. The forces that you exert can cause three things:

- **You can change the shape of an object.** You can stretch or squash a spring. You can bend or break a ruler.
- **You can change the speed of an object.** You can increase the speed of a ball when you throw it. You decrease its speed when you catch it.
- **A force can also change the direction in which something is travelling.** We use a steering wheel to turn a car.

The forces described so far are called **contact forces**. Your hand touches something to exert a force. There are also **non-contact forces**. Gravitational, magnetic and electric forces are non-contact forces. These forces can act over large distances without two objects touching. The Earth pulls you down whether or not your feet are on the ground. Although the Earth is 150 million km away from the Sun, the Sun's gravitational pull keeps us in orbit around it. Magnets also exert forces on each other without coming into contact. Electrostatic forces act between charged objects.

Figure 4.2

■ The size of forces

The unit we use to measure force is the **newton** (N). The box on page 12 will help you to get the feel of the size of several forces.

A force is a **vector** quantity; this means that it has both a size and a direction. We show forces by drawing an arrow in the direction of the force, and next to it we write its size, remembering to show the unit of force, N. Figure 4.3 shows Annabel's weight, which pulls her downwards; Figure 4.4 shows the tension in a rope that is pulling a car forwards.

600 N

Figure 4.3

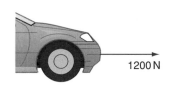

1200 N

Figure 4.4

- The pull of gravity on a fly = 0.001 N
- The pull of gravity on an apple = 1 N
- The frictional force slowing a rolling football = 2 N
- The force required to squash an egg = 50 N
- The pull of gravity on you = 500 N
- The tension in a rope, towing a car = 1000 N
- The frictional force exerted by the brakes of a car = 5000 N
- The push from the engines of a space rocket = 1 000 000 N
- 1000 N = 1 kN (kilonewton)
- 1 000 000 N = 1 MN (mega newton)

■ Some important forces

Weight is the name that we give to the pull of gravity on an object. Near the Earth's surface the pull of gravity is approximately 10 N on each kilogram. We say that the Earth's gravitational field strength is 10 N/kg.

Example. What is your weight if your body has a mass of 50 kg?

$$\text{weight} = \text{pull of gravity}$$
$$= 50 \text{ kg} \times 10 \text{ N/kg}$$
$$= 500 \text{ N}$$

Tension is the name given to a force that acts through a stretched rope; when two teams pull on a rope it is under tension.

When something is squashed it comes under forces of **compression**; the pillars of a building are under compression.

Friction is the contact force that slows down moving things. Friction can also prevent stationary things from starting to move when other forces act on them. Figure 4.5 helps you to understand why frictional forces occur. No surface is perfectly smooth. If you look at a surface through a powerful microscope you will be able to see that it has many rough spikes and indentations. When two surfaces move past each other these rough spikes catch onto each other and slow down the motion.

Figure 4.5 How two surfaces appear when seen through a powerful microscope.

Friction is often a nuisance because the rubbing between two surfaces turns kinetic (motion) energy into heat. Some ways of reducing friction are shown in Figure 4.6. Sometimes, though, friction is useful. Brakes work by using friction to slow down cars. Also, when you walk, the frictional forces between your foot and the floor push you forward.

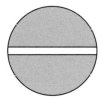

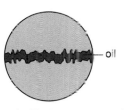

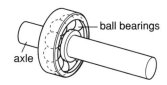

Figure 4.6 Reducing friction
(a) If the surfaces are highly polished, friction is reduced.

(b) A layer of oil between two surfaces acts as a cushion to stop the edges catching.

(c) Steel balls reduce friction by allowing surfaces to roll over each other.

 Now go through the Tutorial *Forces and their effects*.

STUDY QUESTIONS

1 **a)** Give three examples of forces that are pulls, and three examples that are pushes.
 b) For each of the examples of forces you have given, state an approximate value for the size of the force.
 c) Draw a diagram to show the size and direction of the force.

2 How big is the weight of:
 a) a 2 kg bag of sugar
 b) a 1000 kg car?

3 **a)** Explain how a wheel acts to reduce friction.
 b) There is a frictional force between a bicycle wheel and its axle. Explain two ways in which the frictional force can be reduced.

4 In the following diagrams some forces are shown acting on some objects. In each case explain the effect that the forces produce.

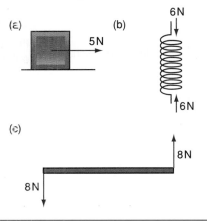

1.5 Forces and vectors

Figure 5.1

If you want to move a chair you have to give it a push. The direction in which the chair moves depends on the direction of your push. A large push gets the chair moving quickly; so both the direction and size of the force are important.

■ Vectors and scalars

Force is an example of a **vector** quantity. Vector quantities have both size and direction. Other examples of vectors are: velocity (the wind blows at 50 km/h from the North); displacement (a car travels 20 km due East). A quantity that has only size is a **scalar** quantity. Some examples of scalar quantities are: mass (3 kg of potatoes); temperature (20 °C); energy (100 joules).

■ Drawing forces

In the previous chapter you met the idea of forces such as weight, friction and tension.

Figure 5.2 shows two examples of forces acting on Michael: (a) his weight (the pull of gravity on him) is 800 N; (b) a rope with a tension of 150 N pulls him forwards.

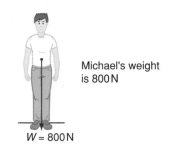

Michael's weight is 800 N

$W = 800\,\text{N}$

(a)

$T = 150\,\text{N}$

The tension in the rope is 150 N

(b)

Figure 5.2

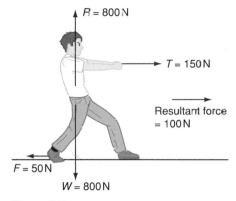

R = 800 N

T = 150 N

Resultant force = 100 N

F = 50 N

W = 800 N

Figure 5.3

It is usual for more than one force to act on something. Then we must show all the forces acting. When Michael is pulled by the rope (Figure 5.3), his weight still acts on him, and the floor supports him too – if the floor did not exert an upwards force on him equal to his weight, he would be falling downwards. The force is called the floor's **reaction force**, R. The floor will also exert a frictional force on him, in the opposite direction to that in which he is moving. All these forces are shown together in Figure 5.3.

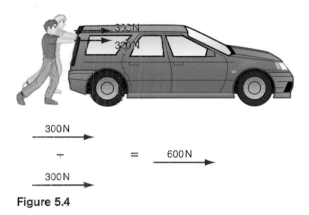

300 N

300 N

300 N

+

300 N

=

600 N

Figure 5.4

■ Adding forces

When two forces act in the same direction, they add up to give a larger **resultant** or **net** force. In Figure 5.4, for example, two people each push the car with a force of 300 N. The resultant force acting on the car is now 600 N.

If forces act in opposite directions they may cancel each other out. In Figure 5.3 Michael's weight, which pulls him downwards, is cancelled by the upwards force from the floor. The resultant force is zero; 800 N – 800 N. We say that these forces are balanced. Michael therefore stays on the floor.

There are other forces that act on Michael; the pull from the rope to the right is 150 N, but the frictional force to the left is 50 N. The resultant horizontal force on Michael is therefore 150 N – 50 N = 100 N, to the right.

■ Resultant force and state of motion

The diagrams in Figure 5.5 show two more examples of how forces add up along a line. In Figure 5.5(a) the dolphin has adjusted his buoyancy so that the upthrust from the water balances his weight; he can now stay at the same depth. In Figure 5.5(b), a car is moving forwards and increases its speed. The push from the road is greater than the wind resistance, so an unbalanced force of 200 N helps to accelerate the car.

(a)

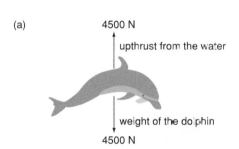

4500 N

upthrust from the water

weight of the dolphin

4500 N

(b)

drag/wind resistance
700 N

900 N

Figure 5.5 (a) The forces balance so the resultant force on the dolphin is zero.
(b) The resultant force on the car is 200 N to the right. This means the car increases its speed.

STUDY QUESTIONS

1 A fisherman has caught a large fish and has to use two balances to weigh it. Look at the diagram to calculate its weight.

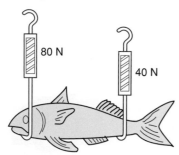

80 N

40 N

2 A golf ball is hit off its tee, 200 m down the fairway. Draw diagrams to show all the forces acting on the ball:
 a) when the ball rests on the tee
 b) while the club strikes the ball on the tee
 c) as the ball is in flight.

3 a) The diagrams below show all the forces acting on a box. In each case, describe what effect these forces have on the box.
 b) For each of the diagrams state the size and direction of the resultant force.

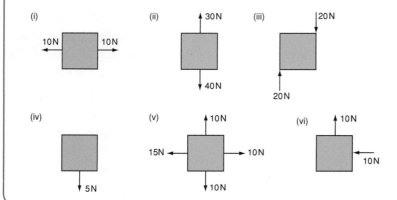

(i) 10N 10N

(ii) 30N 40N

(iii) 20N 20N

(iv) 5N

(v) 10N 15N 10N 10N

(vi) 10N 10N

4 Frank's weight is 800 N and his bike's weight is 2500 N. What upwards force is exerted by the road on his rear wheel?

1100N

5 What is the resultant force on this rocket?

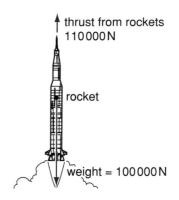

thrust from rockets
110 000 N

rocket

weight = 100 000 N

1.6 Forces in motion

Figure 6.1 The *Saturn V* rocket on its way to the Moon.

Newton's laws of motion allowed scientists to calculate how to land a capsule on the Moon.

Can you state three equations that they used in their calculations?

What important device do you use every day that was developed as a result of the NASA space programme?

■ Newton's first law: balanced forces

Newton's first law of motion states that when no force acts, or balanced forces act on an object, its state of motion will be unchanged. Either a body remains at rest, or it carries on moving in a straight line at a constant velocity.

In Figure 6.2 there are four examples that illustrate Newton's first law:

a) A person is standing still. Two forces act on him: the pull of gravity (his weight) is 750 N; the reaction from the ground is 750 N. These forces balance and he stays still.

b) A spacecraft, *Explorer*, is stationary in space, so far away from the Sun and planets that we can ignore the pull of gravity. There are no forces on *Explorer* and it stays still.

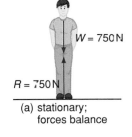

$W = 750\,\text{N}$

$R = 750\,\text{N}$

(a) stationary;
forces balance

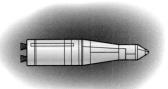

(b) stationary;
no forces act

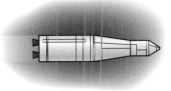

(c) moving at steady speed;
no forces act

driving forces

drag forces

(d) moving at steady speed;
forces balance

Figure 6.2

c) Figure 6.2(c) looks remarkably similar to (b). In this case *Explorer* is moving at a constant speed in outer space, where we can ignore any gravitational pull. In space no resistive or frictional forces act to stop motion, so *Explorer* carries on moving forever.

d) Applying Newton's first law becomes more complicated on Earth because frictional forces act. Here, a car moves at a constant speed along a level road. Its weight is balanced by the reaction from the road, but the forces acting horizontally balance too. There is a forwards push on the wheels, which is balanced by air resistance and friction. When the forwards and backwards forces balance, the car moves at a constant velocity in a straight line. It is necessary to have the engine running so that it can work against the resistive forces.

■ Newton's second law: unbalanced forces

Newton's second law states that when unbalanced forces act on something, then the state of the body changes. An unbalanced force causes acceleration. The body on which the force acts might speed up, slow down, or change direction. A larger unbalanced force causes a larger acceleration; this is part of Newton's second law of motion. Examples of speeding up and slowing down are given in Figure 6.3.

a) *Explorer* has turned on its rocket. There is now a force pushing the spacecraft forward and its speed increases.

b) The driver of the car has seen the traffic slowing down ahead of him. He takes his foot off the accelerator; no forward force acts on the car now, but drag forces continue to act. An unbalanced force acts to slow the car down.

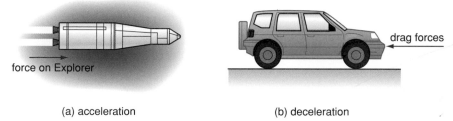

force on Explorer

(a) acceleration   (b) deceleration

Figure 6.3

■ Force, mass and acceleration

You have probably helped push a car with a flat battery. When one person tries to push a car the acceleration is very slow. When three people give the car a push it accelerates quicker.

Acceleration is proportional to the applied force.

You know from experience that large massive objects are difficult to set in motion. When you throw a ball you can accelerate your arm more quickly if the ball has a small mass. You can throw a tennis ball much faster than you put a shot. A shot has a mass of about 7 kg so your arm cannot apply a force large enough to accelerate it as rapidly as a tennis ball.

Acceleration is inversely proportional to the mass.

Figure 6.4 The large force produced by a powerful engine acts on a small mass to give this racing car a large acceleration.

■ *F = ma*

Experiments in the laboratory show you how acceleration depends on the size of the force. Figure 6.5(a) shows the idea. A trolley placed on a table is accelerated by pulling it with an elastic cord. This cord is stretched so that it always remains the same length. The acceleration is measured by attaching a piece of ticker tape to the back of the trolley.

In the first experiment the force acting on one trolley is increased by using extra elastic cords in parallel with the first. You can see that the ticker-tape graphs get steeper as the force increases. The acceleration is getting bigger.

- A 1 kg trolley accelerates at a rate of 1 m/s² with a force of 1 N.
- A 1 kg trolley accelerates at a rate of 2 m/s² with a force of 2 N.
- A 1 kg trolley accelerates at a rate of 3 m/s² with a force of 3 N.

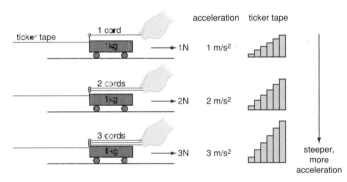

(a) Experiment 1: Keep the mass constant and change the force.

Figure 6.5

In the second experiment, Figure 6.5(b), the mass of the trolley is changed but it is pulled with the same force. As the mass increases the ticker-tape graphs become less steep. The acceleration is getting less.

- A force of 1 N accelerates a 1 kg trolley at 1 m/s².
- A force of 1 N accelerates a 2 kg trolley at ½ m/s².
- A force of 1 N accelerates a 3 kg trolley at ⅓ m/s².

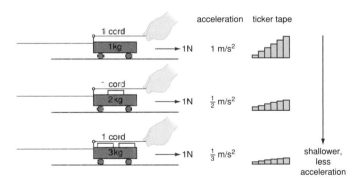

(b) Experiment 2: Keep the force constant and change the mass.

Figure 6.5

This equation fits all of these results:

$$\text{force} = \text{mass} \times \text{acceleration}$$

$$F = ma$$

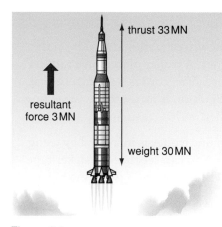

thrust 33 MN

resultant force 3 MN

weight 30 MN

Figure 6.6

The equation defines the newton:

A force of 1 N will accelerate a mass of 1 kg at a rate of 1 m/s².

Example. A sledge has a mass of 10 kg. A boy pulls it with a force of 20 N. What is its acceleration?

$$F = m \times a$$

$$\text{So} \quad a = \frac{F}{m} = \frac{20 \text{ N}}{10 \text{ kg}} = 2 \text{ m/s}^2$$

■ Calculating the resultant force

One common problem arises with the use of Newton's second law. You need to remember that when things accelerate, it is the *resultant* force which causes the acceleration.

Example. A Saturn V rocket (Figure 6.6) of mass 3 000 000 kg takes off; its rockets provide a thrust of 33 000 000 N. What is the rocket's acceleration?

There are two forces acting; the thrust upwards and the weight downwards, which is 3 000 000 kg × 10 N/kg or 30 000 000 N.

$$\text{So acceleration} = \frac{\text{resultant force}}{\text{mass}}$$
$$= \frac{33\ 00\ 000 \text{ N} - 30\ 000\ 000 \text{ N}}{3\ 000\ 000 \text{ kg}}$$
$$= 1 \text{ m/s}^2$$

STUDY QUESTIONS

1 a) A car is stationary on some ice on a road. Explain why the car might have difficulty starting to move on ice.
   b) A sprinter fixes blocks into the ground to help him get a good start. Explain how these assist him.
2 You leave a parcel on the seat of a car. When you brake suddenly, the parcel falls onto the floor. Explain why.
3 The diagram shows the direction of a force on a model car. Which of the following is a possible state of motion for the car? Explain your answers.
   a) Staying at rest.
   b) Beginning to move backwards.
   c) Moving backwards at a constant speed.
   d) Slowing down while moving forwards.

4 Draw all the forces that act on a plane (a) just after take off, (b) while flying at a constant speed at a constant height.

5 Trains accelerate very slowly out of stations. Why is their acceleration very much slower than that of a car?
6 This question refers to the experiments described in Figure 6.5.
   a) How many cords are needed to accelerate a trolley of mass 4 kg at a rate of 0.5 m/s²?
   b) What acceleration is produced by four cords acting on a trolley of mass 3 kg?
   c) The trolley in this experiment has frictional forces acting on it. What effect does friction have on the results?
   d) What can you do to help compensate for friction?
7 You are in a spacecraft in a region where there is no gravitational pull. You have two biscuit tins, one of which has no biscuits (because you have eaten them) and the other is full. How can you tell which is full, without opening the lid?
8 a) What is the acceleration of a mass of 3 kg, which experiences a resultant force of 15 N?
   b) What is the mass of an object that experiences an acceleration of 4 m/s² when a resultant force of 10 N acts on it?

1.7 Applying forces

When you drop something it accelerates downwards, moving faster and faster until it hits the ground. In 1589 Galileo demonstrated to the crowds in Pisa that objects of different masses fall to the ground at the same rate. He dropped a large iron cannon ball and a small one. Both balls hit the ground at the same time. They accelerated at the same rate of about 10 m/s². Aristotle, the Greek philosopher, had previously taught that heavier objects fall more quickly.

Figure 7.1 Galileo demonstrating to the crowds from the Leaning Tower of Pisa.

■ Weight and mass

The size of the Earth's gravitational pull on an object is proportional to its mass. The Earth pulls a 1 kg mass with a force of 10 N and a 2 kg mass with a force of 20 N. We say that the strength of the **Earth's gravitational field**, g, is 10 N/kg.

The **weight**, W, of an object is the force that gravity exerts on it, which is equal to the object's mass × the pull of gravity on each kilogram.

$$W = mg$$

The value of g is roughly the same everywhere on the Earth, but away from the Earth it has different values. The Moon is smaller than the Earth and pulls things towards it less strongly. On the Moon's surface the value of g is 1.6 N/kg. In space, far away from all stars and planets, there are no gravitational pulls, so g is zero, and therefore everything is weightless.

Example. What is the weight of a 70 kg man on the Moon?

$$
\begin{aligned}
W &= mg \\
&= 70 \text{ kg} \times 1.6 \text{ N/kg} \\
&= 112 \text{ N}
\end{aligned}
$$

The size of g also gives us the **gravitational acceleration**, because:

$$\text{acceleration} = \frac{\text{force}}{\text{mass}} \quad or \quad g = \frac{W}{m}$$

EXAM TIP

On the Moon you weigh less than you do on Earth, but your mass stays the same.

■ Falling and parachuting

You have read above that everything accelerates towards the ground at the same rate. But that is only true if the effects of air resistance are small. If you drop a feather you know that it will flutter slowly towards the ground. That is because the size of the air resistance on the feather is only slightly less than the downwards pull of gravity.

The size of the air resistance on an object depends on the area of the object and its speed:

■ The larger the area, the larger the air resistance.
■ The larger the speed, the larger the air resistance.

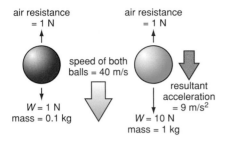

Figure 7.2 At this instant both balls have a speed of 40 m/s. At this speed the weight of the red ball is balanced by air resistance, but the heavier blue ball is still accelerating.

Figure 7.3 The sky diver has reached her terminal velocity. She is in a streamlined position. How could she slow down?

Figure 7.2 shows the effect of air resistance on two balls, which are the same size and shape, but the red ball has a mass of 0.1 kg and the blue ball a mass of 1 kg. The balls are moving at the same speed, so the air resistance is the same, 1 N, on each. The pull of gravity on the red ball is balanced by air resistance, so it now moves at a constant speed. It will not go any faster and we say it has reached **terminal velocity**. For the blue ball, however, the pull of gravity is greater than the air resistance so it continues to accelerate.

Figure 7.4 shows how the speed of a sky diver changes as she falls towards the ground. The graph has five distinct parts:

1   OA. She accelerates at about 10 m/s² just after leaving the aeroplane.
2   AB. The effects of air resistance mean that her acceleration gets less as there is now a force acting in the opposite direction to her weight.
3   BC. The air resistance force is the same as her weight. She now moves at a constant speed because the resultant force acting on her is zero.
4   CD. She opens her parachute at C. There is now a very large air resistance force so she decelerates rapidly.
5   DE. The air resistance force on her parachute is the same size as her weight, so she falls at constant speed until she hits the ground at E.

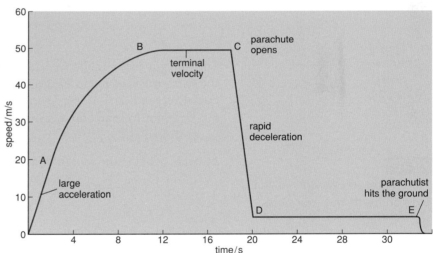

Figure 7.4 Speed–time graph for a parachutist.

■ Driving safely – 1

When you learn to drive, the most important thing you must understand is not how to start, but how to stop. Coming to a halt safely is vital for your own and others' well-being.

Stopping distance

When you are driving you should be aware of your **stopping distance** for a particular speed. The stopping distance is the sum of your **thinking distance** and **braking distance**. The thinking distance is the distance the car travels while you react to a hazard ahead – it takes time for you to take your foot off the accelerator and apply the brake.

thinking distance = speed × reaction time

If you are travelling at 13 m/s, which is just less than 50 km/h (a typical speed in a city) and your reaction time is 0.7 s, your thinking distance will be:

$$\text{thinking distance} = 13 \text{ m/s} \times 0.7 \text{ s}$$
$$= 9.1 \text{ m}$$

You will have travelled about 9 m before you begin to brake.

What affects your reaction time?

You will react more slowly if you are tired, so you should take a break from driving every few hours. Some medicines might make you drowsy, so you should not drive if you are taking these medicines. It is illegal to drive under the influence of alcohol or drugs, both of which slow your reactions and impair your judgement.

Braking distance

Your braking distance depends on your speed. Table 1 shows typical braking distances for a saloon car. There is a gap in the second column, which you will be able to fill in when you answer Study Question 7.

Figure 7.5 Why are variable speed limits imposed on motorways during rush hours?

Table 1

Speed / m/s	Braking distance / m
5	2
10	8
15	17
20	31
25	
30	69
35	94

Certain factors can increase your braking distance:

- Icy or wet roads can reduce the grip on the tyres.
- Gravel, mud or oil on the road can reduce the grip on the tyres.
- Worn tyres can reduce their grip on the road.
- Worn brake pads can reduce the braking force.
- A heavily laden car means there is more mass to slow, so the deceleration is less and the braking distance increased.
- Your stopping distance will be longer if you are going downhill, as gravity is pulling the car forwards.

Visibility

It is dangerous to drive fast when the visibility is restricted by heavy rain, or mist or fog. You need to make sure that you are able to stop within the distance you can see ahead.

STUDY QUESTIONS

1 A student wrote 'my weight is 67 kg'. What is wrong with this statement, and what do you think his weight really is?

2 A hammer has a mass of 1 kg. What is its weight (a) on Earth, (b) on the Moon, (c) in outer space?

3 Explain this observation: 'when a sheet of paper is dropped it flutters down to the ground, but when the same sheet of paper is screwed up into a ball it accelerates rapidly downwards when dropped'.

4 Refer to Figure 7.2 and explain the following.
   a) Why is the red ball falling at a constant speed?
   b) Why does the blue ball fall with an acceleration of 9 m/s²?

5 This question refers to the speed/time graph in Figure 7.4.
   a) What was the speed of the sky diver when she hit the ground?
   b) Why is her acceleration over the part AB less than it was at the beginning of her fall?
   c) Use the graph to estimate roughly how far she fell during her dive. Was it nearer 100 m, 1000 m, or 10 000 m?
   d) Use the information in the graph at point E to make a rough estimate of the acceleration on landing.

6 The graph (right) shows how the force of air resistance on our sky diver's parachute changes with her speed of fall.
   a) How big is the resistive force acting on her if she is travelling at a constant speed of 5 m/s?
   b) Explain why your answer to part (a) must be the same size as her weight.
   c) Use the graph to predict the terminal velocity of the following people using the same parachute:
      i) a boy of weight 400 N
      ii) a man of weight 1000 N.

d) Make a copy of the graph and add to it a sketch to show how you think the air resistance force would vary on a parachute with twice the area of the one used by our sky diver.

e) Why do parachutists bend their legs on landing?

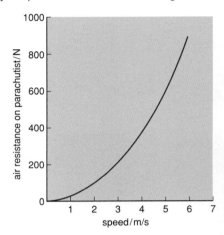

7 Copy Table 1 on page 23 and add to it two further columns headed 'thinking distance' and 'stopping distance'.
   a) Calculate the thinking distances for the speeds listed, assuming your reaction time is 0.7 s.
   b) Now fill in the stopping distances where you can.
   c) Plot a graph to show the stopping distances (y-axis) against the speed (x-axis).
   d) Use your graph to predict the stopping distance for a speed of 25 m/s. Now also fill in the braking distance for a speed of 25 m/s.
   e) What is the maximum safe speed if the visibility is limited to 50 m?
   f) Explain the factors that affect:
      i) the thinking distance for a driver
      ii) the braking distance.

1.8 Collisions and safety

■ Momentum

Momentum is defined as the product of mass and velocity.

$$\text{momentum} = \text{mass} \times \text{velocity}$$

The units of momentum are kilogram metres per second, kg m/s.

Velocity is a vector quantity and therefore momentum is too. You must give a size and a direction when you talk about momentum. Look at Figure 8.2, where you can see two objects moving in opposite directions. One has positive momentum and the other negative momentum.

■ Forces and change of momentum

When a force, F, pushes a mass, m, we can relate it to the mass and acceleration, using the equation:

$$\text{force} = \text{mass} \times \text{acceleration}$$
$$F = ma$$

The acceleration is defined by the equation:

$$\text{acceleration} = \frac{\text{change of velocity}}{\text{time}}$$

These two equations can be combined to give:

$$\text{force} = \frac{\text{mass} \times \text{change of velocity}}{\text{time}}$$

Because (mass × change of velocity) is the change of momentum, the force can be written as:

$$\text{force} = \frac{\text{change of momentum}}{\text{time}}$$

Example

A mass of 7 kg is accelerated from a speed of 2 m/s to 6 m/s in 0.5 s. What force must be applied to do this?

$$
\begin{aligned}
\text{force} &= \frac{\text{change of momentum}}{\text{time}} \\
&= \frac{7\ \text{kg} \times 6\ \text{m/s} - 7\ \text{kg} \times 2\ \text{m/s}}{0.5\ \text{s}} \\
&= 56\ \text{N}
\end{aligned}
$$

Figure 8.1 Why does a shot gun recoil when it is fired?

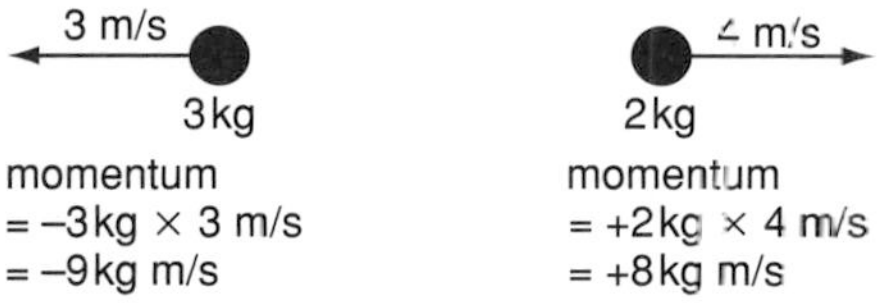

3 m/s
3kg
momentum
= −3kg × 3 m/s
= −9kg m/s

4 m/s
2kg
momentum
= +2kg × 4 m/s
= +8kg m/s

Figure 8.2 In this diagram we have given anything moving to the right positive momentum, and anything moving to the left negative momentum.

■ Momentum and safety

The equation relating force and change of momentum is important when it comes to considering a number of safety features in our lives. If you are moving you have momentum. To stop moving a force must be applied. But the equation shows us that if we stop over a long period of time, the force to slow us is smaller. This way we get hurt less.

Here are some examples of how we protect ourselves by increasing the time we or another object has to stop.

- When we catch a fast ball we move our hands backwards with the ball.
- We wear shin pads in hockey so that the ball has more time to stop when it hits us.
- When we jump off a wall we bend our legs when we land, so that we stop in a longer time.
- Children's playgrounds have soft, rubberised matting under climbing frames, so that a faller takes longer to stop.
- In a bungee jump the elastic rope slows your fall gradually.

> **EXAM TIP**
> Make sure you understand and can explain these examples.

■ Driving safely – 2

Figure 8.3 shows two cars being tested in a trial crash. In the centre of the cars are rigid passenger cells, which are designed not to buckle in a crash. However, the front and back of the cars *are* designed to buckle in a crash – these are the **crumple zones**. These zones absorb energy and also reduce the deceleration by *increasing the time and the distance* to slow the passenger. The force acting on the passenger is less.

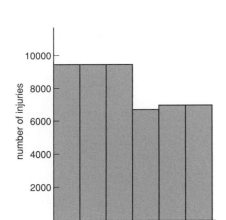

Figure 8.4 The number of serious injuries to front-seat passengers and drivers in cars and light vans in Great Britain. In January 1983 it became compulsory to wear seat belts in the front seats. The number of passengers and drivers wearing seat belts rose from 45% to 95%. The statistics speak for themselves. Will you drive a car without a seat belt?

Figure 8.3 Most of the energy of an impact in a car crash is absorbed by the crumple zones.

Seat belts

Another vital safety feature in a car is a seat belt – you must wear one by law in most countries. Figure 8.4 shows some statistics that illustrate how wearing seat belts has reduced the rate of serious injuries in car crashes.

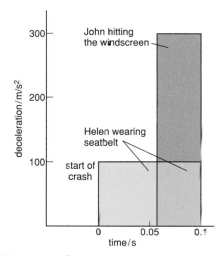

Figure 8.6 Graph to show approximate decelerations in a car crash.

There is some 'give' in a seat belt, which allows the passenger to slow over a longer distance. The seat belt allows you to take advantage of the time it takes the crumple zone to buckle. The graph in Figure 8.6 shows approximate decelerations of two passengers in a car crash. Helen was wearing a seat belt and John was not. Helen decelerated over a period of 0.1 s while the front of the car crumpled. John kept moving forwards until he hit the windscreen. His deceleration was much larger as he stopped in a shorter time. John received very serious injuries.

Figure 8.5 Wearing a seat belt could save your life in an accident. Only dummies forget to put their seat belts on.

STUDY QUESTIONS

1 A car of mass 1200 kg moves at a speed of 30 m/s. What is its momentum?
2 Using your knowledge of momentum, explain:
   a) why you bend your knees when you land after a jump
   b) why cars are designed to have crumple zones.
3 Explain why passengers should wear seat belts in cars and coaches.
4 Explain why it hurts more if you fall over on concrete than it does if you fall over on grass.
5 This question refers to Figure 8.6. John's mass is 80 kg and Helen's mass is 60 kg.
   a) Use the graph to calculate the force that acted on each of them as they decelerated. Explain why John received more serious injuries than Helen.

b) Use the graph (Figure 8.6) and the equation:
$$\text{acceleration} = \frac{\text{change of speed}}{\text{time}}$$
to calculate the speed of the car before the crash.
   c) Helen was driving the car and was responsible for the crash. She was breathalysed by the police and found to be over the drink-drive limit. What measures should governments take to deter drink-drivers?
6 In the UK in 1966, 7985 people were killed in road accidents and 65 000 seriously injured. In 2010, 1857 people were killed in road accidents and 20 800 seriously injured. Give six factors that have improved road safety during this period of time.

1.9 Collisions and explosions

When the firework explodes, chemical energy is transferred to kinetic energy, light energy and sound energy. But the momentum after the explosion is the same as it was before the explosion. Can you explain why?

■ Conservation of momentum

When it comes to calculating what happens in collisions and explosions, momentum is a very useful quantity. Momentum is always conserved.

> When two bodies collide, the total momentum they have is the same after the collision as it was before the collision.

Figure 9.1 Why does this firework explode symmetrically in all directions?

Figure 9.2 shows two ice hockey players colliding on the ice. When they meet they push each other – the blue player's momentum decreases and the red player's momentum increases by the same amount.

Before the collision the total momentum was:

$$\text{momentum of blue player} = 100 \text{ kg} \times 5 \text{ m/s}$$
$$= 500 \text{ kg m/s}$$

$$\text{momentum of red player} = 80 \text{ kg} \times 3 \text{ m/s}$$
$$= 240 \text{ kg m/s}$$

This makes a total of 740 kg m/s.

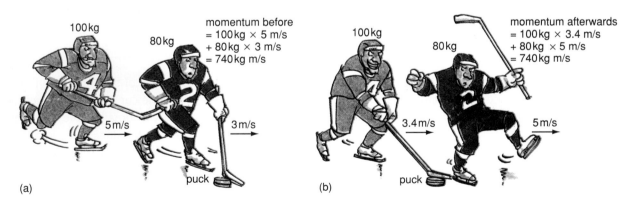

Figure 9.2 The total momentum of the players is the same before and after the collision.

After the collision the total momentum was:

$$\text{momentum of blue player} = 100 \text{ kg} \times 3.4 \text{ m/s}$$
$$= 340 \text{ kg m/s}$$

$$\text{momentum of red player} = 80 \text{ kg} \times 5 \text{ m/s}$$
$$= 400 \text{ kg m/s}$$

This makes a total of 740 kg m/s – the same as before.

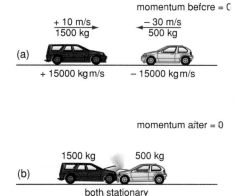

Figure 9.3

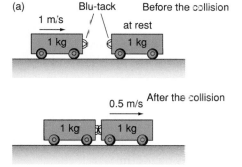

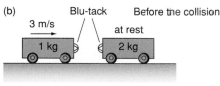

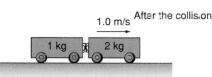

Figure 9.4

EXAM TIP

In a collision between two bodies, where no external force acts on then, momentum is always conserved

Momentum as a vector

Figure 9.3 shows a large estate car colliding head-on with a smaller saloon car. They both come to a halt. How is momentum conserved here?

Momentum is a vector quantity. In Figure 9.3(a) you can see that the red car has a momentum of +15 000 kg m/s and the blue car has momentum of −15 000 kg m/s. So the total momentum is zero before the collision – there is as much positive momentum as negative momentum. After the collision they have both stopped moving and the total momentum remains zero.

Investigating collisions

Figure 9.4 shows how you can investigate conservation of momentum using laboratory trolleys. One trolley is pushed into a second stationary trolley and the speeds measured before and after the collision. These speeds can be measured with light gates and data loggers, or with ticker tape.

In Figure 9.4(a) a trolley of mass 1 kg, travelling at 1 m/s, collides with an identical trolley, which is at rest. They stick together. The momentum before the collision is:

$$1 \text{ kg} \times 1 \text{ m/s} = 1 \text{ kg m/s}$$

The trolleys move off after the collision with the same total momentum of 1 kg m/s, but this is shared by the two trolleys, so they move with a speed of 0.5 m/s.

What happens in Figure 9.4(b)?

The total momentum before the collision is:

$$1 \text{ kg} \times 3 \text{ m/s} = 3 \text{ kg m/s}$$

The momentum after the collision = 3 kg m/s (momentum is conserved). The trolleys stick together to make a new mass of 3 kg, which now carries the momentum. So:

$$3 \text{ kg m/s} = 3 \text{ kg} \times v$$

The unknown speed, v, is therefore 1 m/s.

Newton's third law

Newton's third law of motion states that: to every force there is an equal and opposite force. This law sounds easy to apply, but it requires clear thinking. First, it is important to appreciate that the pair of forces mentioned in the law act on different bodies. Some examples are given in Figure 9.5.

a) If I push you with a force of 100 N, you push me back with a force of 100 N in the opposite direction.

b) When you walk, you push the ground backwards; the ground pushes you forwards.

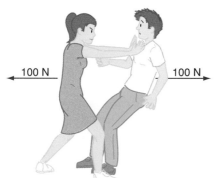

100 N ← → 100 N

(a) Each person experiences the same force when contact is made.

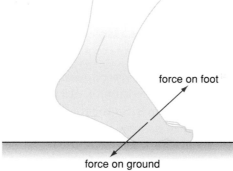

force on foot

force on ground

(b) A foot pushes the ground backwards; the ground pushes the foot forwards.

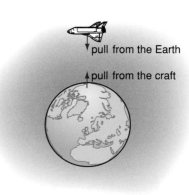

pull from the Earth

pull from the craft

(c) There is an equal and opposite gravitational pull on the craft and on the Earth.

Figure 9.5

c) A spacecraft orbiting the Earth is pulled downwards by Earth's gravity; the spacecraft exerts an equal and opposite gravitational pull on the Earth. This means that as the spacecraft moves, the Earth moves too. But the Earth is so big that it only moves a tiny amount – far too little for us to notice.

■ Taking the plunge

When you go for a swim you need all three of Newton's laws of motion to explain how you get from one end of the pool to the other. Figure 9.7 shows a swimmer at three stages of swimming a length.

a) At the beginning of the length, the swimmer pushes the water; the water pushes her forwards (third law). An unbalanced force acts on the swimmer and she accelerates (second law).

b) In the middle of the length, the forwards push from the water is balanced by resistive forces on the swimmer. She moves at a constant speed (first law).

c) At the end of the length, she stops swimming and drag forces slow her down (second law).

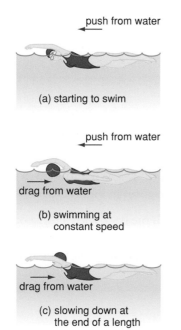

push from water

(a) starting to swim

push from water

drag from water

(b) swimming at constant speed

drag from water

(c) slowing down at the end of a length

Figure 9.7

Figure 9.6 What forces are acting on this swimmer?

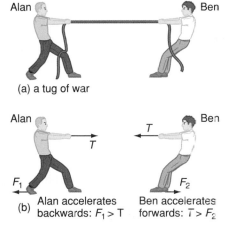

(a) a tug of war

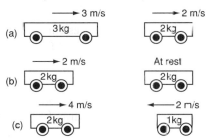

(b) Alan accelerates backwards: $F_1 > T$ Ben accelerates forwards: $T > F_2$

Figure 9.8

■ Tug of war

In Figure 9.8(a) you can see two people engaged in a tug of war. From Newton's third law we know that the force which Alan exerts on Ben must be exactly the same size as, but in the opposite direction to, the force which Ben exerts on Alan

To understand why Alan wins and Ben loses we must draw **free body diagrams** for each person, Figure 9.8(b). Each person pushes on the ground, and the ground pushes him back. Alan is stronger than Ben and pushes the ground harder than Ben. Alan accelerates backwards because $F_1 > T$; Ben accelerates forwards because $T > F_2$. Each has an unbalanced force acting on him. However, they exert the same force on each other.

STUDY QUESTIONS

1 In each of the following experiments shown in the diagrams, the two trolleys collide and stick together. Work out the speeds of the trolleys after their collisions.

(a) → 3 m/s 3kg   → 2 m/s 2kg

(b) → 2 m/s 2kg   At rest 2kg

(c) → 4 m/s 2kg   ← 2 m/s 1kg

2 In Figure 9.3 two cars collided head-on. Each driver had a mass of 70 kg.
   a) Calculate the change of momentum for each driver.
   b) The cars stopped in 0.25 s. Calculate the average force that acted on each driver.
   c) Explain which driver is likely to be more seriously injured.

3 A field gun of mass 1000 kg, which is free to move, fires a shell of mass 10 kg at a speed of 200 m/s.
   a) What is the momentum of the shell after firing?
   b) What is the momentum of the gun just after firing?
   c) Calculate the recoil velocity of the gun.
   d) Why do you think very large guns are mounted on railway trucks?

4 Use the principle of momentum conservation to explain the following:
   a) A gun recoils when fired.
   b) You can swim through water.
   c) Fireworks explode in symmetrical balls.

5 A lorry of mass 18 000 kg collides with a stationary car of mass 2000 kg.

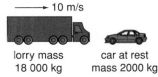

→ 10 m/s

lorry mass 18 000 kg   car at rest mass 2000 kg

   a) Calculate the momentum of the lorry before the collision.
   b) After the collision the lorry and car move off together. What is their combined momentum after the collision?
   c) What is the speed of the lorry and car after the collision?
   d) Each of the drivers of the car and lorry has a mass of 80 kg. Calculate their changes of momentum during the collision.
   e) The collision last for 0.2 s. Calculate the force that acts on each driver during the collision. Explain which driver is more likely to be injured.
   f) Explain why a crumple zone protects the drivers in a collision.

6 Apply Newton's third law of motion to explain the following:
   a) A gun recoils when it is fired.
   b) When you lean against a wall you do not fall over.
   c) You have to push water backwards so that you can swim forwards.

1.10 Rockets and jets

When you go swimming you demonstrate Newton's third law. As you move your arms and legs through the water, you push the water backwards. The water pushes you forwards.

The same idea applies to an aeroplane in flight powered by a propeller (Figure 10.1). The propeller accelerates air backwards, and the air exerts an equal forwards force on the aircraft. As you will see below, rockets and jet engines use the same principle.

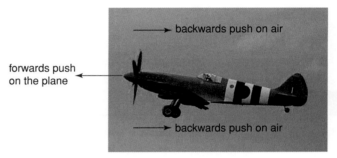

Figure 10.1 The forces acting on an aeroplane powered by a propeller along the flight direction.

■ Rockets

A propeller takes advantage of air resistance. If air did not exert a force on us as we move through it, a propeller would not work. This is why an ordinary aeroplane cannot fly in space, where there is no air for its propellers to push against.

The simplest way to demonstrate the action of a rocket is with an air-filled balloon. If you blow up a balloon and then let it go, it whizzes around the room. It would also whizz around in space where there is no air, because the balloon gets its forwards push from the escaping air. You can explain this by using the principle of conservation of momentum. Before you let go of the balloon, the momentum of the balloon and the air in it is zero. Once the air is allowed to escape from the balloon the *total* momentum is still zero, but the balloon has forwards momentum and the air has backwards momentum (Figure 10.2).

Figure 10.3 shows a simple design for a rocket. The rocket carries with it fuel, such as kerosene, and liquid oxygen (oxygen is needed for the fuel to burn). These are mixed and burnt in the combustion chamber. High pressure gases are then forced out backwards through the nozzle at speeds of about 2000 m/s.

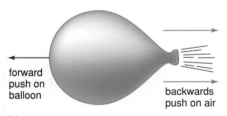

(a) No momentum.

forward push on balloon

backwards push on air

(b) Balloon has momentum to the left. Air has momentum to the right. Total momentum is still zero.

Figure 10.2

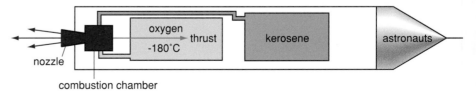

Figure 10.3 A simple rocket.

Figure 10.4 This is a large jet turbine engine. You can clearly see the turbine blades.

■ Jets

Figure 10.5 shows a simplified diagram of the sort of **jet turbine engine** found on an aeroplane. At the front of the engine a rotating compressor sucks in air, acting rather like a propeller, but the air is compressed and as a result it becomes very hot. Some of the heated air then goes through into the combustion chamber and is mixed with the fuel (kerosene). The fuel burns and causes a great increase in the pressure of the gases. The hot gases are then forced out at high speed through the exhaust nozzle. The escaping gases provide a forward thrust on the engine.

The engine is started with an electric motor to rotate the compressor, but once the engine is running some of the energy from the exhaust gases is used to drive a turbine mounted on the same shaft as the compressor.

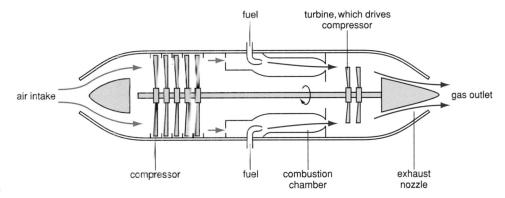

Figure 10.5 The jet turbine engine.

STUDY QUESTIONS

1 a) Explain carefully how a rocket works.
   b) A jet aircraft cannot fly in space. Why?

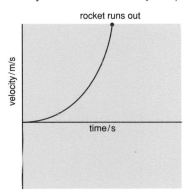

rocket runs out

velocity/m/s

time/s

2 Above you can see a velocity–time graph for a firework rocket. The graph stops at the moment the firework stops burning. A positive velocity on this graph means the rocket is moving upwards.
   a) How can you tell from the graph that the acceleration of the rocket is increasing?
   b) Why does the acceleration rise? (Hint: What happens to the mass as the rocket burns?)
   c) Copy the graph and sketch how the velocity changes until the rocket hits the ground.

3 The diagram shows a homemade water-powered trolley. The idea is that you fill the tank up with water and allow it to flow out of the back.
   a) Explain why the trolley starts to move forwards.
   b) At the start of an experiment the trolley is at rest; its mass is 3 kg, including 2 kg of water. When water is allowed to flow out of the back, it flows at a rate of 0.05 kg/s with a speed of 3.0 m/s. Calculate the backwards momentum of the water that flows out of the trolley in the first 2 seconds.
   c) How much forwards momentum has the trolley gained in this time?
   d) Now calculate the approximate forwards speed of the trolley. (Ignore the mass loss of the water.)
   e) Calculate the trolley's initial acceleration.
   f) Discuss two factors that change the trolley's acceleration as the water level drops.

Summary

 Make sure you can answer all the questions in the *Interactive quiz.*

I am confident that:

✓ **I can recall these facts about forces and motion**
- Average speed = distance/time
- The unit of speed is m/s.
- Acceleration = change of velocity/time
- The unit of acceleration is m/s².
- Average speed = $\frac{u+v}{2}$ where u = starting speed and v = final speed)
- The gradient of a distance-time graph is the speed.
- The area under a velocity-time graph is the distance travelled.
- The gradient of a veolocity-time graph is the acceleration.
- A force is a push or a pull.
- The unit of force is the newton, N.
- Force is a vector quantity.
- Wind resistance increases with speed.
- Newton's first law: if balanced forces act on an object, it remains at rest or moves with constant speed in a straight line.
- Newton's second law: resultant force = mass × acceleration
- Newton's third law: to every force there is an equal and opposite force.

✓ **I can recall these facts about momentum**
- momentum = mass × velocity
- The units of momentum are kg m/s.
- Momentum is a vector quantity.
- force = change of momentum/time
- In collisions, the forces acting are smaller when the time is longer. This is important when designing crumple zones in cars.
- Momentum is conserved in collisions and explosions.

✓ **I can recall these facts about stopping distances**
- Thinking distances are affected by the driver's reaction time.
- The reaction time can be slower if the driver is sleepy or has taken drugs or alcohol.
- Braking distances depend on the speed and mass of the car.
- Braking distances are increased: if the tread on the tyres is worn; if the brakes are worn; if the road is covered with water, ice or mud; if you are going downhill.

Exam-style questions

1 A triathlon race has three parts: swimming, riding a bicycle and running.

a) The diagram shows the force responsible for the forward movement of the athlete in the swimming race.

Copy the diagram and show two other forces acting on the athlete. [2]

b) The table shows the distance of each part of a triathlon race and the time an athlete takes for each part.

Part of race	Distance / m	Time / s
swimming	1500	1200
riding a bicycle	40 000	3600
running	10 000	2000

i) Calculate the athlete's average speed during the swim. [1]

ii) Calculate the athlete's average speed for the whole race. [2]

iii) The graph shows how the distance varied with time for the running part of the race.

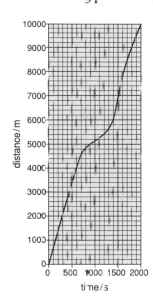

Describe how the athlete's speed changed during this part of the race. [3]

2 The table gives information about a journey made by a cyclist.

Time / hours	Distance / km
0	0
1	15
2	30
3	45
4	60
5	75
6	90

a) Plot a graph using the data in the table. [3]

b) i) Use your graph to find the distance in kilometres that the cyclist travelled in 4.5 hours. [1]

ii) Use the graph to find the time in hours taken by the cyclist to travel 35 kilometres. [1]

c) State the equation that connects average speed, distance moved and time taken. [1]

3 A train travels between two stations. The velocity–time graph shows the train's motion.

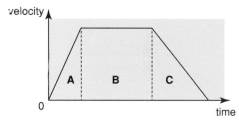

a) How do you know that the train is decelerating in part C? [1]

b) State the features of the graph that represent the distance travelled between the two stations. [1]

c) A second train travels between the two stations at a constant velocity and does not stop. It takes the same time as the first train. Sketch a copy of the graph and then draw a line showing the motion of the second train. [2]

4 a) The diagram shows a lorry. It is travelling in a straight line and it is accelerating. The total forward force on the lorry is F and the total backward force is B.

    i) Which is larger, force F or force B? Explain your answer. [1]

    ii) State an equation that connects acceleration, mass and unbalanced force. [1]

    iii) An unbalanced force of 15 000 N acts on a lorry. The mass of the lorry is 12 500 kg. Calculate the lorry's acceleration and give the unit. [3]

b) The thinking distance is the distance a vehicle travels in the driver's reaction time. The braking distance is the distance a vehicle travels when the brakes are applied.

    i) State one factor that increases the thinking distance. [1]

    ii) State one factor that increases the braking distance. [1]

5 The graph shows the minimum stopping distances, in metres, for a car travelling at different speeds on a dry road.

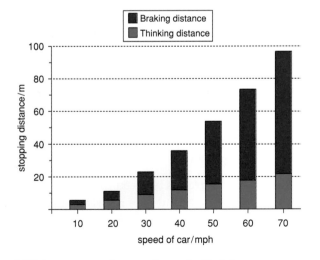

a) Write an equation to show the link between stopping distance, thinking distance and braking distance. [1]

b) Describe the patterns shown in the graph. [2]

c) Use the graph to estimate the stopping distance for a car travelling at 35 miles per hour. [1]

d) To find the minimum stopping distance, several different cars were tested. Suggest how the data from the different cars should be used to give the values in the graph. [1]

e) The tests were carried out on a dry road. If the road is icy, describe and explain what change if any there would be to:

    i) the thinking distance [2]

    ii) the braking distance. [2]

6 The graph shows how the velocity of an aircraft changes as it accelerates along a runway.

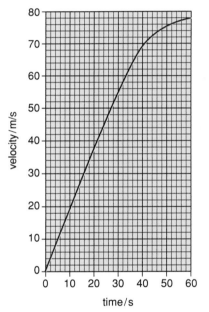

a) Use the graph to find the average acceleration of the aircraft. [3]

b) Explain why the acceleration is not constant, even though the engines produce a constant force. [3]

7 The following graph is a velocity–time graph for the Maglev train, which travels from Longyang Station, on the outskirts of Shanghai, to Pudong International Airport.

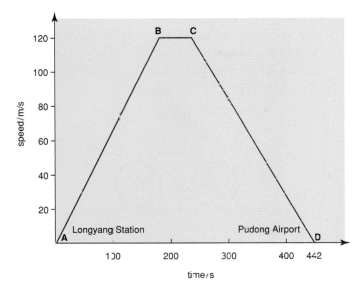

Number of cake cases	Time of fall / s
1	2.7, 2.6, 2.6
1.5	2.2, 2.3, 2.2
2	2.0, 2.0, 1.9
3	1.5, 1.6, 1.7
4	1.4, 1.4, 1.4
6	1.3, 1.3, 1.2
8	1.1, 1.1, 1.2
10	1.1, 1.1, 1.0

a) Use the graph to calculate the train's acceleration over the region AB. Give the unit of acceleration. [4]

b) How far does the train travel at its maximum speed? [3]

c) Use the graph to calculate how far it is from Longyang Station to Pudong Airport. [3]

d) The Trans-Siberian express takes 6 days and 4 hours to travel the 9289 km from Moscow to Vladivostok. Estimate how long it would take to cover the same distance in a Maglev train. [3]

8 Gina plans to investigate drag forces on falling objects. She decides to use a cupcake case as a parachute. The weight of the case can be increased by stacking more cases inside each other. The table shows the times that were recorded for the different numbers of cases stacked together, when they were timed falling a distance of 4 m. Where a number of 1.5 cases is shown, she cut one case in half and put it inside another case.

extra case added to increase the weight

a) Why did Gina record three times for each number of cake cases? [1]

b) Paul said that Gina should have used a more precise stopwatch. Gina replied that her readings were accurate enough, as her reaction time introduced an error anyway. Evaluate this discussion. [2]

c) Copy the table and add two further columns to show:

   i) the average time of fall [2]

   ii) the average speed of fall. [2]

d) Plot a graph of the number of cases on the y-axis against the speed of fall on the x-axis. Draw a smooth line through the points and comment on any anomalous results. [5]

e) Use the graph to predict the speed of fall for a weight of:

   i) 2.5 cases [1]

   ii) 7 cases. [1]

f) Explain what is meant by terminal velocity. [2]

g) Draw a diagram to show the forces that act on a cupcake case, falling at its terminal velocity. [2]

h) Assuming that the cases reach their terminal velocity quickly after release, comment on how the drag force on a falling cupcake case depends on its speed. [2]

i) Paul did an experiment using a cake case with twice the area of Gina's cases. He discovered that one case fell 4 m in a time of 2.63 s. He concluded that 'this means that the area has no effect on the drag force'. Do you agree? Give a reason for your answer. [2]

9 **a)** A car is travelling at 25 m/s. The driver takes his foot off the accelerator and slows down. His deceleration is 2 m/s². How long does it take him to slow down a speed of 15 m/s? [3]

b) The car speeds up from 15 m/s to 30 m/s in 10 s. What was its acceleration? [3]

10 A fly can take off and reach a speed of 3 m/s in a time of 60 milliseconds. What is its acceleration? [3]

11 a) Angela is a skydiver. In part A of the diagram she is falling at a constant speed. How big is the drag force, X, acting on her parachute? [1]

   b) In part B, Angela has just opened her parachute after diving at high speed. Describe how her motion is changing. [2]

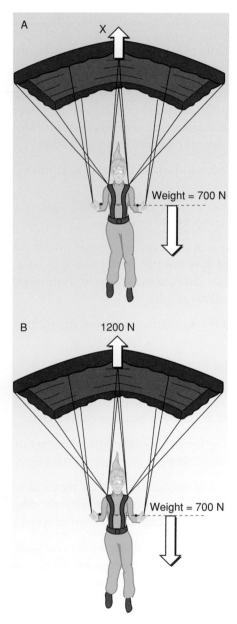

A
X

Weight = 700 N

B   1200 N

Weight = 700 N

12 Andrew is cycling at 5 m/s, and in 5 seconds increases his speed to 7 m/s.

   a) Calculate his acceleration. [3]

   b) The mass of Andrew and his bicycle is 50 kg. The force forwards on the bicycle is 30 N. Calculate the size of wind resistance, R, acting on him. Assume he has the acceleration calculated in part (a). [3]

R

30 N

13 a) There is a parcel on the front seat of a car. The car stops suddenly and the parcels falls off the front of the seat. Use ideas about forces and momentum to explain why this happens. [2]

   b) Explain why you should wear a seat belt when travelling in a car. [2]

14 In some cars air bags are inflated in front of the driver and passenger when there is a crash. Use your knowledge of momentum to explain how these bags can reduce injuries to people in the car. [3]

15 Scientists test the safety features of a car by crashing it into a very large block of concrete. A dummy is placed in the driver's seat and the scientists video the crash.

   a) In one test, the dummy and the car travel at 8 m/s. The mass of the dummy is 72 kg. Calculate the momentum of the dummy. [2]

   b) In another test, the momentum of the dummy changes by 920 kg m/s in a time of 0.17 s. Calculate the average horizontal force acting on the dummy during this time. [2]

   c) These tests help to make our roads safer.

      i) State **two** factors that affect the stopping distance of a car on the road. [2]

      ii) Use ideas about momentum to explain how crumple zones help reduce injuries during a crash. [2]

16 Sketch graphs to show how the *velocity* changes with time for each of the distance–time graphs shown in the diagram. [4]

A

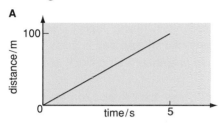

B

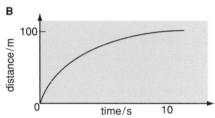

17 A group of students uses a special track. The track is about 2 metres long and is horizontal. Two gliders, P and Q, can move along the track.

The surface of the track and the inside surface of the gliders are almost frictionless. The photograph shows that the gliders can move though two light gates, A and B.

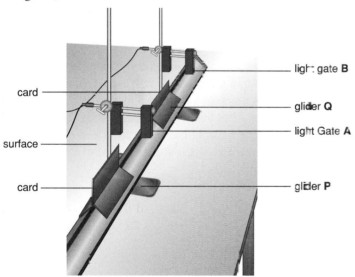

The mass of glider P is 2.4 kg. This glider is moving toward Q at a constant velocity of 0.6 m/s. Glider Q is stationary.

The diagram below shows a side view. Each glider has a card and a magnet attached. Light gate A records the time for which the card is in front of the light gate.

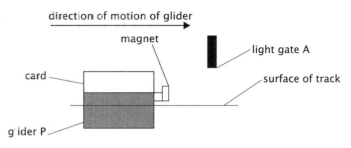

a) i) Apart from the time recorded by the light gate A, state the other measurement that would needed to calculate the velocity of glider P. [1]

ii) Why does the surface of the track need to be frictionless and horizontal? [1]

b) Momentum is a vector quantity.

i) State what is meant by a vector quantity. [1]

ii) Calculate the momentum of glider P. [2]

iii) State the momentum of glider Q. [1]

c) Glider P collides with glider Q and they move off together at a speed of 0.4 m/s.

i) State the combined momentum of P and Q after the collision. [1]

ii) Calculate the mass of glider Q. [2]

iii) Calculate the change in momentum of glider P during the collision. [2]

iv) The time taken for the collision was 0.05 s. Calculate the force that acted on glider P during the collision. [3]

v) State the size of the force acting on glider Q during the collision. [1]

EXTEND AND CHALLENGE

1 a) A rocket has a mass of 3 000 000 kg at take-off. The thrust from the engines is 33 MN. Calculate the initial acceleration.

b) The rocket burns 14 000 kg of fuel per second. What is the mass of the rocket 2 minutes after lift-off?

c) Calculate the acceleration of the rocket 2 minutes after lift-off, assuming that the engines produce the same thrust.

2 This question is about the take-off of a lunar landing craft. Use the data provided: mass of craft 20 000 kg; take-off thrust from engines on craft 52 000 N; Moon's gravitational field strength 1.6 N/kg.

a) What is the craft's weight?

b) At take-off, what is the unbalanced force on the craft?

c) Calculate the acceleration of the craft at take-off.

d) How fast will the craft be travelling after 30 seconds?

e) How far above the Moon's surface will the spacecraft be after 30 seconds?

f) Give two reasons why the craft will actually have travelled slightly further than you estimate.

g) Why could this spacecraft not take off from the surface of the Earth?

3 The graph below shows information about the performance of a high-speed power boat. It has two gears, and you can see how the thrust available from the propellers depends on the speed of the boat. Also shown on the graph is how the drag force depends on the speed. The mass of the power boat with its occupants is 500 kg.

a) What is the boat's top speed in (i) gear 1, (ii) gear 2? Explain how you arrived at your answer.

b) Calculate the boat's acceleration (i) in first gear when the speed is close to zero, (ii) in first gear travelling at 7 m/s.

c) Discuss how a power boat is designed to maximise its speed.

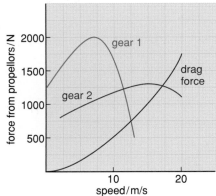

4 You are in outer space, and you are worried that your crew are looking thin. How are you going to work out their mass in a weightless environment? Describe an experiment to calculate an astronaut's mass, using a chair, a large spring balance, a stop clock and a tape measure.

5 Greg test drives his new car. He accelerates rapidly until he reaches a speed of 20 m/s. The mass of the car (with him in it) is 750 kg. The graph shows how the speed changes.

a) Calculate his acceleration over the first 4 seconds.

b) Work out the force acting on the car to accelerate it.

c) Greg invites three friends (total mass 250 kg) into his car to demonstrate its rapid acceleration. Copy the graph, and show how it now accelerates over the first 4 seconds.

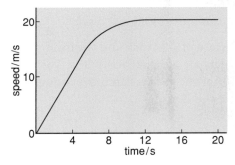

6 The diagram below shows an alpha particle colliding head on with a stationary proton in a cloud chamber. Before the collision the alpha particle has a speed of 10^7 m/s. After the collision its speed is 0.6×10^7 m/s. The mass of the alpha particle is 4 times that of the proton. Calculate the speed of the proton after the collision.

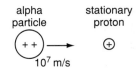

Before the collision

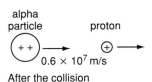

After the collision

Forces and motion 2

The Andromeda Galaxy and its two dwarf companion galaxies. This galaxy is 2.5 million light years away from our galaxy, the Milky Way. The Andromeda Galaxy contains approximately 1 trillion (10^{12}) stars. The Galaxy is bright enough to be seen by the naked eye.

CALCULATE • PRESENT

1 A light year is the distance which light travels in 1 year. Calculate the length of a light year in m. The speed of light is 3×10^8 m/s.
2 Calculate the distance to the Andromeda Galaxy in m.
3 Discuss the feasibility of space travel to another Galaxy or another star in our galaxy.

By the end of this section you should:
* understand what a turning moment is
* be able to recall and use the principle of moments
* understand force–extension graphs for different materials
* know that the Moon orbits the Earth and some planets have Moons
* understand gravitational field strength, g
* know and be able to explain that the gravitational force keeps moons and planets in orbit
* be able to use the relationship between orbital speed, orbital radius and time period
* know the nature of a comet's orbit
* understand the nature of galaxies.

1.11 Turning moments

Figure 11.1

If you have ever tried changing the wheel of a car, you will know that you are not strong enough to undo the nuts with your fingers. You need a spanner to get a large turning effect. You need a long spanner and a large force.

The size of the turning effect a force exerts about a point is called a **turning moment**. The turning moment is increased by applying a large force and by using a long lever.

> turning moment = force applied × perpendicular distance of force from pivot

Perpendicular means 'at right angles'. Figure 11.2 shows you why this distance is important. In Figure 11.2(a) you get no turning effect at all as the force acts straight through the pivot, P. In Figure 11.2(b) you can calculate the turning moment.

$$\text{turning moment} = 100\,\text{N} \times 0.3\,\text{m}$$
$$= 30\,\text{Nm}$$

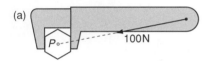

(a)

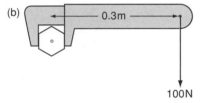

(b)

Figure 11.2

■ Turning forces in action

Figures 11.3 to 11.6 show four examples of how tools can be used to give us large turning moments.

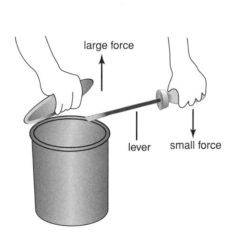

Figure 11.3 A screwdriver can be used to lever off the lid of a paint tin.

Figure 11.4 A screwdriver is used to insert a screw – a broad handle allows us a good grip and leverage.

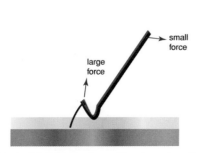

Figure 11.5 A crowbar with a long handle can be used to pull out old nails.

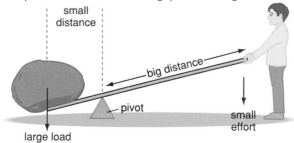

Figure 11.6 A simple lever. The rock can be lifted when its turning effect is balanced by the turning effect of the man's push. With a long lever a small effort can lift a large load.

■ Lifting loads

Turning moments need to be considered when lifting heavy loads with a mobile crane (Figure 11.7). If the turning effect of the load is too large the crane will tip over. So, inside his cab, the crane operator has a table to tell him the greatest load that the crane can lift for a particular **working radius**.

EXAM TIP

The unit of a turning moment is N m or N cm.

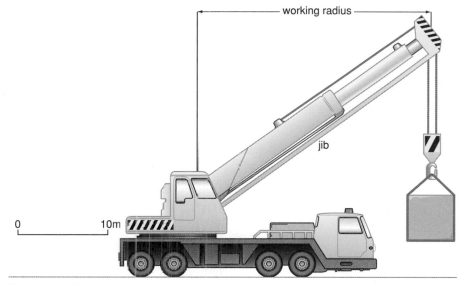

Figure 11.7 A mobile crane.

Table 1 shows you how this works. For example, the crane can lift a load of 60 tonnes safely with a working radius of 16 m. If the crane is working at a radius of 32 m, it can only lift 30 tonnes. You get the same turning effect by doubling the working radius and lifting half the load.

Table 1 A load table for a crane operator

Working radius / m	Maximum safe load / tonnes	load × radius / tonne × m
12	80	960
16	60	960
20	48	960
24	40	960
28	34	952
32	30	960
36	27	972

■ Centre of gravity

Figure 11.8(a) on the next page shows a see-saw that is balanced about its midpoint. Gravity has the same turning effect on the right-hand side of the see-saw, as it has on the left-hand side. The resultant turning effect is zero.

The action of the weight of the see-saw is the same as a single force, W, which acts downwards through the pivot (Figure 11.8(b)). This force has no turning moment about the pivot. As the see-saw is stationary, the pivot must exert an upwards force R on it, which is equal to W.

When the see-saw is not pivoted about its midpoint, the weight will act to turn it (Figure 11.8(c)).

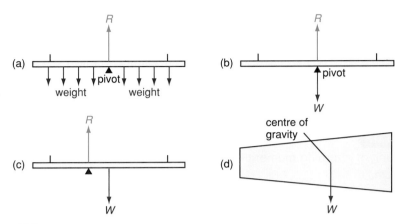

Figure 11.8

Figure 11.9 This rocking toy is stable because its centre of gravity is below the pivot.

The point that the weight acts through is called the **centre of gravity**. The centre of gravity of the see-saw lies at its midpoint because it has a regular shape. In Figure 11.8(d) the centre of gravity lies nearer the thick end of the shape.

Jumping higher

When you stand up straight your centre of gravity lies inside your body. But in some positions you can get your centre of gravity outside your body.

This idea is most important for pole vaulters and high jumpers (Figure 11.10). Suppose a high jumper's legs can provide enough energy to lift her centre of gravity to a height 2 m above the ground. If she can make her centre of gravity pass under the bar, she can clear a bar higher than 2 m (Figure 11.10(b)).

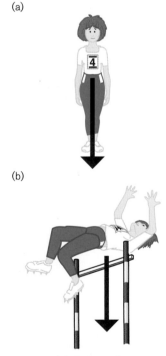

Figure 11.10 (a) Centre of gravity inside the body. **(b)** Centre of gravity outside the body.

Figure 11.11 Why do 'Fosbury-floppers' usually win?

■ Equilibrium, stability and toppling

Something is in equilibrium when both the resultant force and the resultant turning moment on it are zero.

We talk about three different kinds of equilibrium, depending on what happens to the object when it is given a small push.

■ A football on a flat piece of ground is in **neutral equilibrium**. When given a gentle kick, the ball rolls, keeping its centre of gravity at the same height.

- A tall thin radio mast is in **unstable equilibrium**. It is balanced with its centre of gravity above its base. However, a small push (from the wind) will move its centre of gravity downwards. To prevent toppling the mast is stabilised with support wires.
- A car is in **stable equilibrium** (Figure 11.12(a)). When the car is tilted the centre of gravity is lifted, (b). In this position the action of the weight keeps the car on the road. In (c) the centre of gravity lies above the wheels; the car is in a position of unstable equilibrium. If the car tips further, (d), the weight now provides a turning moment to topple the car. Cars are more stable if they have a low centre of gravity and a wide wheel base.

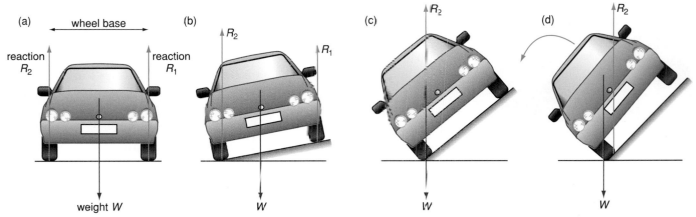

Figure 11.12 R_1 and R_2 are the reaction from the road, which support the car's weight. How does reaction force R_1 change as the car changes its position from (a) to (b) to (c) and to (d)?

 Now watch the animation *Moments*.

STUDY QUESTIONS

1 a) When you cannot undo a tight screw, you use a screwdriver with a large handle. Explain why.
   b) Explain why door handles are not put near hinges.
2 Look at the crane in Figure 11.7.
   a) What is meant by working radius?
   b) Use the scale in Figure 11.7 to calculate the working radius of the crane.
   c) Use the data in Table 1 to calculate the greatest load that the crane can lift safely in this position.
   d) Laura, a student engineer, makes this comment: 'You can see from the driver's table that the crane can lift 960 tonnes, when the working radius is 1 m.' Do you agree with her?
3 a) A crowbar is used to lever a nail out of a block of wood. Use the information in the diagram to calculate the size of the turning moment exerted.

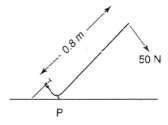

b) A student finds that the minimum force required to lift up the lid of a computer is 6.4 N.

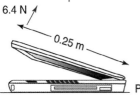

i) Calculate the moment of the force that opens the computer.
ii) Explain why the minimum force required to close the computer lid is likely to be less than 6.4 N.
4 List the glasses shown below in order of stability, starting with the most stable. Explain your answer.

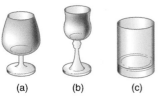

5 a) Explain why people are allowed to stand on the lower deck of a double-decker bus, but not on the higher one.
   b) Explain three features which give Formula 1 cars great stability.

1.12 Balancing forces

Figure 12.1

This tighterope walker is helped if he has a head for heights and an understanding of physics. What conditions must exist for him to remain balanced? How does the pole help him?

■ Balancing

In Figure 12.2 you can see Jaipal and Mandy sitting on a see-saw, which is balanced. It balances because the turning moment produced by Jaipal's weight exactly balances the turning moment produced by Mandy's weight in the opposite direction.

$$\text{Jaipal's anti-clockwise turning moment} = 450\,\text{N} \times 1\,\text{m}$$
$$= 450\,\text{Nm}$$
$$\text{Mandy's clockwise turning moment} = 300\,\text{N} \times 1.5\,\text{m}$$
$$= 450\,\text{Nm}$$

The turning moments balance. The seesaw is in equilibrium.

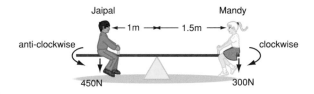

Figure 12.2

In equilibrium:

■ the sum of the anti-clockwise moments = the sum of the clockwise moments
■ the sum of the forces balance.

■ Moments in action

In Figure 12.3 a small crane is being used to load a boat. A counterbalance load on the left-hand side is used to stabilise the crane and to stop it from toppling over.

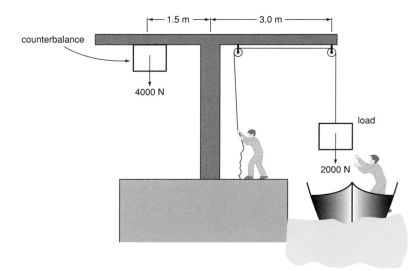

Figure 12.3 Forces acting on a small crane.

The clockwise turning moment from the load being lifted = 2000 N × 3 m
= 6000 Nm

The anti-clockwise turning moment from the counterbalance = 4000 N × 1.5 m
= 6000 Nm

These turning moments keep the beam in equilibrium.

A window cleaner is carrying his ladder (Figure 12.4). The weight of the ladder and the bucket exert a downwards turning moment behind him. He must balance this by pulling down on the ladder in front of him.

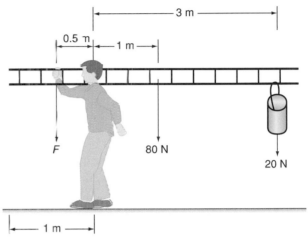

Figure 12.4 Forces on a window cleaner's ladder which is balanced on his shoulder.

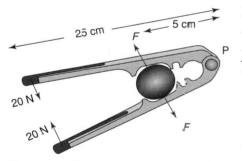

Figure 12.5 Forces acting on a nutcracker.

In Figure 12.5 a nut is being cracked by a nutcracker. How big are the forces F, acting on the nut?

Just before the nut cracks, the turning moments of the forces, F, balance the turning moments of the 20 N forces.

$$F \times 5 \text{ cm} = 20 \text{ N} \times 25 \text{ cm}$$

$$F = 100 \text{ N}$$

This is the force which the nut exerts on the nutcracker. Newton's 3rd law tells us that the nutcracker exerts the same force on the nut, in the opposite direction.

■ Forces on beams

In Figure 12.6 a man is running across a light bridge (which has a negligible weight). How do the forces at A and at B change as he crosses?

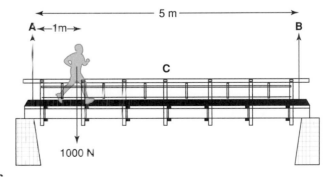

Figure 12.6

There are three easy places where you can use common sense to calculate the forces:

- When he is at A, the upward force at A is 1000 N and the upward force at B is zero.
- When he is at B, the upward force at B is 1000 N and the upward force at A is zero.
- When he is at C, the centre of the bridge, the upward force at each of A and B is 500 N.

When the man is 1 m from A you can use your knowledge of moments to see that A will support more of his weight than B. The exact force can be calculated using the principle of moments.

The turning moment of the man's weight about A is balanced by the turning moment of the upward force at B.

$$1000 \text{ N} \times 1 \text{ m} = (\text{force at B}) \times 5 \text{ m}$$
$$\text{force at B} = 200 \text{ N}$$

The upward force at A is 800 N, as together the two forces A and B must add up to 1000 N.

STUDY QUESTIONS

1 a) Explain why cranes use counterbalances.
  b) In Figure 12.3 the dock workers want to load a heavier weight into the boat. Which way should they move the counterbalance to balance the crane? Explain your answer by referring to turning moments.
  c) A load of 1200 N is now lifted into the boat. Calculate where the counterbalance should be placed now.

2 This question refers to the window cleaner in Figure 12.4.
  a) Calculate the turning moment due to the weight of the bucket about the window cleaner's shoulder.
  b) Calculate the turning moment due to the weight of the ladder about his shoulder.
  c) State the size of the turning moment his arm must produce to balance these turning moments.
  d) Calculate the size of the force, F, which the window cleaner must exert.
  e) A friend suggests that his ladder would be easier to carry if he put the bucket at the other end. Use your knowledge of moments to discuss why this is a good idea.
  f) Can you make a further suggestion, which would make the ladder easier for the man to carry?

3 The diagram shows a pair of cutters.

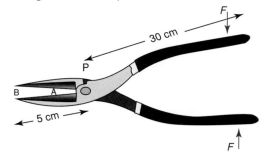

  a) Explain why they have long handles.
  b) You want to cut some thick wire. Use your knowledge of moments to explain whether it is better to put the wire at A or B.
  c) Wire that needs a force of 210 N to cut it is placed at B, 5 cm from the pivot. How big a force will you need to exert at the ends of the handle to cut the wire?

4 This question refers to the man running across the bridge in Figure 12.6.
  a) Calculate the size of the upward forces at A and B when he is 1 m away from B.
  b) Using the information in the text and your answer to part (a), sketch a graph of the way the upward force at A changes as the man runs from A to B.
  c) Calculate the sizes of the forces at A and B when he is 3 m away from A and 2 m away from B.

1.13 Stretching

Our muscles exert forces when they are stretched. An exercise rope helps this woman stretch and tone up her muscles. On most occasions our muscles behave elastically. What does this mean? Describe what happens to a muscle when too much force is applied to it.

Figure 13.1

■ Measuring extension

Figure 13.2 shows a simple experiment to investigate the behaviour of a spring. The spring stretches when a load is hung on it. The increase in length is called the **extension**. This sounds an easy experiment to do, but care must be taken to measure the extension accurately.

Figure 13.3 shows a graph plotted for the force applied to extend a steel spring. The region *AB* of the graph is a straight line passing through the origin up to point B. This shows that the extension is proportional to the load, over the region *AB*. A material that behaves in this way obeys **Hooke's law**.

EXAM TIP

For a material that obeys Hooke's law, the extension is proportional to the load. If the load doubles so does the extension.

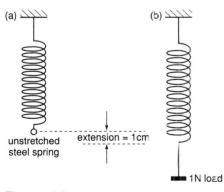

Figure 13.2

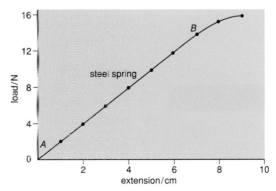

Figure 13.3 Force–extension graph for a steel spring.

■ Elastic limit

Over the region *AB* of the graph (Figure 13.3) the spring shows **elastic** behaviour. This means that when the load is removed from the spring, it returns to its original length and shape. At point *B* the spring has reached its elastic limit. If you increase the load beyond this amount, the spring no longer obeys Hooke's law. If a load of more than 14 N (beyond point *B*) is applied to this spring, it changes its shape permanently. When the load is removed it does not return to its original shape. This is called **plastic deformation**.

When you bounce a hard rubber ball it deforms elastically. How do you think Plasticine deforms?

■ Rubber band

Only some materials obey Hooke's law. You can see from Figure 13.4 that a rubber band certainly does not.

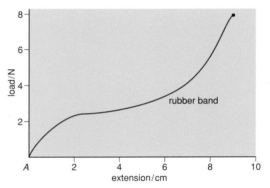

Figure 13.4 Force–extension graph for a rubber band.

■ Springs in series and parallel

Figure 13.5 shows what happens when a load is put on to two springs. When you put two springs in series (Figure 13.5(a)) each one is pulled by the force of 2 N. Each spring is extended by 1 cm, and the total extension is now 2 cm. When springs are put in parallel (side by side) each one supports half of the load. Each spring only extends by 0.5 cm (Figure 13.5(b)).

■ Building materials

Any engineer needs to understand the properties of the materials that are used to build a house or a bridge. Figure 13.6(a) shows a laboratory sample of steel wire with a load applied, and Figure 13.6(b) (red curve) shows how it deformed under tension. When the tensile force reached 1800 N, the sample deformed plastically – it changed shape irreversibly.

On the same graph (Figure 13.6(b)), you can see how an identically shaped sample of cast iron behaved. The iron broke suddenly when the stretching force reached 1100 N. Cast iron is a **brittle** material; this means that it breaks without first bending or stretching out of shape.

In some ways iron and steel are quite similar. They are both **strong** materials, needing a large force to break them; they are also both **stiff** materials because a large force only causes a small change in shape. However, because iron is brittle it is not safe for building large structures. At the end of the nineteenth

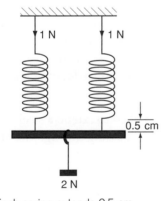

(a) The total extension is 2 cm

(b) Each spring extends 0.5 cm

Figure 13.5

PRACTICAL

Make sure you can describe an experiment to measure the extension of a steel spring as the load varies.

century, the Tay Bridge in Scotland (built of iron) collapsed, plunging a train with its passengers into the river below. Had the bridge been made of steel, it might have buckled, but a brittle fracture would not have occurred with such a catastrophic effect.

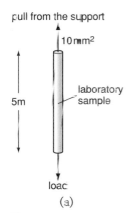

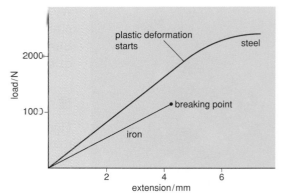

(a)

(b) The load–extension graph for steel and iron samples

Figure 13.6

STUDY QUESTIONS

1 In diagram A, a 2 N weight extends the spring by 4 cm. In each case, B, C and D, calculate the weight hanging on the springs; all the springs are identical.

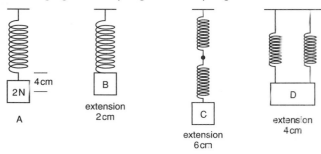

2 Use the information in Figure 13.6(a) and (b) to help you work out the size of the force that this steel girder can support, before it deforms plastically.

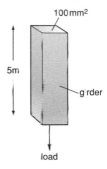

3 Explain in detail how you would carry out an experiment to verify Hooke's law for a steel spring. You should include details of the measurements you would take, how you would tabulate them and how you would plot a graph to show the results.

4 Explain what is meant by the terms:
  a) elastic deformation
  b) plastic deformation.

5 The table below shows how a spring extends when increasing loads are hung on it.
  a) Plot a graph of load (*y*-axis) against extension (*x*-axis).
  b) Up to what load does this spring obey Hooke's law?
  c) What has happened to the spring after a load of 5.0 N has been put on it?

Load / N	Extension / cm
0	0
1.0	2.0
2.0	4.0
3.0	6.0
4.0	8.0
5.0	11.0
6.0	15.0

6 Figures 13.3 and 13.4 in the text show the force–extension graphs for a spring and a rubber band. Use these graphs to work out:
  a) the extension caused by a force of 3 N when the band and spring are in series
  b) the force needed to produce a 4 cm extension when they are in parallel.

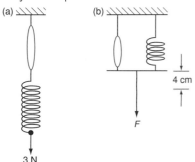

1.14 The Earth in space

Figure 14.1 How many stars can you count here?

We live in an enormous Universe that contains billions and billions of stars, planets and moons. In the daytime the sky is dominated by the Sun, the star that the Earth orbits. At night time you can easily see lots of stars and the Moon; with more skill you can also see some planets.

◼ The sky at night

Figure 14.2 shows the position of the Earth in space; the North Pole tilts towards the Sun in the northern summer and away from the Sun in the northern winter. The Earth rotates every 24 hours around an axis that points towards the Pole Star (or Polaris). Because of this daily rotation of the Earth, the stars appear to rotate each night. For example, Figure 14.3 shows the position of the Plough at 5pm in January; six hours later (11pm) the Earth has completed a quarter of a rotation, so the Plough has rotated through an angle of 90°. If you want to find the Pole Star, you can follow the line of the 'pointers' to help you locate it.

The Plough is a group of stars (constellation) which is 'circumpolar'; this means it appears close to the Pole Star. These stars are visible in the northern hemisphere every night of the year. Stars that are close to the Celestial Equator (Figure 14.2) are not visible all year round.

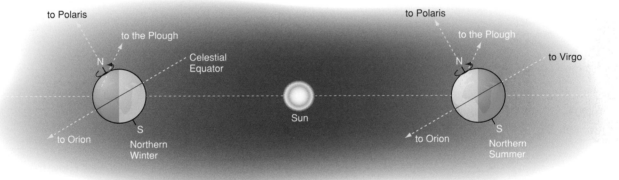

Figure 14.2 The Earth's positions, relative to the Sun, 6 months apart.

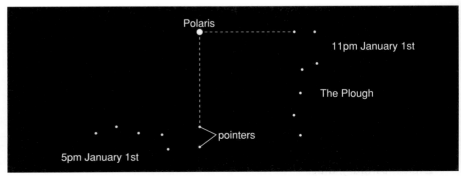

Figure 14.3 The movement of the stars in six hours.

■ The changing Moon

Our nearest neighbour in space is the Moon. The shape of the Moon always seems to be changing. The position of the Moon in the sky also changes from day to day.

The Moon moves around the Earth once a month. This is shown in Figure 14.4. The diagram shows the Moon in eight different places or **phases**. It takes the Moon about 3½ days to move from one position to the next. The Sun shines on the Moon and lights up half of it. In position 1, we cannot see the bright side of the Moon. This is a **new moon**, which is very difficult to see. In position 3, we see a **half moon**, since we can see equal amounts of the dark and bright sides of the Moon. When the Moon is in position 5, we see all of the bright side of it. This is a **full moon**.

Figure 14.5 A waxing gibbous Moon.

Figure 14.6 Looking south on 5 December at 11 pm.

Figure 14.7 Looking south on 6 December at 11 pm.

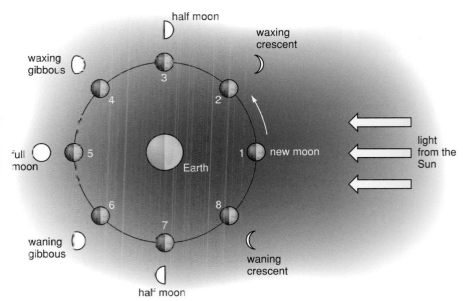

Figure 14.4 Phases of the Moon.

During the first half of the month, the Moon grows from a crescent to a half, to a 'gibbous' and, finally, to a full moon. While the Moon is growing, we say it is **waxing**. In the second half of the month, it is **waning**. During this time it shrinks back to a new moon.

As the Moon moves round us, we see it close to different stars each night. Figure 14.6 shows the view south one night in December in the northern hemisphere. The Moon is near the bright group of stars, the Pleiades. The next night (Figure 14.7) the Moon has moved towards the constellation of Gemini.

STUDY QUESTIONS

1 Draw a diagram to help explain why the Moon appears in different parts of the sky each night.

2 What is meant by a circumpolar star?

3 Figure 14.7 shows the Moon near to the Pleiades on 5 December, viewed from the northern hemisphere. Draw diagrams to show how the Moon and its neighbouring stars looked on the same day when viewed from (a) the Equator and (b) Australia.

4 Explain carefully, with the aid of appropriate diagrams, why we see different stars during different seasons. Look at Figure 14.2 to help you.

5 Copy Figure 14.3 and draw the position of the Plough at (i) 7pm on 1 January, (ii) 2am on 2 January.

6 Look at Figure 14.4 and use it to explain:
   a) why a full moon rises at sunset
   b) why a half moon reaches its highest point in the sky at dawn or sunset.

1.15 The Solar System

Figure 15.1 Four planets in our Solar System.

Identify each of the planets in Figure 15.1.

Why have two planets got cratered surfaces? How were the craters made? How old are the craters?

Which of these planets have moons?

Some planets do not have an atmosphere. Why not?

Where did the Solar System come from? How was it formed?

■ The Sun and planets

The brightest thing you can see in the sky is our **Sun**. The Sun is a star that provides all the heat and light we need to live. The Earth is a **planet** that moves around the Sun in an elliptical path called an **orbit**. In total there are eight planets and many minor planets, comets and meteors, which are kept moving in their orbits by the pull of the Sun's gravitational force.

Planets do not produce their own light like the Sun. We see planets because they reflect the Sun's light. The Sun, planets and moons are known as the **Solar System**. The word 'solar' means belonging to the Sun.

■ The inner planets

The four planets nearest to the Sun, including the third planet – the Earth, have hard, solid and rocky surfaces.

- Mercury is the planet closest to the Sun. It has a cratered surface that looks like the Moon's. During its day the surface is baking hot. Even lead would melt on its surface.
- Venus lies between Mercury and the Earth. It has a thick atmosphere; its clouds are made from burning hot sulphuric acid. Nothing can survive its hot, poisonous surface.
- Mars is the last of the rocky planets. It is colder than the Earth as it is further away from the Sun. Like the Earth, Mars has polar ice caps. Mars once had active volcanoes. The largest mountain is Olympus Mons, which towers 25 km above the surrounding plains.

■ The outer planets

Beyond the orbit of Mars are four giant planets: **Jupiter**, **Saturn**, **Uranus** and **Neptune**. Each of these is much larger than the inner planets – Figure 15.3 shows the relative sizes of the planets. Each of the outer planets has a solid core but the outer surface is made of gas. If you tried to land on one of these planets you would sink into it.

Jupiter is the largest planet in our Solar System. It has a diameter 11 times that of the Earth. The swirling clouds in Jupiter's atmosphere blow around at hurricane wind speeds of more than 300 km/h. Jupiter has at least 66 moons; many of these are very small and have only been discovered recently. Its four largest moons, as large as our Moon, were discovered by

Figure 15.2 Jupiter with its four largest moons – Io, Europa, Ganymede and Callisto. These can be seen with a small telescope.

Figure 15.3 The relative sizes of the Sun and its planets. (Figure 15.5 shows the positions of the planets relative to one another)

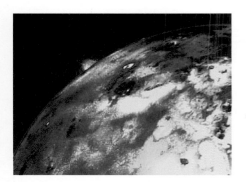

Figure 15.4 This photograph shows the pitted surface of Io. At the top of the photograph you can see a volcano erupting.

Galileo in 1510. These can be seen through a small telescope. One of the large moons, Io, is squeezed by the planet's gravitational field. This causes it to be volcanically active. Figure 15.4 shows a volcano erupting on its surface.

The other giant planets also have large numbers of moons. It seems likely that their strong gravitational pull attracted a lot of rocky material billions of years ago, as the Solar System formed. The table on page 56 gives information about the planets in our Solar System.

■ Gravitational field strength

Every planet, moon or star has a gravitational field at its surface. On the surface of the Earth the **gravitational field strength**, g, is about 10 N/kg. This means that a mass of 1 kg is pulled downwards with a force of 10 N. This force is the object's weight.

The strength of the gravitational field for a planet depends on its radius and density. A larger field is produced by a planet with a larger density and larger radius.

Table 1 shows some examples of gravitational field strengths for various objects in our Solar System. The gravitational field strength is different for each planet and moon.

Table 1

Object	Gravitational field strength / N/kg
Earth	10
Mars	3.7
Jupiter	24.8
Sun	270
The Moon	1.6
Phobos (a moon of Mars)	0.001

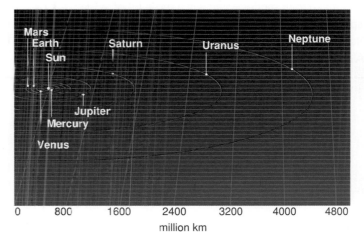

Figure 15.5 The orbits of the planets around the Sun. The four inner planets are very close to the Sun; the gaps between the outer planets are very large.

Table 2 Facts about the planets

Planet	Diameter of planet	Average distance of planet from the Sun	Time taken to go round the Sun	Number of moons	Average temperature on sunny side
Mercury	4900 km	58 million km	88 days	0	350 °C
Venus	12 000 km	108 million km	225 days	0	480 °C
Earth	12 800 km	150 million km	$365\frac{1}{4}$ days	1	20 °C
Mars	6800 km	228 million km	687 days	2	0 °C
Jupiter	143 000 km	780 million km	12 years	66	−150 °C
Saturn	120 000 km	1430 million km	29 years	62	−190 °C
Uranus	52 000 km	2880 million km	84 years	27	−220 °C
Neptune	49 000 km	4500 million km	165 years	13	−240 °C

STUDY QUESTIONS

1 Using Table 2:
  a) Which is the largest planet?
  b) Which planet has a temperature closest to that of our Earth?
  c) Which planet takes just under 2 Earth years to go round the Sun?
  d) Are the temperatures of the planets related to their distance from the Sun? Why do you think Venus is hotter than Mercury?
  e) Is there any pattern in the number of moons that planets have? Try and explain any pattern that you find.
  f) Which planets will go round the Sun more than once in your lifetime?

2 a) Here is something active to do. You can make a model of the Solar System. The scale of your model should be 1 m for 20 million kilometres. Use Table 2 to calculate how far each planet needs to be placed from the Sun. Now go outside and make your model – you will need a lot of space!
  b) Now work out where the nearest star system, Alpha Centauri, should be placed on your model.

Should it be in the next street, the next town or where?
(Alpha Centauri is 9000 times further away from the Sun than Neptune is.)

3 Try and answer these questions about the Solar System. You may need to go to a library or use the Internet to find the answers.
  a) Where is the Sea of Tranquillity?
  b) Which planet has a red spot?
  c) What are Oberon and Titania?
  d) What are 'asteroids'?
  e) Which planet has the shortest day?
  f) How many planets have rings around them?

4 An astronaut has a mass of 110 kg.
  a) Using Table 1, calculate his weight on:
    i) Mars
    ii) Phobos.
  b) The astronaut can jump to a height of 0.3 m Earth in his space suit.
    i) Explain why he can jump to a height of nearly 2 m on the moon.
    ii) What might happen if the astronaut tries to jump on Phobos?

1.16 Orbits

How is it possible for something to travel at a constant speed and to be accelerating all the time? This happens when it follows a circular path. Although the speed is constant, there is a change of direction. So the velocity changes and therefore there is an acceleration.

Figure 16.1 What force keeps these people in their circular path at the funfair?

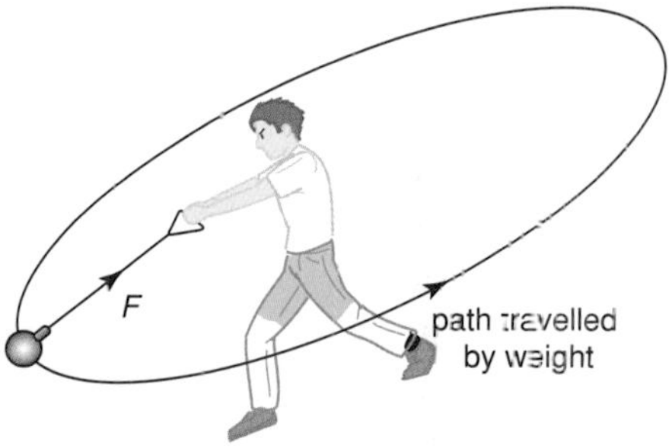

Figure 16.2 A hammer thrower spins the weight around in a circle before releasing it. To keep the weight in its circular path he must exert a force, *F*, towards the centre of the circle.

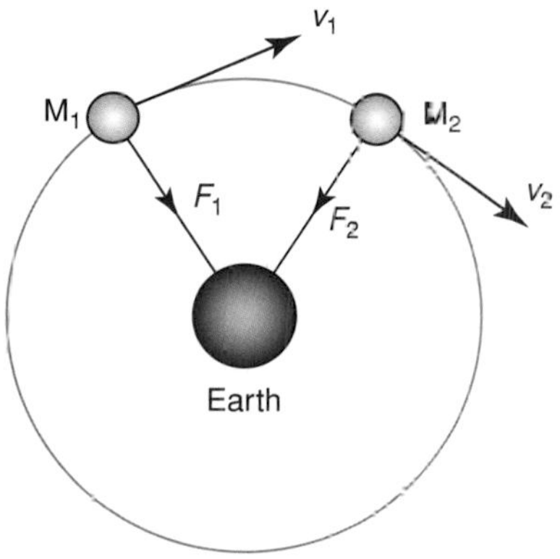

Figure 16.3 The force of gravity directed towards the Earth keeps the Moon in orbit.

■ Throwing the hammer

Figure 16.2 shows an athlete preparing to throw a weight – this event is called throwing the hammer. He spins the weight up to a large speed before releasing it. While the weight is moving in its circular path, the athlete exerts a force, *F*, towards the centre of the circle. When he lets go of the weight it flies off, landing a large distance away.

■ The pull of gravity and orbits

You understand that gravity acts close to the Earth to pull things to the ground. However, gravity is also a force that stretches an enormous distance out into space. Gravity acts on all stars, planets and moons.

- Gravity causes planets and comets to orbit the Sun.
- Gravity causes the Moon and artificial satellites to orbit the Earth.
- Gravity causes stars to orbit around the centre of their galaxies.

Figure 16.3 shows the pull of gravity from the Earth, which keeps the Moon in orbit. In position M_1 the Moon has a velocity v_1. The pull of gravity deflects its motion. Later it has moved to its new position M_2, with a velocity v_2. The force of gravity does not make the Moon travel any faster, but the force changes the direction of motion. The Moon will stay in its orbit for billions of years.

57

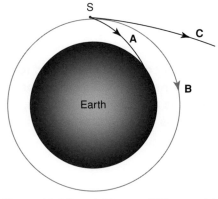

Figure 16.4 Speed C > speed B > speed A.

■ Speed of orbit

Figure 16.4 shows the importance of the speed of orbit. S is a satellite travelling around the Earth.

- If its speed is too great it follows path C and disappears into outer space.
- If its speed is too slow it follows path A and falls to Earth.
- When the satellite moves at the right speed it follows path B and stays in a steady circular orbit.

Planets and moons move in elliptical orbits (see page 60). However, many of the orbits for planets and moons in our Solar System are nearly circular.

The speed of orbit of a moon, planet or satellite can then be related to the radius and time of orbit using the following equation.

$$\text{orbital speed} = \frac{2 \times \pi \times \text{orbital radius}}{\text{time period}}$$

$$v = \frac{2 \times \pi \times r}{T}$$

The equation is a special example of the more familiar equation:

$$\text{average speed} = \frac{\text{distance}}{\text{time}}$$

The distance travelled in one orbit is the circumference of a circle, which is $2 \times \pi \times r$.

■ Orbits near and far

If a planet is close to the Sun the pull of gravity from the Sun is strong. This causes the speed of the orbit to be high. For a planet further away, the Sun's gravity pulls less strongly and the planet moves more slowly.

We can use the data from the last chapter to calculate the orbital speeds for Earth and Mercury.

$$\text{orbital speed of Mercury} = \frac{2 \times \pi \times r}{T}$$

$$= \frac{2 \times \pi \times 58 \text{ million km}}{88 \text{ days}}$$

$$= 4.1 \text{ million km/day}$$

$$\text{orbital speed of Earth} = \frac{2 \times \pi \times r}{T}$$

$$= \frac{2 \times \pi \times 150 \text{ million km}}{365 \text{ days}}$$

$$= 2.6 \text{ million km/day}$$

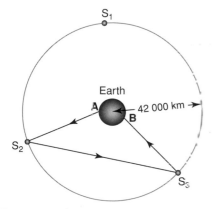

Figure 16.5 Satellites can be put into orbit of radius 4200 km, around the Equator. These satellites have a period of rotation of 24 hours.

Figure 16.6 Heat from the Sun can melt the ice in a comet. Sometimes this causes the comet to develop a spectacular tail.

■ Geostationary orbits

Figure 16.5 shows three satellites in **geostationary orbits** above the Equator. When the radius of the orbit is about 42 000 km, the time of orbit is 24 hours. This means that a satellite always appears in the same position above the Earth's surface. This is important for satellite communication. Positions A and B on the Earth's surface, on the opposite side of the Earth, can always keep in contact by sending signals via satellites S_2 and S_3.

■ Asteroids and comets

Mars is the outermost of four small rocky planets, and Jupiter is the innermost of four gaseous giant planets (Figure 16.7). There is a large gap between these two planets in which thousands of lumps of rock orbit; some of these measure as much as 700 km across. They are known as asteroids, planetoids or minor planets.

Comets, like asteroids, are rocks that orbit the Sun. However, comets have very elongated elliptical orbits (Figure 16.8). We think that at the edge of the Solar System there is a cloud of such comets. Occasionally, one is disturbed in its orbit so that it falls inwards towards the Sun. We notice a comet as it gets close to the Earth and Sun. Heat from the Sun melts ice contained in the rocks. The Sun emits a stream of charged particles called the Solar wind. This wind blows the melted ice away from the Sun, producing the comet's tail; the tail always points away from the Sun.

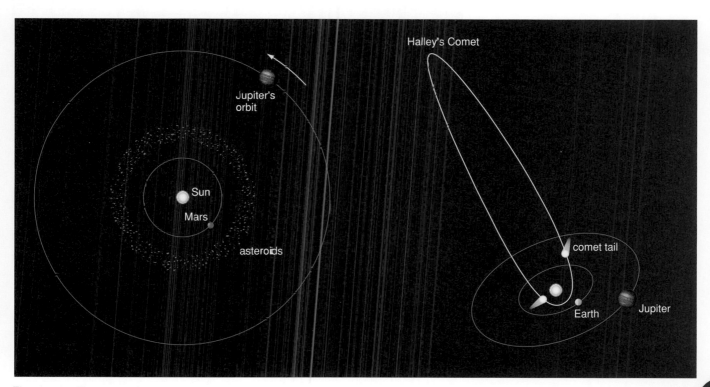

Figure 16.7 The asteroid belt.

Figure 16.8 Comets come from the far edges of the Solar System.

(a)

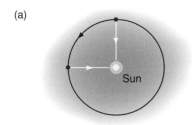

(b)

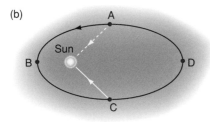

Figure 16.9 Circular and elliptical orbits.

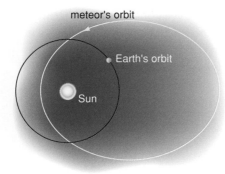

Figure 16.10 Meteors have elliptical orbits around the Sun.

> **EXAM TIP**
>
> You should be able to explain how the speed of a comet changes in its orbit.

■ Elliptical orbits

If a planet orbits the Sun in a circular orbit, it moves at a constant speed. In Figure 16.9(a) you can see that the Sun's gravitational pull is always at right angles to the planet's path.

However, a comet or asteroid in an elliptical orbit does not move at a constant speed. In Figure 16.9(b) the gravitational pull of the Sun on a comet at A is not at right angles to its path. The force does two things: it deflects the comet towards the Sun and speeds it up. At C the pull of the Sun slows the comet down again. At D the comet has low kinetic energy but high potential energy. As the comet falls towards the Sun it increases its kinetic energy to a maximum at B, and decreases its potential energy.

■ Meteors

Meteors are small rock fragments whose elliptical orbit crosses the Earth's orbital path (Figure 16.10). At the same times each year, we see 'showers' of meteors. The meteors enter the Earth's atmosphere travelling at great speeds (20 000 m/s); we see them as streaks of light as they burn up. Sometimes larger fragments of rock hit the ground; these are called meteorites. When you look at the Moon through a telescope, its cratered surface shows plenty of evidence of early meteor bombardment. The Earth, too, would have been cratered with meteor impacts when it formed, but millions of years of weathering has removed the craters. A large crater in the Arizona desert is thought to be only about 20 000 years old (Figure 16.11).

Figure 16.11 This crater in the Arizona desert is thought to have been formed by a meteor impact about 20 000 years ago. It is 200 m deep and 800 m wide.

STUDY QUESTIONS

1 a) What force keeps the Moon in orbit around the Earth?
  b) Explain how this force keeps the Moon moving in a circular orbit.
2 Describe how a comet's orbit differs from that of a planet.
3 a) Make a sketch to show the orbit of a comet around the Sun.
  b) Mark the points on the orbit where the comet has:
    i) the most kinetic energy
    ii) the most gravitational potential energy.
  c) Where is the pull of the Sun strongest on the comet?
  d) Where does the comet travel most slowly?
4 In Figure 16.5 the satellites have an orbital speed of 3054 m/s. Their orbital radius is 42 000 km.
  a) Calculate the time it takes the satellites to orbit the Earth once.
  b) Explain why this time period is useful for communication.
  c) Some satellites go in low orbits over the poles, some 100 km above the Earth's surface.
    i) How will the time period of these satellites compare with the ones in Figure 16.5?
    ii) Explain a use for such satellites.
5 There are over 300 000 known minor planets in orbit around the Sun. Some of these are only about 1 km in diameter. Others are larger, having diameters of about 1000 km.
  The table shows the distances from the Sun and the time periods for the orbits of the planets Uranus and Neptune, and some minor planets in orbit close to them. The orbital radii are quoted in Astronomical Units (AU). 1 AU is equal to the Sun−Earth distance, which is 150 million km.

Planet or minor planet	Radius of orbit / AU	Time of orbit / years
Chiron	14	51
Bienor	17	68
Uranus	19	84
Neptune	32	165
Pluto	39	248
Haumea	43	283
Makemake	46	310
Eris	68	557

  a) Plot a graph of time period of the orbits against the radius of the orbits.
  b) An astronomer has made a mistake in recording radius of orbit for one of the planets. Which one? Suggest what the radius of the orbit should be.
  c) Astronomers think they have discovered a new minor planet with a radius of orbit 55 AU. Use the graph to predict its time period.
  d) Sedna is a minor planet thought to orbit the Sun at a distance of 519 AU, with a period of about 11 400 years. Calculate Sedna's orbital speed in:
    i) millions of km per year
    ii) m/s.

1.17 Beyond the Solar System

Look at the sky on a clear, dark night. How many stars do you think you can see? All of these stars are great distances away from us.

Try to look at the sky on a clear night through binoculars or a small telescope. You will be able to see even more stars. You may be able to see the Milky Way. Many of the stars in the Milky Way have their own solar systems.

Figure 17.1 From the Earth, we see the stars of our galaxy as the Milky Way.

■ Light years

We measure distances to stars in **light years**. A light year is the distance that light travels in one year. This is about 10 million million kilometres. The brightest star in the sky (after the Sun) is Sirius. It is also one of the nearest, but light takes 9 years to reach us from Sirius. Light takes only 6 hours to reach out to the dwarf planet Pluto from the Sun. This makes our solar system look very small.

■ Galaxies

Clusters of millions of stars like the Milky Way are called **galaxies**. The Sun is one of the stars in the Milky Way (Figure 17.2). The Milky Way has about 100 000 million stars in it. If you could see our galaxy from the side, it would look like two fried eggs stuck back to back (Figure 17.2(a)); it is long and thin except for a bulge in the middle. If you could see the galaxy from the top it would look like a giant whirlpool with great spiral arms (Figure 17.2(b)). In fact, the galaxy does spin round. Our Sun takes about 220 million years to go once round the centre of the galaxy. In your lifetime, the pattern of stars that you see each night will not appear to change. But over thousands of years the pattern will change as our Sun moves through the galaxy. Our ancestors who lived 200 000 years ago would have seen slightly different constellations from those we can see today.

(a) Side view of our galaxy   (b) Top view of our galaxy

Figure 17.2 An artist's impression of our galaxy, the Milky Way. The red circle shows the approximate position of our Sun. Why is it not possible to take a photograph of all of the Milky Way?

Figure 17.3 This spiral galaxy lies around 12 million light years away.

■ Groups of galaxies

About 14 000 million years ago there were no galaxies at all, and the Universe was full of hydrogen and helium gas. **Gravity** is a force that acts over enormous distances, even over thousands of millions of light years. Groups of galaxies were formed when gravity gradually pulled large volumes of gas together. After the galaxies were formed, stars were formed inside the galaxies. Look at Figure 17.4. This shows a map of groups of galaxies. Our Local Group is in the middle. There are about 20 galaxies in our Local Group. Some groups of galaxies have as many as 1000 galaxies in them. There are probably about 10 000 million galaxies in the Universe.

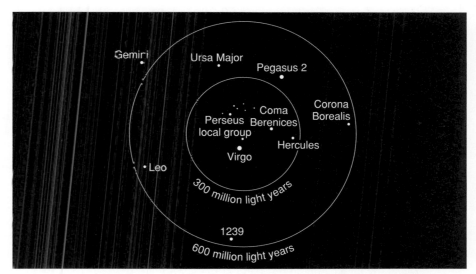

Figure 17.4 This map shows groups of galaxies close to our Local Group. The most distant galaxies in the universe are 14 000 million light years away from us. In this map, a large dot means that the group of galaxies contains more than 50 galaxies.

Figure 17.5 The Virgo cluster of galaxies lies 50 million light years away from us. It consists of about 1000 galaxies spread across 10 million light years.

STUDY QUESTIONS

1 Explain what is meant by each of the following terms. (a) moon, (b) planet, (c) star, (d) galaxy, (e) group of galaxies, (f) Universe

2 Our Sun is about 4600 million years old. Use the information in the text to calculate the number of times the Sun has rotated round the galaxy. Humans have existed on the Earth for about 50 000 years; how many times round the galaxy has the Sun rotated in that time?

3 Voyager 1 was launched in September 1977 and passed Saturn in November 1980. It travelled about 1400 million km to Saturn. It is still travelling near the edge of the Solar System.
   a) Work out its average speed in millions of kilometres per year.
   b) The nearest star to us after the Sun is Proxima Centauri, 4 light years away, in the Alpha Centauri star system. Use the information that light travels at 0.3 million km/s to calculate the distance to Proxima Centauri in millions of kilometres.
   c) Estimate how long Voyager would take to reach Proxima Centauri travelling at the speed calculated in part (a).
   d) Comment on the likelihood of our finding extraterrestrial life.

4 Use the information in the text to estimate the number of stars in the Universe.

5 Imagine that a spacecraft could be launched at the speed of light. How long would it take to reach the following bodies? Select your answer from the list below.
   a) the star Sirius
   b) Jupiter
   c) the Andromeda Galaxy
   d) the far side of the Milky Way
   e) the Sun
   f) Pluto
   g) the cluster of galaxies in Hercules (see Figure 17.4)
   Possible answers:

   10 000 years   9 years
   2.5 million years   8 minutes
   70 000 years   1 minute
   2 seconds   5 hours
   60 000 million years
   40 minutes
   260 million light years

Summary

 Make sure you can answer all the questions in the *Interactive quiz.*

I am confident that:

✓ **I can recall and use these facts about turning forces**

- moment = force × perpendicular distance from the pivot
- The unit of moment is Nm
- The weight of a body acts through its centre of gravity.
- The principle of moments states that in equilibrium the turning moments balance on a body.
- The upward forces on a light beam, supported at its ends, vary with the position of a heavy object placed on the beam.

✓ **I understand and can describe these facts about stretching**

- The extension varies with the applied force for springs, metal wires and rubber bands.
- Hooke's law states that the extension of a spring or wire is proportional to the applied force. This law is associated with the initial linear region of a force–extension graph.
- Elastic materials return to their original shape when a force is removed.

✓ **I understand and can describe these facts about astronomy**

- The Moon orbits the Earth; other planets have moons also.
- The Solar System is part of the Milky Way galaxy.
- A galaxy consists of billions of stars.
- The Universe is a large collection of galaxies.
- The gravitational field strength, g, is different on different planets and moons.
- g has units of N/kg
- The gravitational force causes moons to orbit planets, and planets and comets to orbit the Sun.
- The orbit of a comet differs from that of a planet. Most planets have nearly circular orbits. Comets have elongated elliptical orbits.
- The relationship between orbital speed, orbital radius and time period is:

$$\text{orbital speed} = \frac{2 \times \pi \times \text{orbital radius}}{\text{time period}}$$

Exam-style questions

1 The diagram shows a machine for lifting water out of a lake.

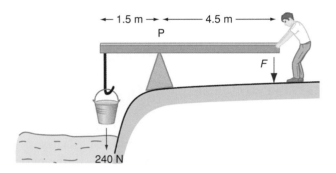

a) Calculate the turning moment of the weight of the bucket, about P. [2]

b) Explain why the man using the machine pushes at the end of the lever. [2]

c) Calculate the minimum size of the force, F, necessary to lift the water. [3]

2 The diagram shows a bus that is being tested for stability. The bus has been loaded with sandbags on the upper deck.

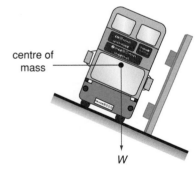

a) The bus has been tilted as far as it can without it tipping over. Explain how the diagram shows you that the bus cannot be tilted any further. [2]

b) Why has loading the upper deck with sandbags decreased the stability of the bus? [2]

c) What will happen to the stability of the bus if the bags are now put on the lower deck? [2]

3 The diagram shows some apparatus being used to find the centre of gravity of a piece of card. Three small holes have been made in the card. There is a retort stand that supports a cork with a pin it. There is also a weight attached to a thin piece of cotton.

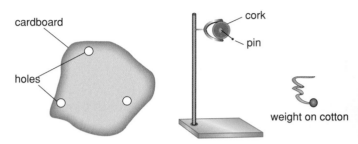

Explain carefully how you would use this apparatus to find the centre of gravity of the card. [5]

4 The diagram shows a crane being used to lift a container into a boat.

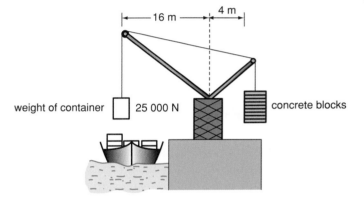

a) Calculate the turning moment of the container, about the pivot P. [3]

b) Explain the purpose of the concrete blocks. [1]

c) What weight of concrete blocks would balance the turning moment of the container? [3]

5 The diagram shows a man climbing a step ladder.

Use the term 'centre of gravity' to explain why the man is unlikely to topple over in this position. [3]

6 The diagram shows a windsurfer in action.

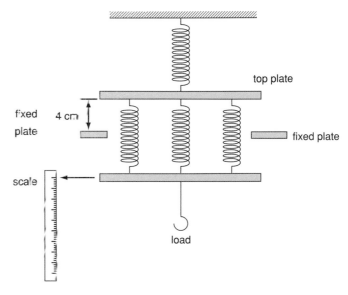

a) Explain why the windsurfer leans out on her sailboard. [2]

b) The weight of the windsurfer is 750 N. Calculate the turning moment caused by this weight about the mast. [3]

c) Explain why the windsurfer leans out further when the wind blows with greater force. [2]

7 A passenger in an airport has a case with wheels.

She decides it will be easier to pull the case if she packs all the heavy items of luggage nearest the wheels.

Explain why this is a good idea. Include ideas about turning moments in your answer. [4]

8 The following diagram shows a device that can be used to measure accurately both small and large weights. When a load of 8 N is applied the top plate rests on the lower fixed plates, so that only the lower three springs can stretch further.

The table shows the total extension of the springs as the load is increased.

Load / N	Extension / cm
2.0	1.0
4.0	2.0
6.0	3.0
8.0	4.0
12.0	4.5
16.0	5.0
20.0	5.5
24.0	6.0
28.0	6.3
32.0	7.0

a) Plot a graph to show the load against the extension of the springs. Draw a line of best fit through the points you have plotted. [4]

b) The physicist doing the experiment has made a mistake with one of the measurements. Can you suggest what the measurement should have been? [1]

c) Two loads are put on the device. One stretches the springs by 1.5 cm, the second stretches them by 5.2 cm. Use your graph to calculate the size of each load. [2]

d) A student says: 'The graph shows that these springs obey Hooke's law'. Comment on this observation. [2]

9 The graph shows the size of the forces required to stretch samples of steel and spider's silk. Both samples are of the same thickness and length.

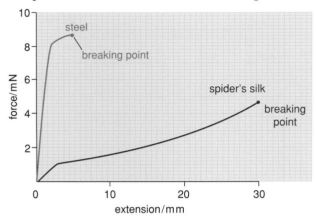

a) Explain why it was decided to use samples of silk and steel that were exactly the same length and thickness. [2]

b) A student observed that neither material obeys Hooke's law. Evaluate this remark. [2]

Both samples break as shown on the graph.

c) How big is the force that breaks the sample of steel? [1]

d) What is the extension of the spider's silk when it breaks? [1]

e) Although the sample of steel is stronger, the spider's silk is less likely to break when catching a fly. Use your understanding of forces and momentum to explain this. [3]

10 The diagram shows the orbits of the Earth and two other bodies about the Sun.

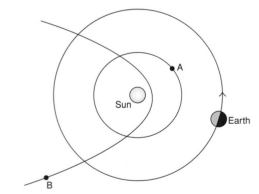

a) Which body could be:

   i) the planet Mercury [1]

   ii) a comet? [1]

b) In which direction does A move around the Sun? [1]

c) **i)** Describe the shape of the orbit of B. [1]

   ii) How does the speed of B change in its orbit? [2]

   iii) What force keeps comets and planets in orbit? [1]

11 a) Astronomers use the term 'Milky Way' to describe part of the Universe. What is the Milky Way? [1]

b) The table below gives information about some of the planets in our Solar System.

Planet	Average surface temperature / °C	Time to orbit the Sun / years	Diameter of the planet / km
Saturn	−190	29	120 000
Uranus	−220	84	51 000
Jupiter	−150	12	143 000

Which planet is nearest to the Sun? Use the information in the table to give two reasons for your answer. [2]

12 The table below shows the gravitational field strength on the surface of some planets.

Planet	Gravitational field strength / N/kg
Earth	10
Mercury	3.7
Jupiter	24
Neptune	11

a) Your mass is 80 kg. What would your weight be on the surface of:

   i) Mercury [1]

   ii) Neptune? [1]

b) What factors affect the size of the gravitational field on the surface of a planet? [2]

13 a) The Moon orbits the Earth at a distance of 384 000 km. One orbit takes 27.3 days. Use this information to calculate the orbital speed of the Moon round the Earth in m/s. [3]

b) A satellite orbits low over the Earth's surface in an orbit of radius 6500 km. Its orbital speed is 7.5 km/s. Calculate the time period of the orbit. [3]

EXTEND AND CHALLENGE

1 The table below shows the properties of some materials used in the manufacturing and building industries. When choosing a material for a particular job, you need to consider the stiffness, strength and density of the material. You need to be aware of the cost too.

   a) Explain why concrete, brick and wood are often used for building houses.

   b) Explain what is meant by **stiffness**.

   Why is the ratio $\dfrac{\text{stiffness}}{\text{density}}$ important?

   c) **Strength** is a measure of what load can be placed on 1 m² of a material before it crumbles or breaks.

   Why is the ratio $\dfrac{\text{strength}}{\text{density}}$ important?

   d) Explain why steel is used for building bridges, but aluminium is used to build aircraft.

   e) GRP (fibre glass) can be used to build small boats, and even small minesweepers for the Naval Forces.

   i) Why is it useful to make minesweepers from GRP?

   ii) Why are large ships not made from GRP?

   f) Turbine blades for aircraft engines need to be strong, stiff and light. Which material in the table would you choose for making the blades?

2 a) State clearly two conditions necessary for a body to be in equilibrium.

   b) The diagram shows a mousetrap. The idea is that as the mouse walks towards the cheese he tips the plank up and then falls conveniently near to Boris the cat. Go through the following calculations to see how far along the plank the mouse can go before it tips up.

   i) Calculate the turning moment of the counterbalance about the pivot.

   ii) The weight of the plank may be taken to act through the 50 cm mark. Calculate the turning moment about the pivot of the cheese and the plank together.

   iii) Use your answers to (i) and (ii) to find where the mouse will overbalance the trap.

   c) Use the information in the diagram to calculate the upwards force that the pivot exerts on the plank, just as the 'trap' overbalances.

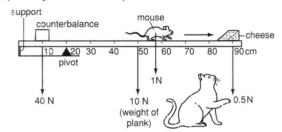

Material	Relative stiffness	Relative strength	Density / kg/m³	Stiffness Density	Strength Density	Cost per tonne / euros
Steel	21 000	40 000	7800	2.7	5.1	100
Aluminium	7300	27 000	2700	2.7	10	400
Wood	1400	2700	500	2.8	5.4	30
Concrete	1500	4000	2500	0.6	1.6	6
Brick	2100	5500	3000	0.7	1.8	10
GRP	2000	50 000	2000	1	25	70
CFRP	20 000	100 000	2000	10	50	1700

GRP: Glass Reinforced Plastic (fibre glass)   CFRP: Carbon Fibre Reinforced Plastic

3 The planet Mars has two moons, Phobos and Deimos. The planet also has an artificial satellite, the *Mars Reconnaissance Orbiter*, which has been in orbit around the planet since 2005.

   a) The speed of a moon (or satellite) around a planet, depends on the strength of the gravitational field of the planet, *g*, and the distance from the centre of the planet, *R*. The speed may be calculated using the formula:

   $$v^2 = gR$$

The table shows the gravitational field strength, distance from the centre of the planet, orbital speed and time period of orbit for each of the moons or satellite.

   i) State an equation that links the orbital speed, distance from the centre of the planet and time period of orbit.

   i) Copy and complete the table. Show separately the working you do for each calculation.

   (b) The Reconnaissance Orbiter orbits Mars in a polar orbit. Explain why this orbit is more suitable for studying the surface of the planet than an equatorial orbit.

Moon or satellite	Gravitational field strength from Mars (N/kg)	Distance from the centre of Mars (m × 10³)	Orbital speed (m/s)	Time of orbit (s)
Reconnaissance Orbiter	1.78	7060		
Phobos		9377		27 550
Deimos			1352	111 670

Electricity 2

1 How would your life have been different had you lived in the same country as you do now, in 1880?

2 How much does it cost to provide electricity to your home each year? How much does it cost to provide electricity to your school each year?

3 What impact does electricity generation have on our environment?

4 What hazards are associated with the use of electricity?

The supply of electricity to our homes and city centres is an essential part of twenty-first century life. Lights in the streets, our homes and offices allow us to be active 24 hours a day. However, electricity comes at a price and care must be taken with how much we use it.

By the end of this section you should:
- know and use the electrical units
- recall the hazards of electricity
- understand the need for insulation, fuses and earthing
- understand that resistors transfer heat
- use the formula: power = current × voltage
- be able to work out the cost of electricity
- understand the difference between a.c. and d.c. supplies
- understand the uses of series and parallel circuits
- understand the factors that affect the current in a series circuit
- describe how the current varies with voltage in various electrical devices
- recall and use the formula: voltage = current × resistance
- know that current is a flow of charge
- recall the definition of a volt
- explain the nature of static electricity
- recall some hazards and uses of static electricity.

2.1 Introducing electricity

The two photographs in Figure 1.1 show how important electricity is in our lives. Electrical devices provide entertainment in the family room and convenience in the kitchen. How many electrical devices do you use every day?

Figure 1.1 Common scenes in the home.

Figure 1.2

■ Electrical energy

Below are two statements about a torch cell connected to its bulb. Which one is correct?

Statement A: The cell is the provider of energy. The cell transfers chemical energy to electricity for it to flow round the circuit. The bulb transfers the electrical energy to heat and light.

Statement B: The cell in an electrical circuit is like a pump in a water circuit. Electricity in the wires is pushed round by the cell, just as water is forced through pipes by a pump.

The answer is that both ideas are correct. The cell provides energy. It is also helpful to compare the flow of electricity with the flow of water. Understanding how water flows will help you to understand how electrical circuits work too.

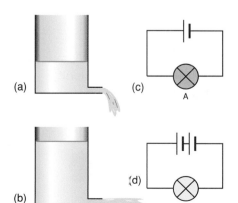

Figure 1.3

Cells and brightness

Figure 1.3(a) shows a tank of water with an outlet pipe at the bottom; water flows out at a slow rate. When the depth of water in the tank is increased, as in Figure 1.3(b), the pressure of water at the bottom of the tank is increased and water flows out at a faster rate.

The cell in an electrical circuit provides an 'electrical pressure' that pushes electricity through the lamp. In Figure 1.3(c) one cell pushes electricity through the lamp at a slow rate and the lamp is dull; electrical energy is being transferred into heat and light energy at a slow rate. In Figure 1.3(d), two cells push the electricity round the circuit more quickly and the lamp is brighter; electrical energy is now being transferred into heat and light energy more quickly.

Figure 1.4 Two men are required to direct this fire hose due to the high pressure of the water.

■ Voltage and current

The words voltage and current are important in describing electrical circuits.

- When describing a stream or river we use the word 'current' to describe the flow of water. When the current is large, this means lots of water flows past us each second.
- In an electrical circuit we use the same word. Current describes the flow of electricity. When the current is large a lot of electricity flows through the circuit.

The unit of current is the **ampere** (A), though this is often shortened to amp.

- Figure 1.4 shows two fire fighters practising to use their hose. The pressure in the hose is high and water flows quickly.
- The voltage of a cell is like an 'electrical pressure.' A high voltage drives a large current around the circuit. High voltages deliver large amounts of energy and can be dangerous.
- Electric shocks delivered from a high voltage source can be very painful, and can even cause death. This is why we are warned about high voltages.

The unit of voltage is the **volt** (V).

■ Electrical hazards

Electricity provided for the home is called the **mains supply**. The voltage of the mains supply differs from country to country but is usually either about 230 V or 120 V. Either voltage is large enough to be dangerous.

Due to the dangers of electricity, we must be on the lookout for hazards. Some of these are listed below:

- Damaged plugs can expose people to high voltages. Plugs are made of plastic, which does not conduct electricity.
- You need to keep an eye on young children and teach them not to play with electrical cables (Figure 1.5).
- If too many plugs are put into one wall socket, a large current might melt or damage wires (Figure 1.6).
- If a cable is frayed or broken it must be replaced. Someone might touch a bare wire and receive a shock.
- A long wire is a trip hazard. If someone trips over a cable they could hurt themselves, or expensive electrical equipment might be pulled over and get damaged.
- You need to be careful if you coil long insulated wires. When you bend the wire you might damage or crack the insulation (Figure 1.7).

Figure 1.5 Children must be educated about the dangers of electricity.

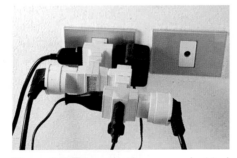

Figure 1.6 This socket has many electrical devices plugged into it. Together they might draw too much current – a large current can melt wires.

Figure 1.7 You need to be careful when coiling wires; if you coil it too tightly you could break the insulation.

Figure 1.8 The electrical elements in toasters are connected to high voltages.

Figure 1.9 Never step on to or across railway lines. As well as the danger from approaching trains, the electrified rails can give you a fatal shock.

- You must keep water away from sockets and plugs. Water conducts electricity, so a wet plug or socket could give you a shock. In most countries you will not find any sockets in bathrooms, except for a special shaver socket
- It is dangerous to push metal objects into electrical sockets. This could give you a shock. It is also dangerous to try and remove toast from a toaster using a knife or a fork, as the wires in a toaster carry a high voltage (Figure 1.8).
- You must also be aware of electrical hazards outside the home. Overhead cables can carry very high voltages so care must be taken near electricity transmission lines and also electric railways (Figures 1.9 and 1.10).

Figure 1.10 Be careful near overhead cables. You could get a shock by flying a kite or carrying a fishing rod too close to them.

Figure 1.11 Keep clear of anything that displays this hazard warning sign.

STUDY QUESTIONS

1 a) Choose three electrical hazards mentioned in the chapter and explain what you would do to remove the danger.
  b) State two electrical hazards that have not been mentioned in the chapter. Explain why we need to be careful of these hazards.
2 Explain what is meant by the following words:
  a) voltage
  b) current.
3 a) Write down the rate of flow of water along pipes A and B.
  b) Write down the electric current flowing along wires A and B and show the direction of the current.

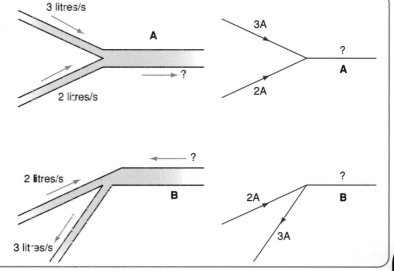

2.2 Using mains electricity

In the home we use electricity for heating, lighting, cooking and powering many other devices, which we use for leisure or tasks.

■ Alternating and direct current

In Figure 2.2(a) and (b) you can see two lamps that are lit by two different electrical supplies. In Figure 2.2(a) the lamp is lit by a 6 V battery. A battery provides a direct current (**d.c.**) – this means that the current flows in one direction at a constant rate. In electrical diagrams a cell is represented by two vertical lines, one long and thin and the other shorter and fat. Here the longer line is on the left. This is the positive side or 'terminal' of the cell. We use the convention that a current flows from the positive terminal to the negative. The current flow is marked with an arrow.

Figure 2.1 Electricity can be used to keep us warm.

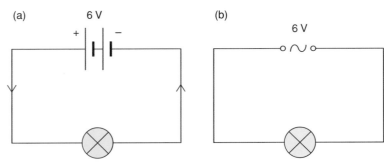

Figure 2.2 (a) In a direct current circuit the current flows at a constant rate in one direction round the circuit.
(b) In an alternating circuit the current constantly changes direction, flowing in one direction then the other.

In Figure 2.2(b) the lamp is lit by an alternating supply (**a.c.**). In an alternating supply, the voltage switches direction many times each second and the current changes direction too.

Figure 2.3 shows graphs of how the a.c. and d.c. supplies change with time. The d.c. supply remains constant at 6 V; the a.c. supply changes from positive to negative.

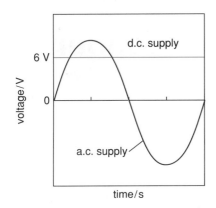

Figure 2.3 Direct and alternating supply voltages.

■ Mains supply

All countries use a.c. supplies for their mains electricity. Most countries use a mains voltage of about 120 V or 230 V. By using a standardised voltage, electrical devices can be used in different countries.

We also describe an alternating current by its **frequency**. The frequency of most mains supplies is either 50 cycles per second or 60 cycles per second. Figure 2.3 shows one cycle of an a.c. supply. So if the frequency of a supply is 50 cycles per second, the current completes each cycle in 1/50 of a second.

The unit of frequency is the **hertz**. A frequency of 50 cycles per second is written as 50 hertz or 50 Hz.

EXAM TIP

Make sure you can explain the difference between an a.c. and a d.c. supply.

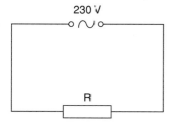

Figure 2.4 A heating element or resistor transfers electrical energy into heat and sometimes light energy.

■ Electrical heating

Figure 2.4 shows a 230 V mains supply. It provides current to a heater, which can also be called a **resistor**. This is shown in the diagram, marked 'R'. The symbol R is used, because we say that the heater offers **resistance** to the flow of electricity.

When a current flows through a resistor, the electrical energy from the supply is transferred into heat energy. The transfer of heat energy to the resistor causes its temperature to rise. Some resistors glow red hot.

Figure 2.5 helps you to understand the idea of resistance by comparing it with the flow of water. In Figure 2.5(a), water flows out of a tank through a long, thin pipe. The flow rate (or current) is low, as the pipe offers high resistance to the flow. In Figure 2.5(b), the flow rate (or current) is high, as a short, wide pipe offers less resistance to the flow.

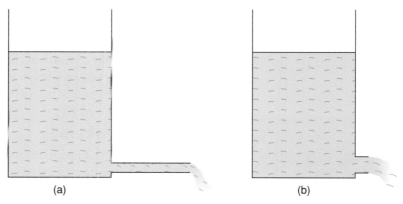

(a)   (b)

Figure 2.5 (a) A long, thin pipe offers high resistance – water flows slowly.
(b) A short, wide pipe offers low resistance – water flows rapidly.

In an electrical circuit the idea of resistance is similar. When different resistors are attached to the mains, different currents flow. A low resistance allows a large current to flow, which will produce a large heating effect. A high resistance allows a small current to flow, which produces a low heating effect.

■ Electricity at home

We use electricity in our homes for several things, e.g. lighting, cooking, heating, computers and TVs. Each electrical device is designed to take a different current, depending on its use. Table 1 shows the size of current that might flow through some electrical appliances attached to a 230 V mains supply.

Table 1 Some electrical appliances and the currents drawn by them

Appliance	Current / A
lamp	0.1
computer monitor	0.5
hairdryer	3.0
toaster	4.0
convector heater	8.5
kettle	12.0

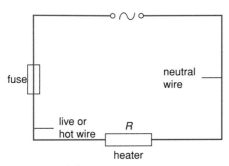

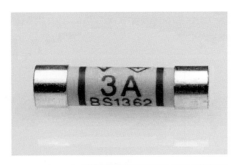

Figure 2.6 A fuse in a circuit.

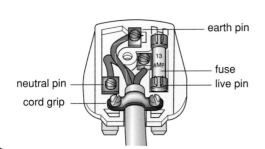

Figure 2.7 Different fuses.

Fuses

Fuses are used with electrical devices for safety. Their main purpose is to prevent a fire.

A fuse contains a thin wire that heats up and melts if too much current flows through it. If this happens we say that the fuse has 'blown'. The rating of a fuse is the maximum current that can pass through it without melting the fuse wire.

You need to choose the correct fuse to put into a plug or fuse board, so that it blows if there is a fault. In the UK it is common to use 3 A or 13 A fuses. Look at the appliances in the table on the previous page. You need to use a 3 A fuse for the lamp and the computer monitor, and a 13 A fuse for the other appliances. A lamp will work with a 13 A fuse but is it safer to use a 3 A fuse. A lamp works on a low current such as 0.1 A or 0.2 A. So, if 3 A flows through a lamp circuit it means there is a fault – a 3 A fuse will blow but a 13 A fuse will not.

Figure 2.6 shows the symbol for a fuse. In most countries mains electricity is supplied by a **live** or **hot** wire, together with a **neutral** wire. The live or hot wire has a large voltage, which supplies the energy. This is the dangerous wire. The fuse is put into the live wire so that it is disconnected when a fuse blows.

Circuit breakers

A circuit breaker is an electromagnetic switch that opens or 'trips' when a current is bigger than a certain value. The advantages of circuit breakers over fuses are that they are sensitive and also they can quickly be reset once a fault has been put right. Circuit breakers are often found in modern houses instead of fuses in the fuse boxboard.

Earthing

Most countries use three-pin plugs for the electrical supply. The third wire is called the earth wire, which as its name suggests is attached to the earth. Figure 2.9 shows a diagram of a correctly wired three-pin plug in use in the UK. The live wire is brown, the neutral wire is blue and the earth wire is green and yellow.

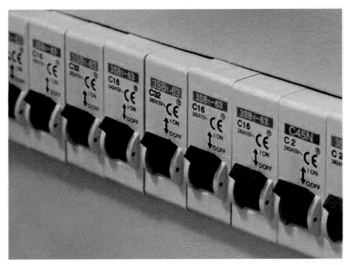

Figure 2.8 Circuit breakers in a modern fuse box.

Figure 2.9 A correctly wired UK plug.

Figure 2.10 explains why the earth wire is an important safety feature. Figure 2.10(a) shows the circuit diagram for an electric heater, which is enclosed in a metal case. The current is flowing from the live wire to the neutral and the fire is working safely. The earth wire is attached to the metal case. When the heater is working correctly the earth wire does not carry a current.

Figure 2.10(b) shows what happens when a fault develops. Now a wire is touching the metal case. Without the earth wire, someone could touch the metal case and get a shock. With the earth wire in place current flows through the earth wire and not the person touching the case. A large current flowing to earth can also blow the fuse, which disconnects the dangerous live wire.

> **EXAM TIP**
>
> The earth wire and fuse together protect the person using an electrical device.

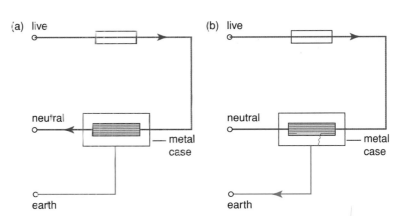

Figure 2.10 (a) The heater works safely. **(b)** A broken wire touches the metal case and the current flows to earth.

Double insulation

Many modern electrical appliances are made out of plastic, which does not conduct electricity. Plastic is an **insulator**. Appliances that are made of plastic can safely be connected to the mains using only two wires. The earth wire is not needed as you cannot get a shock from the plastic.

This method of protection is called **double insulation** and it is shown by the sign ▣. When you see this sign on an appliance you know you do not need an earth wire.

Residual-current circuit breaker (RCCB)

A residual-current circuit breaker (RCCB) is a device that disconnects a circuit when it detects that the current is not the same in the live and neutral wires. When the currents are different there is a small current leaking to earth, which could be through the body of a person who accidentally touches the live wire.

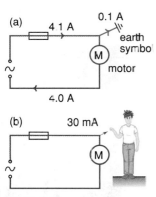

Figure 2.11 (a) An electric lawnmower will continue to work even though a damaged live wire allows a small current to flow to earth.
(b) A small current (30 mA) flows through a person's body. This current is too small to blow a fuse.

Figure 2.11 shows two examples of where there could be an imbalance of current. A gardener is mowing his lawn with an electric mower. The mower is double insulated, so the gardener is protected if the live wire becomes detached inside the mower

It is possible that the wire to the mower becomes damaged – it could be cut by the mower itself. In Figure 2.11(a), a damaged live wire allows a small current to flow to earth. This extra current is not large enough to melt the fuse, so the mower keeps working.

In Figure 2.11(b), the gardener has turned off the mower and picks up the wire. A residual current flows through him. This current is small – only 30 mA, but it could deliver a lethal shock.

An RCCB, which detects an imbalance of currents between the live and neutral wires, will disconnect the supply before an accident happens. RCCBs are widely used in different countries.

 Now watch the video *Comparing the use of fuses to circuit breakers.*

STUDY QUESTIONS

1 **a)** What is the purpose of a fuse in a mains circuit?
   b) What advantages do circuit breakers have over fuses?

2 Explain carefully each of the following:
   a) why the fuse is put into the live or hot wire of a mains circuit
   b) why the rating of a fuse should be slightly higher than the normal working current through an appliance
   c) why appliances with metal cases need to be earthed, but appliances with plastic cases do not need to be earthed.

3 What are the colours of the live, neutral and earth wires in your country?

4 Explain the difference between an a.c. and a d.c. electrical supply.

5 State and explain the energy transfers that occur in an electrical circuit when a battery is connected to a resistor.

6 The diagram shows the trace on an oscilloscope that is being used to measure the voltage of an electrical supply.

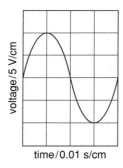

a) What type of supply is it?
b) What is the peak (maximum) voltage of the supply?
c) What is the frequency of the supply?

7 Do some research to find out how an RCCB works.

2.3 Electrical power

Figure 3.1 This car runs on electricity instead of petrol. Here its battery is being charged up from the mains.

How do electric cars shape up against petrol-driven cars? Find out: how long it takes to charge up an electric car; how much it costs to drive 100 km; what the average range of an electric car is.

■ Calculating the power

When you use an electrical appliance at home you are interested in how much energy it provides you with in each second. This determines how bright a light is, or how effective a heater is at keeping you warm. The energy supplied per second in called the **power**.

> power = energy per second

Power is measured in **joules per second** (J/s) or **watts** (W). Sometimes power is supplied in large quantities. An electric fire can transfer 1000 W of electrical power to heat: 1000 W is called a **kilowatt** (1 kW). If you want to talk about the output of a power station you will need to use **megawatts** (MW); 1 MW is a million watts. Some power stations produce 2000 MW of electrical power.

You can work out the electrical power, P, used in a circuit, if you know the voltage, V, of the supply and the current, I, using the formula:

$$power = current \times voltage$$
$$P = I \times V$$

Tables 1, 2 and 3 give examples of electrical appliances with their power, operating voltage and the current supplied.

Table 1 Power used by low-voltage applications

Appliance	Power / W	Operating voltage / V	Current / A
torch LED	0.12	3	0.04
torch lamp	0.9	3	0.3
pocket calculator	0.0003	3	0.0001
car heater	90	12	7.5
electric van	3600	72	50

Table 2 Power used by household appliances with a mains voltage of 230 V

Appliance	Power / W	Operating voltage / V	Current / A
lamp	23	230	0.1
TV	69	230	0.3
fridge	115	230	0.5
hairdryer	690	230	3.0
microwave	1380	230	6.0
electric shower	1955	230	8.5

Table 3 Power used by household appliances with a mains voltage of 115 V

Appliance	Power / W	Operating voltage / V	Current / A
lamp	23	115	0.2
TV	69	115	0.6
fridge	115	115	1.0
hairdryer	690	115	6.0
microwave	1380	115	12.0
electric shower	1955	115	17.0

■ Choosing a fuse

Countries with a 230 V mains supply commonly use 3 A, 5 A or 13 A fuses. It is safest to use a fuse which is just slightly above the maximum current that the appliance uses. In Table 2 the lamp, TV and fridge should be protected with a 3 A fuse, the hairdryer should be protected with a 5 A fuse, and the microwave and shower should be protected with a 13 A fuse.

Example. If you buy a kettle that is marked 230 V 2.4 kW, which fuse should you use in the plug?

You can calculate the current using the formula:

$$power = current \times voltage$$
$$2400 \text{ W} = current \times 230 \text{ V}$$
$$So \ current = \frac{2400}{230}$$
$$= 10.4 \text{ A}$$

EXAM TIP

Remember the formula
$E = I \times V \times t$

You must use a 13 A fuse to protect the kettle because the current will blow a smaller fuse.

■ Paying for energy

When you pay an electricity bill you are paying the electricity company for the energy you have used. You can calculate how much energy has been used with the formula:

$$energy = power \times time$$

or

$$energy = current \times voltage \times time$$

Example. How much energy is used when a 1 kW heater is on for 1 hour?

$$energy \ used = power \times time$$
$$= 1000 \text{ W} \times 3600 \text{ s}$$
$$= 3\,600\,000 \text{ J}$$

Table 4 Cost of electricity in some countries in 2013

Country	Cost of electricity / US cents per kWh
Australia	26
China	16
Iceland	4
Germany	37
Malaysia	9
Russia	11
South Africa	6
Tonga	60
UK	23
USA	12

We can also calculate the energy used in **kilowatt hours** (kWh). Instead of using units of watts and seconds, we use kilowatts and hours. The same example calculation can be done again:

$$\text{energy used} = \text{power} \times \text{time}$$
$$= 1\,\text{kW} \times 1\,\text{h}$$
$$= 1\,\text{kWh}$$

When you use electricity you are billed for the number of kilowatt hours used. The cost of electricity in some countries (in 2013) is shown in Table 4.

STUDY QUESTIONS

1 Calculate the power supplied to each of the following appliances when they are attached to the correct operating voltage.
   a) a 12 V, 5 A light bulb
   b) a 230 V, 2 A heater
   c) a 115 V, 4 A toaster

2 a) Calculate the current flowing in each of the following electrical appliances when they are supplied with the correct operating voltage.
   i) a 230 V, 11.5 W bulb
   ii) a 115 V, 2 kW shower
   iii) a 230 V, 800 W microwave oven
   iv) a 115 V, 460 W TV set
   b) You have available 3 A, 5 A, 13 A and 20 A fuses. Which would you choose for each of the appliances in part a) of the question?

3 a) Make a list of some household electrical appliances that run off the mains supply, for example television, heater, fridge.
   b) Look on the back of the appliance to find out the recommended voltage supply for each, and the power used.
   c) Calculate the current used by each device and recommend a safe fuse to use.

4 A householder goes on holiday for two weeks. To deter burglars she leaves four lights that come on for 6 hours a day. Each bulb is rated at 23 W.
   a) Calculate the energy used over the two weeks in:
      i) joules
      ii) kWh.
   b) Calculate the cost of the electricity (using Table 4) in:
      i) Iceland
      ii) the USA.

5 An electric car battery is charged from a 230 V supply using a current of 65 A. The charging time to fully charge the battery is 3.5 hours.
   a) Calculate the electrical energy used to charge the battery in joules.
   b) 3.6 MJ = 1 kWh. Use this information to express the answer to part a) in kWh.
   c) Calculate the cost of the electricity in the USA when the battery is charged using electricity costing 12 US cents per kWh.
   d) Once fully charged, the range of the car is 300 km. Compare the cost of running the electric car with that of running a petrol-driven car. The cost of the petrol (or gasoline) is 80 cents per litre and the car has a range of 10 km per litre of fuel.

2.4 Electric circuits

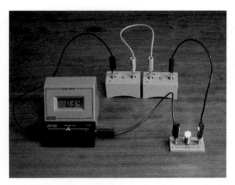

Figure 4.1 A continuous circuit is needed to light this lamp.

■ A continuous circuit

Figure 4.2(a) shows how some components are connected together to make an electrical circuit. This is called a **circuit diagram**. You can see that the current flows from the positive terminal of the cell, through an ammeter and resistor, before returning to the cell. The current flows through all the circuit components, one after another. These components are in **series**.

The ammeter is a device that measures the size of the current – 1 A in this example. In Figure 4.2(a) the switch, S, is closed. This means there is a complete, continuous circuit for the current to flow around. When the switch is open (Figure 4.2(b)), there is a break in the circuit and current cannot flow.

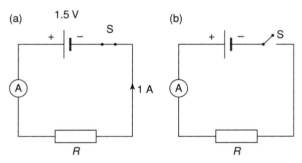

Figure 4.2 Circuit diagrams with the components in series.

EXAM TIPS
• Doubling the voltage doubles the current in a series circuit.
• Increasing the resistance reduces the current.

■ Controlling the current

You can change the size of the current in a circuit by changing the voltage of the cell or battery, or by changing the components in the circuit. Figure 4.3 shows the idea.

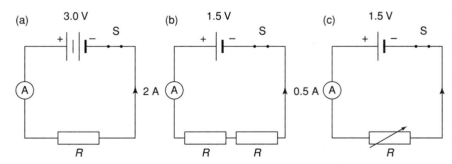

Figure 4.3 Different series circuits.

In Figure 4.3(a), an extra cell has been added to the circuit in Figure 4.2. Now the current is larger.

In a series circuit increasing the voltage increases the current.

In Figure 4.3(b), the voltage of the cell is 1.5 V but now the resistance has been increased by adding a second resistor to the circuit. This makes the current smaller.

In a series circuit increasing the resistance makes the current smaller.

In Figure 4.3(c) a variable resistor has replaced the fixed resistor in the circuit. You can control the size of the current by adjusting the resistor.

Figure 4.4 shows how the variable resistor works. If you use terminals B and C you have a fixed resistor. But if you use terminals A and C you have a variable resistor. The current flows through the thick metal bar at A, then along the resistance wire to C via the sliding contact. The metal bar has low resistance. So the resistance gets lower as the slider moves away from A.

PRACTICAL

You should be able to set up a series circuit and use an ammeter to measure the current.

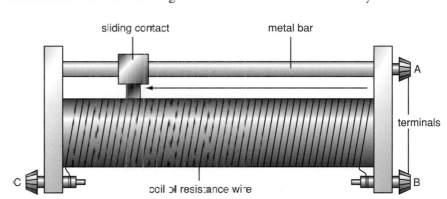

Figure 4.4 A variable resistor.

STUDY QUESTIONS

1 a) Draw a circuit diagram to show a cell connected in series to an ammeter, a diode and a fixed resistor.
  b) Draw a circuit diagram to show how you can control the brightness of a lamp.

2 In the circuit diagrams, lamp A is connected to a single cell. The lamp lights with normal brightness.

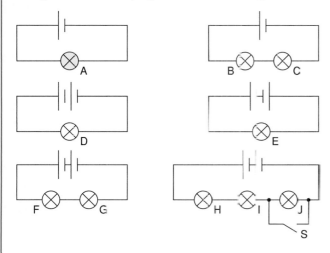

  a) Use the words normal, bright, dim or off to describe the lamps B, C, D, E, F and G.
  b) Describe the brightness of the lamps H, I and J when the switch S is:
  i) open
  ii) closed.

3 a) Which of the lamps in the diagram, K or L, will light?

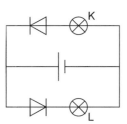

  b) What will happen to the lamps if the cell is turned around?
  c) Draw a new circuit diagram with two diodes and two lamps, so that both lamps light.

EXAM TIP
Make sure you know your circuit symbols.

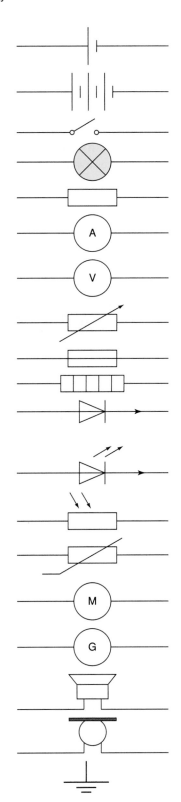

■ Circuit symbols

Figure 4.5 shows the circuit symbols for the electrical components that you will meet in the next few chapters. A brief explanation of the function of each component is given next to each symbol.

A **cell** provides the energy to push the current around a circuit.

A **battery** is two or more cells in series.

A **switch** breaks or rejoins the circuit, turning the current off or on. This switch is open so no current flows.

A **lamp**. When a lamp (or bulb) lights it shows a current is flowing.

A **fixed resistor**. The size of the resistor affects the size of the current.

An **ammeter** measures the current.

A **voltmeter** measures the size of the voltage.

A **variable resistor** allows the size of the current to be varied.

A **fuse** melts (blows) when the current is greater than the fuse's current rating.

A **heater** is a resistor that is designed to transfer electrical energy to heat energy.

A **diode** only allows the current to flow in one direction.

A **light-emitting diode** (LED) emits light when a current flows through it. An LED can be used as an indicator, to show when an appliance is switched on.

A **light-dependent resistor** (LDR). The resistance of an LDR is low in bright light and higher when the light intensity is low.

A **thermistor**. The resistance of a thermistor changes with temperature. The resistance of a (NTC) thermistor is low at high temperatures and high at low temperatures.

A **motor** transfers electrical energy into kinetic energy.

A **generator** transfers kinetic energy into electrical energy.

A **loudspeaker** transfers electrical energy into sound energy.

A **microphone** transfers sound energy into electrical energy.

Electrical appliances are connected to **earth** or ground as a safety measure to prevent anyone who touches the appliance from getting a shock if the appliance becomes live due to an electrical fault.

Figure 4.5 Circuit symbols.

2.5 Calculating the resistance

Figure 5.1

These ceramic discs have a very high resistance so that the power line is insulated from the metal pylon. Each ceramic disc is connected to the next with a metal core to provide strength.

When the ceramic insulators are wet, a small leakage current can flow down the outside of the ceramic discs. Discuss how the design of the discs reduces the size of this current.

What changes would you make to this insulator to make it suitable for a higher voltage power line?

■ Ammeters and voltmeters

Figure 5.2 shows you how to set up a circuit using an ammeter and a voltmeter.

- The ammeter is set up in **series** with the resistor, R. The same current flows through the ammeter and the resistor. The ammeter measures the current in amperes (A), or milliamperes (mA). 1 mA is 0.001 A.
- The voltmeter is placed in **parallel** with the resistor, R. The voltmeter measures the **voltage** across (between the ends of) the resistor. The unit of voltage is the volt (V). The voltmeter only allows a very small current to flow through it, so it does not affect the current flowing around the circuit.

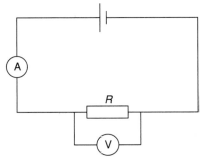

Figure 5.2 Meters in a simple circuit.

■ Resistance

The circuit in Figure 5.2 can be used to calculate the resistance in the circuit. The resistance of a resistor or electrical component is defined using this equation:

$$\text{resistance} = \frac{\text{voltage}}{\text{current}}$$

This equation is usually written as:

$$R = \frac{V}{I}$$

where R is the resistance, V is the voltage across the resistor and I is the current flowing through the resistor.

The unit of resistance is the **ohm** (Ω). Resistances are also measured in kΩ, where 1 kΩ is 1000 Ω.

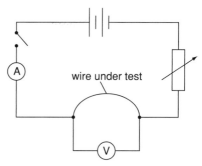

Figure 5.3 Investigating the resistance of a metal wire.

■ Ohm's law

The circuit diagram in Figure 5.3 shows how you can investigate the resistance of a wire. A variable resistor is used to vary the current flowing. You can take pairs of readings of current and voltage. Table 1 shows some typical results.

Table 1

Current / A	0.02	0.04	0.06	0.08	0.1	0.12
Voltage / V	0.5	1.0	1.5	2.0	2.5	3.0

You can then plot a graph to show how the current flowing through the resistor depends on the voltage across it. Figure 5.4 shows the points plotted. This is called a **current–voltage graph**. A straight line has been drawn through the points, which passes through the origin. This shows that the current is *directly proportional* to the voltage. If the direction of the voltage is reversed, the graph has the same shape. The resistance is the same when the current direction is reversed.

When a resistor or wire behaves in this way, it is said to obey **Ohm's law**. This states that:

> For some resistors, at constant temperature, the current through the resistor is proportional to the voltage across it.

The resistor in this case is said to be **ohmic**.

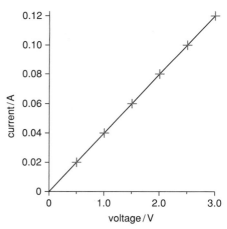

Figure 5.4 A current–voltage graph.

The resistance can be calculated using any voltage and the corresponding current:

$$R = \frac{V}{I} = \frac{20}{0.08} = 25\ \Omega$$

Check that the resistance is the same using another pair of voltage and current readings.

■ The filament lamp

The circuit in Figure 5.3, with the test wire replaced by a filament lamp, can be used to investigate how the current through a filament lamp changes with the applied voltage. The results of the investigation are plotted in a graph, which is shown in Figure 5.5. The line is not straight – it curves away from the current axis (y-axis). The current is not proportional to the applied voltage. So the filament lamp does not obey Ohm's law. We describe the lamp as a **non-ohmic** resistor.

As the current increases, the resistance gets larger. The temperature of the filament increases when the current increases. So we can conclude that the resistance of the filament increases as the temperature increases.

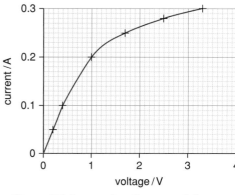

Figure 5.5 A current–voltage graph for a filament lamp.

PRACTICAL

Make sure you can describe an experiment to investigate how the current for a filament lamp or diode changes as the applied voltage changes.

■ The diode

A similar investigation can be carried out for a diode. Figure 5.6 shows a current–voltage graph for a diode.

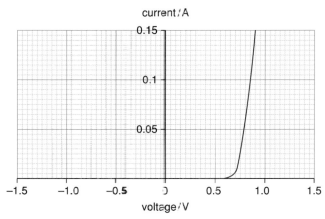

Figure 5.6 A current–voltage graph for a diode; the current only flows for a positive or forwards voltage.

A diode is a component that allows current to flow through it in only one direction. For a 'forward' voltage, current starts to flow when the voltage reaches about 0.7 V. When the voltage is 'reversed', current does not flow at all.

A light-emitting diode (LED) lights up when a current flows through it. This is useful because it allows an LED to be used as an indicator – to show us that a small current is flowing.

■ Changing resistance

Some resistors change their resistance as they react to their surroundings. The resistance of a **thermistor** decreases as the temperature increases. You can control its temperature by putting it into a beaker of warm or cold water, as in Figure 5.7.

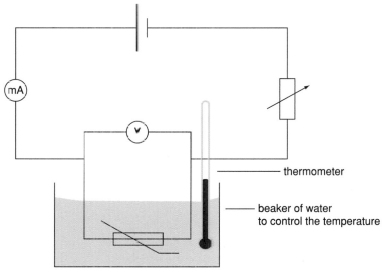

Figure 5.7 Investigating how the resistance of a thermistor changes with temperature.

Figure 5.8 shows how one type of thermistor's resistance changes as the temperature changes.

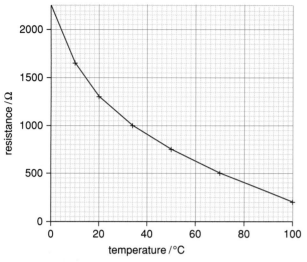

Figure 5.8 A graph to show how the resistance of a thermistor changes with temperature.

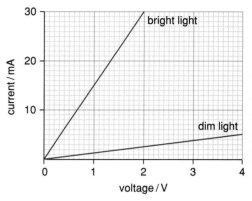

Figure 5.9 A current–voltage graph for a light-dependent resistor in bright and dim light.

The resistance of a **light-dependent resistor** (LDR) changes as the light intensity changes. In the dark the resistance is high but in bright light the resistance of an LDR is low. This is shown in Figure 5.9. A higher current flows through the resistor in bright light because the resistance is lower.

■ Adding resistance

When you add resistors in series you increase the resistance. Here is a simple example. You place a 6 Ω, an 8 Ω and a 12 Ω resistance in series. What is the total resistance? The answer is 26 Ω. You just add up the resistors, as each one limits the current flow.

STUDY QUESTIONS

1 Explain what is meant by an ohmic resistor.
2 This question refers to Figure 5.3. Explain what happens to the current through the ammeter when you increase the resistance of the variable resistor.
3 Figure 5.5 shows the current–voltage graph for a filament lamp.
   a) Calculate the resistance of the filament when the applied voltage is:
      i) 1 V
      ii) 3 V.
   b) Explain what causes this resistance to change.
4 Figure 5.9 shows two current–voltage graphs for an LDR in dim and bright light. Calculate the resistance of the LDR in:
   a) bright light
   b) dim light.

5 a) Draw a circuit diagram to show a cell, a 1 kΩ resistor, and an LED used to show that there is a current flowing through the resistor.
   b) Draw a circuit diagram to show how you would investigate the effect of light intensity on an LDR.
6 The table shows the values of current, voltage and resistance for five resistors, A, B, C, D and E. Use the equation $R = V/I$ to fill in the missing values.

Resistor	Current / A	Voltage / V	Resistance / Ω
A	0.4	12.0	
B		36.0	216
C	0.002		5000
D	10.0	230	
E		115	460

2.6 Current and voltage rules

Some decorative lights are wired in series and some are wired in parallel. Which method is suitable for each of the examples in Figure 6.1? What are the advantages of using a parallel circuit and what are advantages of using a series circuit?

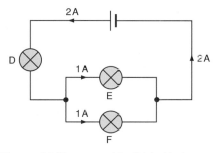

Figure 6.2 A series circuit.

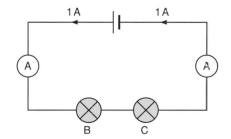

Figure 6.3 The current is divided between two lamps E and F in a parallel circuit.

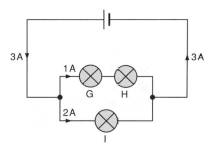

Figure 6.4 A parallel circuit with unequal branches.

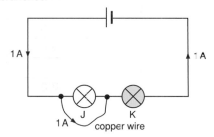

Figure 6.5 A short circuit.

Figure 6.1 (a) These small decorative lights are used to light up lots of trees in the street.

(b) These bright decorative lights spread light around the tree and its surroundings.

Current paths

Figure 6.2 reminds you of the rules about a **series** circuit. In this case the current in the circuit is 1 A. It is the same in each part of the circuit. So the current is 1 A in each of the lamps B and C, and 1 A through both ammeters and the cell. A circuit cannot lose current – in every circuit the current leaving the cell is the same as the current returning to the cell.

Figure 6.3 shows a circuit with branches in it. In this case, 2 A leaves the cell and passes through lamp D. Then, the current splits equally through the identical lamps E and F, and a current of 2 A returns to the negative terminal of the cell. When the current splits between two lamps in this way, we say they are in **parallel**.

The current does not always split equally. Figure 6.4 shows another parallel circuit with three identical lamps. More current flows through lamp I than through lamps G and H. Lamp I provides a lower resistance path. The sum of the currents going in the two parallel paths is 3 A – the same as the current flowing out of and back into the cell.

Figure 6.5 shows an example of a **short circuit**. A copper wire placed across lamp J provides a very low resistance path, so virtually no current flows through the lamp; it all flows through the wire. Lamp J does not light up.

Current rules

The current is the same in all parts of a series circuit.

The same current flows into a junction as comes out of the junction.

■ Adding the voltage

Figure 6.6 shows a car headlamp connected to a 12 V car battery. The battery is the provider of energy in the circuit and the lamp transfers that energy to heat and light. The voltage across the lamp is the same as the battery voltage.

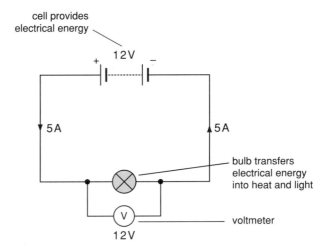

Figure 6.6

EXAM TIP

Remember: voltage is a measure of energy provided by a cell.

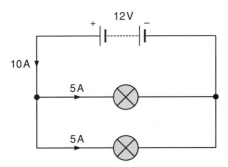

Figure 6.7 A circuit to supply two headlamps from a car battery.

In Figure 6.7 two headlamps are connected in parallel to the car battery; a current of 5 A flows through each. The voltage across each lamp is 12 V because both lamps are connected directly to the battery.

Figure 6.8 can help you understand why the voltage is the same across each headlamp. The voltage is like an 'electrical pressure'. The pressure on the water in each pipe from the water tank in Figure 6.8 is the same. The water tank empties more quickly when water flows through two pipes rather than one. The same idea works for the headlamps in a car. The battery loses energy more quickly when two lamps are on rather than one.

In Figure 6.9 two identical bulbs are connected in series to the car battery. In this example each bulb has a voltage of 6 V across it. As the current flows through the bulbs, it transfers half its energy to each bulb.

Figure 6.8 The pressure on the water in each pipe is the same. These pipes are parallel, like two headlamps connected in parallel.

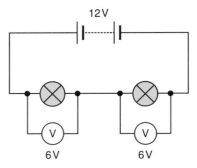

Figure 6.9 Each voltmeter reads 6 V.

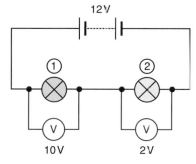

Figure 6.10 The brighter bulb gets the larger voltage.

The voltages do not always split equally. In Figure 6.10, bulb 1 has a larger resistance than bulb 2. There is a larger voltage across bulb 1 than across bulb 2. The current transfers more of its energy to bulb 1, so it is the brighter bulb.

Voltage rules

> The voltage across electrical components in parallel is the same.
>
> The sum of the voltages across electrical components in series adds up to the battery voltage.

■ Uses of parallel circuits

- Light bulbs in a car are placed in parallel across a 12 V battery. Each bulb is designed to work on 12 V. If the bulbs are placed in series they get less than their operating voltage.
- All domestic appliances are designed to work at mains voltage (about 230 V or 120 V in most countries). By putting them in parallel, domestic appliances receive the full mains voltage and can be independently controlled.
- Voltmeters are placed in parallel with appliances to measure the voltage across them.

■ Uses of series circuits

- Decorative lights are an example of a string of small bulbs placed in series. The bulbs are designed to work on low voltages so they share the mains voltage. They can all be turned off with the same switch.
- A switch is placed in series with a light to turn it on and off.
- An ammeter is placed in series with a resistor to measure the current through it.
- A resistor is placed in series with a component such as a diode or thermistor to protect it from overheating.
- A fuse is placed in series with a domestic appliance to protect it. The fuse melts if the current is too large.

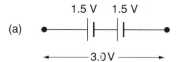

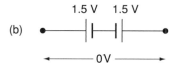

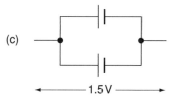

Figure 6.11 Combining cells.

■ Cells and batteries

A battery consists of two or more electrical cells. Figure 6.11 shows three ways in which two cells may be connected.

In series:

a) the voltages add up to produce a larger voltage, provided the cells 'face' the same way;

b) if the cells face in opposite directions the resultant voltage is zero.

In parallel:

c) the voltage produced by the two cells is still 1.5 V, but the battery behaves likes a larger cell, so energy can be provided for longer.

STUDY QUESTIONS

1 Which current in the diagram below is the largest, *p, q* or *r*? Which is the smallest?

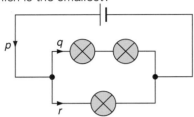

2 Copy the diagrams below and mark in the missing values of current.

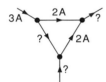

3 In the circuit shown in the diagram, each cell provides a voltage of 1.5 V.

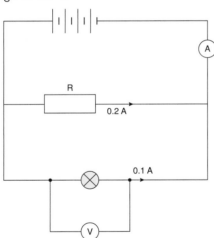

a) What is the total voltage provided by the battery?
b) What is the reading on the voltmeter?
c) What is the current through the ammeter?
d) Calculate the resistance of the lamp.

4 A set of decorative lights has 40 identical lamps connected in series.

Each lamp is designed to take a current of 0.1 A. The set of lights plugs directly into the 230 V mains electricity supply.
a) Write down an equation that links voltage, current and resistance.
b) What is the voltage across one of the lamps?
c) Calculate the resistance of one lamp.
d) Calculate the resistance of the 40 lamps in series.
e) What is the power transformed by the 40-lamp set?

5 The circuit diagram shows a 16 Ω resistor in series with a component X.

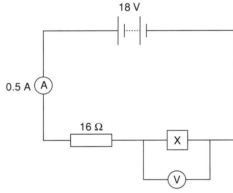

a) Calculate the voltage across the 16 Ω resistor.
b) What is the voltage across the component X?
c) Now calculate the resistance of X.

6 The diagram shows six elements of a car rear-window heater, which are connected in series to a 12 V car battery. The resistance of each element is 2.5 Ω.

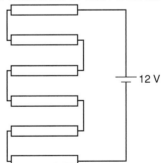

a) Calculate the total resistance of the heater.
b) Calculate the current flowing through the heater.
c) Use the formula: power = voltage × current to calculate the power generated by the heater.
d) A student suggests that the power could be increased by using elements with a greater resistance. A second student suggests that using less resistance would be better because the current would be larger. Who is correct?
e) The elements of some car rear-window heaters are connected in parallel. Suggest an advantage of this different arrangement.

2.7 Circuit calculations

In the previous chapters you have learnt the basic rules about electrical circuits. The best way to make sure that you have understood them is to practise by solving problems. In this chapter, some examples are given, but most of the work is to be done by you.

■ Resistance, voltage and current calculations

You can compare the value of two resistors using an ammeter and a cell; the larger resistor lets less current through. In Figure 7.1(a) the cell pushes a current of 1 A through a 6 Ω resistor; in Figure 7.1(b) the same cell pushes a current of 2 A through a second resistor whose value is not known. Because the current is more than 1 A, the second resistor must have a resistance less than 6 Ω. Can you explain why it is a 3 Ω resistor?

The value of a resistor may be calculated using an ammeter and a voltmeter; for example, in Figure 7.2.

$$R = \frac{V}{I}$$
$$= \frac{10\ V}{2\ A}$$
$$= 5\ \Omega$$

More complicated problems may be solved with the help of the current and voltage rules in Chapter 2.6. For example, you might be asked to calculate the cell voltage in Figure 7.3.

The current flowing through the 12 Ω resistor is:

$$I = \frac{V}{R}$$
$$= \frac{6\ V}{12\ \Omega}$$
$$= 0.5\ A$$

The voltage across the 6 Ω resistor is:

$$V = I \times R$$
$$= 0.5\ A \times 6\ \Omega$$
$$= 3\ V$$

The cell voltage is the sum of the voltages across the two resistors, which is 9 V.

■ Power calculations

Similar care needs to be taken to calculate the power developed in a resistor. For example how much power is produced by the 3 Ω resistor in Figure 7.4?

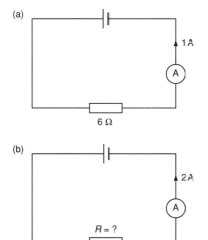

(a)

(b)

1 A

2 A

6 Ω

R = ?

Figure 7.1

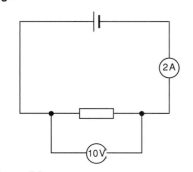

2 A

10 V

Figure 7.2

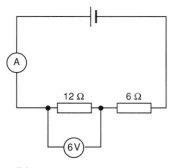

A

12 Ω   6 Ω

6 V

Figure 7.3

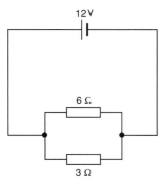

12 V

6 Ω

3 Ω

Figure 7.4

Each resistor has 12 V across it. So the current through the 3 Ω resistor is:

$$I = \frac{12V}{3\,\Omega}$$

$$= 4\,A$$

So the power developed is:

$$P = 12\,V \times 4\,A$$

$$= 48\,W$$

STUDY QUESTIONS

1 The cells in Figures 7.5 to 7.8 are identical; the ammeter in Figure 7.5 reads 1 A.
   a) Calculate the missing values, A_1, A_2 and R_1.
   b) You decide to replace the two resistors in Figure 7.8 with a single resistor. What value are you going to choose? Explain your answer.
   c) Explain how you would use an ammeter and a cell to compare the value of two resistors.

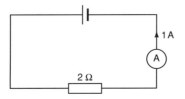

Figure 7.5

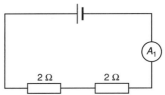

Figure 7.6

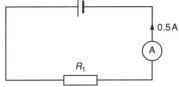

Figure 7.7

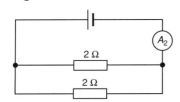

Figure 7.8

2 For each of Figures 7.9–7.13, state which is the larger of R_1 and R_2.

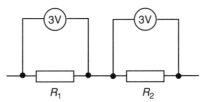

Figure 7.9

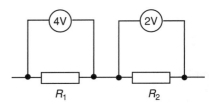

Figure 7.10

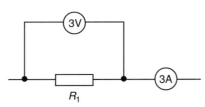

Figure 7.11 Both voltmeters read the same.

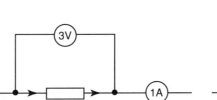

Figure 7.12 Both ammeters read the same.

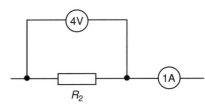

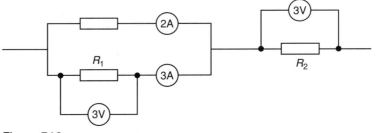

Figure 7.13

STUDY QUESTIONS

3 For each of the circuits in Figures 7.14–7.23, calculate the unknown ammeter or voltmeter readings or missing resistances.
a) Find V_1, V_2 and A in Figure 7.14.
b) Find V_1, V_2 and A in Figure 7.15.
c) Find V_1, V_2 and A in Figure 7.16.
d) Find V_1 in Figure 7.17.
e) Find R and A in Figure 7.18.
f) Find R in Figure 7.19.
g) Find V_1, V_2, A_1 and A_2 in Figure 7.20.
h) Find A_1, A_2 and V in Figure 7.21.
i) Find R_1, R_2 and A_2 in Figure 7.22.
j) Find V in Figure 7.23.

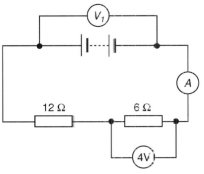

Figure 7.17

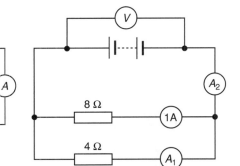

Figure 7.21

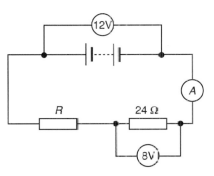

Figure 7.18

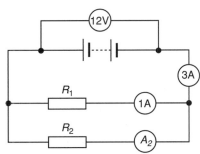

Figure 7.22

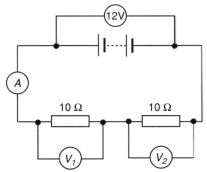

Figure 7.14

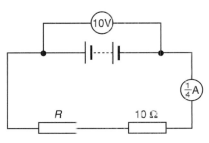

Figure 7.19

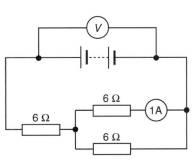

Figure 7.23

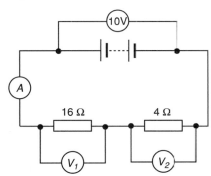

Figure 7.15

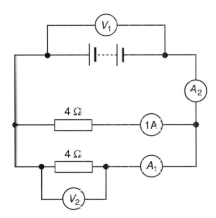

Figure 7.20

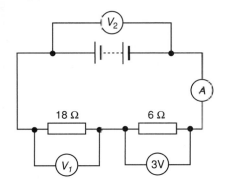

Figure 7.16

2.8 Electric charge

Figure 8.1 This motorbike has been electroplated with chromium, to make it attractive.

Electroplating with metals is a common industrial process. How does electroplating work?
Give two more examples of the use of electroplating.

■ A flow of charge

The apparatus in Figure 8.2 is being used to demonstrate the nature of an electric current. A high-voltage power supply has been used to charge two electric plates. The plate on the right has positive charge and the plate on the left has negative charge. A suspended ball, coated in conducting paint, bounces backwards and forwards between the plates.

When the ball touches the negative plate it becomes negatively charged. It is repelled from the negative plate and attracted to the positive plate, so the ball moves to the right. When the ball touches the positive plate it becomes positively charged. Now the ball is pushed to the left.

A sensitive ammeter, which is connected between the electrical supply and the plates, registers a small current.

> A current is a flow of electric charge.

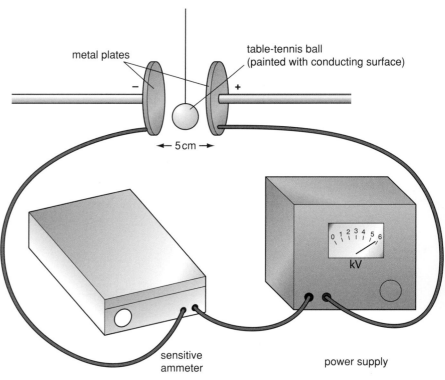

Figure 8.2 Demonstrating that current is a flow of charge.

■ Positive and negative charge

The origin of charge is to be found within atoms. The nucleus of an atom contains protons, which carry one positive charge. The positive charge on the protons is balanced by an equal number of electrons, which carry one negative charge each. You can read more about the charges in atoms in the next chapter in this section, or in Chapter 7.1.

Electrons are very small particles that can be removed or added to an atom relatively easily. Moving electrons carry electric currents.

■ Which materials conduct electricity?

Metals are good conductors of electricity. Most metal atoms have one or two loosely held electrons, which are free to move. When a cell is placed across a metal, the electrons inside it are attracted to the positive terminal of the cell and repelled from the negative terminal. So, electrons move around a circuit, carrying the electric current (Figure 8.3).

Currents can also be carried by positive or negative ions. When an atom gains an electron it is called a **negative ion**. When an atom loses an electron it becomes a **positive ion**. You conduct electricity because your body is full of ions. This is why you can get an electric shock.

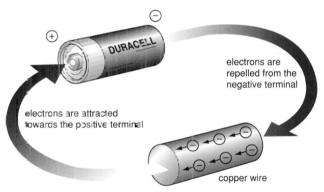

Figure 8.3 In a metal wire current is a flow of electrons.

Materials such as plastics and rubber do not have electrons that are free to move around. These materials do not conduct electricity. They are called **insulators**.

Table 1 Examples of conductors and insulators

Conductors	Insulators
Good:	rubber
metals, e.g. copper, silver, aluminium	plastics, e.g. polythene, PVC, Perspex
Moderate:	china
carbon	air
silicon	
Poor:	
water	
humans	

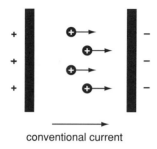

conventional current

(a) Positive particles can carry a current

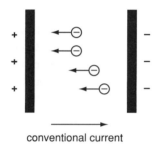

conventional current

(b) Electrons in a metal

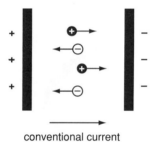

conventional current

(c) Positive and negative ions in a solution

Figure 8.4

■ Which way does current flow?

Before it was appreciated that currents are often carried by the flow of electrons, scientists decided to think of a current as the flow of positive charges. Therefore arrows on circuit diagrams show what we call the **conventional current** flowing from the positive terminal of a battery to the negative terminal. Figure 8.4 shows three examples of a conventional current flowing from left to right. The current can be carried either by positive particles moving to the right, or by negative particles moving to the left, or both.

■ Charge and current

The size of an electric current is the rate of flow of electric charge. In a metal the current is carried by electrons. So, we could measure the charge by counting the number of electrons flowing. When there is a current of 1 A, about six billion billion (6×10^{18}) electrons flow through the ammeter each second. This large number of electrons is one **coulomb** (1 C) of charge. So 1 coulomb per second is 1 amp.

The equation which links charge (Q), current (I) and time (t) is:

$$\text{current} = \frac{\text{charge}}{\text{time}}$$

$$I = \frac{Q}{t}$$

This equation can also be written as follows:

$$\text{charge} = \text{current} \times \text{time}$$

$$Q = I \times t$$

■ Defining the volt

You have already met the idea that voltage is a measure of energy. Voltage is *defined* as the energy transferred for each unit of charge that passes through a component such as a resistor. This allows us to define the volt:

A volt is one joule per coulomb.

$$\text{voltage} = \frac{\text{energy}}{\text{charge}}$$

A worked example will help you understand this idea.

Example. In Figure 8.5 a current of 2 A flows through a resistor. The battery has a voltage of 6 V. How much energy is transferred to the resistor in one minute?

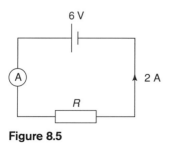

6 V

A

2 A

R

Figure 8.5

EXAM TIP

When calculating the current, remember to turn time in minutes into time in seconds.

First, we must calculate the charge that flows around the circuit in 1 minute.

$$\text{charge} = \text{current} \times \text{time}$$
$$= 2\,\text{A} \times 60\,\text{s}$$
$$= 120\,\text{C}$$

Then the energy is calculated using the equation:

$$\text{energy} = \text{voltage} \times \text{charge}$$
$$= 6\,\text{V} \times 120\,\text{C}$$
$$= 720\,\text{J}$$

STUDY QUESTIONS

1 You are given a number of materials that you have not seen before. Design an experiment to investigate which of the materials conduct electricity. You should explain clearly which electrical components you will use, drawing a circuit diagram to show how you will use these components. You should also explain how you will use your results to draw conclusions.

2 A student decides to copper plate a spoon by placing it in a solution of copper sulfate and passing a current through the solution. The process takes 80 minutes.
   a) Use the information in the diagram to calculate how much charge is passed by the battery during this time.
   b) How much energy is delivered by the battery during the process of electroplating the spoon?
   c) Draw a diagram to show the movement of ions through the copper sulfate solution during the copper plating process.

3 A camera flash bulb is lit for 0.02 s. During this time 0.1 C of charge flows through the bulb. Calculate the average current flowing through the bulb while it is lit up.

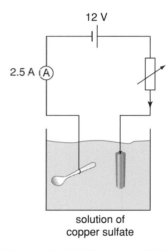

12 V

2.5 A (A)

solution of
copper sulfate

2.9 Electrostatics

Figure 9.1 Using a Van de Graaff generator to demonstrate that like charges repel each other.

The Van de Graaff generator in Figure 9.1 charges the girl up to 250 000 V. Why is it safe to use such a high voltage in these circumstances?

■ Electrical charge

Electricity was discovered a long time ago when the effects of rubbing materials together were noticed. If you pull off a shirt containing nylon you may hear the shirt crackle and in a dark room you may also see some sparks. A well-known trick is to rub a balloon and stick it on to the ceiling. You may have felt an electrical shock after walking across a nylon carpet. In these examples, you, or the balloon, have become charged as a result of **friction** (rubbing).

There are two types of electrical charge, positive and negative. A **positive** charge is produced on a perspex ruler when it is rubbed with a woollen duster. You can put **negative** charge onto a plastic comb by combing it through your hair.

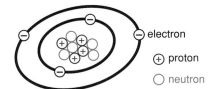

EXAM TIP

Like charges repel; unlike charges attract.

Some simple experiments show us that like charges repel each other, and unlike charges attract each other. These experiments are shown in Figure 9.2.

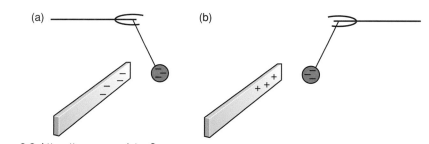

Figure 9.2 Attraction or repulsion?
(a) Like charges repel.
(b) Unlike charges attract.

■ Where do charges come from?

There are three types of small particle inside atoms. There is a very small centre of the atom called the **nucleus**. Inside the nucleus there are **protons** and **neutrons**. Protons have a positive charge but neutrons have no charge. The electrons carry a negative charge and they move around the nucleus. The size of the charge on an electron and on a proton is the same. Inside the atom there are as many electrons as protons. This means that the positive charge of the protons is balanced by the negative charge of the electrons. So the atom is neutral or uncharged (Figure 9.3).

- ⊖ electron
- ⊕ proton
- ○ neutron

Figure 9.3 This beryllium atom is neutral. Four negatively charged electrons balance four positively charged protons.

(a)

woollen duster

perspex ruler

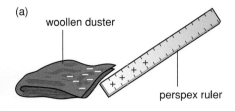

(b)

hair

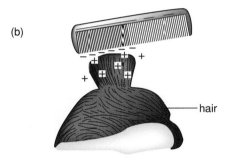

Figure 9.4 Charging by friction.

When you rub a perspex ruler with a duster, some electrons are removed from the atoms in the ruler and are transferred to the duster. As a result the ruler has fewer electrons than protons and so it is positively charged. But the duster has more electrons than protons and is negatively charged (Figure 9.4).

Picking up litter

You can use a plastic comb to pick up small pieces of paper. Figure 9.5 shows the idea. The comb is negatively charged after combing your hair (Figure 9.4(b)). When it is placed close to the paper, electrons in the paper are pushed to the bottom or repelled. The top of the paper becomes positively charged and the bottom negatively charged. The negative charges on the comb attract the top of the paper upwards. The comb's charges repel the bottom, but the positive charges at the top of the paper are closer to the comb. Therefore, the upwards force is bigger than the repulsive downwards force and the piece of paper is picked up.

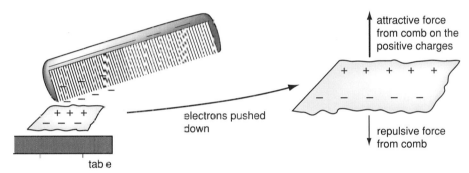

attractive force from comb on the positive charges

electrons pushed down

repulsive force from comb

table

Figure 9.5 Your comb can pick up small pieces of paper. The attractive force on the positive charges is larger than the repulsive force on the negative charges.

The gold leaf electroscope

The construction of a gold leaf electroscope is shown in Figure 9.6. A metal rod and cap are insulated from a metal box. A thin piece of gold leaf is attached to the end of the rod. When the cap is negatively charged, the electrons flow in the metal and the charge is spread out over the electroscope including the gold leaf. Like charges repel, so the leaf moves away from the rod next to it.

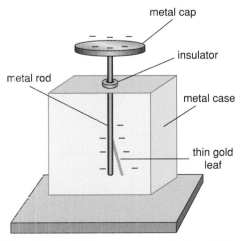

metal cap

insulator

metal rod

metal case

thin gold leaf

Figure 9.6 A gold leaf electroscope is used to investigate charges.

Figure 9.7 shows how a gold leaf electroscope is used to investigate the charges on two plastic rods. In Figure 9.7(a) the electroscope has been charged positively by connecting it to the positive terminal of a high-voltage supply. It has lost electrons and has an overall positive charge.

In Figure 9.7(b) a negatively charged rod is held near the cap. This repels some of the negatively charged electrons from the cap towards the leaf. This neutralises some of the positive charge near the gold leaf, so there is less overall positive charge there. The gold leaf falls.

In Figure 9.7(c) a positively charged rod is held near the cap. This attracts some electrons away from the gold leaf towards the cap, so the overall positive charge near the gold leaf increases. The gold leaf rises further.

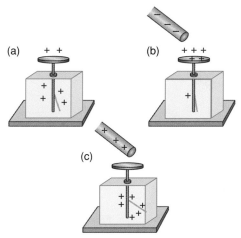

Figure 9.7 (a) Electroscope with positive charge. **(b)** A negatively charged rod repels electrons towards the leaf. Positive charge is neutralised and the leaf falls. **(c)** A positively charged rod attracts electrons from the leaf to the cap. This neutralises the cap and the leaf rises further as there is more positive charge near it.

 Now go through the Tutorial *Static electricity.*

STUDY QUESTIONS

1 a) The diagram below shows two small plastic balls. The balls are charged. What can you say about the charges on the balls?

  b) Draw the forces acting on each ball.

2 a) A plastic rod is rubbed and it becomes positively charged. Explain, in terms of electron movement, what has happened to some of the atoms in the rod.

  b) A plastic rod is rubbed and it becomes negatively charged. Explain, in terms of electron movement,

what has happened to some of the atoms in the rod.

  c) Explain why it is not possible to charge a metal rod that is earthed.

3 Design an experiment to investigate whether a plastic rod has a positive or a negative charge. You can use a gold leaf electroscope and a high-voltage power supply to help you. Describe how you will use the apparatus, and how the result of the investigation will allow you to come to a conclusion.

4 In this chapter you have read that electrons are removed from atoms by rubbing. An electron needs energy to remove it from an atom. Explain, using scientific terms, how rubbing provides this energy.

2.10 Electrostatics at work

During a thunderstorm, a large electrical charge builds up on the base of a cloud until it creates a conducting pathway through the air. The lightning flash occurs when the charge on the cloud flows to the ground or to a tall conducting object.

■ Spark hazards

A sailor who works on board an oil tanker has to wear shoes that conduct electricity. Metals are **conductors** of electricity. Materials like plastic and rubber do not conduct electricity; they are **insulators**. Wearing shoes with rubber soles on board a tanker could be very dangerous.

When the sailor moves around the ship in rubber shoes, charges can build up on him as he works. When he touches the ship, there will be a small spark as electrons flow to neutralise his body. Figure 10.2 explains this process. Such a spark could ignite oil fumes and cause an explosion. Some very large explosions have destroyed tankers in the past. So sailors wear shoes with soles that conduct. Now any charge on him flows away and he cannot make a spark.

Sparks are most likely to ignite the oil when it is being unloaded. To avoid this, the surface of the oil is covered with a 'blanket' of nitrogen. This gas does not burn, so **a** spark will not cause an explosion.

Figure 10.1 A lightning strike on the Eiffel Tower, photographed in 1919.

Figure 10.3 Troy Trice shows the football kit he was wearing when he was struck by lightning. Eyewitnesses say that the bolt burnt through his helmet and blew his shoes off. His breathing stopped, but he was resuscitated and has made a full recovery.

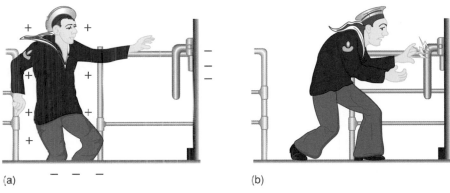

(a)   (b)

Figure 10.2 (a) Jack is positively charged. His charge attracts electrons on to the parts of the ship near to him.
(b) Jack touches the ship with his hand. Electrons flow onto him to neutralise his positive charge. The spark could cause an explosion.

■ Lightning

Large thunderclouds have strong convection currents inside them. Ice crystals are carried up and down by these currents and they can become charged as a result of friction. The bottom of a thundercloud gains a large negative charge.

When a thundercloud passes over a tall building or tree, it can discharge itself with devastating effect. A flash of lightning releases about 1000 million joules of energy. Figure 10.3 shows the sort of damage that lightning can cause.

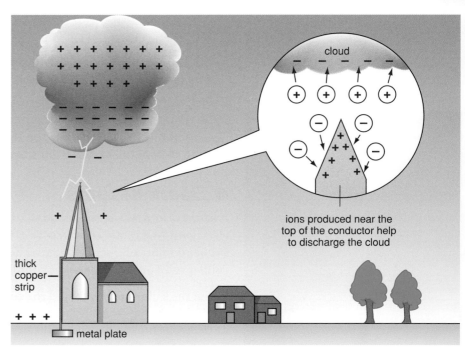

Figure 10.4 How a lightning conductor works.

A tall building is protected by a lightning conductor consisting of a thick metal strip on the outside of the building, which is connected to spikes at the top of the building and a metal plate in the ground (Figure 10.4). When a thundercloud passes overhead, the points of the lightning conductor become positively charged. The large size of the electric forces make positive and negative ions. These ions can help to discharge the thundercloud gradually, so if a lightning strike occurs it is likely to be less energetic and less damaging. Charge passes safely to the ground via the metal strip and plate.

■ Electrostatic precipitation

Many power stations burn coal to produce electrical energy. When coal is burnt a lot of soot is produced. It is important to remove this soot before it gets into the atmosphere. One way of doing this is to use an **electrostatic precipitator**. Inside the precipitator there are wires that carry a large negative charge. As the soot passes close to these wires the soot particles become negatively charged. These particles are repelled away from the

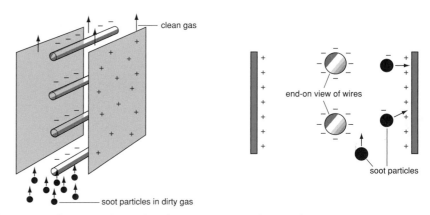

Figure 10.5 Soot particles in dirty fumes are removed in an electrostatic precipitator.

negative wires and are attracted to positively charged plates. The soot sticks to the plates, and can be removed later. Some large precipitators in power stations remove 30 or 40 tonnes of soot per hour.

■ Photocopying

Most offices use photocopying machines. The key to photocopying is a plate that is affected by light. When the plate is in the dark its surface is positively charged. When the plate is in the light it is uncharged.

An image of the document to be copied is projected on to the plate (Figure 10.6(a)). The dark parts of the plate become charged. Now the plate is covered with a dark powder, called **toner**. The particles in the toner have been negatively charged (Figure 10.5(b)), so the toner sticks to the dark parts of the plate, leaving a dark image. Next, a piece of paper is pressed on to the plate. This paper is positively charged, so the toner is attracted to it (Figure 10.6(c)).

Finally, the paper is heated. The toner melts and sticks to the paper, making the photocopy of the document (Figure 10.6(d)).

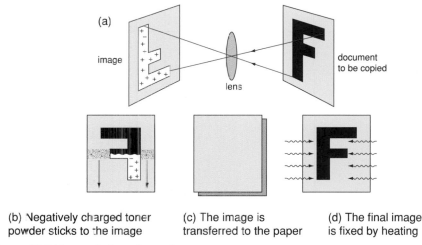

(b) Negatively charged toner powder sticks to the image

(c) The image is transferred to the paper

(d) The final image is fixed by heating

Figure 10.6 How a photocopier works.

■ Electrostatic paint spraying

Electrostatic paint spraying is used to ensure that cars and bicycles get an even coat of paint. Figure 10.7 shows the idea.

- The spray nozzle is charged negatively.
- Paint droplets leaving the nozzle become negatively charged. They repel each other and make a fine mist.
- The droplets are attracted to the positively charged car. The droplets get into places that are difficult to reach.

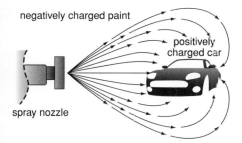

Figure 10.7 Using electrostatic forces to spray-paint a car.

STUDY QUESTIONS

1 When an aircraft is being refuelled it is fitted with a 'ground lug' to electrically connect it to earth. Explain why this is an important safety precaution.

2 a) Explain why a photocopier needs toner powder. Why does the powder need to be charged?
  b) When you get your photocopy out of the copier it is usually warm. Why?
  c) The lens in Figure 10.6(a) produces an image of the document, which is upsidedown and back-to-front. Explain why the final image is the right way round.

3 a) Explain this: When you polish a window using a dry cloth on a dry day the window soon becomes dusty. Why does this not happen on wet days?
  b) Cling film is a thin plastic material that is used for wrapping up food. When you peel the film off the roll it sticks to itself. Can you suggest why this happens?

4 Why should lightning conductors be:
  i) fixed to the ground
  ii) made of metal
  iii) pointed
  iv) at the highest point on a building?

5 a) Electrostatic charges can be dangerous. Name one example of a dangerous situation. Explain what we do to reduce the danger.
  b) Name a process in which electrostatics is put to good use in industry. Give an account of how the process works.

6 Explain in terms of electron movement, why the church spire (in Figure 10.4) becomes positively charged when the thundercloud is overhead.

7 A lightning flash delivers a charge of 5 C. The voltage between the cloud and Earth is 100 million volts.
  a) The flash lasts 0.002 s. Calculate the average current during this time.
  b) Calculate the electrical energy transferred by the flash.
  c) Explain what transfers of energy take place.

Summary

 Make sure you can answer all the questions in the *Interactive quiz*.

I am confident that:

- I can recall the hazards of electricity.
- I can describe the uses of insulation, double insulation, earthing, fuses and circuit breakers.
- I understand that current in a resistor results in an electrical transfer of energy and a rise in temperature.
- I can recall and use the relationship $P = I \times V$
- I can recall and use the relationship $E = I \times V \times t$
- I understand the difference between a.c. and d.c. current supplies.
- I can explain the uses of series and parallel circuits.
- I know that all parts of a series circuit carry the same current.
- I know that components in parallel have the same voltage across them.
- I can describe how current varies with voltage in wires, resistors, filament lamps and diodes.

- I understand how to investigate experimentally how current varies with voltage for a component.
- I understand how changing resistance in a circuit affects the current.
- I can describe the action of an LDR, an LED and a thermistor.
- I can recall and use the relationship: $V = I \times R$
- I understand that current is a flow of change.
- I can recall and use the relationship: charge = current × time
- I can recall that an amp is equivalent to a flow of charge of 1 coulomb per second.
- I can recall that the volt is a joule per coulomb.
- I can identify conductors and insulators.
- I know that insulators can be charged by friction.
- I can explain charging by the gain loss of electrons.
- I know like charges and unlike charges attract.
- I can recall the dangers of electrostatics.
- I can recall some uses of electrostatics.

Exam-style questions

1 The diagram shows an electric mains plug with a fuse and an earth wire.

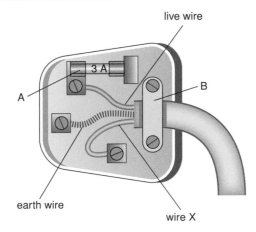

live wire

3 A

A

B

earth wire

wire X

a) Name the third wire X, and the parts labelled A and B. [3]

b) Why is the fuse put in the live wire? [2]

c) The diagram below shows a plug that has been wired dangerously. Explain how you would change the wiring to make it safe. [4]

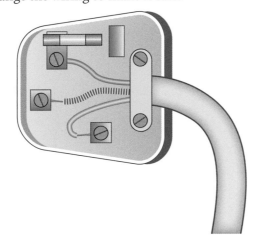

2 Using electricity can be dangerous.

a) Suggest two safety precautions you should take when putting a plug into a mains socket. [2]

b) Mains electricity provides an alternating current (a.c.). A battery provides a direct current (d.c.).

Describe the difference between a.c. and d.c. [2]

c) The photograph shows two mains plugs.

Mains plug A has a connection for an earth wire.

Mains plug B does not have an earth connection.

A   B

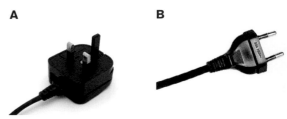

i) Describe how the earth wire can act together with a fuse as a safety device. [2]

ii) Explain why mains plug B can be safe to use even though it has no earth connection. [2]

d) A fuse is rated at 13 A. The mains voltage is 230 V.

Calculate the maximum power that can be supplied using this fuse.

State the correct unit in your answer. [3]

3 An electric iron has been wired without an earth connection. After years of use the live wire becomes loose and touches the metal iron.

a) A man touches the iron and receives an electric shock. Sketch a diagram to show the path of the current through him. [1]

b) Explain how an earth wire would have made the iron safe for him to touch. [2]

c) The mains voltage is 230 V. The man's resistance is 46 kΩ.

Calculate the current that flows through the man. [3]

4 A four-way adaptor is plugged into a mains supply of 230 V. The adaptor has a 13 A fuse. Four appliances may be powered from the adaptor in parallel. The table shows some appliances that might be plugged in to the adaptor and the current that each draws from the mains.

Appliance	Current / A
television	0.5
lamp	0.1
computer	0.3
radio	0.1
iron	4.0
hairdryer	2.5
heater	7.5

a) Explain why appliances are connected to the mains supply in parallel. [2]

b) Calculate the electrical power used when the television, computer, lamp and radio are all plugged in to the adaptor together. [3]

c) Explain what will happen if you plug the iron, the hairdryer and the heater into the adaptor. [2]

d) Explain why we are advised to plug heaters directly in to a mains socket, rather than using an adaptor. [1]

e) Explain why it is important to earth the metal heater. [2]

f) The hairdryer is double insulated. What does this mean? [2]

5 The circuit shown has four ammeters in it.

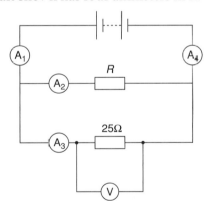

a) Ammeter A_1 reads 0.6 A, and ammeter A_2 reads 0.2 A. What do ammeters A_3 and A_4 read? [2]

b) Is the resistance, R, larger or smaller than 25 Ω? Explain your answer. [2]

c) Calculate the voltage across the voltmeter. Show your working. [3]

d) State the voltage of the battery. [1]

6 A student decides to investigate how the current flowing through a filament lamp changes with the voltage applied across it.

The student uses a 12 V battery, a filament lamp, an ammeter, a voltmeter, a variable resistor, a switch and some connecting wires.

a) Draw a suitable circuit diagram for the experiment. [3]

b) The student obtained the following results.

Voltage / V	0.0	1.0	2.0	3.0	4.0	6.0	8.0	10.0
Current / A	0.0	0.45	0.80	1.05	1.25	1.50	1.75	1.90

  i) Plot a graph of current against voltage. [4]

  ii) Use the graph to find the current when the voltage is 7 V. [1]

  iii) Calculate the resistance of the filament lamp for voltages of 2 V and 6 V. [3]

  iv) Explain why the resistance of the lamp changes as the current increases. [2]

  v) Calculate the power used by the lamp when the voltage across it is 10 V. [3]

7 The diagram shows three lamps connected in parallel to a 12 V battery.

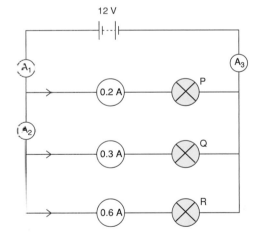

a) Calculate the currents through the ammeters A_1, A_2 and A_3 [3]

b) Calculate the resistance of lamp P. [3]

c) Calculate the power dissipated by lamp R. [3]

8 A filament lamp is connected to a 12 V battery. The current flowing through the lamp is recorded by a data logger when the lamp is switched on. The graph shows how the current in the filament changes with time.

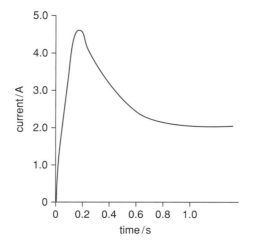

a) Describe how the current in the filament changes with time when it is switched on. [2]

b) Use the graph to determine:

   i) the maximum current in the lamp

   ii) the current after a time of 1 second. [2]

c) The resistance of the filament increases as its temperature rises. Use this information to explain the shape of the graph. [2]

d) The lamp is marked 12 V 24 W. Explain what these markings mean. [2]

9 A strain gauge is a device that detects the way an object changes shape when it is squashed, stretched or bent. The diagram shows how one is made. A thin piece of wire is set into a piece of flexible plastic. When the plastic is bent, the wire stretches. This causes the resistance of the wire to increase.

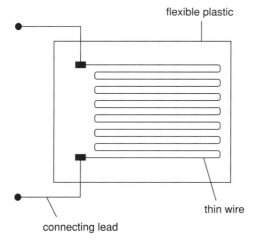

a) Draw a diagram to show how the resistance of the strain gauge can be measured using a battery, ammeter and voltmeter. [2]

b) Before the gauge is stretched it is connected to a 6 V battery. A current of 30 mA flows through it. Calculate the gauge's resistance. [3]

c) Explain why the resistance of the gauge increases when the wire is stretched. [1]

d) What happens to the current in the circuit when the wire is stretched? [1]

10 A student is investigating the relationship between voltage and current.

a) State the equation linking voltage, current and resistance. [1]

b) The meters show the current in a resistor and the voltage across it.

current (mA)   voltage (V)

   i) Copy the results table and add the readings on the two meters to the last column. [1]

Current / mA	0.20	0.60	1.01	1.14	1.81	2.22	
Voltage / V	1.0	3.0	5.0	7.0	9.0	11.0	

   ii) Use the data in the table to draw a graph of current against voltage. [5]

   iii) Circle the anomalous point on the graph. [1]

   iv) How did you decide that this point was anomalous? [1]

   v) Use your graph, or the table, to find the resistance of the resistor that the student used. [2]

c) The student wants to investigate the effect of changing light intensity on a circuit. She sets up equipment outside in a garden for an experiment lasting 24 hours. She uses the circuit shown in the diagram.

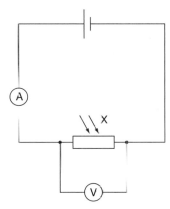

i) Give the name of the component labelled X.

[1]

ii) List the variables that the student should measure. [2]

iii) Explain why the student might need help to take all the readings for this investigation. [2]

iv) The graph below shows some results of the student's investigation.

Copy the graph and label both axes with appropriate quantities and units. [2]

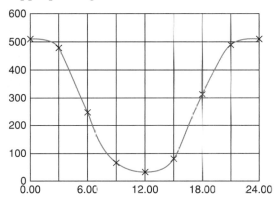

11 A student rubs a plastic rod with a cloth.

a) i) The plastic rod gains a negative charge. Explain why. [2]

ii) Describe experiments the student could do to show that there are two types of electric charge. [4]

b) The teacher uses a Van de Graaff generator to give another student a negative charge.

Use ideas about electric charge to explain why the student's hair stands on end. [3]

12 Burning coal in power stations produces soot, ash and waste gases.

The diagram shows an electrostatic precipitator, which collects the soot and ash particles.

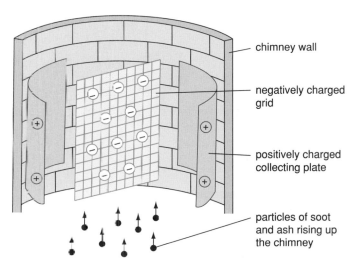

Explain how the electrostatic precipitator prevents the ash and soot escaping to the atmosphere. [4]

13 The diagram shows a car being painted by a process of electrostatic paint spraying.

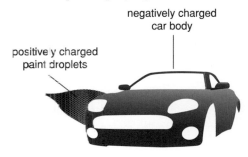

a) Explain why it is important that all the paint droplets are positively charged. [2]

b) Explain why the car must be charged negatively. [2]

14 The diagram shows a thundercloud.

a) Explain why the tree below has a positive charge. [2]

b) The base of the cloud carries a charge of 15 C. The voltage between the cloud and the ground is 800 000 kV.

   i) A flash of lightning discharges the cloud completely in 0.04 s. What is the average current that flows in this time? [3]

   ii) Calculate the maximum energy that could be delivered by this lightning flash. [3]

EXTEND AND CHALLENGE

1 a) The table shows the current in three different electrical appliances when connected to a 230 V a.c. supply.

appliance	current / A
kettle	11.5
lamp	0.05
toaster	4.2

  i) Which appliance has the greatest resistance? How does the data show this?

  ii) The lamp is connected to the mains supply using thin, twin-cored cable, consisting of live and neutral connections. State **two** reasons why this cable should not be used to connect the kettle to the mains supply.

 b) i) Calculate the power rating of the kettle when it is operated from the 230 V a.c. mains supply.

  ii) Calculate the current flowing through the kettle when it is connected to a 115 V mains supply.

  iii) The kettle is filled with water. The water takes 90 s to boil when working from the 230 V supply. Explain how the time it takes to boil changes when the kettle operates on the 115 V supply.

2 The graph shows how the current through a type of filament lamp depends on the voltage applied to it. Three of these lamps are connected into the circuit shown.

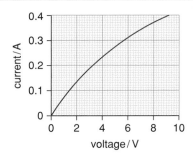

a) The circuit diagram shows 0.2 A flowing through lamp B. Use the graph to find the voltage across it.

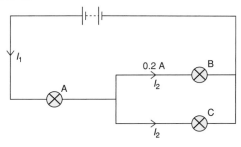

b) Calculate the resistance of bulb B.

c) Work out the currents in: (i) bulb C, (ii) bulb A.

d) Use your answer to part (c) (ii) to calculate the voltage across bulb A.

e) Now calculate the voltage of the battery.

3
Waves

WRITE • CONSIDER

Write down five examples of the use of waves. In each case explain how we use them and how information and energy is carried by the waves.

Sea waves carry a lot of kinetic energy. They also carry some information – about the weather conditions at sea. Energy to set these waves in motion may have travelled thousands of miles, but matter has not been transferred this distance.

Water waves are some of the waves we can see. We make use of many types of waves in our everyday lives, to communicate, to cook and in medicine.

By the end of this section you should:
- be able to describe longitudinal and transverse waves
- know the meaning of amplitude, frequency, wavelength and period of a wave
- know that waves carry energy and information
- recall and use the relationship wave speed = frequency × wavelength
- use the relationship frequency = $\dfrac{1}{\text{time}}$
- understand that waves can be diffracted, reflected and refracted
- understand the nature of light and other electromagnetic waves
- recall the uses and hazards of electromagnetic waves
- be able to construct ray diagrams to show reflection and refraction
- carry out calculations to determine the refractive index and critical angle of materials
- understand the nature of digital and analogue signals
- understand the nature of sound waves
- understand how to use an oscilloscope to investigate the shape of sound waves.

3.1 Introducing waves

Waves do two important things; they carry energy and information. You have seen ocean waves crashing into a sea wall at high tide. Those waves certainly carry energy.

When you watch television you are taking advantage of radio waves. These waves carry energy and information from the transmitting station to your house. Light and sound waves then carry energy and information from the television set to your eyes and ears.

■ Waves on slinkies

One of the best ways for you to learn about waves is to see them moving along on a stretched 'slinky' or spring. Figure 1.3 shows a slinky lying on the floor. When you move your hand from side to side some peaks move away from you along the slinky. Although the wave energy moves along the slinky, the movement of the slinky itself is from side to side. If you tie a piece of string to the slinky, you will see that it moves in exactly the same way as your hand did to produce the waves.

This sort of wave is called a **transverse wave**. The particles carrying the wave in the slinky move at right angles to the direction of wave motion. Water ripples on the surface of a pond and light waves are examples of transverse waves.

You produce a different kind of wave when you move your hand backwards and forwards at the end of the slinky (Figure 1.4). Your hand compresses and then expands the slinky. The wave is made up of compressions and expansions that move along the slinky. This time a piece of string tied to the slinky moves backwards and forwards along it. This sort of wave is called a **longitudinal wave**. The particles carrying the wave in the slinky move backwards and forwards along the direction of wave motion. Sound waves and ultrasound waves are longitudinal.

Figure 1.1 Aerials transmit radio waves. These convey energy and information.

Figure 1.2 Information is a major part of our lives – waves carry this information.

PRACTICAL

Make sure you have observed waves on ropes and slinkies, so that you understand how waves travel.

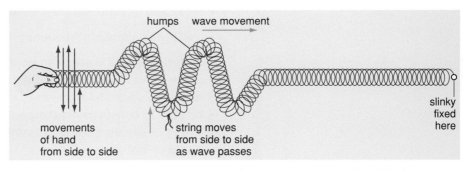

Figure 1.3 A transverse wave: energy is transferred in pulses along the slinky but matter is not transferred.

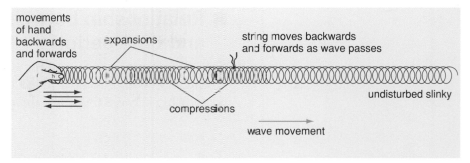

Figure 1.4 A longitudinal wave: energy is transferred in compressions and expansions (decompressions) along the slinky but matter is not transferred.

■ Describing waves

Figure 1.5 is a graph showing the displacement of a slinky coil along its length at one moment for a transverse wave. The arrows on the graph show the direction of the motion of the slinky coil; a larger arrow represents a larger speed.

EXAM TIP

Can you explain the difference between transverse and longitudinal waves?

- **Phase**. Points B and J are moving in phase. They are moving in the same direction, with the same speed. They also have the same displacement away from the undisturbed position of the slinky. F has been displaced in the opposite direction to B and J, and is moving in the opposite direction. F is out of phase with B and J. However, F moves in phase with N.
- The **wavelength** of a wave motion is the shortest distance between two points that are moving in phase. You can think of a wavelength as the distance between two 'humps'. We use the Greek letter λ (*lambda*) for the wavelength.
- The **amplitude** of a wave is the greatest displacement of the wave away from its undisturbed position. You can think of the amplitude as the height of a 'hump'. In Figure 1.5 amplitude is represented by 'a'.
- The **frequency**, f, of the wave is the number of complete waves produced per second. There are two complete waves in Figure 1.5 (A to I, and I to Q). The unit of frequency is waves per second or hertz (Hz); 1 kHz means 1000 Hz; 1 Mhz means 1 000 000 Hz.
- The **time period** of a wave, T, is the time taken to produce one complete wave.

EXAM TIP

Make sure you can define amplitude, wavelength, time period and frequency.

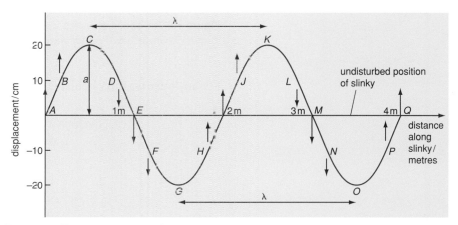

Figure 1.5 The displacement of a slinky along its length. The arrows on the graph show the direction of motion of the slinky.

■ Relationship between frequency and time period

If the frequency of a wave is 10 Hz, 10 complete waves are produced every second. Each wave is completed in a time period of 1/10 s. The general relationship between frequency and time period is:

$$\text{frequency} = \frac{1}{\text{time period}}$$

■ Wave velocity

The **velocity** of a wave, v, is the distance travelled by a wave in 1 second. The velocity of waves down a particular slinky is the same for all wavelengths. Figure 1.6(a) shows waves moving on a slinky with frequency 3 Hz and wavelength 0.4 m. In 1 second three waves have been produced, so the distance travelled by the first wave is $3 \times 0.4 = 1.2$ m. The wave velocity is 1.2 m/s. In Figure 1.6(b) 6 waves have been produced in 1 second and their wavelength is 0.2 m. So in 1 second the first wave travelled $6 \times 0.2 = 1.2$ m. The wave velocity is the same as before, 1.2 m/s.

EXAM TIP

Make sure you can recall an equation linking wave speed to frequency and wavelength.

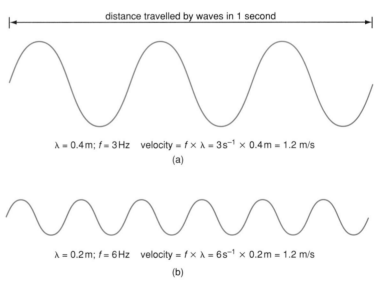

distance travelled by waves in 1 second

$\lambda = 0.4\,\text{m}; f = 3\,\text{Hz}$ velocity $= f \times \lambda = 3\,\text{s}^{-1} \times 0.4\,\text{m} = 1.2$ m/s
(a)

$\lambda = 0.2\,\text{m}; f = 6\,\text{Hz}$ velocity $= f \times \lambda = 6\,\text{s}^{-1} \times 0.2\,\text{m} = 1.2$ m/s
(b)

Figure 1.6 The speed of waves along a slinky is the same for all wavelengths; higher frequency waves have shorter wavelengths.

For any wave we can calculate the wave velocity using the formula:

$$\text{velocity} = \text{frequency} \times \text{wavelength}$$
$$v = f \times \lambda$$

STUDY QUESTIONS

1 Use diagrams to explain what is meant by (i) a longitudinal wave, (ii) a transverse wave. Give two examples of each.

2 How would you use a slinky to demonstrate that waves can transmit both energy and information?

3 Make a sketch of a wave to illustrate what is meant by the terms (i) amplitude, (ii) wavelength.

4 The time periods of two waves are (i) 0.1 s, (ii) 0.25 s. What are their frequencies?

5 a) The length of a railway carriage is 28 m. A passenger at a station counts ten carriages passing him in 14 seconds. How fast is the train travelling?

   b) Waves pass an anchored yacht at a rate of five crests every 20 seconds. The crests are separated by a distance of 7 m. Calculate (i) the frequency of the waves, (ii) the speed of the waves.

6 Copy Figure 1.6(a). Underneath it draw a wave travelling on the same slinky with a frequency of 5 Hz. What is the wavelength of this wave?

7 This question refers to the graph in Figure 1.5.

   a) What is the wavelength of the wave?

   b) What is the amplitude of the wave motion?

c) The frequency of the wave motion is 2 Hz. What is the time period of the wave?

d) Calculate the speed of the wave.

e) Give a point moving in phase with: (i) l, (ii) B, (iii) M.

f) Make a sketch to show what the wave shown in Figure 1.5 looks like a short time afterwards. Use the arrows showing the direction of movement of the particles to help you.

g) In which direction is the wave travelling?

8 A radio station produces waves of frequency 200 kHz and wavelength 1500 m.

   a) What is the speed of the radio waves?

   b) Another radio station produces waves with a frequency of 600 kHz. Assuming that these waves travel at the same speed as the other radio waves, calculate their wavelength.

9 Sound travels at a speed of 330 m/s in air.

   a) A sound wave has a frequency of 660 Hz. What is its wavelength?

   b) A sound wave has a wavelength of 0.2 m. What is its frequency?

3.2 Looking more closely at waves

The dish in Figure 2.1 transmits microwaves to a satellite. Why does the dish have to be so large? Its shape helps direct the beam – how?

Figure 2.1 A large satellite communications dish.

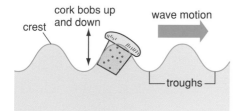

Figure 2.2 Ripples caused by a drop of water.

■ Ripple tanks

You can learn more about the nature of waves by studying ripples that move over the surface of water. It is easy to show that these ripples are transverse waves. If you look at a floating cork you will see it bob up and down as ripples travel along the surface of the water (Figure 2.3).

You can produce water waves in a ripple tank by lowering a dipper into the water (Figure 2.4). A motor vibrates the dipper up and down to produce waves continuously. A beam produces straight waves, and a small sphere produces circular waves. If you shine a light from above the tank you will see bright and dark patches on the screen below. These patches show the positions of the crests and troughs of the waves.

Using a stroboscope

Water waves move quite quickly and it can be difficult to see them. However, if you look through a rotating stroboscope you can make the waves appear

Figure 2.3 Ripples on water are transverse waves.

Waves in a ripple tank can be used to demonstrate wave properties.

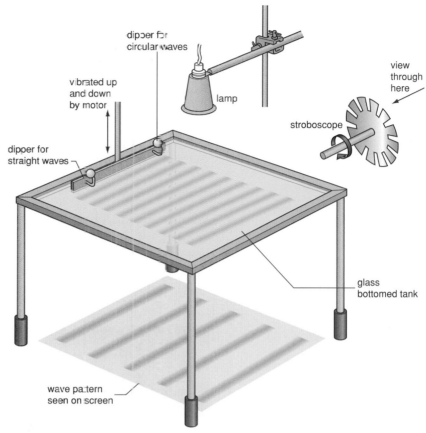

Figure 2.4 A ripple tank.

stationary. The stroboscope is a disc with 12 slits in it. If you rotate the disc twice a second you will see the ripple tank 24 times a second. The waves will appear stationary when the dipper produces waves with a frequency of 24 Hz. Each time there is a slit in front of your eye one wave has moved forwards to the position of the next wave.

■ Diffraction

Make sure you can explain what diffraction is.

When waves pass through a small gap, they spread out. This is called **diffraction**. You can see the diffraction of water waves in a ripple tank. Figure 2.5 shows you what happens when straight waves go through a series of gaps in barriers.

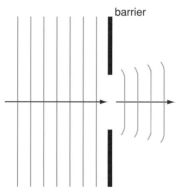

(a) Small wavelength, large gap
Figure 2.5

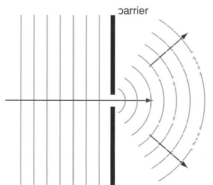

(b) Small wavelength, gap about the size of wavelength

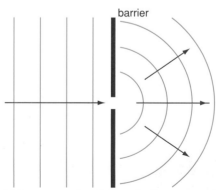

(c) Large wavelength, small gap

119

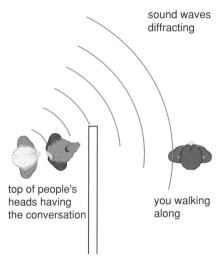

sound waves diffracting

top of people's heads having the conversation

you walking along

Figure 2.6 A 'bird's eye view' of a conversation overheard on the other side of a wall.

In Figure 2.5(a) the gap is large in comparison with the wavelength of the waves. The waves only spread out a little. In Figure 2.5(b) the gap is smaller. The waves spread out more. In Figure 2.5(c) the wavelength is larger than the gap and the waves now spread out completely.

Sound also diffracts. This tells us that sound is carried by waves. Figure 2.6 shows the sort of position you might find yourself in. You are walking down a corridor and you can hear two people talking through an open door or on the other side of a wall, but you cannot see them. The sound waves do not travel in a straight line. They spread out and change direction as they pass the edge of the wall. That is why you can hear them talking even though you cannot see them.

We also think that light is carried by waves. So why can't we see round corners? You cannot see the people talking in Figure 2.6, because light waves have very small wavelengths. This means that when light waves go through a doorway they hardly diffract at all. Sound waves have much longer wavelengths, so they diffract through the doorway.

Figure 2.7 In this photograph you can see water waves diffracting as they pass through a harbour entrance. Water waves have a large wavelength, and so they spread out a lot when they diffract through such a gap.

■ Diffraction of light

Figure 2.8 illustrates how light can be diffracted. A laser beam is directed towards a narrow slit and light spreads out. The illustration in Figure 2.9 shows the result. The wavelength of red light is about 640×10^{-9} m and the slit width is 0.01 mm. So the slit is about 16 times wider than the wavelength of light.

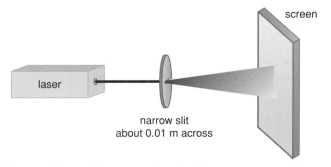

screen

laser

narrow slit
about 0.01 m across

Figure 2.9 Diffraction pattern.

Figure 2.8 Light also diffracts if a beam is directed through a narrow slit.

(a)

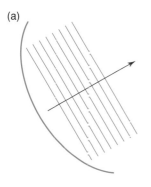

(b)

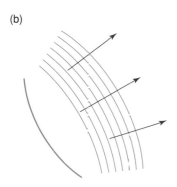

Figure 2.10 (a) A large dish produces a well-directed beam – little diffraction.
(b) With a small dish the waves diffract, so the beam is not well directed and energy is lost.

Design of satellite dishes

The chapter began with the question about a satellite dish – why does it have to be so large? Figure 2.10 gives the answer. If the dish has a large diameter (Figure 2.10(a)), the microwaves leaving it do not diffract much. This means that a well-directed beam of waves is sent out into space towards the satellite. If the dish is small (Figure 2.10(b)), the diffraction effects become significant. Waves spread out and energy is wasted as most of the beam misses the satellite.

Loudspeaker design

Figure 2.11 shows the design of a loudspeaker system. It has two speakers – a woofer and a tweeter. The woofer is the larger speaker; it is designed to produce the bass notes, which have a long wavelength. If the high-pitched notes were sent to the woofer you would only hear them when you were in front of the speaker. This is because they have a short wavelength (5 or 10 cm). They do not diffract well through the woofer as its diameter is too large. The small-diameter tweeter allows the short-wavelength waves to diffract and be heard in all directions.

Figure 2.11 A pair of loudspeakers.

STUDY QUESTIONS

1 Astronomers use radio telescopes to detect radio waves from distant galaxies. Some radio waves have wavelengths a few metres long. Radio telescope dishes can be as wide as 100 m across. This means that the radio waves are only diffracted by a small amount. Explain why.

2 In an experiment in a ripple tank, straight water waves are produced with a frequency of 20 Hz. The waves travel at a speed of 40 cm/s through a gap in a barrier of width 1 cm.
a) Calculate the wavelength of the waves.
b) Draw a diagram to show how the waves would spread through the gap. Explain how you decided what to draw.

c) Draw another diagram to show what happens when the gap is made 4 cm wide.

3 Explain why loudspeaker systems use two speakers: a woofer and a tweeter.

4 The red light used to produce the diffraction pattern in Figure 2.9 has a wavelength of 640 nm (640×10^{-9} m). Sketch a copy of the pattern and add a second pattern to show the diffraction of blue light, wavelength 480 nm, when it goes through the same narrow slit.

3.3 Electromagnetic waves

These people on the beach are exposed to several types of electromagnetic waves. Can you name four types of electromagnetic wave, some of which could be damaging their bodies?

Can you explain what happens to the sunbathers as time passes from morning to afternoon?

Figure 3.1 These sunbathers are exposed to several kinds of electromagnetic waves.

■ The electromagnetic spectrum

You will already have heard of radio waves and light waves. These are two examples of **electromagnetic waves**. There are many sorts of electromagnetic wave, which produce very different kinds of effect. Figure 3.2 shows you the full electromagnetic spectrum. The range of wavelengths in the spectrum stretches from 10^{-12} m for gamma rays to about 2 km for radio waves.

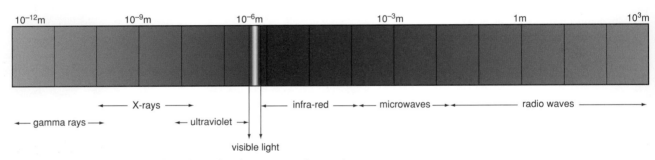

Figure 3.2 The range of wavelengths in the electromagnetic spectrum.

■ Electric and magnetic forces

Many waves that you are familiar with travel through some material. Sound waves travel through air; water ripples travel along the surface of water. Electromagnetic waves can travel through a vacuum; this is how energy reaches us from the Sun. The energy is carried by changing electric and magnetic forces. These changing forces are at right angles to the direction in which the wave is travelling. So electromagnetic waves are transverse waves (Figure 3.3).

■ Wave speed

Electromagnetic waves show the usual wave properties. They can be described by frequency and wavelength. In a vacuum all electromagnetic waves travel at the same speed of 3×10^8 m/s. However, electromagnetic waves travel at slower speeds when they travel in a material. For example, light travels at a slower speed in glass.

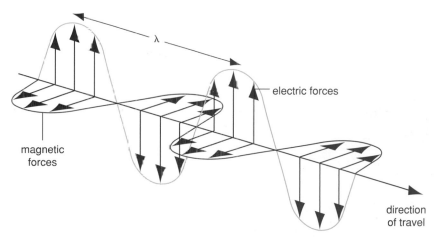

Figure 3.3 In an electromagnetic wave, energy is carried by oscillating electric and magnetic forces. These forces are at right angles to the direction in which the wave travels.

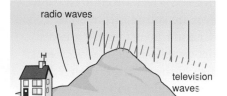

Figure 3.4 Long and medium wavelength radio waves will diffract around hills and houses. However, waves used for TV signals are of short wavelengths. These will not bend around hills so well; this house will have poor TV reception.

■ Radio waves

Radio waves are produced by high-frequency oscillations of electrons in aerials. Radio waves with wavelengths of a few hundred metres are used to transmit local and national radio broadcasts.

Radio waves with wavelengths of a few centimetres are used to transmit television signals and international phone calls. These short-wavelength radio waves are also known as microwaves. Microwaves are also used for mobile internet connection and satellite navigation. When you make a phone call to America, your radio signals are sent into space by large aerial dishes (see Figure 2.1). These signals are received by a satellite in orbit around the Earth. The signals are then relayed to another dish in America. Short wavelengths are used in international communications so that narrow beams can be directed into space (see page 121).

■ Microwaves

Microwaves have wavelengths between radio waves and infra-red waves; but it should be remembered that the distinction between various types of electromagnetic wave is fairly arbitrary. The short-wavelength radio waves described above could also have been described as microwaves.

The other well-known use of microwaves is to heat food in ovens. Microwaves of a particular wavelength are chosen that are absorbed by water molecules. Microwave cooking provides the advantage that the waves can penetrate to the middle of the food, thereby cooking the inside as well as the outside. This is much faster than the conventional method of cooking, where heat is conducted to the inside. Microwave ovens must be made of metal in order to trap the waves inside them; this is important to make sure we do not cook ourselves! Microwaves of certain wavelengths are a hazard that could burn us internally by heating up our body tissues.

■ Infra-red waves

Figure 3.5 A night image taken in infra-red light.

Infra-red waves have wavelengths between about 10^{-4} m and 10^{-6} m. Anything that is warmer than its surroundings will lose energy by giving out infra-red radiation. You lose some heat energy by radiation. You can certainly feel the infra-red radiation given out, or *emitted*, by an electric fire. Prolonged exposure of the skin to infra-red in sunlight can cause skin burns.

Infra-red photography can be used to measure the temperature of objects. The hotter something is, the more infra-red radiation it gives out.

■ Light waves

Light waves form the part of the electromagnetic spectrum to which our eyes are sensitive ('visible' light). Red light has a wavelength of 7×10^{-7} m and violet light a wavelength of 4×10^{-7}. Common uses of light waves include transmitting information along optical fibres (see Chapter 3.4) and taking photographs with cameras. Very bright light can damage the eye. It is more comfortable to wear sunglasses on a bright day and you must avoid looking directly at the Sun.

■ Ultraviolet waves

Ultraviolet waves have wavelengths shorter than visible light – approximately 10^{-8} m or 10^{-9} m. While infra-red waves are emitted from hot objects (1000 °C or so), ultraviolet waves are emitted from even hotter objects 4000 °C and above). The Sun and other stars are sources of ultraviolet 'light'. Exposure to ultraviolet waves can damage your eyes, including snow-blindness, which is sunburn of the retina. Prolonged exposure to ultraviolet light from the Sun can damage your skin and cause skin cancer. Some materials fluoresce when exposed to ultraviolet light. This can have applications in deterring crime (see Figure 3.7).

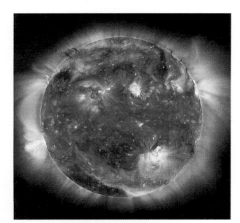

Figure 3.6 This is an ultraviolet image of the Sun. Very hot objects like the Sun produce these waves. Astronomers often 'see' what space looks like in wavelengths other than visible light. Imagine if our eyes detected ultraviolet rather than visible light – how different would the world look?

Figure 3.7 This man has been sprayed with 'smartwater'. Each batch of the water has a special DNA, which determines where a material has come from. The 'smartwater' shows up under UV light. Such materials are now widely used to mark property.

■ X-rays

X-rays have wavelengths of about 10^{-10} m. These rays can cause damage to body tissues, so your exposure to them should be limited. X-rays are widely used in medicine. X-rays of short wavelengths will pass through body tissues but will be absorbed by bone. Such rays can be used to take a photograph to see if a patient has broken a bone or has tooth decay.

Slightly longer wavelength X-rays are used in body scanning. These X-rays are absorbed to different degrees by body tissues, so doctors can build up a picture of the inside of a patient's body. This allows doctors to investigate whether a patient has a disorder in the body.

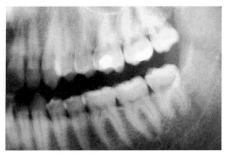

Figure 3.8 Dentists use X-ray photography to check on the health of teeth. X-rays allow dentists to see tooth disease or decay, which are not visible in an ordinary visual check-up.

EXAM TIP

Make sure you know and understand the uses and hazards of the seven types of electromagnetic waves listed here.

Gamma rays

Gamma rays are very short-wavelength electromagnetic waves that are emitted from the nuclei of atoms. Gamma rays are very penetrating and can be very harmful. They can cause mutations in cells leading to cancer. These rays have many industrial, agricultural and medical uses (see Section 7).

The discovery of infra-red and ultraviolet

This is an example of discovery by investigation. In 1800 William Herschel decided to investigate the temperature produced by each colour of the visible spectrum. Figure 3.9 shows how a prism can be used to split white light up into all the colours of the rainbow. Herschel put the bulb of a blackened thermometer in turn into each colour, noting that as he did so, the temperature increased towards the red end of the spectrum. He then put the thermometer just beyond the red end of the spectrum and noted that, although he could see no light, the temperature was even higher. He had discovered invisible heat rays, which we now call infra-red rays. 'Infra' means below – the rays are outside the red end of the spectrum.

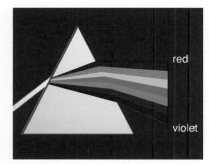

Figure 3.9 A prism splits white light up into the colours of the rainbow.

Inspired by Herschel, a year later in 1801, Johann Ritter investigated the other end of the spectrum. He investigated the effect of light on silver chloride, which was known to be blackened by sunlight. Ritter discovered that the chemical blackened more quickly as he moved towards the violet end of the spectrum. To his surprise, he discovered that the blackening effect was most pronounced just beyond the violet end. So he had discovered ultraviolet rays – 'ultra' means beyond.

 Now watch the animation *Uses and dangers of electromagnetic radiation*.

STUDY QUESTIONS

1 a) How does an electromagnetic wave carry energy? Draw a diagram to help explain your answer.
   b) Electromagnetic waves are emitted from objects when electrons oscillate rapidly backwards and forwards. How do you think electromagnetic waves are detected?

2 a) Why are short-wavelength radio waves needed for mobile phone communications?
   b) Give two reasons why microwave ovens are made from steel.
   c) Which electromagnetic waves cause (i) skin burns, (ii) skin cancer?
   d) Give three examples of how electromagnetic waves are used in your life every day.

3 In the table below you can see some data showing typical values of wavelengths and frequencies for different types of radio wave. The speed of radio waves is 300 000 000 m/s.
   a) Copy the table. Then use the equation $v = f \times \lambda$ to fill in the missing values.
   b) Which wave would you use for (i) a local radio station, (ii) television broadcasts to the USA? Explain your choice.

4 For each of the following types of electromagnetic wave, give an example of a use of the wave and a hazard posed by each: microwave, infra-red, ultraviolet, gamma ray.

Type of radio wave	Wavelength / m	Frequency / MHz
Long	1500	
Medium	300	
Short	10	
VHF		100
UHF		3000

(VHF = very high frequencies, UHF = ultra high frequencies)

3.4 Analogue and digital communications

In the 1820s, William Wordsworth would walk 12 miles from Grasmere to Keswick to see his friend Robert Southey. He would stay a week, before walking back home again. How far do you walk to see a friend? How do you keep in contact now?

Figure 4.1 William Wordsworth (1770–1850).

Figure 4.2 In the past telephone systems transmitted electrical signals through copper wires like these ones.

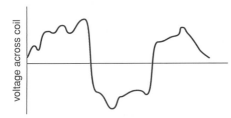

Figure 4.4 The electrical pulses produced by our voice in the mouthpiece make a continuously varying signal. This is called an analogue signal.

■ Analogue signals

Look at Figure 4.3. This shows you the principle of the telephone in your home, which runs on the landline. When you speak your voice produces sound waves, which cause pressure differences in the air. These pressure changes act on the mouthpiece of the telephone, making a cone move in and out. The movements of the cone squeeze some carbon powder. When the carbon is squashed, its electrical resistance becomes slightly less. This allows a larger current to flow from the battery. In this way, the information is carried along the wire by electrical waves.

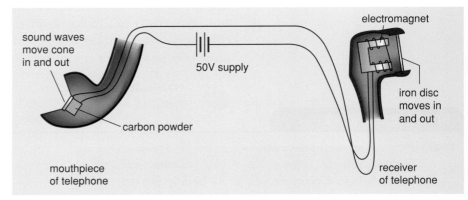

Figure 4.3 A conventional telephone system.

At the other end of the line, someone can listen to your voice. The electrical pulses are turned back into sound waves by the earpiece, which is like a small loudspeaker. The changes in current change the magnetising effect of an electromagnet. This moves a disc in and out to make sound waves. This is called an **analogue signal**, see Figure 4.4.

■ Optical fibres

Modern telephone systems transmit telephone messages by sending pulses of infrared light down glass fibres. **Optical fibres** have several advantages over the old copper wires:

- Optical cables are less bulky than copper cables. The resistance of a thick copper wire is less than a thin wire. So a thick wire has less resistance than a thin wire of the same length. This is why copper cables are so bulky; less energy is lost in a thick, low-resistance cable.
- More messages can be carried at the same time in an optical fibre.

Figure 4.5 Optical fibres are made from thin, flexible glass. Light which has been totally internally reflected emerges from the ends. Light travels along the entire fibre with little absorption. Modern telephone systems use optical fibres in place of copper wires.

- There is less 'crackle' on the line. A signal in one fibre does not affect its neighbour. In a copper wire, the current carrying one conversation can interfere with a conversation being carried by the current in a neighbouring wire.
- Less energy is lost in optical cables. Signals can travel 20 km along an optical fibre without the need for amplification; signals in copper wires need amplification every 2 km.
- Optical fibres are well suited to carrying digital communications (see below).

■ International phone calls

Overseas telephone calls are carried by microwaves (Figure 4.6). The microwaves are transmitted via a satellite. These waves are electromagnetic waves with a frequency of a few gigahertz (1000 million Hz). When you speak to someone via a satellite link, you will notice a delay before they reply. However, for some links undersea optical cables allow a quick connection.

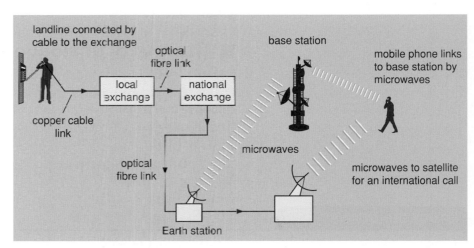

Figure 4.6 How different telephone systems link up. Landlines are connected with local and national exchanges using copper cables and optical fibres. Earth stations connect a country with satellites so that international calls can be made. Mobile phones connect with base stations by microwave links.

■ Digital communications

Figure 4.7 shows an analogue signal that can be transmitted along an electrical cable. But before the signal can be sent along an optical fibre it must be turned into a **digital signal**. A digital signal consists of a series of on-off pulses – like a code.

Analogue signals are converted to digital signals by using a process called pulse code modulation (PCM). The analogue signal is sampled 8000 times a second. In Figure 4.7, for example, the analogue signal might be split up into 35 separate samples. The voltage levels at time t_5, t_{10}, t_{15} and t_{20} are respectively, 8, 17, 22 and 30. Each of these voltage levels can now be turned into a binary code or number (see Table 1). Next to Figure 4.7 you can see the pulses that make up the digital signal. Once the signal has been sent to its destination it can be converted back into an analogue signal.

One significant advantage of using digital signals is that they are less affected by unwanted voltages that are picked up ('noise'). Stray voltages

Table 1 Voltage levels as binary codes

Number (base 10)	Binary code or number				
	(16s)	(8s)	(4s)	(2s)	(1s)
8	0	1	0	0	0
17	1	0	0	0	1
22	1	0	1	1	0
30	1	1	1	1	0

EXAM TIP

Make sure you can explain the advantage of digital communications.

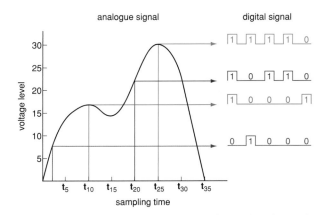

Figure 4.7 Converting an analogue signal to a digital signal.

distort analogue signals but have no effect on digital signals. This is because with a digital signal it is only necessary for the receiver to detect a pulse or the absence of a pulse.

■ The end of analogue TV

Digital signals are now widely used and countries began turning off analogue transmissions to TV sets in around 2010. Digital transmissions can carry much more information than analogue transmission – we now have hundreds of TV channels to choose from.

 Now go through the tutorial *Waves and communication*.

STUDY QUESTIONS

1 Draw a diagram similar to Figure 4.6 to show how a telephone call is transferred from your home landline to a friend in New York. How many different sorts of wave are used in this phone call?

2 Look at the analogue signal in Figure 4.7.
 a) Measure the voltage levels at sample times (i) t_{15} (ii) t_{30}.
 b) Convert these voltage levels to the appropriate binary code (see Table 1 for how it is done).

c) Explain why music needs a higher frequency of sampling than speech.

3 In the diagram you can see two electrical signals (i) and (ii) which leave A and travel to B. The digital signal is sent down an optical fibre, and the analogue signal sent down a copper cable.
 a) Explain which is the analogue signal and which the digital signal.

b) Both signals pick 'noise' and lose energy.
 i) What it meant by 'noise'?
 ii) Why do the signals lose energy?
 iii) Why does the analogue signal lose more energy than the digital signal a long the same length of cable or fibre?

c) X and Y are amplifiers which increase the energy of the signal. Look at the shape of the signals at C.
 Use the diagram to explain two advantages of using digital signals over analogue signals.

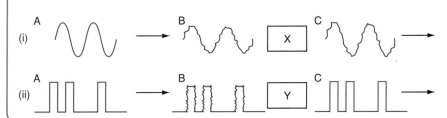

3.5 Rays and shadows

Figure 5.1 A partial lunar eclipse.

In Figure 5.1, the upper left side of the Moon has entered the darkest part of the Earth's shadow (the umbra) and the red tint is due to the filtering effect of the Earth's shadow – the same effect can be seen as the Sun sets. What causes this lunar eclipse?

■ Shadows and eclipses

Shadows are formed when something blocks the path of light. In Figure 5.2 you can see a piece of card held in front of a small source of light. Some light misses the card and travels on, in a straight line, to the screen. A sharp shadow is formed on the screen behind the card.

Not all shadows are so sharp. If the source of light is large then the shadows have two parts. In the middle of the shadow there is a dark part called the **umbra**. Around the edges of the shadow there is a lighter region called the **penumbra**. A good example of the shadow formation is provided by eclipses of the Sun and Moon.

EXAM TIP
Light travels in straight lines – we represent this with light rays.

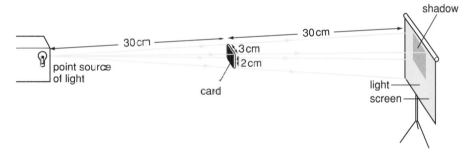

Figure 5.2 Forming a sharp shadow.

SAFETY

Do not look directly at an eclipse of the Sun. Take advice from your teacher before you view an eclipse.

An eclipse of the Sun (a solar eclipse) occurs when the Moon passes between the Earth and the Sun. The Moon is a lot smaller than the Sun but it is closer to us. It is just possible for the Moon to cover the Sun completely. When this happens there is a **total eclipse** of the Sun. During a total eclipse the sky goes black and it is possible to see stars. It is only possible to see a total eclipse of the Sun if you are in the umbra of the shadow (Figure 5.3). If you are inside the penumbra of the shadow you will see a **partial eclipse** of the Sun. Only part of the Sun is covered during a partial eclipse.

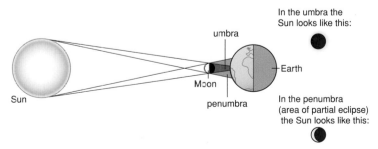

Figure 5.3 An eclipse of the Sun.

PRACTICAL

You can learn about light rays travelling in straight lines by making a pinhole camera.

An eclipse of the Moon (a lunar eclipse) happens when the Moon passes behind the Earth and into the Earth's shadow (Figure 5.4).

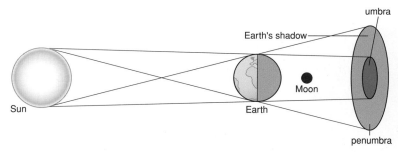

Figure 5.4 An eclipse of the Moon.

■ The pinhole camera

You can make a simple pinhole camera out of a cardboard shoe box. A small hole is put in one end. The other end of the box should be removed and a piece of tissue paper put in its place (Figure 5.5). If you now take the box outside on a bright day and point it at some trees, you will see an image of them on the tissue paper. If you want to take a photograph of the trees, you must use a lightproof box. The photograph is made by allowing the light to fall onto a piece of photographic paper instead of the tissue paper.

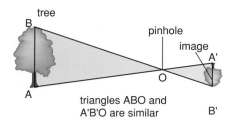

So $\dfrac{AB}{AO} = \dfrac{A'B'}{A'O}$

$AB = \dfrac{A'B'}{A'O} \times AO$

$\quad = \dfrac{10\ cm}{30\ cm} \times 30\ m$

$\quad = 10\ m$

Figure 5.6 Working out the height of a tree from measurements taken using a pinhole camera.

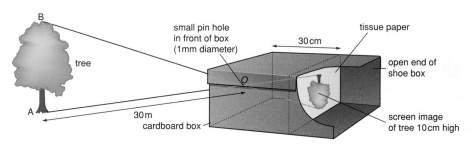

Figure 5.5 The principle of the pinhole camera.

The light from the trees travels through the pinhole in a straight line. This causes the image to be upside down. Provided the hole is small the image of the tree will be sharply defined. If the hole is too big the tree will look blurred.

The size of the image lets you work out the height of the tree, which is 30 m from the pinhole (Figure 5.6).

STUDY QUESTIONS

1 Work out the area of the shadow in Figure 5.2.

2 a) Draw diagrams to illustrate:
   i) an eclipse of the Moon
   ii) an eclipse of the Sun.
   b) The diagram below shows how an 'annular' eclipse of the Sun can happen. During an annular eclipse the Moon is further away from the Earth than in a total eclipse. Sketch how the Sun would appear when viewed from: (i) X and (ii) Y.

3 Venus moves in an orbit closer to the Sun than the Earth's orbit. In the diagram you can see Venus in three positions marked V_1, V_2, V_3. On the right, X, Y and Z show how Venus looked when seen on three occasions through a telescope. Match X, Y and Z to the positions of Venus.

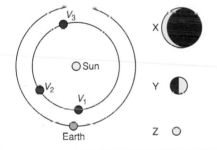

4 a) Explain why making the hole larger in a pinhole camera makes the image more blurred. Illustrate your answer with a diagram.
   A student used a pinhole camera to form an image of the Sun. She investigated how the size of the Sun's image depended on the size of the pinhole. The table below shows her results.
   b) Plot a graph of image size (*y*-axis) against hole diameter (*x*-axis).
   c) The student has made an incorrect measurement of the diameter of the hole. Which measurement is wrong and what should it have been?
   d) Use the graph to predict what the diameter of the Sun's image would be for a very small hole.
   e) Use your answer to part (d) and the extra data provided to calculate the Sun's diameter.
   • distance of Earth to Sun: 150 million km
   • length of pinhole camera: 500 mm

Diameter of Sun's image / mm	6.5	8.0	9.5	11.0	12.5
Diameter of hole / mm	2.0	3.5	4.0	6.5	8.0

3.6 Reflection

Light is a transverse wave, which can be reflected in the same way that water waves are reflected. Studying the way in which water waves behave in a ripple tank will help you to understand the way in which light behaves when it is reflected.

Figure 6.1 How does this trick work?

■ Reflection

In Figure 6.2 you can see a representation of waves approaching a straight metal barrier in a ripple tank. In the diagram, a line is drawn at right angles to the surface of the barrier. This line is called the **normal**. The angle between the normal and the direction of travel before reflection is called the **angle of incidence**, i. The angle between the normal and the direction of travel after reflection is called the angle of reflection, r. When waves are reflected, i always equals r.

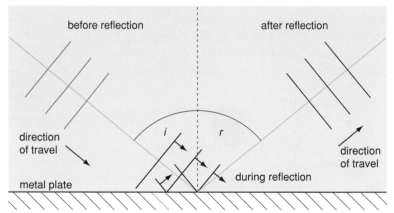

Figure 6.2 Reflection of waves off a plane surface; angle of incidence, $i =$ angle of reflection, r.

■ Reflection of light rays

You may use a mirror every day for shaving or putting on make-up. Mirrors work because they reflect light. In Figure 6.4 you can see an arrangement for investigating how light is reflected from a mirror. A **ray box** is used to produce a thin beam of light. Inside the ray box is a light bulb; light is allowed to escape from the box through a thin slit.

Before the light ray strikes the mirror it is called the **incident ray**. The **angle of incidence**, i, is defined as the angle between the incident ray and the normal. The **normal** is a line at right angles to the surface of the mirror. After the ray has been reflected it is called the **reflected ray**. The angle between the normal and this ray is called the **angle of reflection**, r. Light waves reflect in the same way as waterwaves.

There are two important points about reflection of light rays, which can be summarised as follows:

> The angle of incidence always equals the angle of reflection; $i = r$.
> The incident ray, the reflected ray and the normal always lie in the same plane.

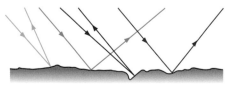

Figure 6.3 Light is reflected from a rough surface in all directions.

All surfaces can reflect light. Shiny smooth surfaces produce clear images. Figure 6.3 shows that light is reflected in all directions from a rough surface so that no clear image can be produced.

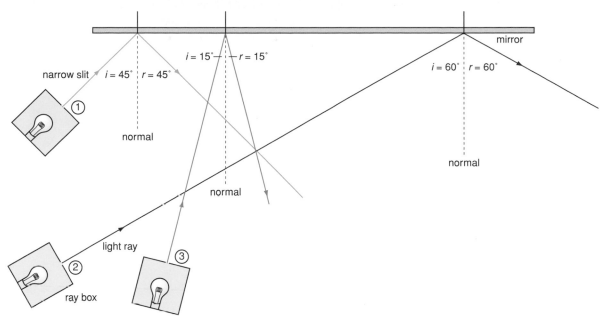

Figure 6.4 Reflection of light rays from a mirror.

■ An image in a plane mirror

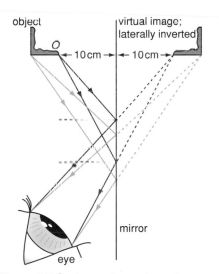

Figure 6.5 Seeing an image in a mirror.

We can use the rules about reflection to find the **image** of an **object** in a plane (flat) mirror. In Figure 6.5 the object is an L shape. Rays from the L travel in straight lines to the mirror where they are reflected ($i = r$). When the rays enter your eye they appear to have come from behind the mirror. This sort of image is called a **virtual image**. Your brain thinks that there is an image behind the mirror, but the L is not really there. You cannot put a virtual image onto a screen. An image that can be put onto a screen (like the one in a pinhole camera) is called a **real image**.

You can see in Figure 6.5 that the image appears to be the same distance behind the mirror as the object is in front of it. The image also appears to be back-to-front. You will have seen this effect when you look into a mirror. When you lift your right hand, your image lifts its left hand. The image is said to be **laterally inverted**.

This is an example of some mirror writing

Figure 6.6 An example of some mirror writing.

An image in a plane mirror is virtual, laterally inverted and the same size as the object.

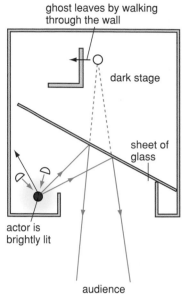

ghost leaves by walking through the wall

dark stage

sheet of glass

actor is brightly lit

audience

Figure 6.7 Pepper's Ghost.

Figure 6.7 shows how it is possible to produce the illusion of a ghost in a play. The technique is known as 'Pepper's Ghost'. A large sheet of glass is placed diagonally across the stage. The audience can see a wall through the glass on the darkened stage. An actor is hidden from the audience in the wings. He is brightly illuminated so that his image is reflected by the glass for the audience to see. When the actor walks off up the stage, his image (the ghost) appears to leave by walking through the wall.

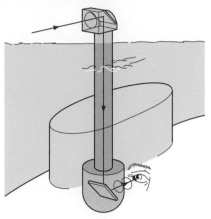

Figure 6.8 Submarines use periscopes so that crew can see above the surface. You can make a simple periscope using two mirrors.

STUDY QUESTIONS

1 a) The image you see in a mirror is virtual and laterally inverted. Describe the nature of the image you see when looking through a periscope as in Figure 6.8.

b) At what angle must the mirrors be fitted into the periscope?

2 John runs towards a mirror at 5 m/s. At what speed does his image approach him?

3 a) How many 10p coins will the eye see reflected in the mirrors below?

b) Draw diagrams to show how each image is formed.

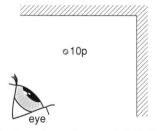

10p

eye

4 Show how the word CALCULATOR would look when reflected in a mirror.

5 Copy the diagrams and complete the paths of the rays after reflections in the mirrors. Use a protractor to draw your diagrams accurately.

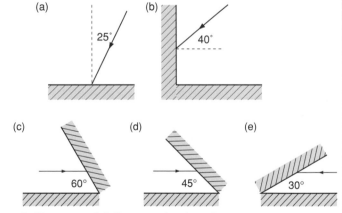

(a) 25°
(b) 40°
(c) 60°
(d) 45°
(e) 30°

6 Draw careful diagrams to show how waves are reflected in the following cases.

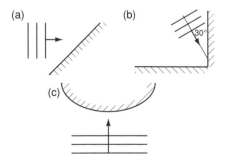

(a)
(b) 30°
(c)

3.7 Refraction

You have already learnt about rays and ray diagrams. Can you draw some ray diagrams to suggest how the direction of the light rays has been altered by the water in the photograph in Figure 7.1?

Figure 7.1 This photograph shows light being refracted (changed in direction) by water in a glass.

■ Refraction of water waves

Figure 7.2 shows a side view of waves passing from a deep region of water in a ripple tank into a shallower region. As the waves pass from deep to shallow water, two things happen: the wavelength of the waves reduces and the speed reduces. The frequency (the number of waves passing a point each second) stays the same.

Figure 7.3 shows the same event from a bird's eye view above the tank. The waves in the deeper water are seen to overtake the waves in the shallow water.

Figure 7.4 shows what happens when the waves meet the region of shallow water at an angle. Now the waves slow down *and* change direction. This is called **refraction**.

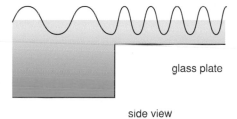

glass plate

side view

Figure 7.2

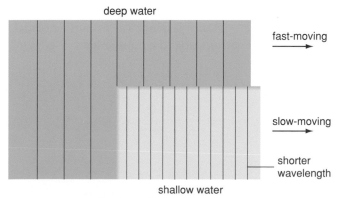

deep water

fast-moving

slow-moving

shorter wavelength

shallow water

view from above

Figure 7.3 Waves going from deep water to shallow water.

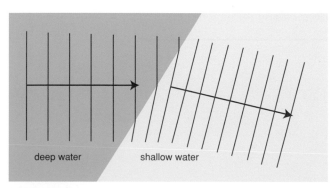

deep water   shallow water

Figure 7.4 Water waves are refracted when they enter shallow water.

Figure 7.5 shows how refraction can be demonstrated by students acting as a platoon of soldiers. The idea is that a platoon (of eight soldiers in this example) walks briskly towards a line, with their arms linked firmly by meter rules. When they cross the line, each in turn slows down. The result is that the platoon slows and their row changes direction. This is a model or an **analogy** of refraction.

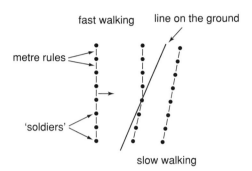

Figure 7.5 Students demonstrate refraction by joining together in a row and slowing down when they cross a line. After crossing the line, the row of students (or 'wavefront') has changed direction.

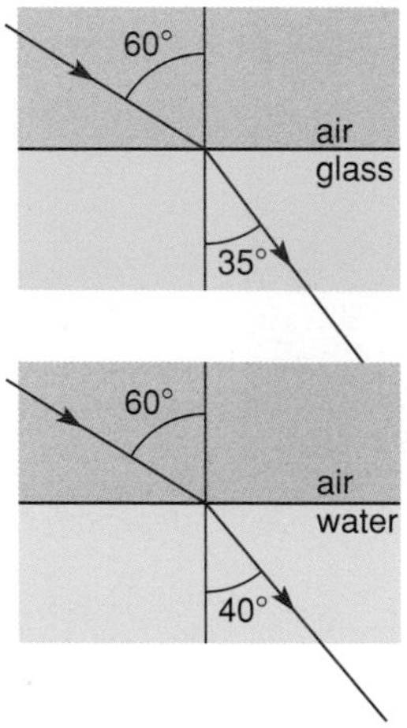

Figure 7.6 Light travels more slowly in glass than it does in water. So a light ray bends more when it goes into glass.

■ Refraction of light

When a light ray travels from air into a clear material such as glass or water, the ray changes direction — it is refracted. Refraction happens because light travels faster in air than in other substances (Figure 7.6).

The amount by which a light ray bends when it goes from air into another material depends on two things:

- what the material is
- the angle of incidence.

Figure 7.7 shows you an experiment to study how light rays bend when they go into a block of glass. The angle i between the normal and the incident ray, AB, is the angle of incidence. The angle r between the normal and refracted ray, BC, is the angle of refraction. The experiment shows these points:

- The light ray is bent towards the normal when it goes into the glass. The angle of incidence is greater than the angle of refraction.
- When the light ray leaves the block of glass it is bent away from the normal.
- If the block has parallel sides, light comes out at the same angle as it goes in.

PRACTICAL

Make sure you understand how to trace the incident rays, how to measure the refracted rays and how to measure the angles of incidence and refraction.

Refraction occurs as light changes speed in passing from one medium to another.

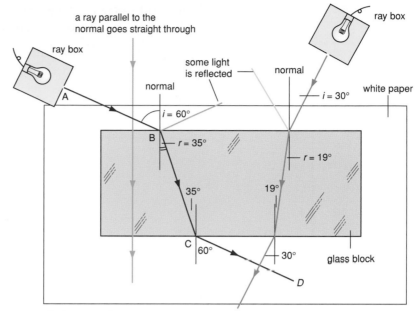

Figure 7.7 Refraction of light rays by a glass block.

■ Refractive index

You can use the apparatus in Figure 7.7 to investigate a relationship between the incident and the refracted rays. Figure 7.8 shows a graph of the investigations for three materials: glass, water and diamond.

There is also a mathematical connection between the incident and refracted rays. This is illustrated in Table 1.

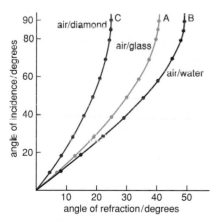

Figure 7.8 These graphs show how r depends on i when light travels from air into A glass, B water and C diamond.

Table 1 Comparison of i and r for glass

Angle of incidence (i)	Angle of refraction (r)	sin i	sin r	sin i/sin r
0	0	0	0	
23	15	0.39	0.26	1.50
34	22	0.56	0.37	1.51
48	30	0.74	0.50	1.48
59	35	0.86	0.57	1.51
80	41	0.98	0.66	1.48

You can see that the ratio of sin i/sin r is approximately constant – in this case its average value is about 1.5. The ratio, 1.5 is the **refractive index** (n) of glass. The refractive index is the **ratio** of the speed of light in air to the speed of light in glass.

$$n = \frac{\sin i}{\sin r}$$

Because n is a ratio of speeds, it has no unit.

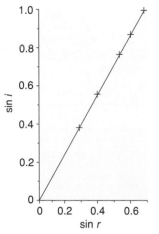

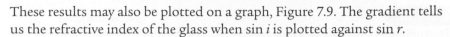

These results may also be plotted on a graph, Figure 7.9. The gradient tells us the refractive index of the glass when sin *i* is plotted against sin *r*.

Example. A light ray is incident on still water at an angle of 45° to the normal. What is the angle of refraction? The water has a refractive index of 1.33.

$$1.33 = \frac{\sin 45}{\sin r}$$

$$\sin r = \frac{\sin 45}{1.33}$$

$$\sin r = \frac{0.71}{1.33}$$

$$\sin r = 0.53$$

$$r = 32°$$

Figure 7.9 The gradient of this graph is the refractive index of glass.

Figure 7.10 James demonstrates refraction in the pool. Why does the pole look bent?

■ Real and apparent depth

When a light ray leaves water and goes into air it is refracted. This effect makes a pond look more shallow than it really is. In Figure 7.11 someone is leaning over a pond to look at a fish. Light rays from the fish travel up to the surface of the water. At the water surface these rays are bent away from the normal. When these rays enter the eye, the person imagines that these rays come from I not O. What is seen is a **virtual image** of the fish. This image is closer to the surface than the fish itself.

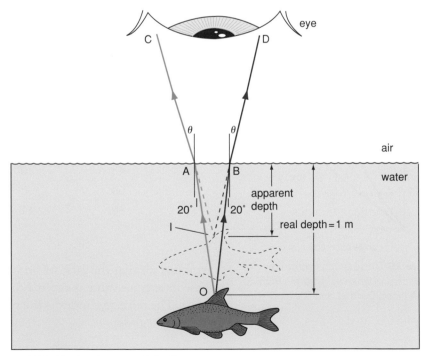

Figure 7.11 Real and apparent depth.

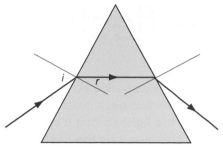

■ Refraction by prisms

You learnt some simple rules about refraction from the experiment shown in Figure 7.7. You can apply these rules to predict what will happen to light rays going into any shape of block. In Figure 7.12 you can see a light ray passing through a triangular glass **prism**. Notice that as the ray goes into the prism it is bent towards the normal; as it leaves the prism it is bent away from the normal.

Figure 7.12 Light is refracted by a triangular prism.

STUDY QUESTIONS

1 What is meant by the term refraction? What causes waves to refract?

2 Draw careful diagrams to show how the waves are refracted in the following cases.

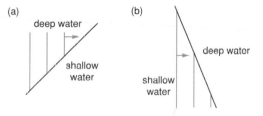

3 When a light ray goes into glass it bends towards the normal; when it comes out it bends away from the normal. Use this rule to sketch the path of the rays through the blocks in these cases.

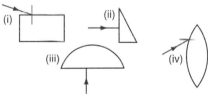

4 a) Make a copy of Figure 7.11. Mark in the rays OB and OA, making sure that the angles between OA and the normal, and between OB and the normal are both 20°.

b) Use the information in Figure 7.8 to work out what the angle θ should be.

c) Now draw in the rays BD and AC.

d) Use your scale diagram to calculate the apparent depth of the fish.

5 Draw diagrams to explain why a swimming pool of constant depth looks shallower at the far end.

6 When a light ray goes from air into a clear material you see the ray bend. How much the ray bends is determined by the refractive index of the material.

a) Look at the table of data below. How is the refractive index of a material related to the speed of light in it?

b) Which bends light more, glass or perspex? The refractive index of perspex is 1.4.

c) A light ray strikes three materials with angle of incidence of 60°. These materials are: (i) glass, (ii) water, (iii) diamond. Use Figure 6.8 to calculate the angle of refraction in each case.

d) Repeat part (c) by calculation using the equation: $n = \sin i / \sin r$.

Material	Speed of light/ 10^8 m/s	Refractive index
Air	3.0	1
Glass	2.0	3/2
Water	2.25	4/3
Diamond	1.25	2.4

3.8 Total internal reflection

Figure 8.1 Why do diamonds sparkle like this?

Diamonds are very popular jewels, because they sparkle so brightly. Diamonds are skilfully cut, so that light is reflected back inside the crystal. This has the effect of concentrating the light so that it comes out brighter from some faces than others. This gives us the sparkle.

In the last chapter you learnt that when a light ray crosses from glass into air, it bends away from the normal. However, this only happens if the angle of incidence is small. If the angle of incidence is too large, all of the light is reflected back into the glass. This is called **total internal reflection**.

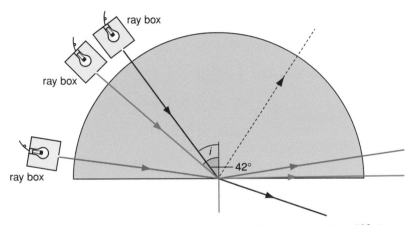

Figure 8.2 Refraction and reflection in a glass block. The critical angle is 42°, the angle between the blue ray and the normal.

Figure 8.2 shows how you can see this effect for yourself in the lab. Three rays of light are directed towards the centre of a semicircular glass block. Each ray crosses the circular edge of the block along the normal, so it does not change direction. However, when a ray meets the plane surface there is a direction change. For small angles of incidence, the ray is refracted (solid red emerging ray). Some light is also reflected back into the block (shown as a dashed red on the diagram).

PRACTICAL

Make sure you understand how to determine the critical angle for glass.

■ Critical angle

At an incident angle of 42° the ray is refracted along the surface of the block (blue ray). This is called the **critical angle**. If the angle of incidence is greater than this critical angle then all of the light is reflected back into the glass (green ray). The critical angle varies from material to material. While it is 42° for glass, for water it is about 49°.

■ Total internal reflection in prisms

An ordinary mirror has one main disadvantage: the silver reflecting surface is at the back of the mirror. So light has to pass through glass before it is reflected by the mirror surface. This can cause several weaker reflections to be seen in the mirror, because some light is internally reflected off the glass/air surface (Figure 8.3(a)).

(a)

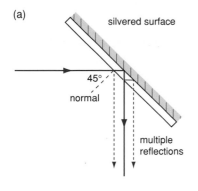

These multiple reflections can be a nuisance, for example in a periscope. We can avoid the extra reflections by using prisms. In Figure 8.3(b) the light ray AB meets the back of the glass prism at an angle of incidence of 45°. This angle is greater than the critical angle for glass, so the light is totally reflected. There is only one reflection because there is only one surface. Total internal reflection by prisms is also put to use inside binoculars and cameras.

■ Critical angle and refractive index

We can calculate the critical angle, c, for a material if we know its refractive index, n, using the equation:

$$\sin c = \frac{1}{n}$$

Example. What is the critical angle for a sample of perspex, with a refractive index of 1.4?

$$\sin c = \frac{1}{1.4}$$

$$= 0.71$$

$$c = 46°$$

(b)

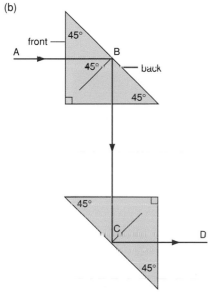

Figure 8.3 (a) Reflection from a mirror. **(b)** Reflection from two prisms to make a periscope.

■ Refraction and reflection on the road

Refraction and reflection are put to good use in your car. It is important that your rear lights are clearly visible to the car behind you. At the same time they must not dazzle the driver of a following car. Figure 8.4 shows how this is achieved. The cover of the rear light is made with a series of points. Any light that is travelling directly backwards is refracted to the side. A similar shape of plastic is used in the reflectors on the back of cars and bicycles. This time the light from the headlights of a car passes straight through a plane plastic surface (Figure 8.5). Then the total internal reflection occurs at the inside surfaces of the pointed plastic.

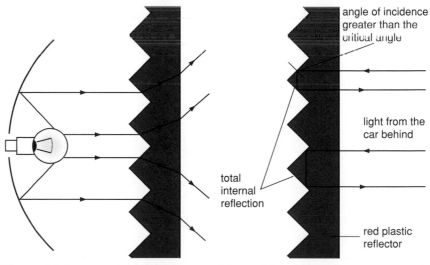

Figure 8.4 A car rear-light cover.

Figure 8.5 A reflector for a car or a bicycle.

141

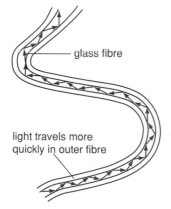

Figure 8.6 Internal reflection traps light inside the glass fibre.

■ Optical fibres

As you read in Chapter 3.4, glass fibres are used for carrying beams of light. The fibres usually consist of two parts. The inner part (core) carries the light beam. The outer part provides protection for the inner fibre. It is important that light travels more quickly in the outer part. Then the light inside the core is trapped due to total internal reflection (Figure 8.6).

Surgeons use a device called an **endoscope** to examine the inside of patients' bodies. This is made of two bundles of optical fibres. One bundle carries light down inside the patient, and the other tube allows the surgeon to see what is there. Optical fibres are also used in telephone networks. A small glass fibre, only about 0.01 mm in diameter, is capable of carrying hundreds of messages, coded as light pulses, at the same time. These fibres have largely replaced the old copper cables in telephone systems.

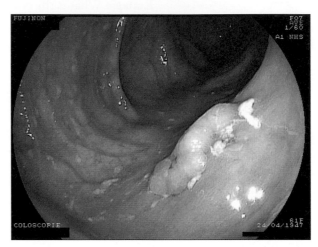

Figure 8.8 This is an image of a patient's lung as seen through an endoscope.

Figure 8.7 This photo shows an endoscope being used to investigate the abdomen. The fibre optic bundle allows the doctor to view inside the patient.

STUDY QUESTIONS

1 Turn back to the last chapter. Explain how the graphs in Figure 7.8 can help you work out critical angles. What are the critical angles of glass, water and diamond?

2 Below, you can see a ray of light entering a five-sided prism (pentaprism) in a camera. The ray undergoes three internal reflections before emerging. Copy the diagram and mark in the ray's path.

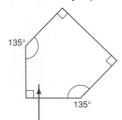

3 Describe in detail three uses for internal reflection. Illustrate your answer with diagrams.

4 The diagram below shows sunlight passing through a prismatic window that is used to light an underground room.

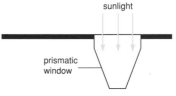

a) Copy the diagram and show the path of the rays through the window.

b) Explain why the window is shaped this way.

5 Diamond has a high refractive index of 2.4. This means that light is internally reflected at shallow angles, which is why diamonds sparkle so much. Use the equation: sin $c = 1/n$ to calculate the critical angle for diamond.

3.9 Sound waves

Sound waves from the festival in Figure 9.1 are diffracted as they come out of the loudspeakers, reflected off solid objects and refracted (change speed) as they pass through layers of air with different densities.

Figure 9.1

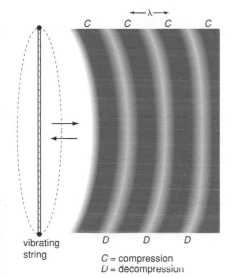

Figure 9.2 A vibrating guitar string.

C = compression
D = decompression

vibrating string

■ Making and hearing sounds

Vibrations

When you pluck a guitar string the instrument makes a noise. If you put your finger on the string you can feel the string vibrating. Sounds are made when something vibrates. The vibrations of a guitar string pass on energy to the air. This makes the air vibrate. Our ears can hear frequencies in the range 20 Hz to 20 000 Hz.

Longitudinal waves

Sound is a longitudinal wave. Molecules in air move backwards and forwards along the direction in which the sound travels. In Figure 9.2, when the guitar string moves to the right it compresses the air on the right hand side of it. When the string moves to the left the air on the right expands. This produces a series of **compressions** and **decompressions**. In a compression the air pressure is greater than normal atmospheric pressure. In a decompression (expansion) the air pressure is less than normal atmospheric pressure.

The ear

Compressions and decompressions travel through air in the same way that compressions and decompressions move along a slinky. Your ear detects the changes in pressure caused by these sound waves. When a compression reaches the ear it pushes the eardrum inwards. When a decompression arrives, the eardrum moves out again. The movements of the eardrum are transmitted through the ear by bones. Then nerves transmit electrical pulses to the brain.

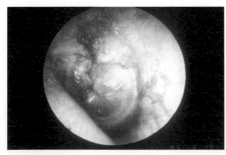

Figure 9.3 This is a photograph of a healthy eardrum. The vibrations carried in sound waves set the membrane in motion.

Table 1

Speeds of sound / m/s	Material
330	air
1500	water
5000	steel

■ Speed of sound

The speed of sound depends on which material it travels through. Sound waves are transmitted by molecules knocking into each other. In air, sound travels at about 330 m/s. In solids and liquids, where molecules are packed more tightly together, sound travels faster (Table 1). In a vacuum there are no molecules at all. Sound cannot travel through a vacuum, although light can.

Figure 8.4 shows a simple way for you to measure the speed of sound through air. Stand about 100 m away from a building and clap your hands. Sound waves will be reflected back to you from the building. When you hear the echo, clap again so that you clap in time with the echo. A friend, watching you clapping your hands, counts 10 claps in 6 seconds. Now you know that the sound took 0.6 s to travel 200 m (to the wall and back again).

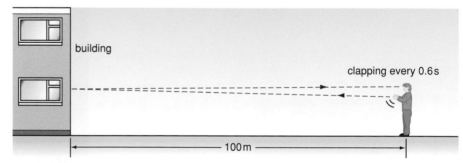

Figure 9.4 Measuring the speed of sound through air.

So the speed of sound is given by:

$$v = \frac{d}{t}$$
$$= \frac{200 \text{ m}}{0.6 \text{ s}} = 330 \text{ m/s}$$

■ Ultrasound

Ultrasound waves are high-frequency sound waves. Like all sound waves, these waves are longitudinal, and their vibrations produce compressions and decompressions (expansions) in the material they travel through. Ultrasound has such a high frequency (above 20 000 Hz) that our ears cannot detect it. The high-frequency waves have a short wavelength. This means that it is possible to produce a narrow beam of ultrasound without it spreading out due to diffraction effects.

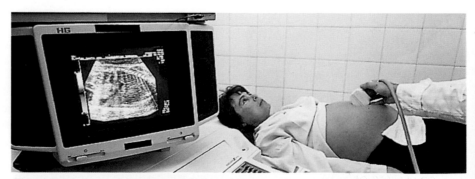

Figure 9.5 In this picture ultrasound emitted by the probe placed on the mother's abdomen is reflected by the foetus. A computer builds up a picture from those reflected waves, which, unlike X-rays, are perfectly safe.

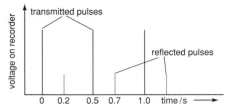

Figure 9.7 Ultrasound pulses for a depth of 150 m.

Ultrasonic depth finding

Ships use beams of ultrasound (or sonar) for a variety of purposes. Fishing boats look for fish; destroyers hunt for submarines; explorers chart the depth of the oceans. Figure 9.6 demonstrates the idea. A beam of ultrasonic waves is sent out from the bottom of a ship. The waves are reflected from the sea bed back to the ship. The longer the delay between the transmitted and reflected pulses, the deeper the sea is (Figure 9.7).

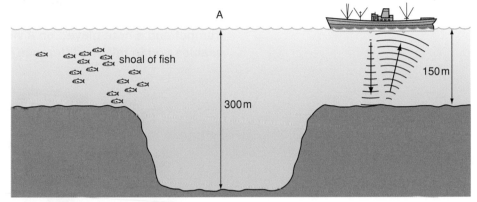

Figure 9.6 Ultrasonic depth finding.

■ Sound waves in medicine

In medicine, controlled shock (or sound) waves can be put to good use. A lithotripter can remove kidney stones without surgery. Sound waves are focused by a reflector onto the kidney stone. Water ensures good transmission of the waves. Without water most of the energy would be reflected off the patient's skin. Pulses of sound energy can shatter the stones and break them into small pieces. The body can then remove the fragments by passing them out in the urine.

STUDY QUESTIONS

1 The frequency of a sound from your mouth is 250 Hz.
   a) Calculate the wavelength of this sound (use Table 1 to find the speed).
   b) Explain why sound is diffracted when it leaves your mouth.

2 a) Ultrasound can be used to examine a baby inside a mother's uterus.
      i) How do the waves help to build up an image?
      ii) Why is ultrasound preferable to X-rays?
   b) Explain how you could use ultrasound waves to check for cracks in railway lines.
   c) A bat can find its supper by using ultrasonic waves for echo-location. Explain how this process works. Could we find our supper through echo-location?

3 The ship in Figure 9.6 sends out short pulses of ultrasound every 0.5 s; the frequency of the waves is 50 kHz (50 000 Hz).

   a) The duration of each pulse is 0.01 s. How many complete oscillations of the ultrasound waves are emitted during that time?
   b) Use the information in Figures 9.6 and 9.7 to show that the ultrasound travels at a speed of 1500 m/s through water.
   c) Sketch a graph, similar to Figure 9.7, to show both the transmitted and reflected pulses when the ship reaches point A.
   d) What difficulties would the sonar operator face when trying to measure depths of around 500 m?
   e) Calculate the wavelength of the ultrasonic waves in water.
   f) i) Why is it important to use a *narrow* beam of ultrasound waves?
      ii) Why is it not possible to produce such a narrow beam of ordinary sound waves?

3.10 Loudness, quality and pitch

Each of these musical instruments can play the same musical notes. However, you can tell the difference between a note played on a trumpet and a note played on a violin. What is it about the notes that enables you to tell the difference?

Figure 10.1

■ Sound energy

Your ears are very good detectors of energy. A disco produces sound energy at a rate of about 40 W. You find this very noisy. If you were to light a disco with one 40 W light bulb, everyone would complain that it was too dark.

Amplitude and loudness

Your ears detect sounds over a wide range of frequencies. You can probably hear frequencies as low as 20 Hz, and as high as 20 000 Hz. Your ears are most sensitive to frequencies of about 2000 Hz. So a note at a frequency of 2000 Hz sounds louder than a note of frequency 10 000 Hz that carries the same energy.

A loud noise makes your eardrums move a long way, while a very quiet noise has only a small effect on your eardrums. The loudness of a noise depends on the pressure change caused by the sound wave. During normal conversation your voice produces a pressure wave of amplitude 1 pascal (Figure 10.2). This is a very small change in comparison with atmospheric pressure (100 000 pascals).

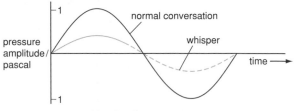

Figure 10.2 Sound waves caused by the human voice.

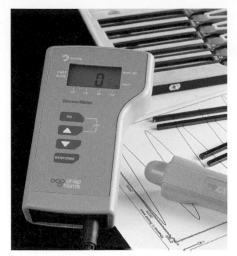

Figure 10.3 This data logger can be used to record the waveforms produced by different instruments.

■ Pitch

We use the term **pitch** to describe how a noise or a musical note sounds to us. Bass notes are of low pitch, treble notes are of high pitch. Men have low-pitched voices, women have voices of higher pitch. The pitch of a note is related directly to its frequency. The higher-pitched notes are the notes with higher frequency.

A data logger and microphone (Figure 10.3) can be used to analyse the waveform of the sound from a tuning fork. Once the data has been collected it can be downloaded and displayed on a computer screen: Figures 10.4(a) and (b) show you that higher-pitched sounds have higher frequencies. The higher-pitched sound, shown in Figure 10.4(b), has more cycles per second than the lower-pitched sound, shown in Figure 10.4(a).

■ Quality

On a piano the note that is called middle C has a frequency of 256 Hz. This note could be played on a piano or a violin, or you could sing the note. Somebody listening to the three different sounds would recognise straight away whether you had sung the note or played it on the piano or violin. The **quality** of the three notes is different. The quality of a note depends on the shape of its waveform. Although notes may have the same frequency and amplitude, if their waveforms are of a different shape you will detect a different sound (Figure 10.5).

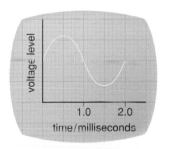

(a) Waveform of tuning fork of low pitch.

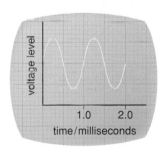

(b) Waveform of tuning fork of higher pitch.

Figure 10.4

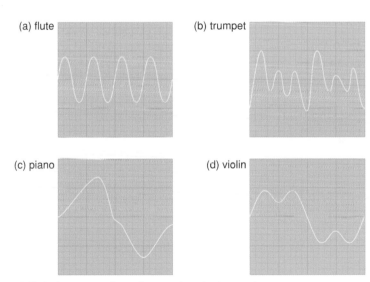

Figure 10.5 Data-logger readings from various instruments.

EXAM TIP

You can use data loggers to display the shape of sound waves, but you also need to know how to use an oscilloscope to measure the frequency of a sound wave. Make sure you understand how to use the *y*-gain and timebase controls.

■ Using an oscilloscope to measure frequency

A microphone is a device that transfers sound energy into electrical energy. The vibrations of a sound move a diaphragm in a microphone backwards and forwards, which generates an a.c. voltage. If the microphone is attached to an **oscilloscope**, we can see how the a.c. voltage changes with time. This is shown in Figure 10.6.

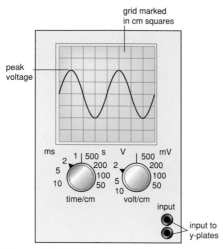

Figure 10.6 A simple waveform on an oscilloscope screen.

Here are some notes on how the oscilloscope works.

The size of the voltage is measured with the y-axis. The y-gain control (on the right-hand side in Figure 10.6) adjusts the sensitivity of the oscilloscope. Here the y-gain is set at 2 V/cm. This means that each centimetre displacement in a vertical direction measures 2 V. So here the peak voltage is 4 V, as the peak is 2 cm above or below the zero voltage level.

The x-axis allows us to measure the time period (and frequency) of the voltage. The timebase (left-hand control in Figure 10.6) is set at 2 ms/cm. This means that each centimetre on the x-axis measures a time of 2 ms. One complete cycle of this voltage takes 4 squares. This is 8 ms or 8/1000 s. Since the frequency of the voltage is equal to 1/time period, the voltage frequency is 1000/8 = 125 Hz.

STUDY QUESTIONS

1 Look at the signal in Figure 10.6. Draw another diagram to show how the trace looks when you make these two separate changes:
  i) increase the y-gain to 1 V/cm
  ii) increase the timebase setting to 1 ms/cm.

2 The diagram below shows a waveform on an oscilloscope creen; the timebase is set to 1 ms/cm and the y-gain control to 2 V/cm. Calculate the peak voltage and frequency of the a.c. supply

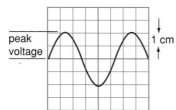

3 **a)** Use Figure 10.4 to calculate the frequencies of the sounds emitted from the two tuning forks.
  b) Using the same scales as Figure 10.5, sketch the forms of notes from tuning forks of frequencies
    i) 2000 Hz
    ii) 750 Hz.

4 Look at Figure 10.5. The data logger collected information about the four musical instruments for the same length of time in each case.

a) Which note has the highest frequency?
b) Which instrument is played most loudly?
c) Which instrument is played most softly?
d) Which two instruments are playing notes of the same pitch?

5 An electronic synthesizer produces the two pure notes A and B as shown below. It produces a third note C by adding the two waveforms together.
a) Copy the two waveforms onto some graph paper.
b) Add the two waveforms together to produce the waveform of C.
c) Does C sound louder than A or B?
d) How does the frequency of C compare with:
  i) A,
  ii) B?
e) Does C have the same quality as A or B?

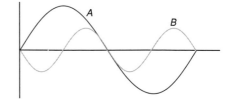

Summary

 Make sure you can answer all the questions in the *Interactive quiz*.

I am confident that:

✓ I understand the properties of waves
- Describe longitudinal and transverse waves.
- State and describe the meaning of amplitude, frequency, wavelength and period of a wave.
- wave speed = frequency × wavelength
$$v = f \times \lambda$$
- frequency $= \dfrac{1}{\text{time period}}$
$$f = 1/T$$
- Waves are diffracted when they pass an edge or go through a gap.

✓ I can recall the electromagnetic spectrum
- All electromagnetic waves travel at the speed of light.
- Recall the uses of: radio waves, microwaves, infra-red, visible light, ultraviolet, X-rays, gamma rays.
- Recall the detrimental effects of: microwaves, infra-red, ultraviolet, gamma rays.
- Understand the difference between digital and analogue signals.
- Understand the advantages of digital signals.

✓ I can recall and describe the properties of light
- Light can be reflected, refracted and diffracted.
- The angle of incidence (i) equals the angle of reflection (r).
- Describe experiments to demonstrate the refraction of light.
- Refractive index, $n = \dfrac{\sin i}{\sin r}$
- Describe an experiment to determine the refractive index of glass.
- Describe the role of total internal reflection in transmitting information along fibres and in prisms.
- The relation between the critical angle, c, and the refractive index, n, is:
$$\sin c = \frac{1}{n}$$

✓ I can recall and describe the properties of sound
- Sound can be reflected, refracted and diffracted.
- The range of human hearing is 20 Hz to 20 000 Hz.
- Describe how to measure the speed of sound in air.
- Understand how an oscilloscope can be used to display a sound wave.
- The pitch of a sound is related to its frequency.
- The loudness of a sound is related to its amplitude.

Exam-style questions

1 The diagram shows a wave on the sea.

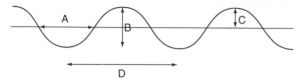

a) i) Which letter shows the wavelength of the
wave? [1]

ii) Which letter shows the amplitude of the
wave? [1]

b) What type of wave is shown in the diagram?
Describe how energy is transmitted by the
water. [2]

c) A man watches some waves pass his boat. He sees
the crest of a wave pass him every 4 s.
Calculate the frequency of the waves. [2]

d) He sees that the wavelength is the same length as
his boat, which is 5 m long. Calculate the speed of
the waves. [2]

2 A teacher and two students are measuring the speed
of sound.

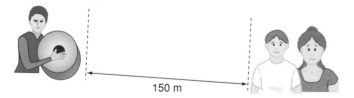

150 m

The teacher makes a sound by hitting two cymbals
together. Each student starts a stopwatch when they
see the teacher hit the cymbals. They each stop their
stopwatch when they hear the sound.

a) Describe how a sound wave moves through the
air. [3]

b) The students repeat the experiment and record
their readings in a table.

Student	Time / s
Andrew	0.44, 0.46, 0.44, 0.48, 0.43
Kefe	0.5, 0.6, 0.4, 0.4, 0.6

i) State the precision of Andrew's readings. [1]

ii) State the equation linking speed, distance
travelled and time taken. [1]

c) The teacher was standing 150 m from the
students. Use the experimental data recorded by
each student to calculate:

i) the average measured time for each student [2]

ii) the speed of sound calculated by each
student. [2]

Write each answer to an appropriate number of
significant figures.

d) The students look in a data book and find that
the speed of sound in air is given as 341 m/s.

The students discuss their results:

Andrew: 'My experiment was more accurate
because my answer was closest to 341 m/s.'

Kefe: 'No, you did not allow for reaction time.
My result is the best that you can get
with this method.'

Andrew: 'No, reaction time didn't matter because
I had to react twice and it cancelled out.'

Evaluate these conclusions. [5]

3 A student is investigating refraction of light.

a) What is refraction? [1]

b) The diagram shows a ray of light travelling from
air to glass.

Copy the diagram and add labels to show the angle
of incidence, *i*, and the angle of refraction, *r*. [2]

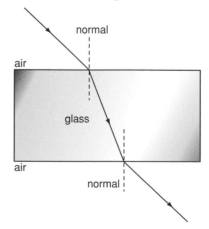

c) The student wants to find the refractive index of
the glass.

i) State the equation linking refractive index,
angle of incidence and angle of refraction. [1]

ii) The student has available the following pieces of apparatus: a rectangular glass block, a protractor and a ray box.
Describe how the student should carry out the experiment. You should include:

- what the student should measure

- how the measurements should be made

- how the student should use a graph to find the refractive index. [6]

4 Light from an object forms an image in a plane mirror.

a) State which **two** statements in the box below are correct. [2]

> The image in a plane mirror is virtual.
> Light from the object passes through the image in a plane mirror.
> Light waves are longitudinal.
> The angle of incidence equals the angle of reflection.
> The incident ray is always at right angles to the reflected ray.

b) i) Copy the diagram and use words from the box to label the numbers on the diagram. [2]

mirror	normal	ray	reflection

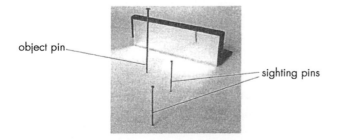

(1)........................

(2)........................

ii) Write *r* on your diagram to show the angle of reflection. [1]

c) A student investigates the formation of the image in a plane mirror, using the apparatus shown below.

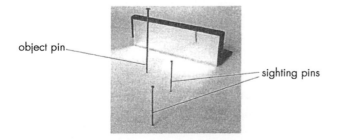

object pin

sighting pins

She uses the holes that the pins make to construct this diagram.

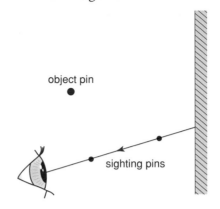

object pin

sighting pins

i) Copy the diagram and add to it to show how the student should find the position of the image. [3]

ii) Explain how the student could confirm that the position of the image is correct. [2]

5 **a)** State the law of reflection. [1]

b) A student is playing in goal in a football match. The window of a nearby building reflects sunlight into his eyes.

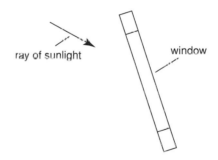

ray of sunlight

window

i) Copy and complete the diagram to show the reflection of the ray from the front of the window. [2]

ii) Suggest how you could stop sunlight being reflected into your eyes from this window. (*Although the most obvious answers include comments such as 'closing your eyes' or 'wear a cap or sunglasses' these would get no mark.*) [1]

iii) Light is part of the electromagnetic spectrum. State a feature that all parts of the spectrum have in common. [1]

6 a) The diagram shows a ray of light directed at a semicircular glass block.

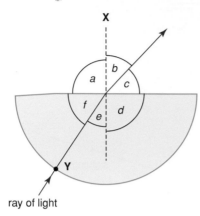

ray of light

i) Name line **X**. [1]

ii) State which letter, *a, b, c, d, e* or *f*, is the angle of incidence. [1]

iii) Name angle *b*. [1]

iv) State an equation that relates angle of incidence, angle of refraction and refractive index of glass. [1]

v) At point **Y** light passes from air to glass but refraction does not take place.
How can you tell this from the diagram? [1]

vi) Why does refraction not take place at point **Y**? [1]

b) Glass with a critical angle of 42° was used to make the blocks shown below.

(i)

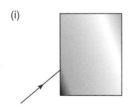

(ii)

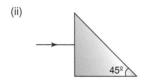

i) Copy and complete the diagram to show how the ray of light passes through the rectangular block and out into the air. [3]

ii) Copy and complete the diagram to show how the ray of light passes through the triangular glass block and out into the air. [2]

7 This question is about radiations in the electromagnetic spectrum.

radio waves	micro-waves	infra-red	A	ultraviolet	B	gamma rays

a) Name the two parts of the spectrum that are missing (A and B). [1]

b) Which electromagnetic radiation is used for heating and night vision equipment? [1]

c) Which electromagnetic radiation is used for cooking and satellite transmission? [1]

d) Which end of the electromagnetic spectrum has the highest frequency? [1]

e) Exposure to excessive electromagnetic radiation can be harmful to the human body. For two named types of radiation, describe:

i) a harmful effect [2]

ii) how the risks of exposure can be reduced. [2]

8 a) Music can be stored on a plastic disc in a single spiral groove.

The groove varies in width and depth. As the disc rotates, a diamond needle moves through the groove. The needle moves up and down following the shape of the groove.

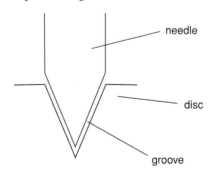

The shape of the groove determines the amplitude and frequency of movement of the needle. The movements are changed into electrical signals and then into sound waves.

i) The needle moves through a part of the groove that causes it to move up and down rapidly through a large vertical distance. Describe and explain the sound that can be heard. [2]

ii) Explain why such discs can only be used a certain number of times before the quality of sound deteriorates. [2]

b) Compact discs (CDs) were first used in the 1980s to store music in a digital form.

   i) Which of the signals below is digital and which is analogue? [1]

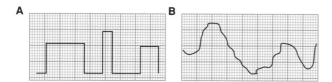

A   B

   ii) Explain your choice in part (i). [2]

   iii) State **one** advantage of using digital rather than analogue signals. [1]

   iv) Give another everyday use of a digital signal, apart from music recording. [1]

c) The diagram shows a recent invention called an atomic force microscope that can be used to scan the surface of a material. The movement of the tip causes the path of the ray of light to alter. Images of the atoms on the surface of the material are produced from the light received by the detector.

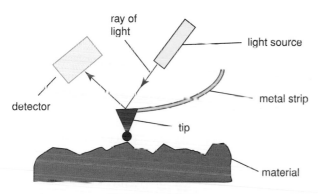

The bottom of the tip is negatively charged. It is attracted or repelled by the charge on the surface of the material.

   i) Explain what sign of charge on the surface of the material would cause the tip to move upwards. [2]

   ii) Explain why the metal strip should be elastic and obey Hooke's law. [3]

   iii) Explain why it is important for the top surface of the tip to be perfectly flat. [2]

   iv) The same tip is used many times. Explain why the quality of the images produced does not deteriorate. [2]

9 The diagram shows a ray of light incident at point **A** inside a glass optical fibre. The ray of light is totally internally reflected at **A** and eventually passes out into the air from point **B**.

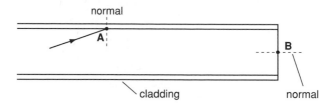

a) Copy then draw on the diagram the path taken by the ray of light:

   i) between **A** and **B** [1]

   ii) as it passes into the air from **B**. [2]

b) Explain carefully:

   i) why the light is totally internally reflected inside an optical fibre [1]

   ii) why the light is able to emerge at **B**. [1]

10 The electromagnetic spectrum is the name given to a family of waves that includes light, infra-red and ultraviolet radiations. All members of the family can travel through a vacuum with the same high velocity.

Electromagnetic waves are produced when the energy of electrically charged particles is changed in some way. The greater the change in energy, the shorter the wavelength of the electromagnetic wave produced. Radio waves, with a wavelength of up to 10 km, and gamma (γ) rays, with wavelengths of a thousand millionths of a millimetre, are found at opposite ends of the electromagnetic spectrum.

a) Name **one** part of the electromagnetic spectrum:

   i) that is not mentioned in the above passage [1]

   ii) that has a wavelength shorter than that of visible light. [1]

b) Give **one** reason why radio waves have a longer wavelength than gamma (γ) rays.

c) State **one** practical use of

   i) infra-red radiation [1]

   ii) ultraviolet radiation. [1]

11 A student investigates total internal reflection of light inside semicircular blocks. The illustration shows the path followed by a ray of light in a plastic block.

a) The student draws this diagram of the apparatus.

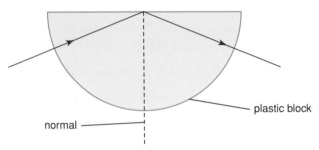

i) Copy the diagram. Mark and name the **two** angles that the student should measure. [2]

ii) Describe how the student should measure and record the angles. [3]

iii) State how these two angles are related. [1]

b) The student repeats the experiment with a glass block rather than a plastic one. The light emerges from a different place, as shown in the next diagram.

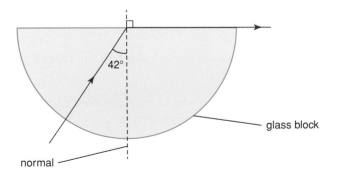

i) What is the name given to the angle marked 42° in the diagram? [2]

ii) Calculate the refractive index of the glass. (sin 42° = 0.6691) [3]

12 In recent years there has been a rapid growth in the number and use of mobile phones. These use radio waves for transmitting speech. They have to use frequencies that are not already used by radio stations.

a) Radio waves used for mobile phones have a typical wavelength of 0.30 m. Calculate the frequency of these radio waves, given that their speed is 3.0×10^8 m/s. [3]

b) The diagram below shows how a dish aerial is used to focus waves and transmit them to a satellite. Focusing the radio waves minimises the effects of diffraction.

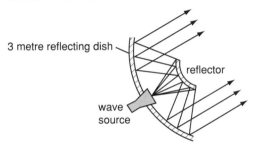

i) Explain why it is important to minimise the effects of diffraction. [2]

ii) What **two** factors affect the amount of diffraction that takes place when a wave passes through an opening? [2]

iii) The waves used for satellite transmission have a much shorter wavelength than the 0.30 m used by mobile phones. Suggest why a wavelength of 0.30 m is unsuitable for satellite transmission. [2]

c) Transatlantic telephone calls can be carried either using satellite links or by optical fibres on the seabed. Describe how optical fibres can be used to carry telephone calls. Suggest **one** advantage and **one** disadvantage of using optical fibres rather than satellite links. [4]

EXTEND AND CHALLENGE

1 Read the article below about whales, then answer the questions.

a) Explain why the reflection and refraction of waves shown in the diagram help the whales to communicate over large distances.

b) Explain why creatures living at the bottom of the sea cannot communicate over long distances.

c) Wallis, an amorous bull whale, is prepared to swim for a day to find a mate. After singing for half an hour, he gets a response from Wendy 7 minutes after he stops. How far away is she, and will Wallis bother to make the journey? (Assume Wendy replies as soon as Wallis finishes his serenade.)

- Wallis can swim at 15 km/h.

- Sound travels at about 1500 m/s in water.

Whale song

Not only are blue whales the largest animals in the world, but they are also the noisiest. They give out low frequency sounds that allow them to communicate over distances of thousands of kilometres.

The whales are helped in their long-distance communications because the sounds they give out are trapped in the upper surface layers of the ocean. Sounds that hit the surface of the sea at a shallow angle are reflected back. Sounds that travel downwards are turned back upwards. At greater depths sound travels faster, because the water is more compressed. This causes sound waves to be refracted as shown in the diagram. This is similar to the refraction of light waves on a hot day, which allows us to see a mirage. Only in the top layers of the ocean does sound travel a long way. The sounds are trapped, rather like light waves in an optical fibre.

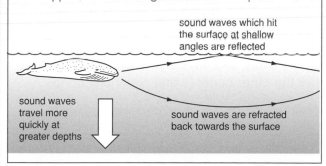

sound waves which hit the surface at shallow angles are reflected

sound waves travel more quickly at greater depths

sound waves are refracted back towards the surface

d) Why are there long pauses in whale conversations?

e) Explain carefully how the refraction of sound waves shown in the diagram tells us that sound travels faster at greater depths. Draw a diagram to show what would happen to whale sounds if sound travelled more *slowly* at greater depths.

f) On a hot day, it is common to see a mirage on a road as you drive along. The mirage is an image of the sky. Draw a diagram to explain how mirages occur. (Hint: light travels slightly faster in the hot air just above the road surface.)

2 An earthquake produces seismic waves which travel around the surface of the Earth at a speed of about 6 km/s. The graph shows how the ground moves near to the centre of the earthquake as the waves pass.

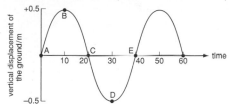

a) What is the time period of the waves?

b) What is the frequency of the waves?

c) Calculate the wavelength of the seismic waves.

d) Explain why the ground is moving most rapidly at times C and E.

e) When is the ground accelerating at its greatest rate?

f) Use the graph to estimate the vertical speed of the ground at the time marked C.

g) Make a sketched copy of the graph. Add to it a second graph, to show the ground displacement caused by a second seismic wave of the same amplitude but twice the frequency.

h) Discuss whether high-frequency or low-frequency seismic waves will cause more damage to buildings.

i) The diagram shows seismic waves passing a house. The waves produce ground displacements that have a vertical component YY$_1$ and a horizontal component XX$_1$. Which component is more likely to make the house fall down? Explain your answer.

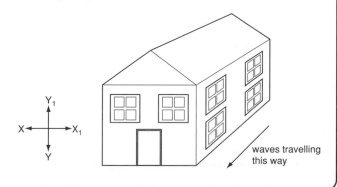

waves travelling this way

155

4
Energy resources and energy transfer

CALCULATE • PRESENT

1 How much electrical energy is used by your country each year?
2 What fraction of electricity is generated in your country using fossil fuels?
3 What is the total electrical energy generated each year in the world?

Drax power station in Yorkshire, UK. The plumes from this coal-fired power station are illuminated by the station's own lighting. The wide cooling towers are releasing water vapour into the atmosphere, which is harmless. The thin combustion tower to the left is fitted with flue-gas desulfurisation equipment, to reduce the pollution that escapes into the atmosphere due to the burning of coal. Power stations like this one operate 24 hours a day, 365 days a year to provide us with heating, lighting and all the other benefits that electricity brings.

By the end of this section you should:
- be able to define work
- understand that energy is used to do work
- know some different energy forms, and know how one form can be transferred to another
- understand that energy is always conserved
- be able to define power
- be able to do calculations involving energy transfers
- be able to define efficiency
- understand that electricity can be produced in many different ways, be able to appreciate the differences between them and know the difference between renewable and non-renewable fuels.

4.1 Energy

Figure 1.1

When you fill a car up with fuel, do you think about the principle of the conservation of energy?

- What type of energy is stored in the fuel?
- Where did that energy come from in the first place?
- When the fuel is used, its energy is transferred to other types of energy. Can you name three other types of energy?

■ What is energy?

What does it do for us? Why do we have to pay for it? We cannot see energy, but we can see what it does for us. Energy has the capacity to do a job of work for us. For example, there is chemical energy stored in petrol; this can be released in an engine, which can push a car along a road, or in a crane that lifts a load for us. When a force moves something this is called work – see Chapter 4.5.

Energy is valuable to us, not only because it enables us to do jobs of work, but also because it provides the heating and lighting for our homes, schools and places of work. Energy resources are limited and we pay for the energy we use.

The unit we use to measure energy is the **joule** or **J**. This is named after the physicist James Joule. Larger quantities of energy are measured in kJ (a thousand joules) or MJ (a million joules).

■ Different types of energy

Several different types of energy are listed below and on the next page.

- **Chemical energy.** Food has chemical energy stored in it, which is released by chemical reactions inside our bodies. Food provides the energy to keep us warm and to enable us to move around. The burning of petrol and other fuels are also examples of chemical reactions that release energy to do useful work.
- **Gravitational potential energy.** When a rock is placed at the top of a hill, it has some stored energy; this is gravitational potential energy. When the rock is sent rolling down the hill, this energy is released and can set other things in motion too. Water stored in a high-level dam helps us to generate electrical energy. The stored gravitational potential energy has the capacity to keep the generators moving when the water flows downhill.
- **Kinetic energy.** This is the name given to the energy of motion. All moving objects have kinetic energy. A moving hammer has kinetic energy, which can be used to do a useful job of work, for example knocking in a nail.
- **Thermal (or heat) energy.** The hotter something is, the more thermal energy it possesses; this energy is stored in the vibrational or random kinetic energy of the molecules.
- **Elastic potential (or strain) energy.** If you have used a bow, you will know that you have to pull hard on the string before you can shoot the arrow. In bending the bow you have strained it, and it stores elastic potential energy. That stored energy can be used to shoot the arrow and give it kinetic energy.

Figure 1.2 (a) Chemical energy stored in the coal is being transformed into thermal and light energy. **(b)** Potential energy is stored in this water. **(c)** Elastic potential energy is stored in this stretched catapult, which is used to hurl a projectile.

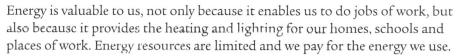

Figure 1.3 This ride in a theme park demonstrates one way to transfer potential energy to kinetic energy.

- **Electrical energy.** This energy is used to cause a current to flow, which can then turn that energy into heat or light energy. It can be stored in a battery.
- **Light energy.** This is emitted by hot objects such as a lamp or the Sun. These objects emit thermal energy too.
- **Sound energy.** This is the energy of sound waves, transmitted through the air by objects that are vibrating. We detect this energy when it sets our eardrums vibrating.
- **Nuclear energy.** This is the energy locked up by the strong forces that hold a nucleus together. This can be released in nuclear reactions to produce great amounts of thermal energy. The process of thermonuclear fusion in a star is an example.
- **Electromagnetic energy.** This is carried as waves by moving electric and magnetic fields. Light is an example of electromagnetic energy. Other electromagnetic waves carry energy too: radio waves carry energy and information; infra-red waves carry energy that warms you in sunlight, for example.
- **Magnetic energy.** This energy is stored in magnets; when you put two magnets together, they either pull each other together or push each other apart.

■ The principle of conservation of energy

As you will see in the examples that follow, one energy type can be transferred to another type. When such a transfer takes place, there is no loss of energy, but it has changed to another form. This is summarised by the **principle of conservation of energy**.

Energy cannot be created or destroyed, but it can be transferred from one form to another.

Figure 1.4 These thermonuclear reactions are transferring nuclear energy into thermal energy, light energy and other electromagnetic energy forms.

■ Energy transfers

In Figure 1.5, chemical energy in Wally's muscles allows him to pull up the box. Now the box has potential energy. When Wally slips, the potential energy turns into kinetic energy. When the box hits the ground the kinetic energy turns into heat energy, and sound energy.

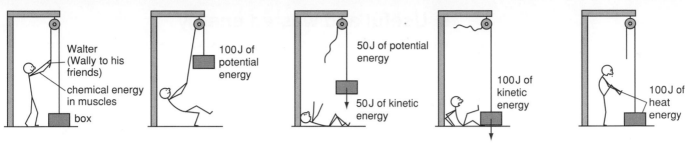

Figure 1.5

In Figure 1.6, you can see how kinetic energy can be turned into potential energy, then back to kinetic energy again.

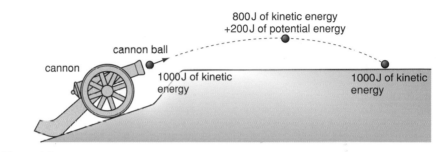

Figure 1.6

In Figure 1.7, a skier falls through a height of 10 m. He ends up with the same kinetic energy whether he falls straight down or accelerates more smoothly down the slope. In each case he loses the same potential energy.

In Figure 1.8, a cat called Boris is catching his supper. Chemical energy is used to create elastic potential energy in Boris' muscles. This elastic potential energy is converted to kinetic energy when Boris pounces on the mouse.

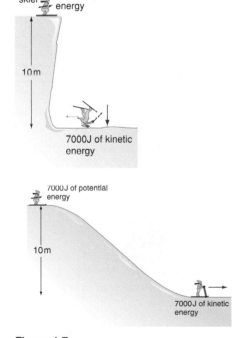

Figure 1.7

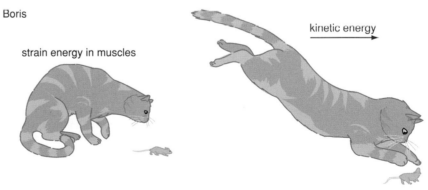

Figure 1.8

Some energy transfers are more complicated than the ones described above. For example, this is what happens when a car is driven: chemical energy in petrol is transferred to heat, sound and kinetic energy in the pistons and engine. The kinetic energy in the pistons is transferred to the body of the car to work against drag and frictional forces. This work transfers energy to heat.

■ Useful and wasted energy

When we use an energy source, we usually want to turn it into a useful form of energy. For example, we may use a crane to lift a heavy load for us. What we want to do is to use the chemical energy stored in the petrol to transfer gravitational potential energy to the load we are lifting. Unfortunately, when we use an engine it produces unwanted energy. You know from experience that a car engine makes a noise and gets hot. So it produces two forms of unwanted energy – heat energy and sound energy.

■ Efficiency

When a machine wastes energy in this way we say that it is inefficient. We can express **efficiency** as a percentage or a fraction. In the case of a petrol engine, only about 25% of the available energy is usefully used to lift a load or drive a vehicle forwards. The other 75% of the chemical energy is wasted as heat and some as sound. We calculate efficiency using the equation:

$$\text{efficiency} = \frac{\text{useful energy output}}{\text{total energy input}}$$

A steam engine is rather less efficient than a petrol engine. What is the efficiency of a steam engine that gets 18 kJ of useful energy from 150 kJ of chemical engine from the coal in its furnace?

$$\text{efficiency} = \frac{18\,\text{kJ}}{150\,\text{kJ}} = 0.12 \text{ or } 12\%$$

Figure 1.9 shows how we can show the same information in a **Sankey diagram**. Such a diagram shows how the energy put into a machine is used usefully or dissipated as heat.

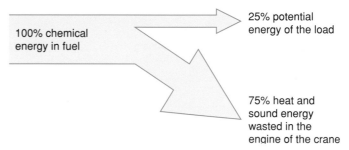

100% chemical energy in fuel

25% potential energy of the load

75% heat and sound energy wasted in the engine of the crane

Figure 1.9 A Sankey diagram to show the fate of the chemical energy used in a crane to lift a load.

Now watch the animation *Energy, power and efficiency.*

STUDY QUESTIONS

1 In the question below, state clearly all the energy transfers which occur. Do not just write the forms of energy, but explain precisely where the energy is at each stage.
   a) A golfer hits a ball down the fairway.
   b) An electric motor lifts a load.
   c) A firework rocket flies into the air and explodes.
   d) A car brakes and comes to a halt without skidding.
   e) A car brakes and skids to a halt.

2 Explain what is meant by the principle of conservation of energy.

3 In the diagram below, a ball falls to the ground. Near the ball, in positions A to E are marked some values of its kinetic energy (KE) and potential energy (PE). Copy the diagram and fill in the missing values (you may ignore wind resistance.)

	KE	PE
A •	0	50 J
B •	10 J	
C •		25 J
D •	35 J	
E •		0

4 A student compares two engines, A and B. Both machines have the same energy input. She discovers that A wastes less energy as heat than B does. Which engine is more efficient?

5 a) A car's engine is supplied with a kilogram of diesel, which contains 45 MJ of energy. The engine is 36% efficient. How much useful energy is available to drive the car forwards?
   b) Draw a Sankey diagram to show how the energy in the diesel is turned to other forms.

6 a) An electric crane, with an efficiency of 30%, produces 240 J of useful gravitational potential energy in lifting a load. How much energy was put into the motor to do this job?
   b) Draw a Sankey diagram for this process to show how the energy put into the motor was transferred to other types of energy.

4.2 Conduction

Table 1 Comparing conductivity

Material	Conductivity / W/mK	
copper	385	good conductors
iron	72	
con-crete	5	
glass	1	
brick	0.6	
water	0.6	
fat	0.046	
wool	0.04	
air	0.025	poor conductors

When you walk around your house in bare feet you will notice that your feet feel warm as long as you stay on a carpet. But if you go into a kitchen which has tiles on a concrete floor your feet will soon feel cold. You notice this effect because the tiles are good conductors of heat. A good conductor of heat will carry heat away from your body quickly; this makes you feel cold. Why do some materials conduct heat well?

Figure 2.1

(a) Heat is conducted quickly by fast-moving electrons.

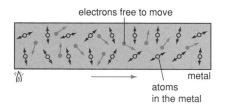

(b) Heat is conducted slowly by atoms bumping into each other.

Figure 2.2

■ Insulators and conductors

Table 1 shows you materials that conduct heat well (those with high **conductivity**) and materials that are poor conductors or **insulators** (low conductivity). All metals are good thermal conductors and materials such as plastic, wood and air are insulators. When heat is transferred by conduction, hot atoms pass some of their kinetic energy to colder neighbouring atoms. Metals contain electrons that are free to move. When one end of a metal rod is heated, energy can be carried away from the hot end of the rod by fast-moving electrons (Figure 2.2(a)). In a thermal insulator there are few electrons that are free to move, and heat is transferred more slowly by vibrating atoms bumping into neighbouring atoms (Figure 2.2(b)).

Polyethylene foam has a very low conductivity; this makes it a good insulator between the walls of a house.

Figure 2.3 Trapped air in this foam makes it an excellent insulator for this house.

Figure 2.4 This robin has fluffed out its feathers to trap a layer of air. Air is a poor conductor of heat and so the bird manages to keep warm even in cold weather.

■ Keeping warm

If you look at Table 1 you can see that fat, wool and air are all poor conductors of heat. It is no surprise then, that these three substances are important for keeping warm-blooded animals (including us) at the right temperature. When you go swimming, your skin is in contact with cold water and you lose heat by conduction. In really cold Arctic waters you could not survive more than a few minutes. Seals, however, spend all of their lives in cold water. They are protected from losing heat by conduction by a very thick layer of fat (blubber) which surrounds their body.

Birds have feathers and other animals have fur or hair. Fur and feathers are poor conductors of heat, but the way they reduce heat loss is by trapping a thick insulating layer of air. Our clothes trap air to keep us warm.

■ Heat exchange

Figure 2.5 shows a double-pipe heat exchanger that is being used in a laundry. Hot dirty water from the washing goes through the central pipe. Clean cold water flows around the outside of the pipe. The idea is to warm up the clean water using heat from the dirty water. This helps to reduce the laundry's heating bill.

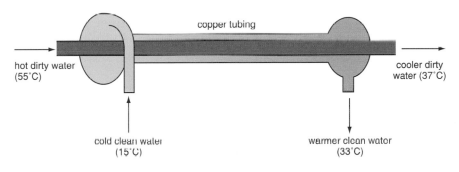

Figure 2.5 A heat exchanger for a laundry.

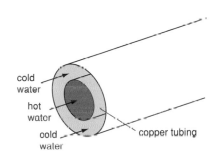

Figure 2.6 The heat exchanger wall is made of thin metal.

Figure 2.6 shows part of the heat exchanger. The following points make sure that as much heat is removed from the hot liquid as possible:

- The wall between the hot and cold water should be made from a good conductor (usually metal).
- The wall should be thin, so that heat is conducted rapidly.
- The surface area should be large to conduct more heat.
- The temperature difference between the cooling water and the hot liquid should be large.
- More heat is extracted from the hot liquid if it flows slowly through the heat exchanger.

Figure 2.7 This radiator has lots of fins to increase the surface area for heat exchange.

STUDY QUESTIONS

1 Here is part of a conversation between Peter, Ramesh and Lorraine, who are talking about keeping warm in winter.

Peter: I think string vests are ridiculous, they are just full of holes. How can they possibly keep you warm?

Ramesh: I heard on the radio that it was better to wear two vests than one. How can they do any good?

Lorraine: It's not the vest that keeps you warm, it's the air underneath them.

Comment on this conversation.

2 This question refers to the laundry's heat exchanger shown in Figure 2.5. What effect will the following changes have on the final temperature of the clean water that is being warmed up?

a) Iron tubing is used instead of copper.

b) Thinner copper tubing is used for the wall of the heat exchanger.

c) The length of the heat exchanger is increased.

d) The hot dirty water is made to run faster.

3 Find out why power stations need heat exchangers.

4 a) Explain in terms of the motion of particles how
   i) a metal conducts heat
   ii) wood conducts heat.

b) The diagram below shows a piece of wood with a ring of brass round part of it. A piece of paper has been stuck partly across the wood and partly across the brass. A flame is now applied gently underneath the paper as the wood is turned slowly. The paper over the wood turns black and burns. The paper over the brass discolours slightly and does not burn. Explain why.

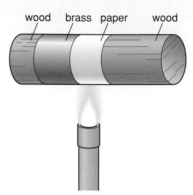

5 a) Explain why a woollen sweater keeps you warm.

b) Explain why it is dangerous to put your bare hand on to metal when the temperature is −15 °C, but it is safe to make a snowball.

4.3 Convection

Figure 3.1 This buzzard soars upwards with very little effort. How does it manage this?

■ Convection currents

To make a hot air balloon fly you need a burner which heats up the air inside the balloon. When air is heated it expands and its density becomes less. When hot air is surrounded by colder, more dense air, it rises. This is the same principle as a cork submerged in water floating to the surface.

Figure 3.2 shows how air circulates if you stand, with most of your clothes off, in the middle of a room. Your body heats up air next to it, which then rises. Colder air flows down near the walls to replace the warmer air. The currents of air that flow are called **convection currents**.

■ Heat transfer by convection

Heat can be transferred by convection in *liquids* and *gases*, but not in solids. Although most liquids and gases do not transfer heat very well by conduction, they do transfer heat quickly by convection. Convection currents allow large quantities of hot liquid or gas to move and give heat energy to a colder part. If we wore no clothes our bodies would lose lots of heat by convection. By wearing clothes we trap a layer of air which acts as an insulator.

Exactly the same idea is used to reduce heat losses from a house in a cold country. The loft (roof space) is full of air and convection currents there can cause a large amount of heat loss. Lofts can be insulated with felt or fibreglass. To stop convection in the cavity between inner and outer walls, it is possible to pump in polystyrene foam. The foam has lots of air trapped in it and so is a poor conductor of heat. Double glazing also traps air, in a layer between two pieces of glass (Figure 3.3).

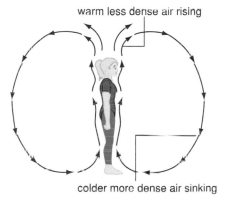

warm less dense air rising

colder more dense air sinking

Figure 3.2 Convection currents near a person in a room.

EXAM TIP

Make sure you understand how houses are insulated to keep them warm.

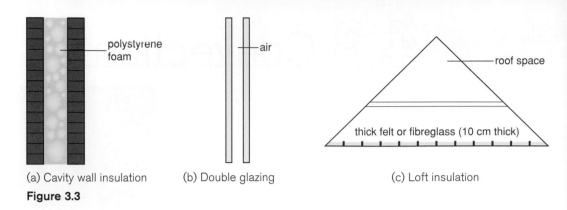

(a) Cavity wall insulation   (b) Double glazing   (c) Loft insulation

Figure 3.3

■ Sea breezes

Convection currents also play an important part in our weather systems. Winds are convection currents on a large scale. You have probably noticed when you have been sunning yourself on the beach that there is usually a sea breeze (Figure 3.4). In the daytime the land warms up quickly. This causes a rising air current and so a breeze blowing in from the sea. Seabirds are quick to take advantage of these rising currents of air, and can soar upwards without flapping their wings.

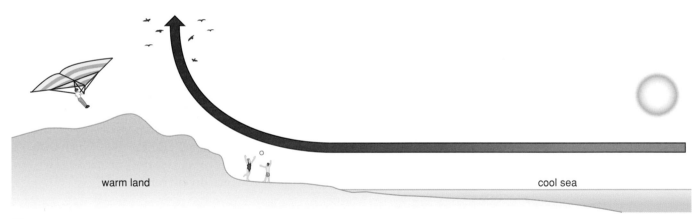

warm land   cool sea

Figure 3.4 The sea takes lots of heat energy to warm up, so it remains cooler than the land. The land warms quickly, and warm air rises above the land.

■ Convection in water

When water is heated it too will transfer heat energy by convection. Figure 3.5 shows a simple way that you can show this in a laboratory. Place some potassium permanganate crystals at the bottom of a flask of water. When heat is supplied from underneath the dissolved potassium permanganate rises, showing the path of the currents.

It is possible to circulate water around the heating system of a house using convection currents. Figure 3.6 shows such a heating system. The boiler must be put at the lowest point in the house. The hot water rises upwards to the roof. The water then feeds the radiators and finally the cool water is returned to the boiler.

PRACTICAL

Make sure you can explain how you can see convection currents in water.

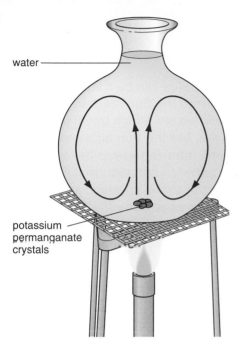

water

potassium permanganate crystals

Figure 3.5 A laboratory experiment to show convection currents in water.

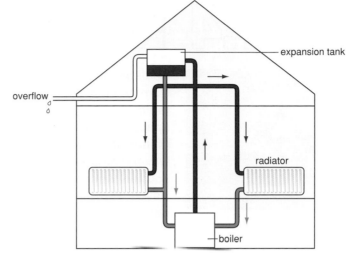

expansion tank

overflow

radiator

boiler

Figure 3.6 This system of circulating water is suitable for a small house only. In a large house a pump is used to help push the water round.

STUDY QUESTIONS

1 Heat cannot be transferred by convection in a solid. Explain why.

2 Figure 3.4 shows the direction of a sea breeze in daytime. At night, the land cools down more quickly than the sea. Draw a diagram to show the direction of the breeze at night.

3 Explain how glider pilots can manoeuvre their gliders to great heights without using an engine.

4 Over a hundred years ago in tin mines, fresh air used to be provided for the miners through two ventilation shafts shown below.

a) To improve the flow of air, a fire was lit at the bottom of one of the shafts. Explain how this worked.

b) One day, Mr Trevethan, the owner of the mine, had an idea. To make the ventilation even better he lit another fire at the bottom of the second shaft. Comment on this idea.

5 This question is about the cost of insulating a house. At the moment the house has no loft insulation, cavity wall insulation or double glazing.

a) Use the data in the box to decide which method of insulation provides the best value for money.

b) How many years do you have to wait before the double glazing has paid for itself?

6 Explain why a candle will not light in a weightless spacecraft in outer space, even if it has a plentiful supply of oxygen.

- Yearly heating bill for house: €700
- Cost of double glazing: €5000 This would reduce the fuel bill by 20% a year
- Cost of loft insulation: €450 This would reduce the fuel bill by 30% a year
- Cost of cavity wall insulation: €1800 This would reduce the fuel bill by 25%

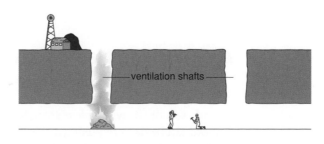

ventilation shafts

4.4 Radiation

Figure 4.1 The Sun emits various types of electromagnetic wave.

Radiation is the third way by which heat energy can be transferred from one place to another. Heat energy from the Sun reaches us by radiation. The Sun emits electromagnetic waves, which travel through space at high speed. Light is such a wave, but the Sun also emits a lot of infra-red waves (or infra-red radiation). Infra-red waves have longer wavelengths than light waves. It is the infra-red radiation that makes you feel warm when you lie down in the sunshine. Infrared radiation travels at the same speed as light; as soon as you see the Sun go behind a cloud you feel cooler.

■ Good and bad absorbers

Infra-red radiation behaves in the same way as light. It can be reflected and focused using a mirror. Figure 4.2 shows the idea behind a solar furnace. The shiny surface of the mirror is a poor absorber of radiation, but a good reflector. Radiation is absorbed well by dull black surfaces. So the boiler at the focus of the solar furnace is a dull black colour.

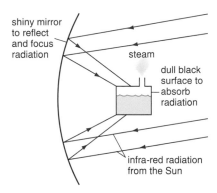

shiny mirror to reflect and focus radiation

steam

dull black surface to absorb radiation

infra-red radiation from the Sun

Figure 4.2 A solar furnace.

> **EXAM TIP**
> Don't forget that heat can be transferred by three methods: conduction, convection and radiation.

Figure 4.3 Solar panels in this house provide the householder with electrical energy. The blackened surface allows infra-red radiation to be absorbed efficiently.

■ Good and bad emitters

Figure 4.4 shows an experiment to investigate which type of teapot will keep your tea warm for a longer time. One pot has a dull black surface, the other is made out of shiny stainless steel. Radiation that is emitted from the hot teapots can be detected using a thermopile and a sensitive ammeter. If you do the experiment you will find that, when the teapots are filled with hot water at the same temperature, the black teapot emits more radiation than

Figure 4.4 A sensitive instrument called a thermopile can detect radiation.

the shiny surface. So a shiny teapot will keep your tea warmer than a black teapot.

- Black surfaces are good absorbers and good emitters of radiation.
- Shiny surfaces are bad absorbers and bad emitters of radiation.

EXAM TIP

Make sure you know which surfaces are good emitters and absorbers of radiation.

■ The greenhouse effect

In Italy, where the average temperature in the summer is high, tomatoes grow very well. It is a great help to tomato growers in a cooler country if they use a greenhouse. On a warm day the temperature inside a greenhouse can be 10 °C or 15 °C higher than outside (Figure 4.5). Infra-red radiation from the Sun passes through the glass of the greenhouse, and is absorbed by the plants and soil inside. The plants radiate energy, but the wavelength of the emitted radiation is much longer. The longer wavelengths of radiation do not pass through the glass and so heat is trapped inside the greenhouse. The temperature rises until the loss of heat through the glass by conduction balances the energy absorbed from the Sun.

A similar greenhouse effect occurs in our atmosphere, and there is concern that the effect is increasing and leading to global warming. As we continue to burn fossil fuels we are filling our atmosphere with carbon dioxide and other chemicals. As these chemicals absorb long-wavelength radiation emitted from the Earth's surface, the average temperature of the Earth increases. The planet Venus has a greenhouse effect on a large scale. Its atmosphere is mostly carbon dioxide and its average surface temperature is about 460 °C, hot enough to melt some metals.

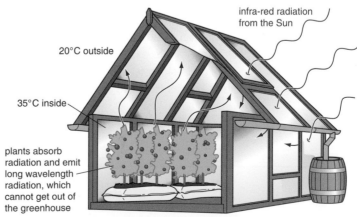

Figure 4.5 Explaining the greenhouse effect.

■ Vacuum flask

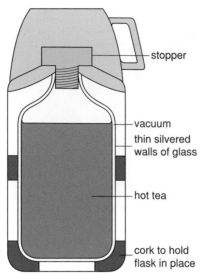

Figure 4.6 A vacuum flask.

A vacuum flask (Thermos flask) keeps things warm by reducing heat losses in all possible ways. The flask is made with a double wall of glass and there is a vacuum between the two walls. Conduction and convection cannot take place through a vacuum. The glass walls are thin, so that little heat is conducted through the glass to the top. Heat can be radiated through a vacuum, but the glass walls are silvered like a mirror so that they are poor emitters of radiation. The stopper at the top prevents heat loss by evaporation or convection currents (Figure 4.6).

STUDY QUESTIONS

1 Explain why each of the following is true, in terms of heat transfer.
   a) A concrete floor feels much colder than a wooden floor when walked on with bare feet, although the temperature of each floor is the same.
   b) Clean snow does not melt quickly in bright sunshine, though dirty snow does.
   c) Some casserole dishes that are used in ovens are black, but the outside of an electric kettle is shiny.
   d) After finishing a marathon, athletes may be wrapped in aluminium-coated plastic sheets.
   e) In hot countries many houses are painted white.
2 Explain three ways in which a vacuum flask helps to keep drinks warm.
3 The diagram above right shows how the Earth receives radiation from the Sun in daytime and re-radiates energy at night.
   a) Explain why, although the Earth has been receiving radiation from the Sun for millions of years, its temperature remains roughly the same.
   b) Why is the density of radiation received at A higher than at B or C? Use this fact to explain why the Earth has a hot equator and cold poles.
   c) Where is the greatest radiation loss from the Earth at night?

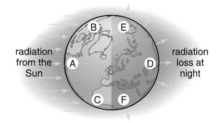

   d) The diagram below shows three convective masses of air in the northern hemisphere. Explain the directions of the rising and falling air.

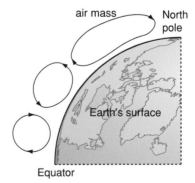

   e) Do some research to find out how many similar masses of rising and falling gases there are on Jupiter. Why do you think this planet has more of these than Earth?

4.5 What is work?

You agree to help a friend move a heavy load. What two factors determine how hard the job will be?

Figure 5.1

■ A job of work

Tony works in a supermarket. His job is to fill up shelves when they are empty. When Tony lifts up tins to put them on the shelves he is doing some work. The amount of work Tony does depends on how far he lifts the tins and how heavy they are.

We define **work** like this:

$$\text{work done} = \text{force} \times \text{distance} = F \times d$$

Work is measured in **joules** (J). 1 joule of work is done when a force of 1 newton moves something through a distance of 1 metre, in the direction of the applied force.

$$1\,\text{J} = 1\,\text{N} \times 1\,\text{m}$$

Example. How much work does Tony do when he lifts a tin with a weight of 20 N through a height of 0.5 m?

$$\begin{aligned} W &= F \times d \\ &= 20\,\text{N} \times 0.5\,\text{m} \\ &= 10\,\text{J} \end{aligned}$$

Tony does the same amount of work when he lifts a tin with a weight of 10 N through 1 m.

You will notice that the unit of work, J, is the same as that used for energy, J. This is because when work is done, energy is transferred. In the case of the tins, the work done by Tony is transferred to the tins as gravitational potential energy.

$$\text{work done} = \text{energy transferred}$$

Following on from Chapter 4.1, we can now also provide an easy way to understand energy.

$$\text{Energy is the capacity to do work.}$$

■ Does a force always do work?

Does a force always do work? The answer is no. In Figure 5.2 Martin is helping Salim and Teresa to give the car a push start. Teresa and Salim are pushing from behind; Martin is pushing from the side. Teresa and Salim are doing some work because they are pushing in the right direction to get the car moving. Martin is doing nothing useful to get the car moving. Martin does no work because he is pushing at right angles to the direction of movement.

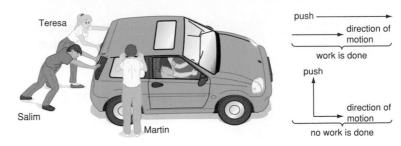

Figure 5.2

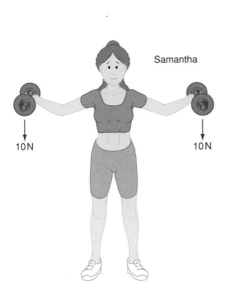

Figure 5.3

In Figure 5.3 Samantha is doing some weight training. She is holding two weights but she is not lifting them. She becomes tired because her muscles use energy, but she is not doing any work because the weights are not moving. To do work you have to move something, for instance lifting a load or pushing a car.

■ Paying for the fuel

When you want a job done you usually have to pay for it. This is because you have to buy fuel. This provides energy for the job to be done. The supermarket manager has to pay Tony to do his work. The most important thing that Tony buys with his money is food. Food gives him the energy to do his work.

Figure 5.4 shows a crane at work on a building site. The crane runs on diesel fuel.

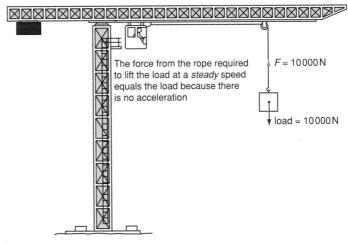

Figure 5.4

Table 1

Load lifted / N	Distance moved / m	Work done / J	Diesel used / litre
10 000	1	10 000	0.01
10 000	2	20 000	0.02
20 000	2	40 000	0.04
40 000	3	120 000	0.12

Table 1 shows the amount of diesel used by the crane in Figure 5.4 for some jobs. You can see that to lift a heavier load, or to move it further, more diesel is used. The work done by the crane is transferred into gravitational potential energy of the load.

Now go through the tutorial *Work done*.

STUDY QUESTIONS

1 In which of the following cases is work being done?
  a) A magnetic force holds a magnet on a steel door.
  b) You pedal a cycle along a road.
  c) A pulley is used to lift a load.
  d) You hold a 2 kg weight, but without moving it.
2 Calculate the work done in each case below.
  a) You lift a 20 N weight through a height of 2 m.
  b) You drag a 40 kg mass 8 m along a floor using a force of 80 N.
3 Table 2 below shows some more jobs done by the crane in Figure 5.4. Copy the table and fill in the missing values.

Table 2

Load lifted/N	Distance moved/m	Work done/J	Fuel used/ litre
5000	2		0.01
10 000	4		
	10	40 000	
6000			0.06
	5		0.1
25 000		90 000	

4 Joel is on the Moon in his spacesuit. His mass including his suit is 120 kg. The gravitational field strength on the Moon is 1.6 N/kg.
  a) Calculate Joel's weight in his spacesuit.

b) Joel now climbs 30 m up a ladder into his spacecraft. How much work does he do?
5 Mr Hendrix runs a passenger ferry service in the Caribbean . He has three ships, which are all the same. Sometimes he has problems with the bottoms of the ships, when barnacles stick to them. This increases the drag on the ships, and they use more fuel than usual.
  a) Explain why a larger drag makes the ships use more fuel.
  b) Table 3 below shows the amount of fuel used by Mr Hendrix's three ships, on recent journeys.
    i) Calculate how much fuel is used per km travelled for each ship.
    ii) The drag force on the *Caribbean Princess* is 50 000 N. Compare this with the drag force on *Windward Beauty* and on *Island Queen*. Which ship has barnacles on her bottom?

Table 3

Ship	Journey	Distance/ km	Fuel used/ litre
Island Queen	Vieux Fort–Bridgetown	175	1050
Windward Beauty	Plymouth–Kingstown	220	1100
Caribbean Princess	Bridgetown–St. George's	255	1275

4.6 Calculating energy

In Figure 6.1, how much work is done in lifting 110 kg through 2 m? Can you estimate the total kinetic energy of the vehicles shown in Figure 6.2? On the vampire roller coaster in Figure 6.3, you can fall a height of 15 m. If you start from a very low speed what is the speed you will reach by the bottom of the fall?

Figure 6.1

■ Gravitational potential energy

When a weightlifter lifts his weights he does some work. This work increases the gravitational potential energy (GPE) of the weights. The total mass of the bar is m. How much work does he do when he lifts the bar a height h? (m is in kilograms and h is in metres.) The pull of gravity on the bar (its weight) is $m \times g$. We call the pull of gravity on each kilogram g; this is 10 N/kg.

$$\text{work done} = F \times d$$
$$= mgh$$

The work done is equal to the increase in potential energy.

$$\text{gravitational potential energy} = mgh$$

Figure 6.2

■ Kinetic energy

The kinetic energy of a moving object is given by the formula:

$$\text{kinetic energy} = \tfrac{1}{2}\,mv^2$$
(m is the mass of the object in kg, and v is its velocity in m/s.)

This formula is very important for working out the stopping distance of a moving car. When cars are travelling very quickly, they need a large distance to stop in. Table 1 shows the stopping distances for a car travelling at different speeds. Next time you are travelling down the motorway at 30 m/s (110 km/h) remember that your car needs about 72 m to stop in.

Figure 6.3 These riders get a thrill when potential energy is transferred to kinetic energy.

Table 1 The faster the car travels, the greater the distance it needs to stop

Speed / m/s	Thinking distance / m	Braking distance / m	Total stopping distance / m
10	6	6	12
20	12	24	36
30	18	54	72
40	24	96	120

When a driver sees a hazard, there is a small delay before he presses the brake pedal. In this time the car moves forward at its original speed. This is the *thinking distance*, which depends on the car's speed. When the brakes are applied, work is done by the braking force to reduce the car's kinetic energy. Since the car's kinetic energy depends on v^2, the *braking distance* depends on v^2. This means that when the car's speed doubles from 10 m/s to 20 m/s, the braking distance increases by a factor of 4. You can read more about stopping distances in Chapter 1.7.

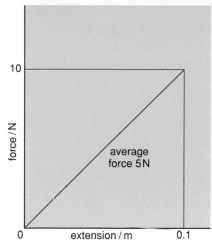

Figure 6.3

■ Elastic potential energy

When a spring is stretched it stores strain energy. This energy can be obtained from the spring when it is released, provided that it has not been stretched past its elastic limit.

Figure 6.3 shows a force-extension graph for a spring. How much energy is stored when the spring is stretched 0.1 m?

> energy stored = work done in stretching the spring
> = average force × distance

When the spring is stretched the force pulling it changes, so we have to average the force. The average force is half of the final force (10 N) stretching the spring. So:

$$\text{energy stored} = 5\,\text{N} \times 0.1\,\text{m}$$
$$= 0.5\,\text{J}$$

■ Using equations to calculate the energy changes

Now that you have learnt some formulae for various types of energy, you can use them together with the principle of conservation of energy to do some calculations. Some examples are given below.

1 A car, with a mass of 1200 kg and travelling at 30 m/s, is slowed by its brakes to a speed of 20 m/s. The brakes are applied for a distance of 75 m. What force do the brakes apply in slowing the car down?

We solve this by thinking of energy transfers. Work is done by the brakes in transferring the car's kinetic energy to thermal energy in the brake blocks.

$$\text{work done by the brakes} = \text{kinetic energy transferred (or lost to other forms)}$$
$$Fd = \tfrac{1}{2}mv_1^2 - \tfrac{1}{2}mv_2^2$$
$$F \times 75 = \tfrac{1}{2}(1200 \times 30^2) - \tfrac{1}{2}(1200 \times 20^2)$$
$$F \times 75 = 600 \times 900 - 600 \times 400$$
$$F \times 75 = 540\,000 - 240\,000$$
$$F = \frac{300\,000}{75}$$
$$= 4000\,\text{N}$$

EXAM TIP

Look at the calculation for the change of kinetic energy. Work out the first value for kinetic energy, then subtract the second value for kinetic energy.

2 A ball of mass 100 g is thrown vertically upwards with a speed of 12 m/s. What is the maximum height it will reach?

As the ball rises, its kinetic energy will be transferred to gravitational potential energy. So we can use equations for those quantities to solve the problem. (The gravitational field strength g is 10 N/kg.)

$$mgh = \tfrac{1}{2}mv^2$$
$$0.1 \times 10 \times h = \tfrac{1}{2} \times 0.1 \times 12^2$$
$$10h = \tfrac{1}{2} \times 144$$
$$h = 7.2\,\text{m}$$

3 This problem refers to energy transfers in a bungee jump. Figure 6.4 shows a jumper, Chloe, launching herself off the Victoria Falls Bridge,

Figure 6.4

which crosses over the Zambezi River at a height of 128 m. Chloe has a mass of 60 kg. Clearly, the bungee rope is designed so that she does not fall into the river. Figure 6.5 shows the elastic potential energy stored in the rope as it stretches; the unstretched length of this rope is 90 m.

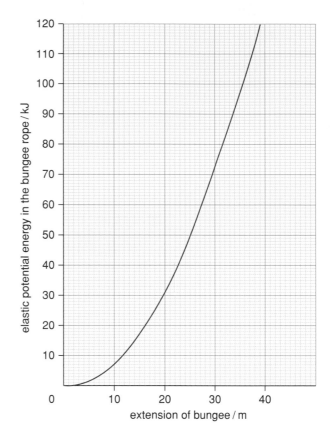

Figure 6.5

We can use this data to calculate the maximum speed of the jumper and to check that she falls a total of only 120 m and so avoids falling into the river.

She reaches her greatest speed after she has fallen 90 m, just before the rope begins to slow her down. So her potential energy has been transferred to kinetic energy.

$$mgh = \tfrac{1}{2}mv^2$$
$$60 \times 10 \times 90 = \tfrac{1}{2} \times 60 \times v^2$$
$$v^2 = 2 \times 900$$
$$v^2 = 1800$$
$$v = 42 \text{ m/s}$$

When Chloe falls a total of 120 m the gravitational potential energy transferred is:

$$\text{GPE converted} = mgh$$
$$= 60 \times 10 \times 120$$
$$= 72\,000 \text{ J}$$

You can see from the graph (Figure 6.5) that when the rope is stretched by 30 m, it stores 72 000 J of elastic potential energy, so she stops there, having fallen a total of 90 m + 30 m, which is 120 m, 8 m above the river.

STUDY QUESTIONS

1 A charging rhinoceros moves at a speed of 15 m/s and its mass is 750 kg. What is its kinetic energy?

2 What is the thinking time of the driver whose thinking distances are shown in Table 1?

3 a) Use the data in Table 1 to plot graphs of:
   i) the thinking distance against speed
   ii) the braking distance against speed.
   Draw the best fit line through the points for each graph.
   b) Comment on the shape of each graph.

4 Figure 6.3 shows a graph of force against extension for a spring. The same spring is extended by 0.05 m.
   a) Calculate the force required to cause this extension.
   b) Calculate the energy stored in the spring now.

5 A car of mass 750 kg slows down from 30 m/s to 15 m/s over a distance of 50 m.
   a) What is its change in kinetic energy?
   b) What is the average braking force that acts on it?

6 A car of mass 1000 kg does an emergency stop when it is travelling at 15 m/s; it brakes to a stop in a distance of 20 m.
   a) Calculate the change in kinetic energy for the car.
   b) Calculate the force which acts to slow it down.
   c) The car is now heavily loaded and has a mass of 1250 kg. It is travelling at 15 m/s. Explain why the braking distance is now larger than the distance you calculated in part (a).

d) On another day the car is travelling at 30 m/s; if the brakes exert the same force, calculate the braking distance now. (The mass is still 1000 kg).

e) What will happen to your braking distance if:
   i) the road is icy
   ii) you are going downhill?

7 A catapult stores 10 J of elastic potential energy when it is fully stretched. It is used to launch a marble of mass 0.02 kg straight up into the air.
   a) Calculate how high the marble rises.
   b) How fast is the marble moving when it is 30 m above the ground? (Ignore any affects due to air resistance.)

8 a) Gregg has a mass of 90 kg.
   i) Calculate the gravitational potential energy transferred if he falls 128 m.
   ii) Use the graph in Figure 6.5 to calculate the elastic potential energy stored when the rope has extended 38 m.
   iii) Discuss whether the rope is safe for Gregg to use in the bungee jump.
   b) What change or changes would you make to ensure a safe jump for someone of Gregg's mass?

4.7 Power

Figure 7.1

Alice and David are lifting some bricks. They each lift 20 bricks through a height of 5 m. This means that they do the same amount of work. However, David is large and powerful and he lifts all of his bricks in one go. Alice, who is a small girl, lifts her bricks one at a time. We use the word powerful to describe someone who can do the work quickly.

■ Power formula

Power is the rate of doing work or transferring energy.

$$\text{power} = \frac{\text{work done or energy transferred}}{\text{time taken}}$$

From the equation above you can see that power is measured in J/s. But we give power its own unit called the **watt**. 1 watt (1 W) is equal to a rate of working of 1 J/s. Power ratings can be very large; then we use the units of kW (kilowatt or 1000 W) and MW (megawatt or 1 000 000 W).

■ Body power

Alice measures her personal power output by running up a flight of steps. She takes 8.4 s to run up a flight of steps of total height 6 m. Her mass is 14 kg. What power does she develop? She has done some work to lift her weight of 140 N through a height of 6 m.

$$\text{work done} = \text{force} \times \text{distance}$$
$$= 140\,\text{N} \times 6\,\text{m} = 840\,\text{J}$$
$$\text{power} = \frac{\text{work done}}{\text{time}}$$
$$= \frac{840\,\text{J}}{8.4\,\text{s}} = 100\,\text{W}$$

Alice is transferring energy at about the same rate as an old-style filament light bulb.

■ Power of an express train

Figure 7.2 shows a *Eurostar* express train approaching a station at a steady speed. When the train moves at a constant speed, the driving force from the wheels is exactly balanced by opposing frictional forces. These opposing forces are caused by friction in the axles of the wheels and by wind resistance. So the train does work against these frictional forces.

How much power does the train have to produce when it is running at 40 m/s?

$$\text{power} = \frac{\text{work done}}{\text{time}} = \frac{\text{force} \times \text{distance}}{\text{time}}$$
$$= F \times \frac{d}{t}$$

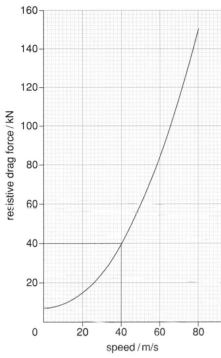

Figure 7.3 Graph to show the resistive force acting on a *Eurostar* train as the speed increases.

So the power developed is equal to the driving force × the distance travelled per second. But the distance travelled per second is the speed, *v*.

$$\text{power} = F \times v$$

The resistive force on the train travelling at 40 m/s can be found from Figure 7.3; you can see it is 40 kN.

$$\begin{aligned}\text{power} &= 40 \text{ kN} \times 40 \text{ m/s} \\ &= 40\,000 \text{ N} \times 40 \text{ m/s} \\ &= 1\,600\,000 \text{ W or } 1.6 \text{ MW}\end{aligned}$$

Figure 7.2

STUDY QUESTIONS

1 What is the unit of power?
2 David runs up the same flight of steps as Alice in a time of 5 seconds. The steps are 6 m high and David's mass is 100 kg. Calculate his power. How many times more powerful is he than Alice, whose power is 100 W?
3 A weightlifter lifts 280 kg above his head. In the last part of the lift he raises the bar through 1.0 m in 1.5 s.
   a) How much work does he do?
   b) How much power does he develop?
4 a) Use the graph in Figure 7.3 to estimate the resistive drag force on a *Eurostar* train when it is travelling at:
     i) 60 m/s
     ii) 80 m/s.
   b) Show that the power that the engine produces to pull the train at 60 m/s is about 5 MW.
   c) Calculate the power the engine produces when the train runs at 80 m/s.
   d) Use the formula $W = F \times d$ to calculate the work done against resistive forces when the train goes 2 km travelling at:
     i) 40 m/s
     ii) 80 m/s. Give your answers in MJ.
   e) Now explain why you save on petrol costs if you drive at 80 kph rather than at 110 kph.
5 Here is part of an answer written by a student to explain the motion of a cricket ball. She has made some mistakes. Rewrite what she has written, explaining and correcting her errors.
   'When a batsman hits a cricket ball he gives it a certain force. As the ball rolls over the grass this force is used up and eventually the ball stops. All the power that the batsman used in hitting the ball ends up as heat.'
6 Read this extract from a magazine article: *The hind legs of a locust are extremely powerful. The insect takes off with a speed of 3 m/s. The jump is fast and occurs in a time of 25 milliseconds. The locust's mass is about 2.5 g.*
   Use the information to answer the problems below.
   a) Calculate the locust's average acceleration during take off. (25 milliseconds = 0.025 s)
   b) Now work out the average force exerted by the locust's hind legs (remember to turn the mass into kg).
   c) The locust's legs extend by 5 cm (0.05 m) during its jump. Calculate the work done by its legs.
   d) How much power does the locust develop in its muscles?
   e) Calculate the power/mass ratio for the locust and compare this with David's power/mass ratio (from question 2).

4.8 Electrical energy production

All of these devices can be turned on with the flick of a switch. How does the electricity company cope, when we all come home and turn everything on at the same time?

Figure 8.1 What are the consequences of being able to turn all of these on at the flick of a switch?

Many power stations use coal as their source of energy. When coal is burnt its stored chemical energy is released as heat energy. This heat energy boils water at high pressure to make superheated steam at temperatures of about 700 °C. The kinetic energy in the superheated steam is used to drive **turbines**. These are connected to the electricity generator's large coils, which rotate inside a strong magnetic field (see Chapter 6.8).

Figure 8.2 shows the principle behind the production of electrical energy in a power station.

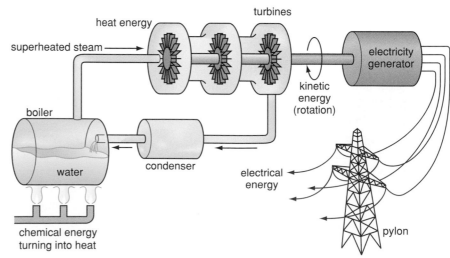

Figure 8.2 The principle of a power station.

Figure 8.3 This shows several 600 megawatt generators inside the coal-fired Drax power station. Superheated steam is used to drive the generators.

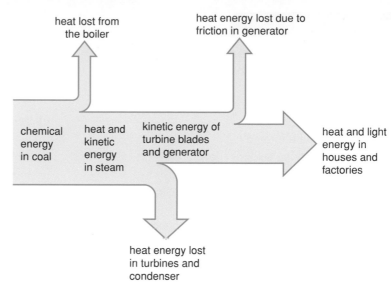

Figure 8.4 Energy transfers in a power station.

Figure 8.4 is a Sankey diagram showing how energy is used in the process of electrical energy generation. There is a lot of heat lost in the power station. The electrical energy itself is also converted to heat energy in factories and houses.

There are two problems that arise from the production of electricity that worry a lot of people.

1 **Pollution.** Burning coal makes the gases carbon dioxide and sulphur dioxide. These pollute the atmosphere. When sulfur dioxide dissolves in water, an acidic solution is formed containing sulfuric acid.

$$\text{water} + \text{sulfur dioxide} \rightarrow \text{sulfuric acid}$$

So when sulfur dioxide gets into rain, the rain becomes acidic. We call this **acid rain**. Acid rain damages stonework in buildings. It is thought that acid rain is also killing trees in Scandinavia. It is likely that sulfur dioxide produced in Britain is blown across to Scandinavia by the prevailing south-westerly winds.

2 **Global warming.** Heat energy is always produced when we make electrical energy. People worry that we will warm the Earth up, as we increase our use of electrical energy. This warming is caused by extra carbon dioxide in the atmosphere trapping heat in, so that the Earth's temperature will rise slowly. This phenomenon is called the **greenhouse effect** (see Chapter 3.3). An increase in the Earth's temperature could have very serious consequences. An increase of 1 °C or 2 °C to the Earth's average temperature would melt a large amount of ice from the polar ice caps and cause great changes in regional climates and weather patterns.

Although we get great benefits from electrical energy, we have to consider its effect on the environment. If we are not careful we will damage the world that we live in.

Figure 8.5 A hydroelectric dam.

STUDY QUESTIONS

1 a) Explain why smog is sometimes seen in large cities. If necessary, use the Internet to find out what smog is.

  b) Why do large cities have smokeless zones?

2 a) Explain what acid rain is.

  b) How is acid rain formed?

  c) What effects does acid rain have on the environment?

  d) What would you do to reduce the problems caused by acid rain?

3 Give a detailed account of the energy changes that occur to generate electricity in a coal-fired power station.

4 Figure 8.6 shows the layout of a pumped storage power station. Water from the high level lake produces electrical energy by flowing through the turbine generators. These are placed just above the low level lake. When there is a low demand for electricity, the generators are driven in reverse to pump water back into the high level lake. This means there will be enough water to generate electricity again, the next time demand is high.

a) Why is this sort of power station useful to electricity companies?

b) Would this pumped storage power station pollute the atmosphere when it generates electricity?

c) Where does the energy come from to pump the water back up the hill again?

d) What energy changes occur as water flows from the high level lake to the low level lake?

e) Calculate the loss of gravitational potential energy of the water in 1 second. (Use the information in Figure 8.6.)

f) The turbines are 60% efficient. Calculate the electrical power output of this station. Give your answer in MW.

For the next two questions, look at Figure 8.7.

g) At what times of day will the pumped storage power station be producing electricity?

h) Explain the shape of the graph in Figure 8.7. Why does it reach a maximum at about 6 pm?

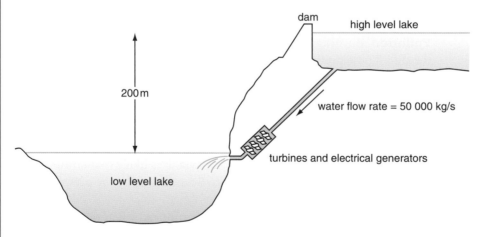

Figure 8.6 A pumped storage power station.

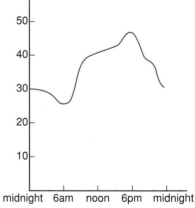

Figure 8.7 The typical use of electrical energy on a winter's day.

4.9 The world's energy resources

A large city might use 10^{14} J of energy in one day. We need to burn 10 000 tonnes of coal to provide this amount of energy. The Sun is the major energy source for the Earth. The Sun provides heat and light to make our lives possible, as well as providing energy for the growth of foods that we eat. Fossil fuels, which we burn, originally derived their energy from the Sun too.

Figure 9.1

■ Fossil fuels

At the moment the world faces an energy crisis. This may seem surprising; you have learnt that energy cannot be lost. The problem is that we are burning fuels such as coal, oil and gas. These fuels produce electricity, warm our houses and provide energy for transport. The end product of these fuels is heat energy. We cannot recapture the heat and turn it back into coal or oil. These fuels are known as **non-renewable energy sources**. Once we have burnt them they have gone forever.

Coal, oil and gas are known as **fossil fuels**. They are the remains of plants and animals that lived hundreds of millions of years ago. Supplies of these fuels are limited. We use coal mainly for the production of electrical energy. If we go on using coal at its present rate, it will last for about another 300 years.

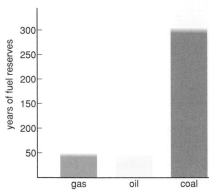

Figure 9.2 How long will our fossil fuels last?

We get petrol from oil. So this energy source is vital for running cars and also aeroplanes. At our present rate of use, known reserves of oil will last us about 50 years. Gas will last for about the same time.

As current supplies of oil and gas become depleted, they get more expensive to extract. The price of oil and gas continues to rise; the shortage of fossil fuels is a problem that will have to be faced in our lifetime. It is important that we use fossil fuels carefully, and we must also look for other sources of energy.

■ Other energy sources

Nuclear power

Nuclear power is used to generate about 17% of the worlds electricity. France generates 78% of its electrical energy using nuclear power. Until the Fukoshima disaster of 2011, Japan generated about one-sixth of its electricity using nuclear power. In 2012 the Japanese Government took the decision to abandon the use of nuclear power while the country assessed the safety of the nuclear programme.

The nuclear fuel used is uranium. This is also a non-renewable energy source. But nuclear power could provide our energy for a few thousand years. Nuclear power worries people because of the possibility of accidents such as that in Fukushima, and because of the radioactive waste that is produced. This is discussed further in Section 7, Chapter 8.

Some further sources of energy are described below; these are **renewable energy sources**. In these cases we extract energy from the environment and these energy sources will always be available to us.

Biomass

Biomass is the name we use when talking about plants in the sense that we can extract energy from them. The most common way of extracting energy from biomass is to cut down a tree and burn it. Trees are a renewable energy source so long as forests are looked after properly. Unfortunately, in Africa,

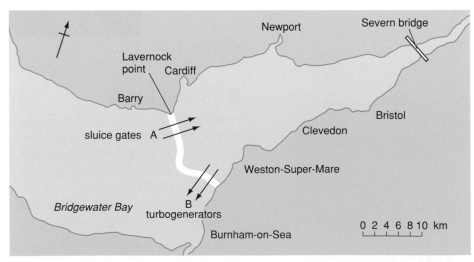

Figure 9.3 The possible Severn Barrage in the UK. The cost is estimated at £30 billion. The barrage would be able to produce 7000 MW of power. This amounts to about 5% of the national need.

Asia and South America trees are being cut down far faster than they are being replanted. It is thought that cutting down large forests has changed our climate by reducing rainfall in some parts of the world and by affecting the carbon dioxide levels in the atmosphere.

In some countries vegetable oils are widely used as fuels in farm machinery and cars.

Tidal power

Figure 9.3 shows a map of the Severn estuary in the UK, which is a suitable position for a tidal barrage. The idea is that water flows in through the sluice gates at A at high tide. At low tide water flows out through the turbogenerators at B. We are using the potential energy of the water to generate electrical energy. If the Severn estuary barrage is built it will produce about 7000 MW of power.

Hydroelectric power

This form of generation is widely used in Scandinavia, where a lot of water flows down the mountains from melted snow. The principle is the same as tidal power: the potential energy of the water is used to generate electrical energy.

Wind power

Energy from the wind can also be used to generate electricity. Figure 9.4 shows a wind farm. Wind power is considered in more detail in the next chapter.

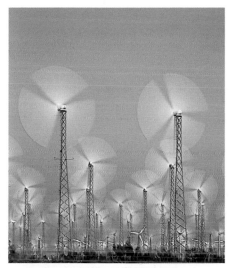

Figure 9.4 A large wind farm. Each wind turbine has three blades and can produce a power of up to 3 megawatts. Such a large farm can be equivalent to a coal-fired power station.

Geothermal power

Energy can be obtained from a hot spring. As the water in the spring boils, the steam formed is used to drive electrical turbines. In some countries: Iceland, New Zealand and China for example, warm water (50 °C) is pumped out of the ground directly into factories and houses to provide central heating.

Solar power

Energy from the Sun can be used directly to warm up water in panels in the roofs of houses. It can also be used to generate electricity using panels of photocells. Solar panels on the roofs of houses are now a common sight.

STUDY QUESTIONS

1 Explain the difference between a renewable and a non-renewable fuel.

2 a) Why are air fares likely to be extremely expensive in 50 years' time?

  b) Government ministers sometimes talk of introducing 'Green Taxes'. What are they, and do you agree that they should be introduced?

  c) Why is petrol wasted if a car accelerates or brakes rapidly?

3 Explain carefully the energy transfers which occur to produce a fossil fuel; remember to explain where the energy came from in the first place.

4 Describe three advantages and disadvantages of large scale electricity production using (i) coal, (ii) a combination of renewable energy sources such as wind and tidal power. In your answer consider factors such as cost, the environmental impact and supply of the energy resource.

5 Discuss the advantages and disadvantages of the use of nuclear power to generate electricity.

4.10 Large-scale electricity production

Figure 10.1 On average each person in this photograph uses 25 MJ of electrical energy every day. How much is used by the whole world every day, and how much will we use in 2050?

In about 2011, the world's population reached 7 billion people; the population was 5 billion in the early 1980s and it is projected to be 9 billion by 2040 or 2050. This rapidly growing population brings with it many problems for us to solve: we need to provide more housing in safe places; we need more food; we need to produce more electricity to light and heat our homes. The need for electricity is growing, not just because of the growing population, but due to the urbanisation and industrialisation of countries, which were until recently less reliant on modern technology.

This chapter looks in some detail at the way in which some countries produce electricity, and discusses the advantages and disadvantages of the methods of production.

■ Energy use by country and per person

Table 1 shows the electrical energy used by a number of countries, listed by the total energy used, and also by the energy used per head of population. You can draw two obvious conclusions from the data – large countries need more energy and rich countries use more. The data was recorded in 2011.

The contrast between the energy available in the industrialised world and the African World is quite pronounced. There can be difficulties when countries try to agree targets for carbon emissions: China and India use a lot of coal

EXAM TIP

The use of coal to generate electricity is discussed in Chapter 4.8, and the use of nuclear power is discussed in detail in Chapters 7.8 and 7.9.

EXPLANATION

A TW (terrawatt) is 10^{12} W (a million million W).
A TWh is the energy used when 1TW of power is used for 1 hour.

Table 1 Electrical energy used by country

Country	Total energy used per year / TWh	Energy used per head of population per year / kWh
China	4 400	2 600
USA	4 400	13 500
Russia	1 000	7 000
India	900	600
France	600	8 900
Brazil	500	2 300
UK	400	6 100
Norway	100	31 000
Iceland	12	39 000
Kenya	6	137
Ethiopia	4	44
Somalia	0.3	31
Rwanda	0.1	10

to produce electricity but their populations are very large. The amounts of electrical power used per head in Norway and Iceland are large because each country generates nearly all of their electricity by using cheap, renewable sources (hydroelectric and geothermal), which do not produce greenhouse gases.

■ Means of electrical power generation

Each country solves its energy production according to the sources they have available. Some countries have a plentiful supply of fossil fuels; others have natural resources available such as wind and wave power. Table 2 shows some countries and the major sources of their electrical generation.

Table 2 Sources of electricity generation by country

Country	Coal / %	Gas / %	Oil / %	Nuclear / %	Hydro / %	Geothermal / %	Others – wind, power, bio-mass, tidal / %
China	70	6	4	2	18	0	0
USA	45	23	1	20	7	0	4
France	4	4	2	78	11	0	1
UK	33	40	0	19	3	0	5
Brazil	1	13	4	2	75	0	5
Norway	0	0	0	0	99	0	1
Iceland	0	0	0	0	70	30	0
Kenya	0	12	5	0	70	13	0

In the paragraphs that follow we look at the advantages and disadvantages of three examples of power generation on a large scale in different countries.

■ China's Three Gorges Dam

Figure 10.2 illustrates a problem caused by the growing production of electricity – with so many coal-fired power stations, smog in industrial areas is a health hazard. China is committed to producing more of its energy by renewable means. The Three Gorges Dam is the largest hydroelectric plant in the world, being able to generate 21 GW (21 000 MW) of power. This and other hydroelectric power stations have the advantage of being clean and non-polluting. However, the building of the dam had its disadvantages: the lake behind the dam caused 2 million people to be displaced from their homes; archaeological and cultural sites were flooded; farmland and fish breeding habitats were destroyed. A further disadvantage is that the plant rarely runs at its maximum capacity. The Three Gorges Dam lies on the

> **EXPLANATION**
>
> A GW (gigawatt) is 10^9 W (a thousand million W).

Figure 10.2 Smog in a city.

Figure 10.3 This photograph shows the Three Gorges Dam under construction.

Yangtze River, whose source is in the Tibetan Plateau. The flow of water is at a low point over the winter months as water is frozen into the glaciers in the Himalayan Mountains. In the summer months the river flows rapidly, so the production of electricity is at its greatest then (see Figure 10.4).

The principle behind generating electricity with water is shown in Figure 10.3. Gravitational potential energy stored in the water behind the dam is used to rotate the turbines attached to a generator. The Three Gorges Dam has 32 such generators.

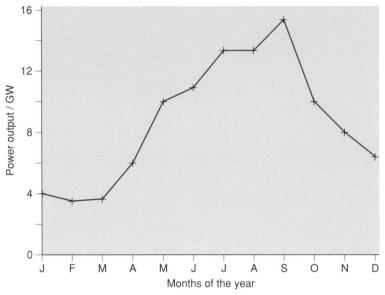

Figure 10.4

■ Iceland's geothermal plants

Iceland takes advantage of the volcanic activity on the island, which generates underground hot-water sources. Some hot water is used directly to warm houses, and some hot water or steam is used to drive turbogenerators (Figure 10.5). This form of electricity production has the advantage of being clean, there is no need to mine fossil fuels, and geothermal energy will not run out in the foreseeable future. The only disadvantage is that it is only available in a small number of countries.

Figure 10.5

Wind power

Figure 10.6 illustrates the growth in the world's capacity to generate electricity with wind power over the last 15 years. The advantage of wind power is that it provides a continuous free and clean source of energy. People point to the disadvantage that the wind does not blow all the time. However, if the UK had wind turbines installed all across the country, it is highly likely that many of the turbines would be working on most days. When the turbines are working they reduce the need to burn fossil fuels.

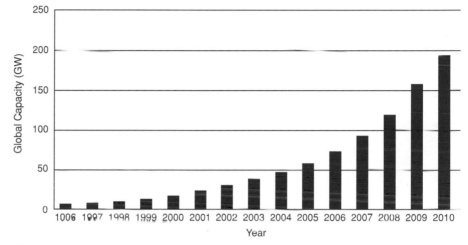

Figure 10.6

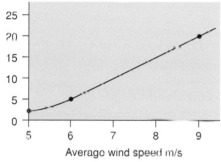

Figure 10.7 The y axis shows the percentage of time the wind generator works at full power (3.0 MW)

Figure 10.7 shows how well a wind turbine works, depending on the average wind speed: for example an average wind speed of 7 m/s means the generator is at full capacity for 10% of the time; an average wind speed of 9 m/s means the generator is working at full capacity for 20% of the time. Some people complain that the wind turbines are unsightly and that they make a noise, which is annoying if you live close to one.

STUDY QUESTIONS

1 a) In Table 1, two different units of energy are used – TWh (terawatt hours) and kWh (kilowatt hours). Explain what these two units mean.

   b) Explain what is meant by the unit of power, the gigawatt or GW.

2 Use the information in this chapter to summarise the advantages and disadvantages of electrical generation using:

   i) hydroelectric power

   ii) wind power

   iii) geothermal power.

3 Do some research to enable you to summarise the advantages and disadvantages of electrical generation using:

   a) solar power

   b) nuclear power.

4 Choose one country from China, USA, France and the UK. Discuss the advantages and disadvantages of the main way in which that country generates its electrical supply (see Table 2).

5 a) Use the information in Figure 10.4 to work out the average power generated by the generators of the Three Gorges Dam.

   b) Now work out the average energy output of the generators, per year, in TWh.

6 The UK needs to generate an average of 30 GW of electrical power to provide for the country's needs.

   a) How many 3 MW wind turbines would the country need to produce this power:

      i) if they worked at full power all the time

      ii) if the average wind speed near them is 6 m/s? Use Figure 10.7 to help you answer these questions.

   b) Where you would site these turbines in the country?

Summary

 Make sure you can answer all the questions in the *Interactive quiz*.

I am confident that:

✓ **I can recall these facts about energy**
- The principle of conservation of energy: energy cannot be created or destroyed.
- Energy can be transferred from one type of energy to another.
- Energy is the capacity to do work.
- Efficiency = $\dfrac{\text{useful energy}}{\text{energy put in}}$

  Efficiency is expressed as a fraction or a percentage.
- Types of energy include: gravitational potential, kinetic, elastic, chemical, heat, electrical, light, sound and nuclear.
- Heat energy can be transferred by conduction. Metals are good conductors of heat. Trapped air is a poor conductor (or insulator).
- Heat energy can be transferred by convection. Warm air is less dense than cold air, so it rises. This difference of density causes convection currents.

- Heat energy can be transferred by infra-red radiation, which travels at the speed of light. Black surfaces are good emitters and absorbers of radiation; shiny surfaces are poor emitters and absorbers of radiation.
- Work = force × distance moved in direction of force
- 1 joule = 1 newton × 1 metre
- Gravitational potential energy =
  mass × gravitational field strength × height
  $$GPE = mgh$$
- Kinetic energy = ½ mass × velocity²
  $$KE = \tfrac{1}{2}mv^2$$
- Power = $\dfrac{\text{energy transferred}}{\text{time}}$

  1 watt = 1 joule/second
- The advantages and disadvantages of the generation of electricity using renewable and non-renewable energy resources.

Exam-style questions

1 People can take various actions to reduce heat loss from their homes. Describe one thing that can be done to reduce heat loss through:

a) the gaps around the doors [1]

b) the glass in the windows [1]

c) the outside walls [1]

d) the roof. [1]

e) The diagram shows three pieces of aluminium, each with a different surface. They each have a drop of water placed on them, then they are heated by a radiant heater placed about 30 cm above them. Explain the order in which the water drop on each piece of aluminium will dry.

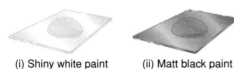

(i) Shiny white paint   (ii) Matt black paint

(iii) Shiny unpainted metal [3]

2 A conveyor belt is used to lift bags of cement on a building site (see diagram above right).

a) A 30 kg bag of cement is lifted from the ground to the top of the building. Calculate its gain in gravitational potential energy. (1 kg has a weight of 10 N.) [3]

b) The machine lifts five bags per minute to the top of the building. Calculate the useful energy delivered by the machine each second. [2]

c) The machine is 20% efficient. Calculate the input power to the machine while it is lifting the bags. [3]

5.8 m

3 A car and its passengers have a combined mass of 1500 kg. It is travelling at a speed of 15 m/s. It increases its speed to 25 m/s.

a) Calculate the increase in kinetic energy as a result of this increase in speed. [3]

b) Explain why the increase in kinetic energy is a much greater fractional increase than the increase in speed. [1]

4 The diagram shows a Pirate Boat theme park ride, which swings from A to B to C and back.

a) As the boat swings from A to B a child gains 10 830 J of kinetic energy. The child has a mass of 60 kg and sits in the centre of the boat. Calculate the speed of the child as the boat passes through B. [3]

b) Sketch a graph to show how the child's gravitational potential energy changes as the boat swings from A to B to C. [3]

c) By using the concept that gravitational potential energy is converted to kinetic energy as the child falls, calculate the height change of the ride. [3]

A

B

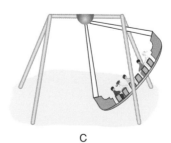

C

5 In the following cases explain carefully the energy changes or transfers that occur. Do not just write something like 'potential to kinetic', be specific: Where is the energy? Is the energy given to another object?

a) You pluck a guitar string and your friend hears a sound. [3]

b) You throw a ball vertically upwards. [3]

c) You kick a football along the ground; it comes to a halt. [3]

d) Energy is transferred from the Sun to warm you up while sunbathing. [3]

e) You accelerate a car, then bring it to rest using the brakes. [3]

f) A firework rocket takes off, explodes and falls back to the ground. [3]

6 A hot liquid loses heat by conduction, convection, radiation and evaporation. The vacuum flask shown below is designed to prevent hot liquids becoming cold.

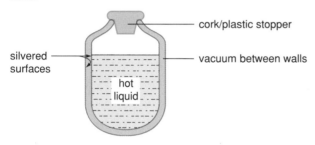

a) Explain how the vacuum between the walls reduces the heat loss. [2]

b) Explain how and why the cork/plastic stopper reduces the heat loss. [2]

c) Explain how the silvered surfaces reduce heat loss. [2]

7 The diagram below shows radiation from the Sun arriving at the Earth's surface at two places and the possible movement of an air mass between the North Pole and the Equator.

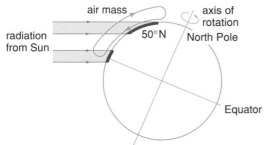

a) How does the intensity of radiation arriving at the Equator compare with that arriving at latitude 50° North? [1]

b) State how this affects the average surface temperatures at the Equator and at latitude 50° North. [1]

c) The diagram shows the possible movement of air between the North Pole and the Equator. Explain how the circulation of the air shown is produced. [2]

8 The next diagram shows how energy from the Sun can be used to heat a house.

Water from the storage tank is pumped through the solar panel.

In the solar panel, the water passes through copper pipes that are painted black.

The water is then returned to the storage tank.

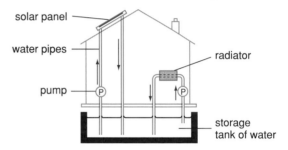

a) i) Explain why the pipes in the solar panel are painted black. [1]

ii) Plastic pipes are cheaper than copper pipes. Explain why copper pipes are used in the panel rather than plastic ones. [1]

b) Write down **one** advantage and **one** disadvantage of using solar panels rather than gas to heat a house. [2]

c) The solar panel takes water from the bottom of the storage tank. The radiator takes water from the top of the storage tank. Explain why. [2]

d) The house is heated by pumping warm water from the storage tank through radiators. The diagram below shows the position of a radiator in a room. Describe how the radiator heats the room. Copy the diagram and add to it to illustrate your answer. [2]

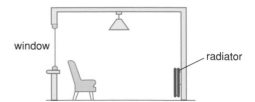

9 The diagram shows a section of track near a railway station. The track at the station is slightly higher than the rest of the track. What advantage does this give? Explain your answer in terms of energy changes. [3]

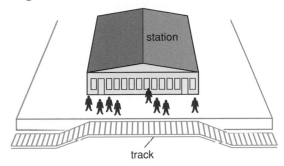

10 Which of the following forces are doing work?

a) A magnetic force holding a magnet onto a steel door. [1]

b) A force driving a car forward. [1]

c) A weightlifter holding a weight stationary. [1]

d) A paper weight holding down a pile of paper. [1]

e) A crane applying a force to lift a load. [1]

f) The pull of gravity holding a satellite in a circular orbit around the Earth. [1]

11 The Eiffel Tower in Paris is 300 m high and can be climbed using its 1792 steps. Jacques decided to climb the tower; he took 15 minutes to do it and he has a mass of 60 kg.

a) How much work did he do climbing the steps? [3]

b) What was his average power output during the climb? [3]

c) A croissant provides Jacques with 400 kJ of energy when digested. How many croissants should Jacques eat for breakfast if his body is 20% efficient at transferring this energy into useful work? [3]

d) Explain where most of the energy from Jacques' food goes. [1]

12 a) The diagram (above right) shows a wind turbine with a rotor 100 m across, used to generate electricity.

i) Estimate the total area of the rotor blades. [2]

ii) The wind has a velocity of 10 m/s. The force it can cause on a surface of 1 m² is 90 N. How much work can this wind do on 1 m² in 1 s? (work = force × distance) [3]

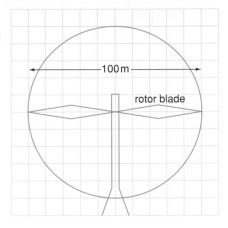

iii) Wind is used to turn the rotor blade. The effective work done on 1 m² of the blade is 50% of that calculated in (ii). Find how much energy is transferred to the rotor in 1 s. [1]

iv) Calculate the maximum electrical power, in watts, that would be generated by this wind turbine. [2]

v) A conventional power station generates about 900 MW of electrical power (1 MW = 1 000 000 W).

How many of these wind turbines would be needed to replace a power station? [2]

b) In Chapter 4.9 you saw where a barrage could be built across the estuary of the River Severn. This would make a lake with a surface area of about 200 km² (200 million m²).

The diagram below shows that the sea level could change by 9 m between low and high tide; but the level in the lake would only change by 5 m.

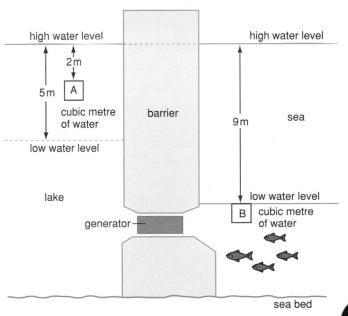

i) What kind of energy is given up when a cubic metre of water falls from position A to position B? [1]

ii) A cubic metre of water has a mass of 1000 kg. The acceleration due to gravity is 10 m/s². Calculate the force of gravity on a cubic metre of water. [1]

(force = mass × acceleration)

Calculate the work that this can do as it falls from A to B. [2]

(work = force × distance)

iii) How many cubic metres of water could flow out of the lake between high and low tide? [2]

iv) Use your answers to parts (ii) and (iii) to find how much energy could be obtained from the tide.

Assume that position A is the average position of a cubic metre of water between high and low levels in the lake. [2]

v) The time between high and low tide is approximately 20 000 seconds (about 6 hours). Use this figure to estimate the power available from the dam. Give your answer in megawatts. [3]

c) Explain the advantages and disadvantages of the wind turbine and the Severn Barrage as sources of power. [4]

13 Three physics students decide to compare the force of wind resistance on their cars. They decide to carry out a fair test to see how far each car can travel, at a constant speed of 70 km per hour, using only 5 litres of petrol. The table shows their results.

Car	Distance travelled / km
Renault Clio	75
Astra 1.3 l	70
Volvo 440	50

a) Which car do you think is the most streamlined? [1]

b) Compare the resistive forces on the Renault and Volvo, when they travel at 70 km per hour. [2]

c) Their teacher tells them it is not really a fair test. What factors have they forgotten? [2]

14 An electric winch is used to pull a coal truck up an inclined plane, as shown in the diagram.

a) How much useful work is done in lifting the load through 15 m? [3]

The winch uses a 6 kW electrical supply, and pulls the truck up the slope at a rate of 5 m/s.

b) How long does it take to pull the truck up the slope? [2]

c) How much work is done by the winch? [2]

d) Calculate the efficiency of the machine. Where do you think unwanted energy transfers occur? [3]

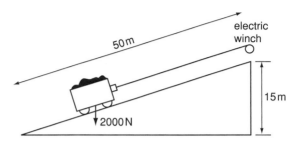

15 The Highway Code states how the braking distance for a car, with good brakes on a dry road, depends on the speed of the car. The braking distance is the distance travelled by a car from the time when the brakes are first applied, until the car stops.

The table below shows the braking distances for different speeds.

Speed / m/s	8	12	16	20	24	28	32
Braking distance / m	5	11	20	31	44	61	

a) Plot a graph of the braking distance (y-axis) against the speed (x-axis). [5]

b) From the graph determine the braking distance for a car travelling at 10 m/s. [1]

c) Predict the braking distance for a car travelling at 32 m/s. Explain why this prediction is less accurate than your calculation in part (b). [2]

The time taken for the driver to react before he applies the brake is called the thinking time, and the distance he travels during this time is the thinking distance. The thinking time for a driver is usually about 0.6 s.

d) i) What is the thinking distance for a car travelling at 20 m/s? [2]

ii) What is the total stopping distance at this speed? [1]

e) i) State two factors which affect the thinking distance. [2]

ii) State two factors which affect braking distance. [2]

f) Calculate the kinetic energy of a car with mass 1500 kg, travelling at 20 m/s. [3]

g) Using the table of braking distances, calculate the average braking force on the car, as it comes to a halt. [3]

EXTEND AND CHALLENGE

1 You can see the profile of a fairground ride in the diagram. A car leaves point A and arrives later at point F. The mass of the car, including occupants, is 200 kg.

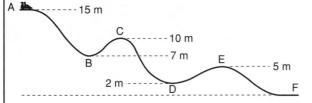

a) Calculate the car's gravitational potential energy at each of the points A to F.

b) Now calculate the car's speed at each of the points B to F. Assume its speed was very small at A.

2 *Voyager 1* was launched on 5 September 1977. After a journey of nearly two years it reached Jupiter. On 30 January 1979 *Voyager* was 35.1 million km away from Jupiter, and on 5 March *Voyager* was 2.81 million km from Jupiter. The table below shows this data. The times recorded are from 0.00 h GMT on 30 January 1979.

a) During all of the approach to Jupiter, the motors on *Voyager* were turned off. So the only force acting on *Voyager* was the gravitational pull of Jupiter. Explain why *Voyager's* speed increased as it approached Jupiter.

b) Work out the acceleration of *Voyager* between points:
  i) 1 and 1A
  ii) 2 and 2A.
  Express your answers in m/s^2. (Hint: 1 hour = 3600 s.)

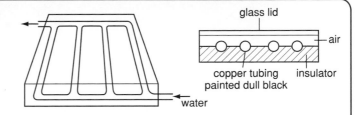

a) Why is thin copper tubing used and why has it been painted black?

b) Why does a glass lid improve the efficiency of the solar panel?

c) Which material would you choose to insulate the bottom of the panel?

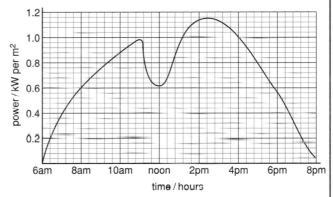

d) The graph shows how the power of sunlight falling on 1 m^2 of solar panel varies throughout a bright summer's day.
  i) Explain the variation through the day. What do you think happened round about noon?

	Distance from Jupiter's centre R / millions of km	Velocity v / m/s	Time from 00.00 h GMT 30 Jan 1979		Date
			Days	Hours	
1	35.10	10 900	0	00	30 Jan
1A	34.71	10 904	0	10	
2	2.81	14 212	32	15	5 Mar
2A	2.76	14 271	32	16	

c) Now work out the force acting on *Voyager* at points 1 and 2. *Voyager's* mass is about 2000 kg. Explain why the force changed.

d) Work out *Voyager's* increase in kinetic energy as it moved from point 1 to point 2. Where did this increase in kinetic energy come from?

3 The diagrams show a simple solar panel. Water is pumped slowly through thin copper tubing, which has been painted a dull black colour. The tubing has been embedded in an insulating material.

ii) Use the graph to estimate the total energy absorbed by the panel during the day. Assume the panel absorbs 20% of the incident radiation; express your answer in kWh.

iii) A typical house needs about 10 kWh of energy per day. Estimate the size of panel needed to supply energy to a house through the summer months.

e) Comment on the limitations of solar power in a Northern European country.

5
Solids, liquids and gases

A hot air balloon works on the principle that the density of hot air is less than the density of cold air. So, when hot air is put into the balloon from the burners, the cold air surrounding the balloon causes the balloon to rise.

CONSIDER • CALCULATE

1 How does the speed of the air molecules inside the balloon compare with that of the air molecules outside the balloon?

2 How does the spacing of the air molecules inside the balloon compare with that of the air molecules outside the balloon?

3 Do some research to find out:
   a) the average temperature of the air in a hot air balloon
   b) how big a balloon has to be to lift a load of 3000 kg – the typical mass of five passengers, the basket, the burners and the balloon itself.

By the end of this section you should be able to:
- **recall and use the relationship: density = mass/volume**
- **describe an experiment to measure density**
- **recall and use the relationship: pressure = force/area**
- **recall and use the relationship: pressure = height × density × g**
- **understand that matter can change between states**
- **know the molecular structures of solids, liquids and gases**
- **understand the significance of Brownian motion**
- **understand the Kelvin scale of temperature**
- **understand the relationship between the speed of gas molecules and temperature**
- **use and understand the gas laws**

5.1 Density

Figure 1.1 Eurofighter Typhoon F1.

Table 1

Material	Density / kg/m³
gold	19 300
lead	11 400
steel	8000
aluminium	2700
glass	2500
Kevlar	1440
water	1000
lithium	500
cork	200
air	1.3 } at standard temperature and pressure
hydrogen	0.09

Figure 1.2

The Eurofighter Typhoon is made from low-density materials to keep its weight to a minimum and allow it to climb or change direction quickly. It is made up mainly of the following materials: carbon-fibre composites such as Kevlar; lightweight alloys such as aluminium/lithium alloy; glass-reinforced plastics. Find out how much more expensive these materials are than aluminium and steel. Why would steel be a very poor choice for this purpose?

■ What is density?

A tree obviously weighs more than a nail. Sometimes, you hear people say 'steel is heavier than wood'. What they mean is this: a piece of steel is heavier than a piece of wood with the same volume.

To compare the heaviness of materials we use the idea of **density**. Density can be calculated using this equation:

$$\text{density} = \frac{\text{mass}}{\text{volume}} \quad \text{or} \quad \rho = \frac{m}{V}$$

The Greek letter ρ (rho) is used to represent density. Density is usually measured in units of kg/m³. Some typical values of density are in Table 1.

■ Measuring density

You can calculate the density of an object by measuring its mass and calculating its volume. Figure 1.2 shows a regularly shaped piece of material. Its dimensions have been measured carefully with an accurate ruler. Its mass has been measured on an electronic balance and found to be 173.2 g.

What is its density in kg/m³?

$$\text{volume} = 0.101\,\text{m} \times 0.048\,\text{m} \times 0.013\,\text{m}$$
$$= 0.000\,063\,\text{m}^3$$

$$\text{density} = \frac{\text{mass}}{\text{volume}}$$

$$= \frac{0.1732\,\text{kg}}{0.000\,063\,\text{m}^3}$$

$$= 2750\,\text{kg/m}^3$$

This method has limitations:

- A ruler can only measure to an accuracy of 0.1 cm, so the volume may not be calculated exactly.
- The shape of the block may not be regular.

The volume of an irregularly shaped object can be calculated by immersing it in water. This is illustrated in Study Question 5 on page 199.

5.3 Pressure in liquids

This scuba diver is enjoying warm tropical waters, where she can see brightly coloured fish in the coral reefs. Although the water looks clear and safe, there are hidden dangers. One danger is the pressure of the water itself. For every 10 m below the surface of the sea, there is an increase in pressure equal to 1 atmosphere pressure. When the pressure increases on your body gases dissolve in your blood, which can be very painful and dangerous to your health. You have to take care to change depth slowly, as rapid changes of pressure can cause injuries to your ears or lungs.

- Calculate the pressure 20 m below the surface of the sea.
- Safety guidelines advise that it is safe to dive for 55 minutes to a depth of 18 m, and for 20 minutes to a depth of 30 m. Can you explain why you should dive for a shorter time at greater depths?
- Find out what is meant by the 'bends'.

Figure 3.1 This diver is 20 m below the surface of the sea.

■ Transmitting pressures

When you hit a nail with a hammer the pressure is transmitted downwards to the point. This happens only because the nail is rigid.

When a ruler is used to push a lot of marbles lying on a table, they do not all move along the direction of the push. Some of the marbles give others a sideways push. The marbles are behaving like a fluid.

In Figure 3.2 you can see a cylinder of fluid that has been squashed by pushing a piston down. The pressure increases everywhere in the fluid, not just next to piston. The fluid is made up of lots of tiny particles, which act rather like the marbles to transmit the pressure to all points.

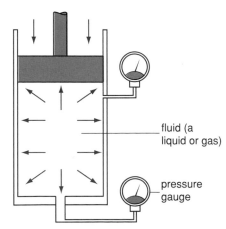

fluid (a liquid or gas)

pressure gauge

Figure 3.2 The pressure in a fluid acts equally in all directions.

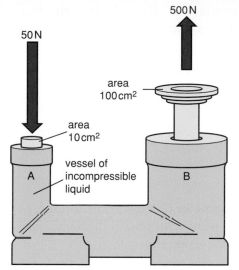

Figure 3.3 The principle of a hydraulic jack.

Hydraulic machines

We often use liquids to transmit pressures. Liquids can change shape but they hardly change their volume when compressed. Figure 3.3 shows how a hydraulic jack works.

A force of 50 N presses down on the surface above **A**. The extra pressure that this force produces in the liquid is:

$$P = \frac{F}{A}$$
$$= \frac{50\,\text{N}}{10\,\text{cm}^2} = 5\,\text{N/cm}^2$$

The same pressure is passed through the liquid to **B**. So the upwards force that the surface **B** can provide is:

$$F = P \times A$$
$$= 5\,\text{N/cm}^2 \times 100\,\text{cm}^2 = 500\,\text{N}$$

With the hydraulic jack you can lift a load of 500 N by applying a force of only 50 N. Figure 3.4 shows another use of hydraulics.

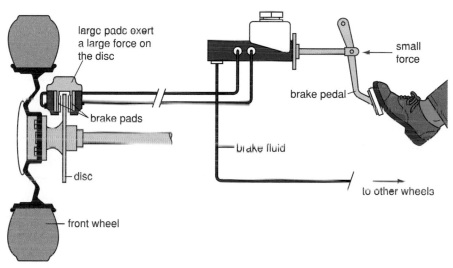

Figure 3.4 Cars use a hydraulic braking system. The foot exerts a small force on the brake pedal. The pressure created by this force is transmitted by the brake fluid to the brake pads. The brake pads have a large area and exert a large force on the wheel disc. The same pressure can be transmitted to all four wheels.

Increase of pressure with depth

The pressure of a liquid below the surface depends on three things:

- **depth**, h
- **density**, ρ
- the **pull of gravity** per kilogram, g ($g = 10$ N/kg)

The pressure that acts on a diver depends on the weight of water above him. As he goes deeper the weight of water on him increases, so the pressure also increases.

The diver feels a bigger pressure under 10 m of sea water than under 10 m of fresh water. Sea water has a higher density than fresh water.

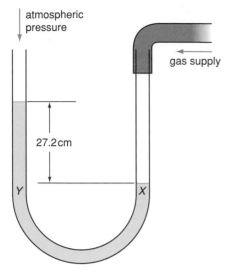

atmospheric pressure

gas supply

27.2cm

Y

X

Figure 3.5 A manometer.

The strength of the gravitational pull on the diver affects the force that the water exerts on the diver. The Earth gives a downwards pull of 10 N per kilogram.

To calculate the pressure P under a liquid you can use this formula:

$$P = h \times \rho \times g$$

The units of these quantities in the equation are: P, N/m²; h, m; ρ, kg/m³; g, N/kg.

■ The manometer

Figure 3.5 shows how you can use a **manometer** to measure the pressure of a gas supply. The two points X and Y are at the same level in the liquid. This means that the pressures at X and Y are the same.

Pressure at X = gas supply pressure.
Pressure at Y = atmospheric pressure + pressure due to 27.2 cm of water.

So the gas supply pressure is greater than atmospheric pressure, by an amount equal to the pressure due to a column of water 27.2 cm high. We say that the extra pressure (above atmospheric pressure) of the gas supply is '27.2 cm of water'.

STUDY QUESTIONS

1 This question refers to the gas supply in Figure 3.5.
   a) One day you notice that the difference in height between the water levels at X and Y has increased to 30.2 cm. Explain what has happened.
   b) The water is replaced by oil. Use the information in the table to explain what will happen to the difference in height now.

Liquid	Density / kg/m³
Water	1000
Oil	800

2 Sometimes, after a road accident, the Fire and Rescue Service uses inflated air bags to lift a vehicle, to free passengers who have become trapped. Explain how such bags can lift a large load easily.

3 a) Use the equation $P = h\rho g$ to calculate the pressure acting on a diver at depths of (i) 10 m, (ii) 30 m.
   The density of the water is 1000 kg/m³. You will need to include the pressure of the atmosphere at the surface of the sea, which is 100 000 N/m².
   b) Calculate the force exerted by the pressure on the diver's mask at a depth of 30 m. His mask has an area of 0.02 m².
   c) Explain why the diver's mask is in no danger of breaking under this pressure.

4 The diagram shows the principle of a hydraulic jack. Two cylinders are connected by a reservoir of oil. A 200 N weight resting on piston A can be used to lift a larger load on piston B.
   a) Calculate the extra pressure at x, due to the 200 N weight.
   b) Explain why the pressure at y is the same as the pressure at x.
   c) Why would the jack not work if the oil were replaced by a gas?
   d) Calculate the size of the load, W, which can be lifted.
   e) If you need to lift W by 0.5 m, how far do you need to move piston A?

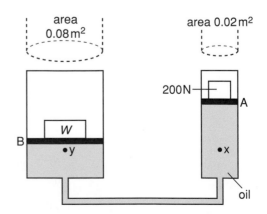

area 0.08 m²

area 0.02 m²

200N

A

W

B

•y

•x

oil

5.4 Atmospheric pressure

Figure 4.1 How can such a large piece of glass be put in place using only suction pads?

One of the most effective ways of moving large pieces of glass on a building site is to pick them up using large suction pads. The idea is simple: you evacuate the air from inside the pad and atmospheric pressure pushes the pad firmly in place against the glass.

■ Atmospheric pressure is 100 000 N/m². You want to lift a piece of glass which weighs 1000 N. Calculate the minimum area of suction pad you need.

■ Size of atmospheric pressure

Figure 4.2 shows a hollow metal cylinder, which comes apart in two pieces. When the air is pumped out of it, a large force is needed to pull the two halves apart. You can measure the size of this force by attaching weights to the bottom half of the cylinder.

Example. You might find that a total mass of 50 kg is needed to pull the halves apart. When this happens, the force from the weight of the 50 kg balances the force of atmospheric pressure on the bottom surface.

So atmospheric pressure, $P = \dfrac{F}{A}$

$$= \frac{500\ \text{N}}{50\ \text{cm}^2}$$

(Remember, the gravitational pull is 10 N on each kg.)

$$= 10\ \text{N/cm}^2\ or\ 100\,000\ \text{N/m}^2\ (\text{Pa})$$
$$(\text{since}\ 1\ \text{m}^2 = 10\,000\ \text{cm}^2)$$

This is a very large pressure. The atmosphere exerts a force of about 100 000 N (the weight of 100 large men) on the outside of a window (area about 1 m²). The window does not break because air inside the house pushes back with a force of the same size.

■ Using atmospheric pressure

Piles that anchor the foundations of buildings are usually knocked into the ground by a large pile driver. However, circular or ring piles can be driven into the ground by atmospheric pressure (Figure 4.3). The idea is to place a

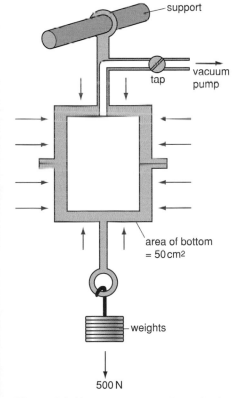

Figure 4.2 You can measure atmospheric pressure using this apparatus.

EXAM TIPS

- Atmospheric pressure acts in all directions.
- Atmospheric pressure is large – 100 000 Pa.

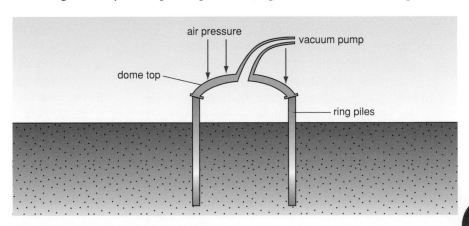

Figure 4.3 Driving in piles with air pressure.

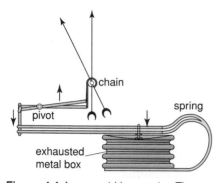

Figure 4.4 An aneroid barometer. The expansion of the metal box, when the atmospheric pressure drops, causes the movement of a pointer.

dome over the top of the piles. Then a vacuum pump takes the air out of the space under the dome. There is now a large pressure difference between the inside and outside, which pushes the piles into the ground.

■ Measuring atmospheric pressure

Instruments that measure atmospheric pressure are called **barometers** (see Figures 4.4 and 4.5). The most accurate type is the mercury barometer (Figure 4.5). The pressure at the points x and y is the same. So the pressure due to 760 mm of mercury, Hg, is equal to the atmospheric pressure. This is the average pressure of the atmosphere, written as 760 mm Hg.

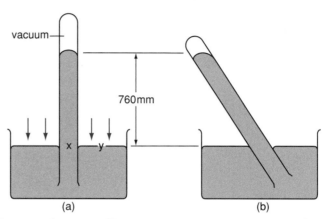

Figure 4.5 A mercury barometer. The average atmospheric pressure is 760 mm of mercury. It does not matter if the barometer is tilted, as the vertical height of the mercury column stays the same.

STUDY QUESTIONS

1 Describe two experiments which show that atmospheric pressure is very large.
2 Explain why atmospheric pressure is less at the top of a mountain, in comparison with sea level.
3 Use the formula $P = h \times \rho \times g$ and the information in the text about the mercury barometer to calculate atmospheric pressure. You will also need to know that the density of mercury is 13 600 kg/m³ and the gravitational field strength, g, is 10 N/kg. (If you wish to do the calculations more precisely you can use the more accurate value of $g = 9.81$ N/kg.)
4 This question is about driving piles in using atmospheric pressure (Figure 4.3).
   a) Use the diagram on the right and the scale to check that the area of the top of the dome (which is circular) is about 12 m².
   b) Use your answer to work out the force with which the atmosphere pushes down on the dome top. (Atmospheric pressure is 100 000 Pa.)
   c) The pile sinks into the ground when the air pressure beneath the dome is reduced to 35% of atmospheric pressure. What force then pushes upwards on the dome?

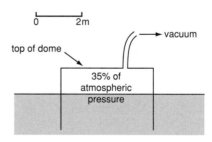

   d) What is the maximum load that can be allowed to rest on these piles?
   e) The atmosphere also acts on the sides of the dome. Why do you not need to include this effect in your calculations?
5 You take the apparatus shown in Figure 4.2 to the planet Zeta, where the pull of gravity is 25 N on each kilogram. When you evacuate the apparatus, as described earlier, you find that a mass of 40 kg is needed to pull apart the two halves of the cylinder.
   a) How big is the pull of gravity on the 40 kg mass?
   b) Calculate the atmospheric pressure on Zeta.

5.5 Atoms and molecules

A male Emperor moth uses his very large antennae to detect the scent of a female. A male Emperor moth can be attracted by the scent of a female at a distance as far as 10 km. The female produces only a small quantity of scent. This suggests that tiny particles of her scent are constantly on the move and spread out through the air.

Figure 5.1 Emperor moth.

■ Atoms, elements and molecules

Everything we touch, swallow and breathe is made out of tiny particles. The smallest particles are **atoms**. There are only about 100 different types of atom. Materials that are made from only one type of atom are called **elements**. For example, aluminium contains only aluminium atoms. Some other common elements are oxygen, hydrogen, nitrogen and carbon.

The small particles in lots of materials are **molecules**. Atoms combine chemically to make molecules. For example, a water molecule is made up of two hydrogen atoms and one oxygen atom, while a carbon dioxide molecule contains one carbon and two oxygen atoms.

Atoms and molecules are far too small for us to see directly. But Figure 5.2 shows you some molecules seen through a powerful electron microscope. Electron microscopes show us that oil molecules are about 0.000 000 1 cm (10^{-7} cm) long. That means that 10 000 000 molecules put end to end would be about 1 cm long.

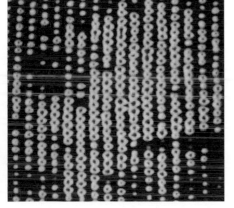

Figure 5.2 This electron micrograph shows the alignment of molecules in enzyme catalase.

■ Discovering molecules

The idea that things were made from atoms and molecules was thought of over two hundred years ago, long before electron microscopes were invented. Below are some examples which suggest that **matter** is made up of small particles. Matter is the name which we use to describe all solids, liquids and gases.

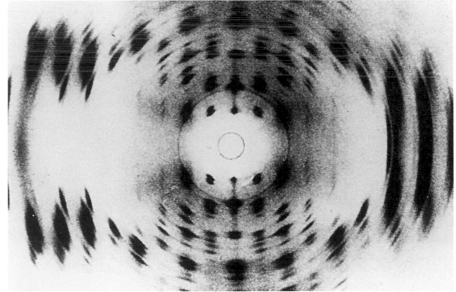

Figure 5.3 This is an X-ray diffraction photo of DNA. The dark spots are caused by X-rays being diffracted by DNA molecules. A photograph like this one played a vital part in the unravelling of the complex structure of the DNA molecule.

Figure 5.5

- There is a simple experiment that you can do for yourself, which shows that liquids are made up of very small particles. You can take a small drop of blue ink and put it into a glass of water. If you stir the water it will turn a very pale blue. The small particles in the ink have now been spread further apart.
- Figure 5.4 shows how you can grow a crystal. You dissolve some copper sulfate in water to make a strong solution. Then a small crystal of copper sulfate is placed in the solution. During a week or so, this crystal grows very slowly into a larger one. This can be explained by saying that the solution contains very small particles of copper sulfate. These particles stick to the crystal so that it grows larger.

Growing a crystal is a bit like making a neat pile of oranges. As another orange is added the pile grows. You can see in Figure 5.5 that the shape of a pyramid of oranges is the same as the shape of an alum crystal in Figure 5.6.

Figure 5.6 The shape of the alum crystal suggests that the molecules in it are stacked neatly in rows like the oranges above.

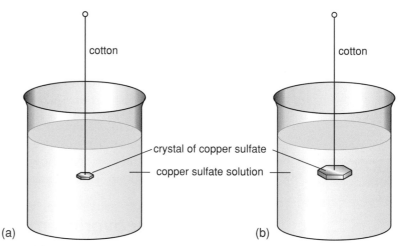

Figure 5.4 (a) A small crystal of copper sulfate is placed in a copper sulfate solution. **(b)** a week later a large crystal has grown.

STUDY QUESTIONS

1 When you cook a curry the aroma spreads right through the house. Why does this suggest that the curry powder is made up of small particles?

2 Explain carefully why growing crystals supports the theory that solids are made up of tiny particles.

3 The South American golden poison-dart frog produces the world's most lethal poison, batrachotoxin. Only 0.002 g of this substance is enough to kill an average adult human (mass 70 kg).
   a) Work out the lethal dose of this poison per gram of human flesh.
   b) What leads you to think that this poison is made up of small particles?

4 In a laboratory experiment a drop of oil, volume 0.5 mm³, is dropped onto the surface of some water covered with a thin powder. The oil spreads, pushing the powder out of the way, as shown in the diagram.
   a) Use the diagram to estimate the area covered by oil in mm².

b) Now calculate the thickness of the oil in mm.
c) Explain how this experiment helps to show that oil particles are very small.
d) Some people claim that the oil film is only one molecule thick. Do you think this is likely?

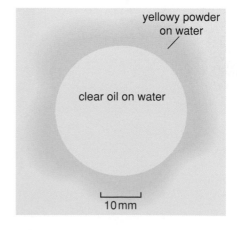

yellowy powder on water

clear oil on water

10 mm

5.6 Melting and evaporation

You may not be thinking of science when you put perfume or aftershave on. But to explain why you smell nice wearing this needs a good knowledge of molecules.

- When you press the spray nozzle on the top of a perfume bottle, why is a fine spray of liquid produced?
- The perfume does not stay as a liquid on your face – why not?
- Later in the day, people can still smell the perfume. How does the aroma reach them?

Figure 6.1 Spraying perfume.

■ The kinetic theory of matter

When something is moving it has **kinetic energy**. Molecules of matter are always on the move. This idea is called the **kinetic theory**. The most important points in the theory are:

- Every kind of material is made of small particles (molecules or atoms).
- The sizes of particles are different for different materials.
- The particles themselves are very hard. They cannot be squashed or stretched, but the distance beween particles can change.
- The particles are always moving. The higher the temperature of a substance, the faster the average speed of its particles.
- If two different particles are at the same temperature then they have the same kinetic energy, so the heavier particle moves more slowly than the lighter particle.

Figure 6.2 (a) Water appears in different states . . . ice . . .

(b). . . water . . .

(c). . . vapour and steam. Geysers are formed when water deep in the Earth is heated under pressure. The water finds a route to the surface and boils to form a jet of steam sometimes as much as 70 metres high.

Solids, liquids and gases

Ice, water and steam are three different **states** of the same material. We call these three states solid, liquid and gas. You will now see how the kinetic theory helps us to understand them.

- **Solid.** In a solid the particles are packed, in a regular structure, into rows just like apples or oranges stacked in shops (Figure 6.3(a)). The particles can never move out of their rows, but they vibrate around their fixed positions. As the temperature of a solid is raised the particles vibrate more and the material expands. This means that the distance between particles has increased a little.

  In a solid the particles are very close to each other and held in position by very strong forces. This makes it very difficult to change the shape of a solid by squashing it or pulling it.

- **Liquid.** In a liquid the particles are also very close to each other, which means that liquids are also very difficult to compress (Figure 6.3(b)). The particles in a liquid have a close-packed, irregular structure and can move around at random. A liquid can change shape to fit into any container, but its volume will remain constant at a given temperature. As a liquid warms it also expands a little, due to its particles vibrating more.

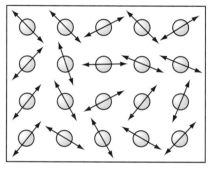 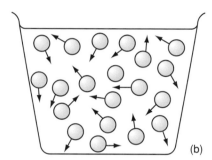 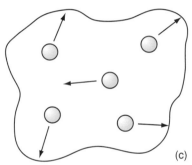

(a)   (b)   (c)

Figure 6.3 (a) Particles in a solid are arranged in neat rows. The particles can vibrate but do not leave their positions in the rows. **(b)** Particles in a liquid are close together, but free to move around within a close-packed, irregular structure. **(c)** Gas particles are free to move into any available space. They move quickly and there are large distances between them.

- **Gas.** In a gas the particles are separated by big distances (Figure 6.3(c)). The forces between gas particles are very small. It is easy to compress a gas because there is so much space between the particles. The gas particles are in a constant state of rapid random motion. This makes a gas expand to fill any available space.

Changing solid to liquid

When a solid such as ice is heated, the molecules inside it vibrate more and more quickly. If enough heat is supplied the molecules will break away from their fixed positions and start to move around. The solid has melted (Figure 6.4). The temperature at which this change happens is called the **melting point** of the material.

When a substance changes from one state of matter to another (for example solid to liquid) this is called a **change of state**.

Most materials expand when they melt, because molecules are a little further apart in the liquid state. Water is an unusual substance because it expands when it freezes. Water is at its most dense at 4 °C, so when a pond freezes over there is a layer of dense water at 4 °C at the bottom. Ice is less dense than water, which is why we see ice on the surface of ponds.

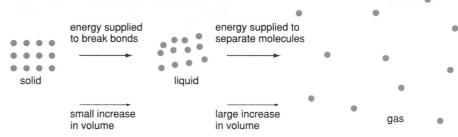

Figure 6.4 Change of state as heat energy is supplied.

The expansion of water on freezing can be a nuisance. It causes pipes to burst in houses or in cars. To prevent freezing in car cooling systems, drivers add antifreeze. This lowers the melting point of water. Similarly, salt is put onto icy roads in winter to lower the melting point.

Figure 6.5 shows a simple experiment to record how the temperature changes as ethanamide turns from a liquid to a solid. The tube of liquid cools quickly from about 100 °C to about 80 °C (Figure 6.6), then the temperature remains constant for a few minutes as the ethanimide solidifies (or freezes). This is the reverse process of melting. When a substance melts, heat is supplied to break molecular bonds; when a substance freezes, heat is given out as the bonds form. Only when all the ethanamide has frozen does the temperature continue to drop.

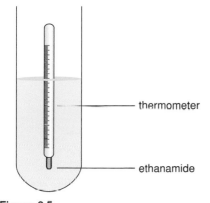

Figure 6.5

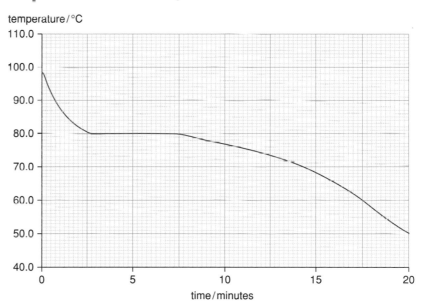

Figure 6.6 Cooling curve for ethanamide. The horizontal position indicates a change of state.

■ Evaporation

As a liquid warms up, the average speed of the molecules in it gets greater. However, not all of the molecules in the liquid will be travelling at the same speed. Figure 6.8 shows that some will be travelling slowly and some more quickly. Some molecules near to the surface of the liquid have enough energy to escape. They evaporate from the liquid to form a vapour (water in the gaseous state). Evaporation from the surface of a liquid can happen at any temperature. But as the temperature gets higher more molecules have enough energy to escape. So evaporation happens at a faster rate.

Figure 6.7 This wine cooler has been soaked in water before the wine bottle was placed in it. Evaporation of the water through the porous pot takes heat away from the wine and keeps it cool.

211

As a liquid is heated, eventually the temperature rises to the **boiling point** of the liquid. At this point, evaporation also happens inside the liquid. Bubbles of vapour form inside the liquid and rise to the surface. Heat applied to a boiling liquid gives the molecules enough energy to evaporate.

Evaporation causes cooling. This is because it is the faster molecules that escape, leaving behind the slower molecules, resulting in a colder liquid. The evaporation of sweat from your skin keeps you cool on a hot day. But this can also be dangerous. You can lose heat from your body very rapidly in dry and windy conditions.

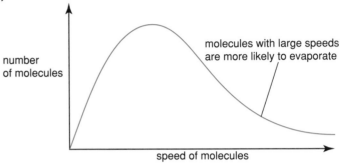

Figure 6.8 The molecules in a liquid do not all travel at the same speed.

When a gas cools, the molecules condense to form a vapour which is made of small liquid drops. Clouds are made of water vapour and when the drops get large they fall as rain.

 Now go through the tutorial *Energy transfers*.

STUDY QUESTIONS

1 Use the kinetic theory to help you explain the following:
   a) Some solids, like metals, are very stiff and difficult to bend.
   b) A liquid can be poured.
   c) If a gas pipe has a small hole in it, gas will escape from the pipe and you will be able to smell it a few metres away from the leak.
2 Describe carefully the differences between solids, liquids and gases in terms of:
   a) how the molecules are arranged in the material
   b) how the molecules move
   c) the separation of the molecules.
3 a) Why do you hang out washing, rather than leaving it in a pile to dry?
   b) Why does washing dry faster on warm, windy days?
   c) Why does the amount of water in the atmosphere (humidity) affect the drying rate?
4 Explain why a saucepan will come to the boil more quickly if it is covered by a lid.
5 This question is about the water cycle – how water is carried from

the sea, to fall as rain, before returning to the sea again.
   a) At A in the diagram sunlight causes water to evaporate; explain what this means.
   b) At B water vapour has condensed to form clouds of water droplets. Explain the difference between water vapour and water droplets.
   c) At C the clouds rise as they approach a mountain: explain what happens to the temperature of the air, and then why rain falls at D.
6 Explain, in terms of molecular motion, why the pressure in a gas decreases if the gas is allowed to expand into a larger volume (without changing its temperature).

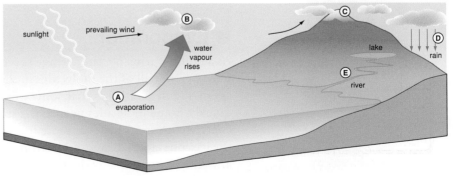

5.7 Physics in the kitchen

When salt is added to water, the boiling point of the water is increased. You often add salt to water when you cook vegetables. Does this make the vegetables cook more slowly or more quickly?

■ Changing boiling points

When water boils, bubbles of water vapour form inside the liquid. The pressure inside these bubbles is equal to the pressure of the air above the water. This means that when the air pressure changes, the water boils at a different temperature. If the air pressure is greater than 1 atmosphere, water boils above 100 °C; if the pressure is lower than 1 atmosphere, water boils below 100 °C.

Figure 7.1 shows a graph of how the boiling point of water changes with pressure. You would notice this effect if you lived somewhere like Mexico City, which is 3000 m above sea level. The air pressure there is only about 0.7 atmospheres, and water boils at 90 °C. At the top of Mount Everest, 8848 m above sea level, a kettle would boil at only 70 °C.

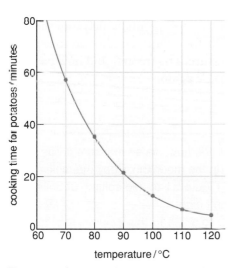

Figure 7.2 Graph to show how the cooking time for potatoes decreases as the temperature is raised.

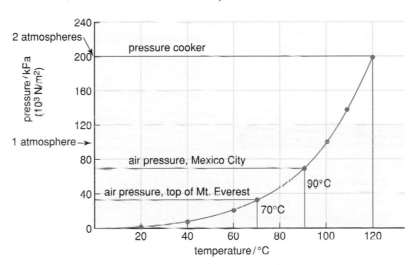

Figure 7.1 Graph showing how the boiling point of water changes with pressure.

In a pressure cooker the air pressure is increased to about 2 atmospheres. The cooker has an airtight lid except for a small hole at the top. Weights are put on top of this hole so that the air pressure inside must be greater than atmospheric pressure before steam will escape. The advantage of cooking at high pressure is that the boiling point of water is raised and cooking times are considerably reduced (Figure 7.2, Figure 7.3).

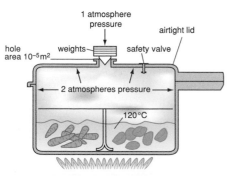

Figure 7.3 A pressure cooker.

■ Refrigeration

When you go to the doctor for an injection, your arm gets cleaned with some alcohol. This evaporates quickly, making your arm cold. A refrigerator (fridge) in your kitchen cools your food in a similar way. Figure 7.4 shows a refrigerator. The cooling in a refrigerator is done by chemicals called freons, which boil at low temperatures (about –30 °C). The cooling occurs in the freezer compartment where boiling freons evaporate. The freons evaporate because they absorb heat energy from the contents of the refrigerator. The freon gas then reaches the compressor, which squashes the gas to a high pressure. The compression also warms the gas. From here the freon gas passes through a condenser, which cools the gas down. The gas turns back into liquid freons as it cools.

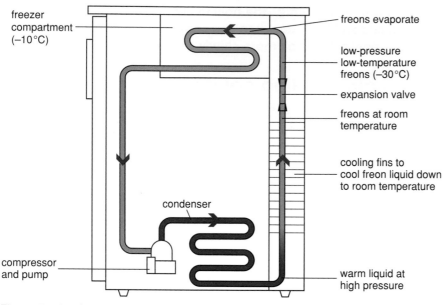

Figure 7.4 A refrigerator.

On the back of your refrigerator you will see cooling fins, which cool the liquid back to room temperature. Then the freon liquid is allowed to expand, further reducing its temperature and pressure. The freon liquid now passes through the ice box to start the cooling cycle again.

STUDY QUESTIONS

1 **a)** The area of the hole in the top of the pressure cooker in Figure 7.3 is 10^{-5} m. What weight must be put on top of the hole to keep the pressure inside the cooker at 2 atmospheres (2×10^5 N/m²)? Remember the pressure outside is 1 atmosphere.
  b) What is the pressure inside the cooker when a weight of 0.5 N is used?

2 This question is about the time taken to cook your potatoes as you climb Mount Everest. The higher you get the longer it takes.

Table 1

Height above sea level / m	Air pressure / kPa	Boiling point of water / °C	Cooking time for potatoes / min
0	100		
2000	79		
4000	62		
6000	47		
8000	36		

  a) Table 1 shows you how the air pressure drops as you climb up the mountain. Copy the table and then use Figure 7.1 to add column of boiling points for each height.
  b) Use Figure 7.2 to add a further column, for cooking times.
  c) Now plot a graph to show how your cooking times (y-axis) change with your height above sea level (x-axis).
  d) Use your graph to predict cooking times at (i) 5000 m (ii) 8500 m.
  e) Would your cooking times have changed so much if you used a pressure cooker to cook your potatoes? Explain your answer carefully.
  f) Calculate the cooking time for your potatoes at a height of 8000 m, when you use the pressure cooker (Figure 7.3) with a weight of 1 N.

5.8 Molecules on the move

Robert Brown was a British botanist who became famous for his use of the microscope. In 1827, he examined some small particles of pollen, which were floating in water. He noticed that the pollen particles had a continual jittery motion. Can you explain what causes this motion?

Figure 8.1 Robert Brown (1773–1858).

■ Diffusion

In Chapter 5.5 you read how a male Emperor moth can detect a female moth's scent at a great distance. This supports the idea that the scent is made up of molecules and also the idea that the molecules in a gas are moving. Here are some simple experiments to show you more about the movement of molecules. In Figure 8.2(a) you can see a long tube with all the air pumped out of it. It is closed with a tap. On the other side of the tap is attached a small capsule of bromine inside some rubber tubing. The capsule is broken and then the tap is opened. As soon as the tap is opened the bromine vapour fills the long tube (Figure 8.2(b)). This tells us that the bromine molecules are moving quickly. They are actually moving at a speed of about 200 m/s.

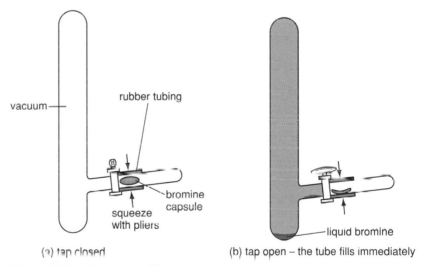

vacuum
rubber tubing
bromine capsule
squeeze with pliers
liquid bromine

(a) tap closed

(b) tap open – the tube fills immediately

Figure 8.2 Bromine vapour filling a vacuum.

Figure 8.3 shows what happens when the experiment is repeated with air inside. This time when the tap is opened the bromine does not fill the tube quickly. After about 20 minutes the bottom half of the tube is coloured dark brown, but the top is only light brown. So although the bromine molecules travel very quickly it takes a long time for them to reach the top.

The reason for this is that the air molecules are also moving quickly. The air molecules get in the way of the bromine molecules. When two molecules bump into each other they change direction. The bromine molecules keep changing direction and so take a long time to reach the top (see Figure 8.4).

This process of one substance spreading through another is called **diffusion**.

Diffusion also occurs in liquids. Figure 8.5 shows an example of ink spreading through water. Diffusion is very important for all living things. When animals

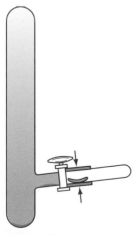

Figure 8.3 After 20 minutes bromine molecules are just beginning to reach the top of the tube; this is because they have had millions of collisions with air molecules.

215

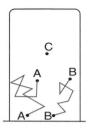

Figure 8.4 Many collisions with air molecules means that the bromine molecules take a long time to move up the tube.

Figure 8.5 Place some ink in a glass of water. After an hour or so the water is evenly coloured throughout. Diffusion works more slowly in liquids, which suggests that molecules move more slowly in liquids than in gases.

have eaten a meal, food is digested and diffuses into the blood. Blood then carries the food all round the body. Plants need nitrogen, potassium, phosphorus and other elements. These diffuse from the soil into the plants' roots.

■ Brownian motion

Robert Brown looked through his microscope at some grains of pollen which were in water. He noticed that the grains of pollen were moving around randomly. They jiggled from side to side.

You can see the same sort of **Brownian motion** if you look through a microscope at smoke particles. Figure 8.6 shows a typical experimental arrangement. A small puff of smoke is put into a smoke cell under the microscope. Light from a small bulb shines onto the cell. The smoke particles show up as tiny specks of light through the microscope. Figure 8.7 shows the sort of path a smoke particle follows.

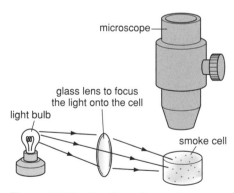

Figure 8.6 Viewing Brownian motion.

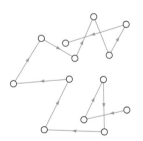

Figure 8.7 The path of a smoke particle as seen through the microscope.

This is an important experiment as it shows that air molecules are hitting the smoke particles. The smoke particles move randomly because they are being randomly knocked by moving air molecules. These air molecules are too small to see through the microscope, but they are moving so quickly that they can deflect a much larger smoke particle.

The path that smoke particles follow is sometimes called a 'random walk'. This is the same sort of path that the bromine molecules follow in the experiment described earlier.

■ Gas pressure

The idea that gas molecules are always moving rapidly in random directions helps us to understand why a gas exerts a pressure on the walls of its container: the molecules of the gas exert a force every time one hits the wall. The pressure caused by the gas depends on the following factors:

- the number of collisions that the particles have with the container walls per second
- how hard the particles hit the walls.

The pressure inside a container of gas can be increased in three ways:

- Putting more molecules in the container. The number of collisions that the molecules make with the walls each second is now larger.
- Making the volume of the container smaller. The same number of molecules make more collisions with the walls, because they travel less distance between collisions.
- Heating the container. The molecules travel faster and they now hit the container walls harder and more often.

EXAM TIP

Make sure you can explain why Brownian motion provides evidence for the existence of molecules.

STUDY QUESTIONS

1 Figure 8.4 shows two bromine molecules moving in a jar full of air. Both molecules reach the top after a while.
   a) Copy the diagram and complete the paths of A and B, to show a possible way by which they could reach the top.
   b) Explain why bromine molecules move in this way.
2 a) Describe how you would set up an experiment to observe Brownian motion.
   b) What would you see in this experiment?
   c) What evidence does Brownian motion provide for the existence of molecules?
3 a) Explain what diffusion is.
   b) Why does diffusion take so long, even though molecules travel at high speeds such as 200 m/s?
4 A bottle of air is sealed at room temperature and atmospheric pressure. The bottle is now placed in a refrigerator. Which of the following statements about the air in the bottle is incorrect?

   a) The average kinetic energy of the molecules has reduced.
   b) The molecules are moving more slowly than at room temperature.
   c) The molecules hit the wall of the container less often than before.
   d) The molecules hit the walls with less force.
   e) There are fewer molecules in the bottle than at room temperature.
5 a) Explain, in terms of molecules, how a gas exerts a pressure on the walls of its container.
   b) The air inside an old tin is heated with a Bunsen burner. The lid is pressed firmly on. Explain why the pressure inside the tin increases.
   c) If the tin is heated enough the lid flies off. Explain why.
   d) The experiment is now repeated, but with a small amount of water placed in the tin. Explain why the lid flies off at a lower temperature.

5.9 The gas laws

When we walk past pipes in a factory or refinery we assume that they are all perfectly safe. But someone will have calculated that they are. What factors need to be taken into account when checking the safety of these pipes?

Figure 9.1 What factors affect the pressure of the gases in these pipes?

PRACTICAL

Make sure you understand how to investigate how the pressure of a gas depends on its temperature. What are the independent, dependent and constant variables in this investigation?

■ Linking the pressure of a gas to its temperature

Figure 9.2 shows apparatus that can be used to investigate how the pressure of a gas changes as it is heated up. To make it a fair test, the volume of the gas is kept constant. The pressure of the gas is measured with a pressure gauge as the temperature of the water bath is raised.

The results of such an experiment are shown in Figure 9.3. As the temperature is raised from 0 °C to 100 °C the pressure rises steadily from

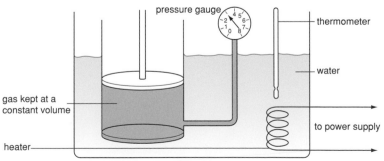

Figure 9.2 Investigating how the pressure of a gas depends on temperature.

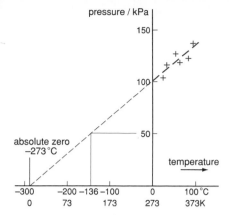

Figure 9.3 Results of the experiment shown in Figure 9.2.

about 100 kPa to about 137 kPa. We are able to draw a straight line through these results. If this line is extended below 0 °C you can predict what will happen to the pressure at lower temperatures. You can see that the pressure will be about 50 kPa at −136 °C; this is half of the pressure at 0 °C. At a temperature of −273 °C the gas pressure has reduced to zero.

We can begin to make sense of these results when we think about the theory of gases described in Chapter 5.8. The theory tells us that molecules are constantly on the move and exert a pressure by hitting the walls of their container. We can explain the results as follows.

- At 0 °C moving molecules exert a pressure of 100 kPa because they hit the walls of their container.
- At 100 °C the molecules are moving faster, so they hit the walls of the container harder and more often; the pressure rises to 137 kPa.
- At −136 °C the molecules have slowed down, so the collisions with the container walls are less frequent and less forceful; the pressure drops to 50 kPa.
- At −273 °C the graph predicts that the pressure will be zero. The conclusion we draw from this is that at this temperature the molecules stop moving altogether. If the molecules have stopped moving, they do not hit the walls of their container at all, so no pressure is exerted.

This means that −273 °C is the lowest possible temperature. The temperature of an object depends on the random kinetic energy of its molecules. At −273 °C molecules stop moving, so we cannot cool them any further below that. We call −273 °C **absolute zero**.

■ The Kelvin scale

We use an **absolute temperature scale** to help us predict how the pressure of a gas changes with temperature. Absolute temperatures are measured in **Kelvin** or **K**. Absolute zero is 0 K; 0 °C is 273 K. The size of a Kelvin is the same size as 1 °C. Note that we do not use a degree sign with Kelvin: we write 77 K, *not* 77 °K. Note also that K is a capital letter; the lower case k is used denote kilo (1000), so 'above 100 kPa' means a pressure of more than 100 000 Pa.

We convert degrees Celsius to Kelvin by adding 273; we convert degrees Kelvin to Celsius by subtracting 273.

For example:

$$150\,K = (150 - 273)\,°C$$
$$= -123\,°C$$
$$200\,°C = (200 + 273)\,K$$
$$= 473\,K$$

The Kelvin scale is helpful is enabling us to see the pressure change more clearly. If the Kelvin temperature doubles then we know that the pressure of the gas also doubles (provided the volume of the gas remains constant).

■ Boyle's law

Figure 9.4 shows a very similar apparatus to that used in the previous experiment. But now the piston is moved to allow the volume of the gas to change; the cylinder is leak-tight so that no air can escape or enter. To make it a fair test, the piston is moved slowly to ensure the temperature of the gas remains the same throughout the experiment. When the volume of the air

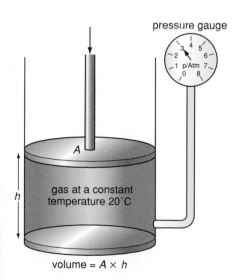

Figure 9.4 Investigating how the pressure of a gas depends on its volume.

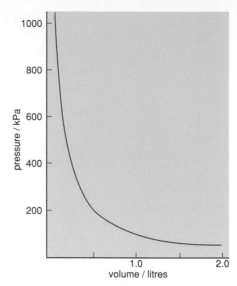

Figure 9.5 As the volume of the gas is halved, the pressure doubles.

Table 1

Pressure / kPa	Volume of air / l
50	2.0
100	1.0
200	0.5
400	0.25
1000	0.1

in the cylinder is changed, by moving the piston, the pressure in the cylinder also changes. Figure 9.5 shows in graph form how the changes between pressure and volume are linked.

Table 1 shows the sort of results you can expect to get if you do the experiment; when the gas is compressed to half its volume the pressure doubles. Note also from the values in the table that if you multiply the pressure and volume together, you always get the same number. (What is it in this example?)

So, for a constant mass of gas, at a constant temperature:

$$P_1V_1 = P_2V_2$$

This is known as **Boyle's law**.

We can also make sense of this in terms of molecular motion. When the volume of a gas is reduced, the pressure increases because the molecules hit the walls of the container more often.

■ Calculating the pressure

Here we look again at the results of the experiment using the apparatus in Figure 9.2. The results are plotted again, using only the Kelvin scale, in Figure 9.6. We can now see more clearly the relationship between the pressure of the gas and the Kelvin scale. The straight line drawn through the data passes through the origin. So we can say that the pressure of a fixed mass of gas at a constant volume is directly proportional to the Kelvin temperature. This means that the ratio of pressure to temperature (in K) for the gas is always the same.

We can use this equation to calculate the pressure or temperature:

$$\frac{P_1}{P_2} = \frac{T_1}{T_2}$$

Remember this is for a change at constant volume.

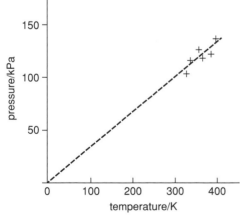

Figure 9.6 The pressure is proportional to the absolute temperature.

EXAM TIP

When calculating the pressure of a gas, make sure you have changed the temperature into Kelvin.

For example, the graph in Figure 9.6 shows us that the pressure is 110 kPa at a temperature of 300 K. What will the pressure be when the container is heated to a temperature of 600 K? Using T_1 as 600 K, T_2 as 300 K and P_2 as 110 kPa, we can substitute those numbers into the equation to give:

$$\frac{P_1}{110} = \frac{600}{300}$$
$$P_1 = 2 \times 110 \text{ kPa}$$
$$= 220 \text{ kPa}$$

■ Kelvin temperature and kinetic energy

A further important point that comes from the Kelvin scale is that the kinetic energy of the molecules in a gas is directly proportional to the Kelvin temperature. We can put this the other way round: the Kelvin temperature of a gas is a measure of the average random kinetic energy of its molecules.

STUDY QUESTIONS

1 This question refers to the experiment shown in Figure 9.4. Use Table 1 or Figure 9.5 to work out the volume of the air when the pressure was:
   a) 300 kPa
   b) 800 kPa

2 a) Explain what is meant by absolute zero.
   b) Why is it not possible to have a temperature of −300 °C?

3 a) Convert these temperatures to degrees Kelvin: 100 °C, 327 °C, −173 °C, −50 °C.
   b) Convert these absolute temperatures to °C: 10 K, 150 K, 350 K, 400 K.

4 This question refers to the experiment described in Figure 9.2.
   a) Use the graph in Figure 9.3 to predict the pressure in the cylinder at:
   i) a temperature of −200 °C
   ii) a temperature of 173 K.

5 The diagram shows a gas holder. It is filled with gas from the grid pipeline where the pressure is 800 kPa. In the gas holder, the volume of gas is 160 000 m³ and the pressure is 100 kPa. What was the volume of gas when it was in the pipeline?

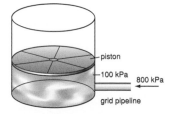
piston
100 kPa   800 kPa
grid pipeline

6 a) Explain what happens to the speed of the molecules in a gas as the temperature increases.

   b) Explain why the pressure of a gas increases as the temperature rises.

7 A gas in a container of a fixed volume has a pressure of 200 kPa at a temperature of 200 K. What will the pressure be at:
   a) 100 K   b) 600 K   c) 350 K?

8 A cylinder of gas has a pressure of 450 kPa at a temperature of 27 °C.
   a) Express 27 °C in Kelvin.
   b) Now calculate what the pressure in the gas will be at:
   i) 177 °C   ii) −73 °C.

9 a) What happens to the temperature of a gas in Kelvin if the average kinetic energy of the molecules doubles?
   b) What happens to the temperature of gas in Kelvin if the average speed of its molecules is doubled?

10 An airtight cylinder of gas has a volume of 0.4 m³ and a pressure of 250 kPa at 20 °C.
   a) The cylinder expands slightly but the temperature of the gas does not change. What happens to the pressure of the gas?
   b) The cylinder is then warmed to 100 °C without changing its volume. What is the pressure after it has been heated?

11 Devise an experiment to investigate the relationship between the volume and temperature of a fixed mass of gas when its pressure is kept constant. Explain what apparatus you would use, what measurements you would take and how you would control the variables.

Summary

Make sure you can answer all the questions in the *Interactive quiz.*

I am confident that:

✓ **I can recall these facts and concepts about density and pressure**
- I can recall and use the equation: $\text{density} = \dfrac{\text{mass}}{\text{volume}}$
- I know that the unit of density is kg/m^3
- I know and can describe how to measure density
- I can recall and use the equation: $\text{pressure} = \dfrac{\text{force}}{\text{area}}$
- I know that the unit of pressure is N/m^2 or pascal (Pa)
- I can recall and use the relationship:

$$\text{Pressure difference} = \text{height} \times \text{density} \times g$$

✓ **I can recall these facts and concepts about change of state**
- I understand that a substance can change state from solid to liquid by the process of melting.
- I understand that a substance can change state from a liquid to a gas by the process of evaporating or boiling.
- I know that particles in a liquid have a random motion within a close-packed irregular structure.
- I know that particles in a solid vibrate about fixed positions within a close-packed regular structure.

✓ **I can recall these facts and concepts about ideal gas molecules**
- I understand the significance of Brownian motion.
- I know that molecules in a gas have a random motion.
- I know that molecules exert a pressure by hitting the walls of their container.
- I understand that absolute zero is $-273\,°C$.
- I can convert temperatures between the Kelvin and Celsius scales.
- I understand that the Kevin temperature of the gas is proportional to the average kinetic energy of its molecules.
- I can use the relationship between the pressure and Kelvin temperature for a fixed mass of gas at a constant volume:

$$\frac{P_1}{T_1} = \frac{P_2}{T_2}$$

- I can use the relationship between the pressure and volume of a fixed mass of a gas at a constant temperature: $P_1V_1 = P_2V_2$

Exam-style questions

1 a) Write down the formula that connects density, mass and volume. [1]

b) Explain how you would use a measuring cylinder, electronic balance and some glass marbles to calculate the density of glass. [5]

2 The side of a cube of wood is 4.0 cm; the mass of the cube is 32.0 g. Calculate the density of wood in g/cm³. [3]

3 A customer buys a 'gold' ornament from a second-hand shop. He decides to check whether the ornament is really made of solid gold.

The results of his measurements are shown below.
■ mass of the ornament = 910 g
■ volume of the ornament = 70.0 cm³

a) Suggest how the customer took the measurements. [2]

b) Calculate the density of the ornament. [3]

c) Use the data below to suggest what the customer might find if he cuts his ornament in half. [1]
■ density of gold = 19.3 g/cm³
■ density of lead = 11.6 g/cm³

4 Use the idea of pressure to explain the following.

a) A saw has a jagged edge. [2]

b) A knife cuts more easily when it has been sharpened. [2]

c) You should not walk over a wooden floor wearing stiletto heels. [2]

d) Canadians wear snow shoes to help them get around in winter. [2]

e) A tank has caterpillar tracks on it. [2]

5 Diagrams A, B and C show three boxes. Calculate which box would you use and how would you position it to exert:

a) the greatest pressure on the ground [2]

b) the smallest pressure on the ground. [2]

A   weight = 18 000 N

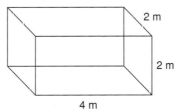

B   weight = 24 000 N

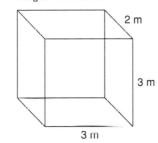

C   weight = 5000 N

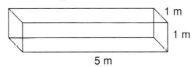

6 a) The diagram shows a piece of glass being lifted by a suction cup. The area of the cup is 0.005 m² and the pressure inside the cup has been reduced to 0.7 atmospheres. (1 atmosphere pressure is 100 000 Pa.) What is the greatest weight you could lift safely with this cup? [3]

b) What possible changes could you make in order to lift a heavier piece of glass? [2]

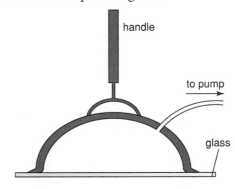

7 Below, you can see two oil wells. Oil, salt water and natural gas are trapped by oil-proof layers of rock.

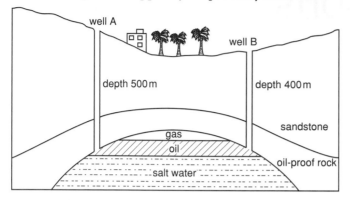

a) i) Why is the salt water lying below the oil?

   ii) Why is the natural gas lying above the oil? [2]

b) When well A is drilled, oil shoots 10 m above the ground. When well B is drilled, oil shoots much higher above the ground. Explain why oil shoots much higher from well B. [2]

c) As the oil escapes from the wells, what happens to

   i) the volume of the natural gas

   ii) the pressure of the natural gas? [2]

d) After a few months, oil can still be obtained from well A but it has to be pumped out. Explain why the oil does not shoot out by itself. [1]

8 **a) i)** State what is meant by **pressure**. [1]

   ii) A suitable unit for pressure is the pascal (Pa). State another unit used to measure pressure. [1]

b) Explain briefly, in terms of pressure, why:

   i) the sharp edge of a knife, and not the blunt edge, is used for cutting [2]

   ii) the thickness of the wall of a dam, used to store water, is greater at the base than at the top [2]

   iii) a tin can collapses when the air is removed from it [2]

   iv) aneroid barometers may be used as altimeters (height meters) in aircraft. [2]

c) The diagram shows a simple type of hydraulic braking system. The areas of cross-section of the small cylinder and large cylinder are 0.0004 m² and 0.0024 m² respectively. The brake pedal is pushed against the piston in the small cylinder with a force of 90 N.

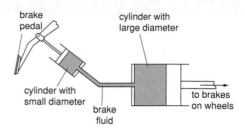

i) Determine the pressure exerted on the brake fluid. [3]

ii) Determine the force exerted by the brake fluid on the piston in the large cylinder. [2]

9 Colonel Carruthers has been murdered at Campbell Castle. Inspector Grappler of the Yard has been sent to investigate. He finds old Carruthers dead in the library. Outside the library window there are some footprints in the flower bed (exhibit A). This is an important clue; the inspector realises that he can estimate the suspect's height. Inspector Grappler carries out an experiment in the flower bed. He uses a wooden square (exhibit B) and some weights. He piles the weights onto the square and measures how far the square sinks into the flower bed. His results are in the table.

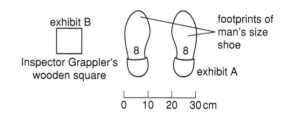

Mass of the inspector's weights / kg	Depth of the hole made by the square / mm
5	7
10	14
15	20
20	25
25	30

a) Estimate the area of the suspect's shoes. [3]

b) Inspector Grappler measured that the shoes had sunk 23 mm into the flower bed. Use the data in the table and your answer to part (a) to make an estimate of the suspect's mass. [3]

c) Exhibit C shows roughly how the height of a man depends on his mass. Exhibit D shows roughly how a man's shoe size depends on his height. Use these graphs to make an informed guess of the suspect's height. [2]

d) Of Colonel Carruthers' servants (see exhibit E), which one do you suspect? [2]

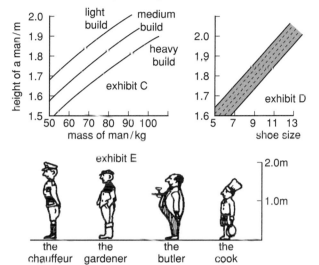

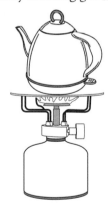

exhibit E

the chauffeur   the gardener   the butler   the cook

10 The kinetic theory assumes that gases are made up of small, fast-moving molecules, which move in random directions. Explain how the observation of Brownian motion supports this theory. [4]

11 A kettle is being heated on a camping stove. The heat is provided by burning gas from the cylinder.

a) Water in the kettle boils at 100 °C and steam is produced. Convert this temperature to a temperature on the Kelvin scale. [1]

b) Explain **one** difference between the molecules in steam and the molecules in water. [1]

c) Explain how the molecules in the steam exert a pressure on the kettle walls. [2]

d) The wind blows the flame out and 520 cm³ of gas, at a pressure of 135 kPa, escapes from the cylinder. As the gas escapes, its pressure reduces to 100 kPa. Calculate the volume of the escaped gas at a pressure of 100 kPa. [3]

e) After the tap is closed to prevent further loss of gas, the cylinder is left in the sunshine and it warms up. Explain what happened to the gas in the cylinder. [2]

12 When a drop of ether is placed on the skin, the skin feels cold. Explain why. [3]

13 a) Explain one difference between the ways in which molecules are arranged in water and in ice. [1]

b) Explain why an ice cube at a temperature of 0 °C is more effective in cooling a drink than the same mass of water at a temperature of 0 °C. [2]

c) Explain why ice cubes float on water. [1]

d) Ice cubes in a glass of water melt to form more water. What happens to the level of water in the glass? [1]

14 As an athlete runs, he gets hot. To avoid overheating his body sweats. The sweat evaporates and cools his body.

a) Use your ideas about molecules to explain why evaporation leads to cooling. [2]

b) At the end of a marathon race, runners are given shiny foil sheets to wear, to stop them cooling down too quickly.

i) Explain why the runner might cool quickly at the end of a marathon. [2]

ii) Explain how the foil reduces heat loss. [2]

15 This question is about hanging your washing out to dry. Explain why the towel will dry more quickly if:

a) the towel is spread out on the line, not folded [1]

b) it is a warm day [1]

c) there is a wind blowing. [1]

16 These questions are about a scuba diver and the pressure in his body. You will need the following information to help you answer them:

The density of water is 1000 kg/m³; the pull of gravity is 10 N/kg; on the day of the dive, the atmospheric pressure is 100 kPa.

a) The diver descends to a depth of 25 m.

i) Use the formula $P = h \times \rho \times g$ to calculate the extra pressure on his body caused by the water.

ii) Calculate the total pressure on the diver's body. [3]

b) When the diver is at a depth of 25 m his lungs can hold 5 litres of air.

i) What volume would this air occupy at normal atmospheric pressure?

ii) Explain why divers must breathe out as they rise to the surface. [4]

17 At the beginning of the compression stroke in the cylinder of a diesel engine, the air is at a temperature of 127 °C and a pressure of 120 kPa.

a) Convert this temperature to degrees Kelvin. [1]

b) During the compression stroke the volume of the air is squashed to 1/20th of its original volume, then its temperature is raised to 727 °C.

i) Calculate the pressure in the air after it has been compressed to 1/20th of its volume.

ii) Calculate the final pressure after the air has been warmed to 727 °C. [4]

18 Cylinders of gas that are caught in the flames of a burning building can be a significant hazard. At a temperature of 20 °C the pressure in a cylinder of gas is 300 kPa – this is three times normal atmospheric pressure. The temperature of a fire might reach 1200 °C.

a) Explain why the pressure rises in the cylinder, in terms of molecular motion. [2]

b) i) Calculate the pressure in the cylinder at a temperature of 1200 °C.

ii) Explain why this is a dangerous pressure. [4]

19 The diagram shows Boris in a diving bell. He is just about to explore the depths of the black lagoon. As the bell is lowered into the sea, water rises to fill the bell.

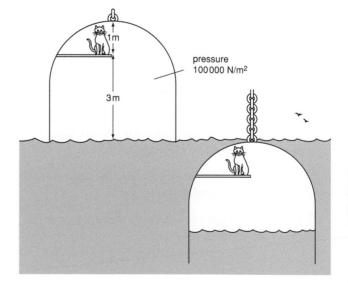

pressure
100 000 N/m²

a) Explain why water starts to fill the bell as it is lowered. [1]

b) the pressure below the surface of the sea is given by the formula: $P = (100\ 000 + 10\ 000\ d)\ N/m^2$; d is the depth below the surface in metres. What is the pressure of air in the diving bell at a depth of 10 m? [2]

c) How deep can the bell go, before Boris gets his feet wet? [3]

20 A balloon seller has a cylinder of helium gas which he uses to blow up his balloons.

The volume of the cylinder is 0.10 m³.
It contains helium gas at a pressure of 1.0×10^7 Pa.
The balloon seller fills each balloon to a volume of 1.0×10^{-2} m³ and a pressure of 1.2×10^5 Pa.

a) Explain, in terms of particles, how the helium in the cylinder produces a pressure. [2]

b) Calculate the total volume that the helium gas will occupy at a pressure of 1.2×10^5 Pa. You can assume that there is no change in the temperature of the helium gas. [3]

c) Calculate the number of balloons of volume 1.0×10^{-2} m³ that the balloon seller can fill using the gas. [2]

21 The diagram below shows a method of observing the diffusion of bromine in air.

When the bromine is released it forms a brown gas which is seen to diffuse slowly up the diffusion tube.

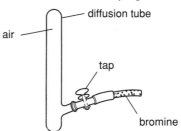

a) Although the average speed of a bromine molecule is 350 m/s, the bromine gas only travels about 10 cm through the air in 500 s. Draw a diagram to show the path a bromine molecule takes as it travels through the air and use it to explain why diffusion is a slow process. [2]

b) When food is being cooked at home the smells from the cooking soon travel through the house. If diffusion is such a slow process, how can you explain this? [2]

22 Can you explain why bubbles rising in a glass of a fizzy drink get larger as they rise to the surface? [2]

EXTEND AND CHALLENGE

1 In the diagram below, you can see the planet Mars in an elliptical orbit around the Sun. At its closest (position A) Mars is about 200 million km away from the Sun. At its most distant (position B) Mars is about 250 million km away from the Sun.

Mars has a thin atmosphere which is mostly carbon dioxide. The pressure of the atmosphere changes from winter to summer. The table below shows some details of the Martian climate. The data were taken by the Viking Lander, near to the equator in 1977.

a) Convert the temperatures into Kelvin.

b) Use these temperatures to explain why the average pressure of the atmosphere changes so much.

	Average daily temperature / °C	Average pressure / N/m²
Position B (winter)	−73	50
Position A (summer)	−13	65

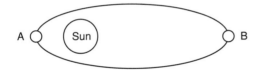

2 The diagram above right shows a piece of apparatus used to investigate how gas pressure varies with temperature, at constant volume. The table shows a set of results.

Temperature / in °C	26	50	65	80	100
Pressure reading / kPa	102	110	115	120	127

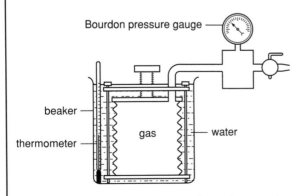

a) Plot a graph of pressure, *P* (*y*-axis), against temperature, *T*, in °C (*x*-axis). Choose a scale on the *x*-axis which runs from −300 °C to 100 °C. Use it to find the pressure of the enclosed gas at 70 °C.

b) The graph enables you to make predictions about the pressure outside the range of values plotted. How?

c) If the gas pressure continued to vary in the way suggested by the graph, what pressure would you expect at (i) 200 °C, (ii) 0 °C, (iii) −200 °C?

d) Is it correct to say that the pressure is proportional to temperature? Why?

e) Where does the line cross the temperature axis (it should be between −270 and −280 °C). What will the gas pressure be at this temperature?

3 Below you can see Boris, Vladimir and Leonid. Boris is twice as tall, twice as long and twice as wide as Vladimir, but they have the same density.

(a) How many times more massive than Vladimir is Boris?

(b) The area of Boris's paw is greater than the area of Vladimir's paw. By how many times is it bigger?

(c) Is the pressure bigger under Boris's paws or under Vladimir's paws? By what factor does the pressure differ under the two cats' paws?

(d) Leonid the lion is a distant cousin to Boris. Lions, as you know, are much bigger than domestic cats. Can you use the result of part (c) to explain why a lion's legs are proportionately thicker than a cat's?

Boris (cat)

Vladimir (kitten)

Leonid (lion)

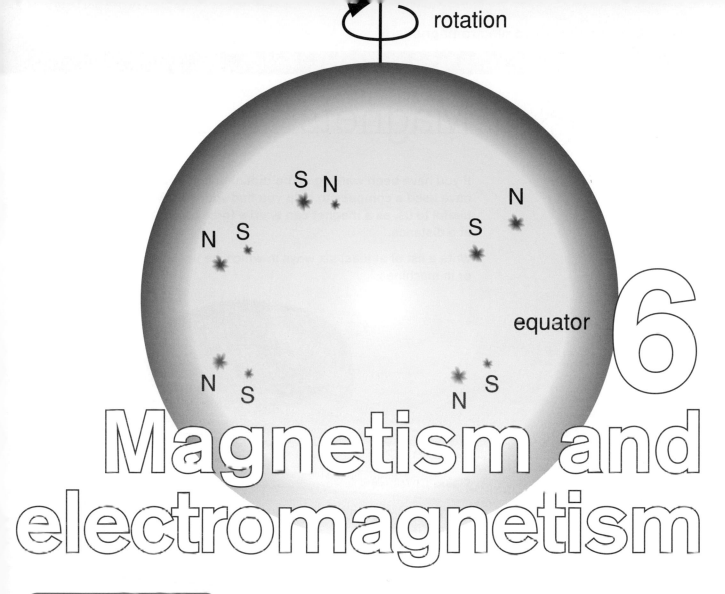

rotation

S N

N S

N

S

N

S

equator

6

Magnetism and electromagnetism

CALCULATE • PRESENT

Use the internet to help you to answer the following questions:

1 What is the average surface temperature of the Sun?
2 What is the surface temperature of a sunspot?
3 How can you tell from the photograph that sunspots are colder than the rest of the Sun's surface?

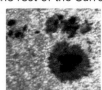

4 How long is the sunspot cycle?
5 Use the information in the photograph and text on this page to sketch the magnetic field lines close to a pair of sunspots. The diagram at the top of the page shows how sunspots are paired.

The Sun has a strong magnetic field. This is produced by the movement of charged particles (a plasma) caused by convection currents in the Sun's core. The outer and inner layers of the Sun rotate at different rates, causing the Sun's magnetic field to get twisted.

At the surface, the magnetic field emerges from pairs of sunspots, one of which is a north pole and the other a south pole.

Sometimes convection currents lead to eruptions in the surface of the Sun. Charged material flies into space but it is trapped by the Sun's magnetic field and flows in great arches.

By the end of this section you should:
• know what a magnetic field is
• know that an electric current can produce a magnetic field
• know how an electric motor works
• understand how electromagnets work and why they are useful
• know what electromagnetic induction is
• understand how generators work
• understand how transformers work and explain how electricity is transmitted.

6.1 Magnets

If you have been walking in the mountains or in the forest, you might have used a compass to help you find your way. Magnets are very useful to us, as a magnet can exert a force on another magnetic object at a distance.

Write a list of at least six ways in which we use magnets in the home or in machines.

Figure 1.1 This is a simple everyday device, but can you explain how it works?

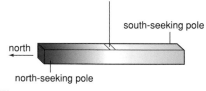

Figure 1.2

In Figure 1.2 you can see a bar magnet that is hanging from a fine thread. When it is left for a while, one end always points north. This end of the magnet is called the **north-seeking pole**. The other end of the magnet is the **south-seeking pole**. We usually refer to these poles as the north (N) and south (S) poles of the magnet.

■ Poles

Some metals, for example iron, cobalt and nickel, are **magnetic**. A magnet will attract them. If you drop a lot of pins on to the floor the easiest way to pick them all up again is to use a magnet.

The forces on pins, iron filings and other magnetic objects are always greatest when they are near the poles of a magnet. Every magnet has two poles that are equally strong.

When you hold two magnets together you find that two north poles (or two south poles) repel each other, but a south pole attracts a north pole (Figure 1.3).

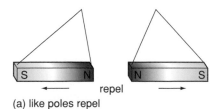
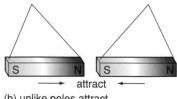

(a) like poles repel

(b) unlike poles attract

Figure 1.3

■ Magnetic fields

There is a magnetic field in the area around a magnet. In this area there is a force on a magnetic object. If the field is strong the force is big. In a weak field the force is small.

The direction of a magnetic field can be found by using a small plotting compass. The compass needle always lies along the direction of the field. Figure 1.4 shows how you can investigate the field near to a bar magnet, using a plotting compass. We use magnetic field lines to represent a magnetic field. Magnetic field lines always start at a north pole and finish on a south pole. Where the field lines are drawn close together, the field is strong. The further apart the lines are, the weaker the field is.

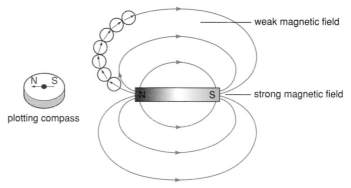

Figure 1.4 Plotting magnetic field lines around a bar magnet.

■ Combining magnetic fields

The pattern of magnetic field lines close to two (or more) magnets becomes complicated. The magnetic fields from the two magnets combine. The field lines from the two magnets never cross. (If field lines did cross, it would mean that a compass would have to point in two directions at once.)

Figure 1.5 shows the sort of pattern when two north poles are near each other. The field lines repel. At the point X there are no field lines. The two magnetic fields cancel out. X is called a neutral point.

Figure 1.6 shows the pattern produced by a north and south pole. Notice that there is an area where the field lines are equally spaced and all point in the same direction. This is called a uniform field.

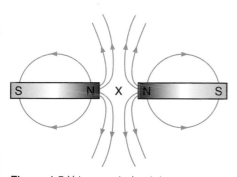

Figure 1.5 X is a neutral point; a compass placed here can point in any direction.

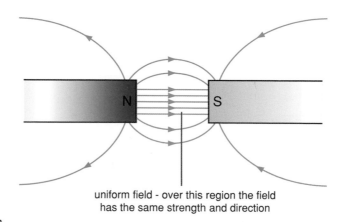

uniform field - over this region the field has the same strength and direction

Figure 1.6

There is a magnetic south pole near the geographic North Pole.

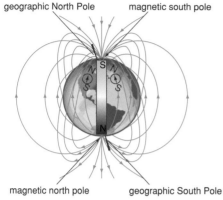

geographic North Pole   magnetic south pole

magnetic north pole   geographic South Pole

Figure 1.8 The Earth's magnetic field.

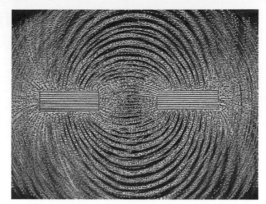

Figure 1.7 Computer artwork of the magnetic field around two magnets, as revealed by iron filings.

■ The Earth's magnetic field

Figure 1.8 shows the shape of the Earth's magnetic field. The north (seeking) pole of a compass points towards geographic North. Unlike poles attract. This means that geographic North behaves like a magnetic south pole.

However, magnetic south is not in the same place as the geographic North Pole. At the moment magnetic south is in the sea north of Canada. Over a period of centuries the direction of the field alters.

STUDY QUESTIONS

1 a) The diagram shows a bar magnet surrounded by four plotting compasses. Copy the diagram and mark in the direction of the compass needle for each of the cases B, C, D.

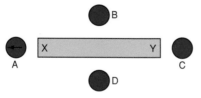

    b) Which is a north pole, X or Y?

2 Draw carefully the shape of the magnetic field between and surrounding these two magnets. Mark in any neutral points.

3 Two bar magnets have been hidden in a box. Use the information in the diagram (above right) to suggest how they have been placed inside the box.

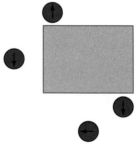

4 Give **three** examples of where you might use permanent magnets in the home. Describe each situation.

5 Refer to Figure 1.8 showing the Earth's magnetic field.
    a) Compare the strength of the magnetic field at the Equator and at the geographic North Pole. Which is stronger? Give a reason for your answer.
    b) Why is a compass very difficult to use near to the Earth's magnetic poles?

6 Pins can be attracted to a magnet but they are not permanent magnets. Explain how you would demonstrate that something which is magnetic is a *permanent* magnet.

6.2 Currents and magnetism

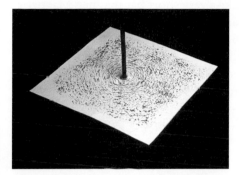

Figure 2.1 Iron filings are arranged in circles around this wire, which is carrying a current. What can you deduce from this? Can you identify any North and South poles?

■ The magnetic field near a straight wire

An electric current in a conductor produces a magnetic field around it.

In Figure 2.2, a long straight wire carrying an electric current is placed vertically so that it passes through a horizontal piece of hardboard. Iron filings have been sprinkled onto the board to show the shape of the field. Below are summarised the important points of the experiment:

- When the current is small, the field is weak. But when a large current is used the iron filings show a circular magnetic field pattern.
- The magnetic field gets weaker further away from the wire.
- The direction of the magnetic field can be found using a compass. If the current direction is reversed, the direction of the magnetic field is reversed.

Figure 2.3 shows the pattern of magnetic field lines surrounding a wire. When the current flows into the paper (shown ⊗) the field lines point in a clockwise direction around the wire. When the current flows out of the paper (shown ⊙) the field lines point anti-clockwise. **The right-hand grip rule** will help you to remember this (Figure 2.4). Put the thumb of your right hand along a wire in the direction of the current. Now your fingers point in the direction of the magnetic field.

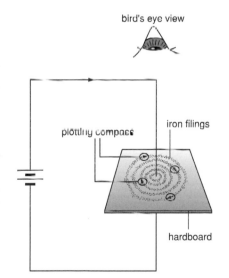

Figure 2.2 This experiment shows there is a magnetic field around a current-carrying wire.

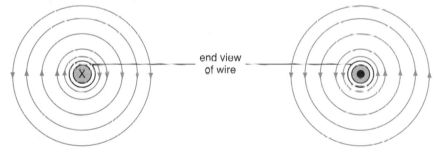

Figure 2.3 The magnetic field pattern around a current-carrying wire.

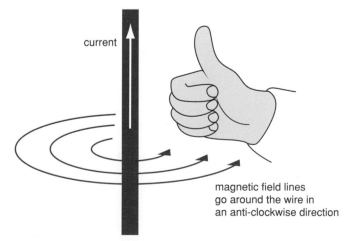

Figure 2.4 The right-hand grip rule.

PRACTICAL

Use the right-hand grip rule at A to check that the field lines go around the wire in an anti-clockwise direction. Why do they go in the opposite direction at B?

■ The magnetic field near coils of wire

Figure 2.5 shows the magnetic field around a single loop of wire that carries a current. You can use the right-hand grip rule to work out the field near to each part of the loop. Near A the field lines point anti-clockwise as you look at them, and near B the lines point clockwise. In the middle, the fields from each part of the loop combine to produce a magnetic field running from right to left. This loop of wire is like a very short bar magnet. Magnetic field lines come out of the left-hand side (north pole) and go back into the right-hand side (south pole). Figure 2.6 shows the sort of magnetic field that is produced by a current flowing through a long coil or **solenoid**. The magnetic field from each loop of wire adds on to the next. The result is a magnetic field which is like a long bar magnet's field.

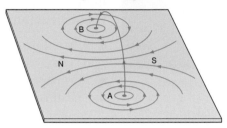

Figure 2.5 The magnetic field near a single loop of wire.

■ Producing large magnetic fields

The strength of the magnetic field produced by a solenoid can be increased by:

■ using a larger current
■ using more turns of wire
■ putting some iron into the middle of the solenoid.

But there is a limit to how strong you can make the magnetic field. If the current is made too large the solenoid will get very hot and start to melt. For this reason large solenoids must be cooled by water. There is also a limit to the number of turns of wire you can put into a space.

Nowadays, the world's strongest magnetic fields are produced by **superconducting magnets**. At very low temperatures (about 4 K) some materials, such as niobium and lead, become superconductors. A superconductor has no electrical resistance. This means that a current can flow without causing any heating effect. So a large magnetic field can be produced by making enormous currents (5000 A) flow through a solenoid, which is kept cold in liquid helium.

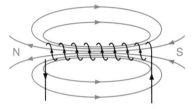

Figure 2.6 The magnetic field near a long solenoid.

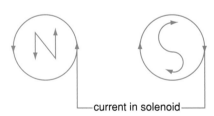

Figure 2.7 This is a good way to work out the polarity of the end of a solenoid.

Figure 2.8 The iron filings show the shape of the magnetic field around a solenoid.

EXAM TIP

A long solenoid and a bar magnet both produce a magnetic field of the same shape.

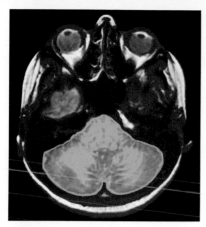

Figure 2.9 A coloured three-dimensional magnetic resonance imaging scan of a healthy human brain, seen from the front. This technique, using strong magnetic fields generated by superconducting electromagnets, allows doctors to examine organs non-intrusively.

Figure 2.10 Some superconducting magnets are so strong that the can lift the weight of a train. The Maglev (derived from magnetic levitation) in Shanghai is lifted and driven by superconducting magnets.

STUDY QUESTIONS

1 The diagram below shows two plotting compasses, one above and one below a wire. Draw diagrams to show the position of the needles when:
   a) there is no current
   b) the current is very large (30 A)
   c) the current is small (1 A). A current of 1A produces a magnetic field near the wire, which is about the same size as the Earth's magnetic field.

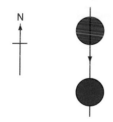

2 The diagram shows a long perspex tube with wire wrapped around it to make a solenoid.
   a) Copy the diagram and mark in the direction of the compass needles 1–6, when the current flows through the wire.

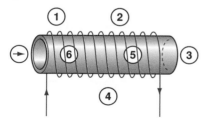

   b) Which end of the solenoid acts as the south pole?
   c) In which direction do the needles point when the current is reversed?
   d) Copy the diagram again, leaving out the compasses. Draw magnetic field lines round the solenoid.

3 The diagram represents a wire placed vertically, with the current flowing out of the paper towards you. Copy it and draw the magnetic field lines round the wire, showing how the field decreases with distance.

4 Diagram A below shows an electron moving around the nucleus of an atom.

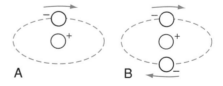

   a) Explain why this atom is magnetic. (Remember: a moving electron produces a current.)
   b) Sketch the shape of the magnetic field near the atom.
   c) What happens to the magnetic field if the electron moves the opposite way?
   d) What can you say about the atom in diagram B? Is it more or less magnetic than the other atom?

6.3 Magnetising

Millions and millions of pieces of information are stored in the magnetic field pattern in this computer's hard disk.

How is this information retrieved from the disk?

Do some research to find out about the size of computer memories in 1970, 1990 and 2010.

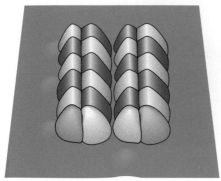

Figure 3.1 This scanning tunnelling microscope image shows two atomic-scale bits. Each bit consists of twelve iron atoms. The magnetisation direction of each iron atom is opposite to its neighbour. The bit on the left stores one piece of information (1); the bit on the right stores another piece of information (0). This is the world's smallest magnetic storage unit.

■ Magnetic domains

Steel can be a permanent magnet; once a piece of steel has been magnetised it remains a magnet. Iron can be a temporary magnet; iron is only magnetised when in a magnetic field. This field can be provided by a magnet or by a coil of wire carrying a current, which also produces a magnetic field (see Chapter 6.2). A magnetically **hard** material becomes a permanent magnet when it is magnetised; a magnetically **soft** material will make a temporary magnet.

The insides of magnetic materials are split up into small regions, which we call **domains**. Each domain acts like a very small magnet. In any iron or steel bar there are thousands of domains. The idea helps us to understand permanent and temporary magnets.

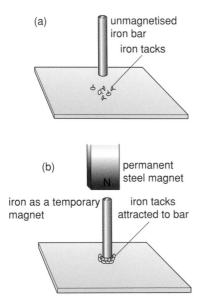

Figure 3.2 An iron bar will act as a magnet when there is a permanent magnet near it.

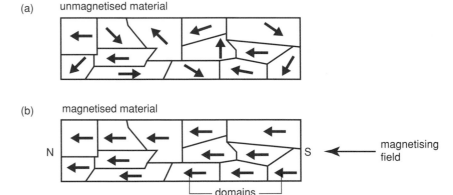

Figure 3.3 Domains in a magnetic material become aligned in a magnetic field.

In an iron bar the domains are jumbled up when there is no magnet near (Figure 3.3(a)). But as soon as a magnet is put near to the bar the domains are made to line up (Figure 3.3(b)). So an iron bar will be attracted to either a north or south pole of a permanent magnet.

In a steel bar, once the domains have been lined up, they stay pointing in one direction.

Magnetically soft materials are temporary magnets. Permanent magnets are magnetically hard materials.

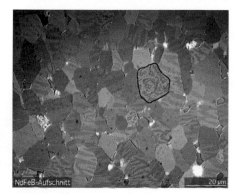

Figure 3.4 Magnetic domains.

■ Magnetic memories

We use magnetic materials to store information; this can be in the form of data on a computer, or a film or music. From the 1960s, music was recorded on magnetic tapes and then played back. The information was stored in crystals of ferric oxide (Fe_2O_3), which were inserted in the tape and protected with a plastic coating. Before DVD players, films were recorded on magnetic video tapes and played on video recorders. These were common in the 1980s through to this century.

Such devices were analogue; these have now been replaced with digital recording methods (see Section 3.4).

The same principle of storage is still used in computer hard drives; information is stored and 'remembered' by permanent magnets. The hard drive is coated in a thin layer of magnetic material. The direction of magnetisation in this layer can be changed by applying a strong magnetic field. Information can be stored digitally in the pattern of the magnetic field (see Figure 3.1). The information can be stored indefinitely and retrieved when necessary or erased if no longer needed.

■ Magnetising

One way to make a magnet from an unmagnetised steel bar is to stroke it repeatedly with a permanent magnet. The movement of the magnet along the steel bar is enough to make the domains line up (Figure 3.6(a)).

A magnet can also be made by putting a steel bar inside a solenoid. A short but very large pulse of current through the solenoid produces a strong magnetic field. This magnetises the bar (Figure 3.6(b)).

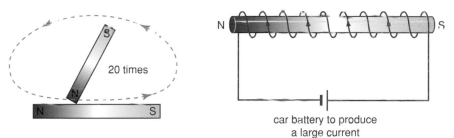

Figure 3.6 (a) Magnetisation of a steel bar by stroking. **(b)** Magnetisation using a solenoid.

Figure 3.7 This photograph shows the design of a practical laboratory electromagnet. It is made strong by two coils with many turns of wire to increase the magnetising effect of the current. When the current is switched off the iron filings will fall off the magnet.

The apparatus shown in Figure 3.6(b) can be used as an **electromagnet** if an iron bar is used instead of a steel bar in the solenoid. When a current is switched on the iron becomes magnetised; when the current is switched off the iron is no longer magnetised. The presence of iron greatly increases the strength of the solenoid's magnetic field. Electromagnets are widely used in industry.

■ Demagnetising

To make a steel bar lose its magnetism you need to jumble up the domains inside the bar. There are three ways to do this:

■ Hit the bar with a hammer.
■ Put the bar inside a solenoid that has an alternating current supply. The alternating current produces a magnetic field that switches backwards and forwards rapidly. The domains are left jumbled up after the current has been reduced gradually to zero. This principle can be used to erase information from computer memories.
■ Heat the bar to about 700°C. At low temperatures the atoms inside the steel line up to magnetise each domain. At a very high temperature the atoms vibrate at random so much that each domain is no longer magnetised.

Figure 3.8

STUDY QUESTIONS

1 a) Tracey has magnetised a needle as shown below. She then cuts the needle into four smaller bits as shown. Copy the diagram and label the poles A–H.

   b) Tracey says 'This experiment helps to show that there are magnetic domains in the needle'. Comment on this observation.

2 The diagram below shows an electromagnet. As the current increases the magnet can lift a larger load because the domains in the iron core line up more and more.

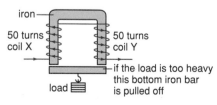

Maximum load (N)	Current (A)
0	0
5.0	0.5
8.5	1.0
12.0	2.0
14.0	3.0
14.8	4.0
15.0	5.0

   a) Use the data provided to draw a graph of the load supported (y-axis) against current (x-axis).
   b) Use the graph to predict the load supported when the current is:
      i) 1.5 A   ii) 6.0 A.
   c) Sketch on your graph how the load varies with current when each of the coils X and Y has:
      i) 25 turns   ii) 100 turns.
   d) What happens when you reverse the windings on coil X?
   e) Make sketches to show how the domains are lined up when the current (in the original diagram) is:
      i) 0   ii) 0.5 A   iii) 5 A.
   f) Use your answer to part (e) to explain why there is a maximum load that an electromagnet can lift.

3 The diagram shows the magnetic field close to a bar magnet, and an iron tack below it.
   a) Draw a diagram to show how the domains are aligned in the tack.
   b) Explain carefully why the tack is attracted to the magnet. Will the tack be attracted when the field is uniform?
   c) What happens if a south magnetic pole replaces the north pole close to the tack? Explain your answer.

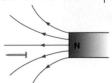

4 Explain how music or data can be stored in magnetic material.

6.4 The motor effect

What do the two machines in Figure 4.1 have in common? Answer – they both use electric motors to do work and make our lives easier. Can you name six other household machines that use electric motors?

In Figure 4.2 you can see a piece of aluminium foil that was positioned between the poles of a strong magnet. A current through the foil has caused it to be pushed down, away from the poles of the magnet. Reversing the current makes the foil move upwards, away from the poles of the magnet. This is called the **motor effect**. It happens because of an interaction between the two magnetic fields, one from the magnet and one from the current.

■ Combining two magnetic fields

In Figure 4.3 you can see the way in which the two fields combine. By itself the field between the poles of the magnet would be nearly uniform. The current through the foil produces a circular magnetic field. The magnetic field from the current squashes the field between the poles of a magnet. It is the squashing of the field that catapults the foil, upwards in this case.

Figure 4.1 Two common household appliances.

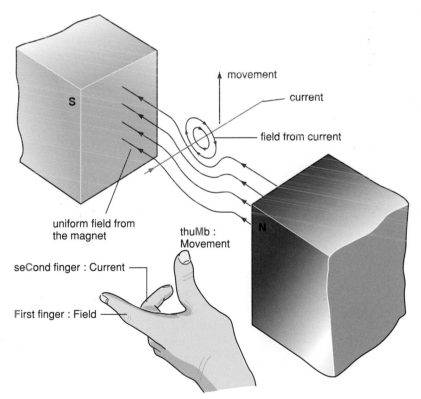

Figure 4.3 Left-hand rule: you can use the left hand to predict the direction of movement of this wire.

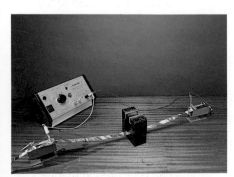

Figure 4.2 Aluminium foil carrying a current is pushed out of a magnetic field.

The force acting on the foil is proportional to:

- the strength of the magnetic field between the poles
- the current
- the length of the foil between the poles.

■ The left-hand rule

To predict the direction in which a straight conductor moves in a magnetic field you can use the **left-hand rule** (Figure 4.3). Spread out the first two fingers and the thumb of your left hand so that they are at right angles to each other. Let your first finger point along the direction of the magnet's field, and your second finger point in the direction of the current. Your thumb then points in the direction in which the wire moves.

This rule works when the field and the current are at right angles to each other. When the field and the current are parallel to each other, there is no force on the wire and it stays where it is.

■ Ammeters

Figures 4.4 and 4.5 show the idea behind a moving-coil ammeter. A loop of wire has been pivoted on an axle between the poles of a magnet. When a current is switched on, the left-hand side of the loop moves downwards and the right-hand side moves upwards. (Use the left-hand rule to check this.) If nothing stops the loop, it turns until side *DC* is at the top and *AB* is at the bottom. However, when a spring is attached to the loop it only turns a little way. When you pass a larger current through the loop, the force is larger. This will stretch the spring more and so the loop turns further.

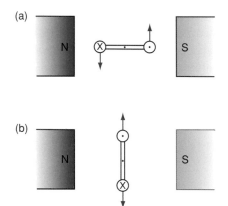

Figure 4.5 (a) The end-on view of the wire loop in Figure 4.4. The turning effect is maximum in this position. **(b)** In this position the forces acting on the coil produce no turning effect.

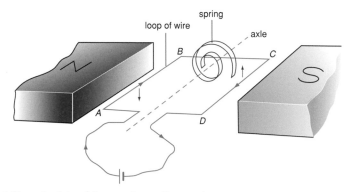

Figure 4.4 The principle of the moving-coil ammeter.

Figure 4.6 shows how a model ammeter can be made using a coil of wire, a spring and some magnets.

An ammeter is sensitive if it turns a long way when a small current flows through it. The sensitivity of an ammeter will be large when:

- a large number of turns is used on the coil
- strong magnets are used
- weak springs are used.

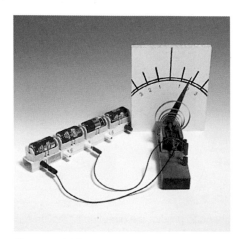

Figure 4.6 This shows a model ammeter. The coil turns in the magnetic field and is constrained by a spring.

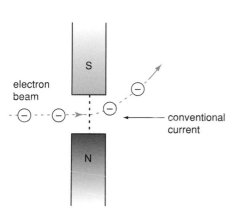

electron
beam

conventional
current

Figure 4.8 Use the left-hand rule to check that electrons are deflected by this magnetic field into the plane of the paper.

Figure 4.7 An ammeter coil.

■ Deflection of charged particles

An electric current is a flow of charged particles (usually carried by electrons in wires). You have just read that a wire carrying a current experiences a force in a magnetic field. In the same way, a beam of moving charged particles can be deflected by a magnetic field (Figure 4.8).

The size of the force depends on:

- the strength of the magnetic field
- the speed of the particles
- the charge on the particle.

The direction of the deflecting force on the particles can be predicted using the left-hand rule. Particles that are moving parallel to the magnetic field do not experience a deflecting force.

EXAM TIP

Remember that if an electron beam is moving to the right, conventional current is towards the left.

STUDY QUESTIONS

1 a) The diagrams show: (A) a pair of magnets, (B) a wire carrying a current into the paper. Sketch separate diagrams to show the magnetic fields near each of (A) and (B), when they are well separated.

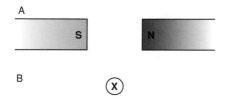

b) The wire is now placed between the poles of the magnets. Sketch the combined magnetic field. Add an arrow to show the direction in which the wire moves.
c) Which way does the wire move when:
   i) the current is reversed,
   ii) the north and south poles are changed round?
d) Give two ways in which the force on the wire could be increased.

2 This question is about the model ammeter shown in Figure 4.6. The graph shows the angle that the coil turns through, against the current flowing through the coil.

a) Use the graph to work out the current when the angle is:
   i) 30°   ii) 50°.
b) Make a sketch of the graph. Add to it further graphs to show the deflection for different currents when the ammeter is made:
   i) with stronger springs
   ii) with twice the number of turns on its coil.
c) Could this ammeter be used to measure alternating currents? Explain.
d) (Quite hard) Why is the graph not a straight line?

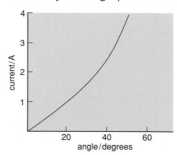

6.5 Electric motors

What are the advantages and disadvantages of replacing petrol driven cars with electric cars?

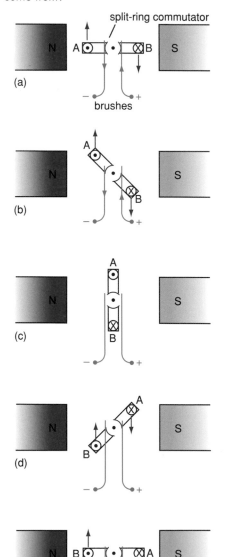

Figure 5.1 This electric bike carries a city worker to her office. What does it have in it to make it work? Where does the energy come from?

■ The principle of the motor

In the last chapter you learnt that a coil carrying a current rotates when it is in a magnetic field. However, the coil can only rotate through 90° and then it gets stuck. This is not good for making a motor. We need to make a motor rotate all the time.

Figure 5.2 shows the design of a simple motor which you can make for yourself. A coil carrying a current rotates between the poles of a magnet. The coil is kept rotating continuously by the use of a **split-ring commutator**, which rotates with the coil between the carbon brush contacts. This causes the direction of the current in the coil to reverse, so that forces continue to act on the coil to keep it turning.

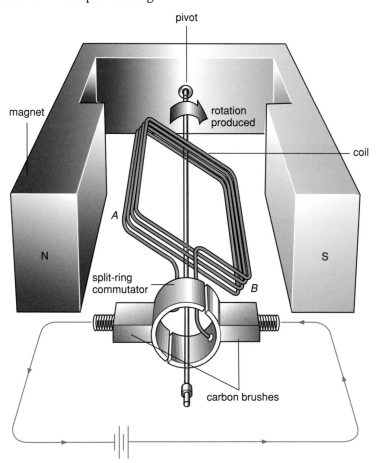

Figure 5.2 A design for a simple motor.

How the commutator works

Figure 5.3 explains the action of the commutator. The steps are explained on the next page.

Figure 5.3

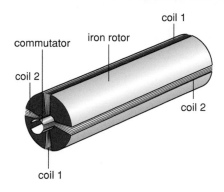

(a)

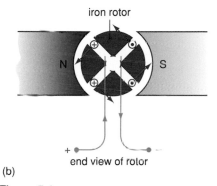

end view of rotor

(b)

Figure 5.4

(a) A current flows into the coil through the commutator so that there is an upwards push on side A, a downwards push on B.

(b) The coil rotates in a clockwise direction.

(c) When the coil reaches the vertical position no current flows through the coil. It continues to rotate past the vertical due to its own momentum.

(d) Now side A is on the right-hand side. The direction of current flowing into the coil has been reversed.

(e) Side A is pushed down and side B is pushed upwards. The coil continues to rotate in a clockwise direction.

■ Commercial motors

You use electric motors every day. Every time you put your washing into the washing machine or use a vacuum cleaner, you are using an electric motor. Your car also uses an electric motor to get it started. For these sorts of use, motors need to be made as powerful as possible.

Here are some of the ways to make a motor more powerful (see Figure 5.4):

- A large current should be used.
- As many turns as possible should be put on the coil.
- More than one coil can be used. Each coil then experiences a force, so the total force turning the motor is larger.
- The coils can be wound on an iron rotor to increase the magnetic field.
- Curved pole pieces make sure that the magnetic field is always at right angles to the coils. This gives the greatest turning effect.

 Now go through the tutorial *Generating electricity.*

STUDY QUESTIONS

1 What two properties of carbon make it a good material to use for motor brushes?
2 a) Look at Figure 5.3. Which position is the motor likely to stick in?
  b) Explain why the motor shown in Figure 5.4 is less likely to stick.
3 Copy Figure 5.4(b) and draw in some field lines to show the shape of the magnetic field.
4 The motor shown below is used to lift up a load.
  a) Use the information in the diagram to calculate the following:
    i) the work done in lifting the load
    ii) the power output of the motor while lifting the load
    iii) the electrical power input to the motor.

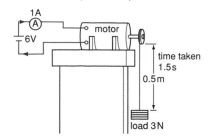

  b) Calculate the efficiency of the motor.
  c) Explain carefully the energy changes which occur during the lifting process.
5 The next diagram shows how an electric motor can be made using an electromagnet. You can see the forces acting on the coil when a current flows.

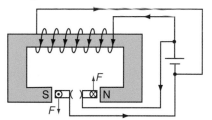

  a) The battery is now reversed. What effect does that have on:
    i) the polarity of the magnet?
    ii) the direction of current in the coil?
    iii) the forces acting on the coil?
  b) Would this motor work with an a.c. supply? Explain.
  c) Why are the electromagnet and coil run in parallel from the battery, not in series?

6.6 Electromagnets in action

Figure 6.1 Electromagnets are widely used in cars.

Electromagnetic devices are widely used, for example in cars. Research and explain three uses of electromagnets in cars, such as the starter motor, the ignition switch or the door locks.

■ Reed switches

Two reeds made of magnetic materials are enclosed inside a glass tube. Normally these reeds are not in contact so the switch is open (Figure 6.2(a)). When a magnet is brought close to the reeds they become magnetised so

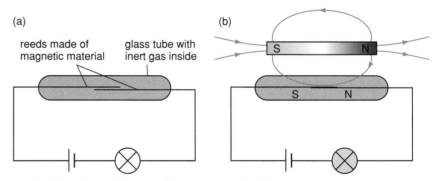

Figure 6.2 A reed switch is operated by a magnetic field.

that they attract each other. The switch is now closed (Figure 6.2(b)). These switches can be used to work circuits using a magnetic field. This field can be supplied using a permanent magnet or a solenoid (Figure 6.3).

■ Relays

A car starter motor needs a very large current of about 100 A to make it turn round. Switching large currents on and off needs a special heavy-duty switch. If you had such a large switch inside the car it would be a nuisance since it would take up a lot of space. The switch would spark and it would be unpleasant and dangerous. A way round this problem is to use a **relay**.

Figures 6.4(a) and 6.4(b) show how a car starter relay works.

Inside the relay a solenoid is wound round an iron core. When the car ignition is turned, a small current magnetises the solenoid and its iron core. The solenoid is attracted towards the heavy-duty electrical contacts, which are also made of iron. Now current can flow from the battery to the starter motor. The advantage of this system is that the car engine can be started by turning a key at a safe distance.

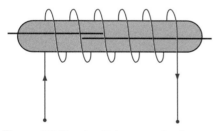

Figure 6.3 Reed switches can also be opened and closed using the magnetic field from a solenoid. This device is sometimes called a reed relay.

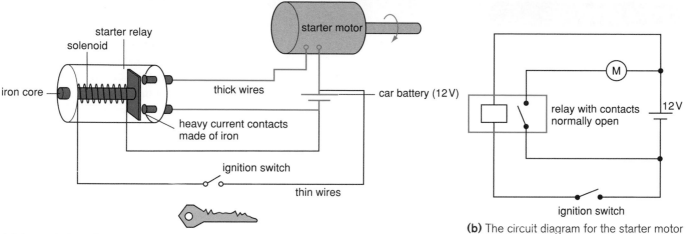

(a) A car starter relay
Figure 6.4

(b) The circuit diagram for the starter motor

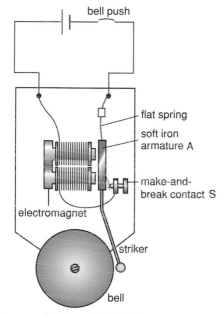

Figure 6.5 An electric bell.

■ Electric bells

Figure 6.5 shows the idea behind an electric bell. When the bell push is pressed the circuit is completed and a current flows. The electromagnet becomes magnetised and the soft iron armature A is attracted to the electromagnet. The movement of A causes the striker to hit the bell. As the bell is hit, A moves away from the contact S and the circuit is broken. The electromagnet is now demagnetised and a spring pulls A back to its original position. The circuit is remade and the process starts over again. The striker can be made to hit the bell a few times every second.

■ The moving-coil loudspeaker

The loudspeaker in your radio and television is probably made like the one shown in Figure 6.6. A loudspeaker is an example of a **transducer**. Transducers transfer one form of energy into another.

Electrical signals from the receiver cause the current flowing in the coil to change. A change in the current causes a change in the magnetic force acting on the coil. In this way the paper cone is made to move in and out. The vibrations of the cone produce sound waves.

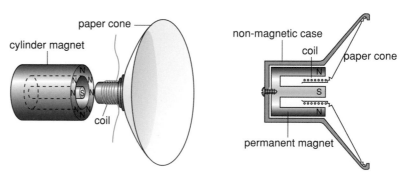

Figure 6.6 Two views of the moving-coil loudspeaker.

STUDY QUESTIONS

1 The diagram below shows the detonator circuit for a magnetic mine. This sort of mine is placed on the seabed in shallow water. The detonator is activated when it is connected across the battery. Explain how a ship can trigger the mine.

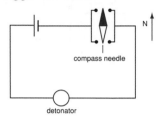
compass needle
detonator

2 This question is about the relay circuit in Figures 6.4(a) and 6.4(b).
  a) Why is the coil made of insulated wire?
  b) Explain why iron is used in the centre of the solenoid.
  c) When the ignition switch is turned the motor starts, which in turn starts the petrol engine. Explain, step by step, how this process works.

  d) i) The current through the motor is 100 A. Why is it important to use thick wires?
     ii) The resistance of the relay coil is 48 Ω. Calculate the current that flows through it when connected to the car battery in Figure 6.4(a).
     iii) Why is it an advantage to use thin wire in the relay circuit?

3 a) Use the left-hand motor rule to explain why a current causes the coil to move in or out in Figure 6.6.
  b) Now explain how an alternating current can cause a loudspeaker cone to vibrate.
  c) How is the intensity of the emitted sound controlled?
  d) How is the pitch of the sound controlled?

4 Explain how a relay could be used to lock a car door.

5 Draw a circuit diagram to explain how a reed switch can be used to switch off the power to a laptop computer when the lid is closed.

6.7 Electromagnetic induction

The device shown in Figure 7.1 is used at airports to check that passengers are not carrying any guns or bombs. Metal objects set off an alarm. How does this system work?

Electric motors work because forces act on current-carrying wires that are placed in magnetic fields. A motor transfers electrical energy into mechanical energy. The process can be put into reverse. If you turn a small motor by hand, you can generate a voltage. This voltage can make a current flow in a circuit. Then mechanical energy has been transfered into electrical energy. This is called **electromagnetic induction**.

Figure 7.1

■ Direction of movement

You can investigate which direction you must move the wire in to make a current flow around the circuit in Figure 7.2. You can move the wire backwards and forwards along the directions XX', YY' or ZZ'.

The outcome will be that you only induce a voltage and make a current flow when you move the wire up and down along XX'. The wire must cut across the magnetic field lines.

- ■ Reversing the direction of motion reverses the direction of the voltage. If moving the wire up makes the meter move to the right, moving the wire down will make the meter move to the left.
- ■ Reversing the direction of the magnetic field reverses the direction of the voltage.

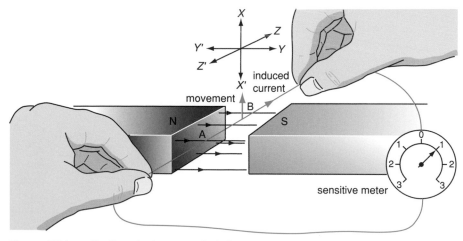

Figure 7.2 Investigating electromagnetic induction.

EXAM TIP

To generate an electric current you must keep the wire moving across magnetic field lines. Remember this can also be achieved by the *magnet* moving.

EXAM TIP

When you move a magnet to generate a current, a force acts to slow the magnet's movement.

■ Size of the induced voltage

You can also investigate what happens when you make each of these three separate changes: moving the wire faster; using different magnets; using more loops of wire.

The outcomes are as follows:

■ Moving the wire more quickly induces a greater voltage. When the wire is stationary no voltage is induced.
■ Using stronger or bigger magnets induces a greater voltage for the same speed of movement.
■ Looping more turns of wire though the same magnetic field and moving the wire at the same speed induces a larger voltage.

■ Energy changes

In Figure 7.3(a) a current is being produced by moving a magnet into a solenoid. When the current flows a compass needle is attracted towards end Y. So end Y behaves as a south pole and end X as a north pole. This means that as the magnet moves towards the solenoid there is a magnetic force that repels it. There is a force acting against the magnet, so you have to do some work to push it into the solenoid. The work done pushing the magnet produces the electrical energy.

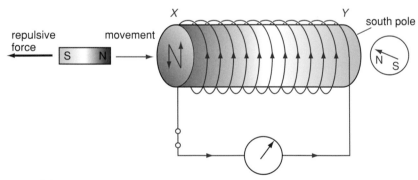

Figure 7.3(a) Lenz's law of electromagnetic induction says: 'When a current is induced it always opposes the change in magnetic field that caused it.' The end X of the solenoid is a north pole. So the effect of the induced current is to push the magnet back. This opposes the motion of the magnet, and agrees with Lenz's law.

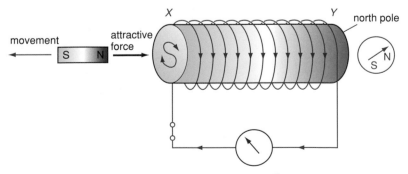

EXAM TIP

When the switch is opened, there is no current. So the magnet can move in and out of the coil without any repulsion or attraction.

Figure 7.3(b) Now the magnet moves away. X is now a south pole so the magnet is attracted to the solenoid. This opposes the motion and so agrees with Lenz's law.

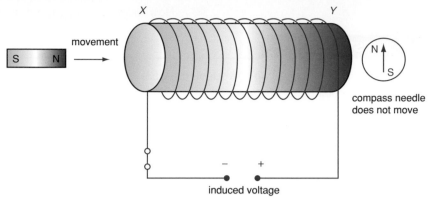

Figure 7.3(c)

In Figure 7.3(b) the magnet is being pulled out of the solenoid. The direction of the current is reversed and now there is an attractive force acting on the magnet. The pulling of the magnet still does work to produce electrical energy.

When a current is produced by electromagnetic induction, some other form of energy is transferred to electrical energy. In the example described in Figure 7.3 the energy originally came from the muscles pushing the magnet.

In Figure 7.3(c) a magnet is moved towards the coil as before, but the meter has been removed leaving a gap in the circuit, so now no current can flow. However, a voltage is induced across the ends of the wire. Because there is no current, the magnet does not experience an attractive or repulsive force and no energy is transformed.

■ An electromagnetic flow meter

Figure 7.4 shows a way to measure the rate of flow of oil through an oil pipeline. A small turbine is placed in the pipe, so that the oil flow turns the blades round. Some magnets have been placed in the rim of the turbine, so that they move past a solenoid. These moving magnets induce a voltage in the solenoid which can be measured on an oscilloscope (Figure 7.4(b)). The faster the turbine rotates, the larger is the voltage induced in the solenoid. By measuring this voltage an engineer can tell at what rate the oil is flowing.

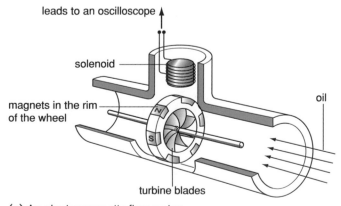

(a) An electromagnetic flow meter.

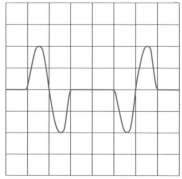

(b) The oscilloscope trace. The timebase is set so that the dot crosses the screen at a rate of one square every 0.02 seconds.

Figure 7.4

Now watch the video *Electromagnetic induction.*

STUDY QUESTIONS

1 In Figure 7.2 the wire moves up at a speed of 2 m/s. This makes the pointer of the meter kick one division to the right. Say what will happen to the meter in each of the following cases:
  a) The wire moves up at 4 m/s.
  b) The wire moves down at 6 m/s.
  c) The wire moves along YY' at 3 m/s.
  d) The magnets are turned round and the wire is moved up at 3 m/s.
  e) A larger pair of magnets is used so that the length of the wire AB in the magnetic field is doubled.

2 In the diagrams below, explain which arrangement will produce a larger deflection on the meter when the wires are moved between the poles of the magnets.

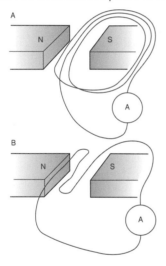

3 This question refers to the flow meter shown in Figure 7.4.
  a) The poles on the wheel rim are arranged alternately with a north, then south pole facing outwards. Use this fact to explain the shape of the oscilloscope trace.
  b) Sketch the trace on the oscilloscope for the following (separate) changes:
    i) The number of turns on the solenoid is made 1.5 times larger.
    ii) The flow of oil is increased, so that the turbine rotates twice as quickly.
  c) i) Use the information in Figures 7.4(a) and 7.4(b) to show that there is a time of 0.08 seconds between each magnet passing under the solenoid.

  ii) How long does it take for the turbine to rotate once?
  iii) How many times does the turbine rotate each second?

4 The diagram below shows a heavy copper pendulum suspended from a wire, which swings backwards and forwards from A to C, between the poles of a strong magnet. As the wire moves, a current is made to flow through the resistor R; a data logger is used to record how the voltage changes across R.
  a) Give two reasons why you would expect the current to be greatest as the pendulum moves past B.
  b) Sketch a graph to show what voltage the data logger records as the pendulum swings from A to C and back again. Mark your graph clearly to show the points A, B and C.
  c) On the same axes sketch the voltage you would observe when:
    i) the pendulum is released from a greater height
    ii) the polarity of the magnets is reversed.
  d) Explain carefully the energy changes which occur when the pendulum swings from A to B:
    i) with S closed
    ii) with S open.
  e) It is observed that the pendulum swings take longer to die away when the switch is open, than when the switch is closed. Explain why.
  f) The pendulum is replaced by a heavier one; it is released again from A. What effect will you notice on:
    i) the graph drawn in part (b)
    ii) the time taken for the swings to die away? Explain your answer.

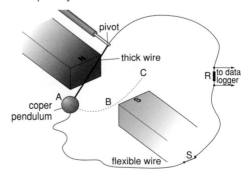

6.8 Generators

Find out how many power stations there are in your country.

Figure 8.1 The same principles of electromagnetic induction apply in power stations but the scale is much bigger. The generator shown in Figure 8.1 can deliver 200 MW of power.

■ The a.c. generator (alternator)

Figure 8.2 shows the design of a very simple **alternating current (a.c.)** generator. By turning the axle you can make a coil of wire move through a magnetic field. This causes a voltage to be induced between the ends of the coil.

You can see how the voltage waveform, produced by this generator, looks on an oscilloscope screen (Figure 8.3(a)). In position (i) the coil is vertical with AB above CD (Figure 8.3(b)). In this position the sides CD and AB are moving parallel to the magnetic field. No voltage is generated since the wires are not cutting across the magnetic field lines.

When the coil has been rotated through a ¼ turn to position (ii), the coil produces its greatest voltage. Now the sides CD and AB are cutting through the magnetic field at the greatest rate.

In position (iii), the coil is again vertical and no voltage is produced. In position (iv) a maximum voltage is produced, but in the opposite direction. Side AB is moving upwards and side CD downwards.

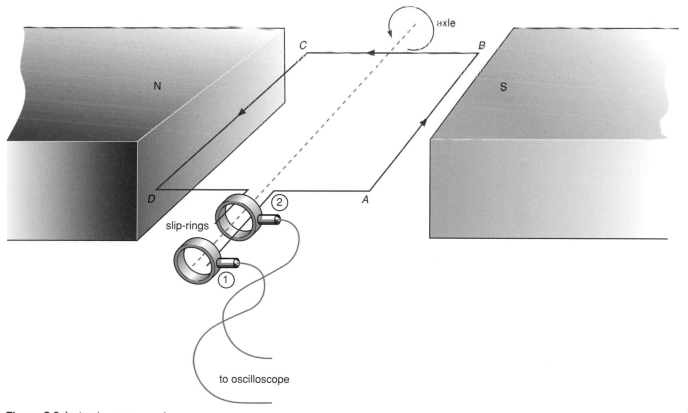

Figure 8.2 A simple a.c. generator.

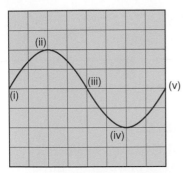

Figure 8.3(a) Voltage waveform.

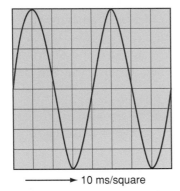

→ 10 ms/square

Figure 8.4 The generator is turned twice as fast.

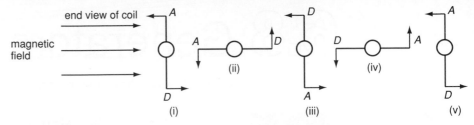

Figure 8.3(b) Position of coil.

■ The size of the induced voltage

The size of the induced voltage can be made larger by:

- rotating the coil faster
- using stronger magnets
- using more turns of wire
- wrapping the wire round a soft iron core.

Figure 8.4 shows the voltage waveform when the generator is rotated twice as quickly. There are two effects: the maximum voltage is twice as large; the frequency is doubled, i.e. the interval between the peaks is halved.

■ Producing power on a large scale

The electricity that you use in your home is produced by very large generators in power stations. These generators work in a slightly different way from the simple one you have seen so far.

Instead of having a rotating coil and a stationary magnet, large generators have rotating electromagnets and stationary coils (see Figure 8.5). The advantage of this set-up is that no moving parts are needed to collect the large electrical current that is produced.

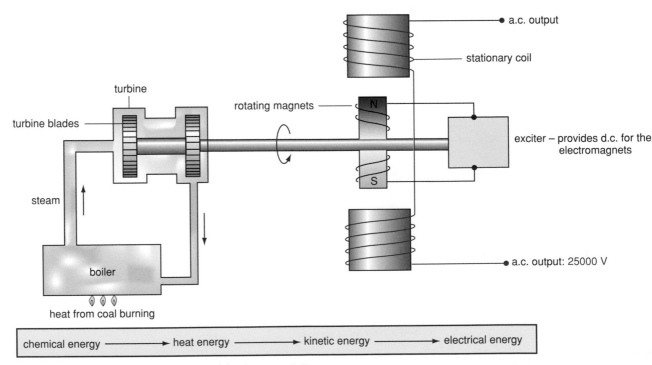

Figure 8.5 Electricity generation in a coal-fired power station.

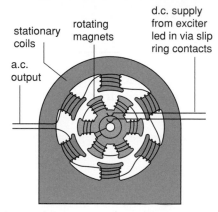

Figure 8.6 A section through a large generator.

The important steps in the generation of electricity in a coal-fired power station (Figure 8.5) are these:

1 Coal is burnt to boil water.
2 High-pressure steam from the boiler is used to turn a turbine.
3 The drive shaft from the turbine is connected to the generator magnets, which rotate near to the stationary coils. The output from the coils has a voltage of about 25 000 V.
4 The turbine's drive shaft also powers the **exciter**. The exciter is a direct current (d.c.) generator that produces current for the rotating magnets, which are in fact electromagnets.

STUDY QUESTIONS

1 The circuit diagram is for a 'shake-up' torch. A magnet is placed in a coil of wire, which is linked to a rechargeable battery and a light-emitting diode (LED). The magnet is free to slide backwards and forwards, down inside the coil.

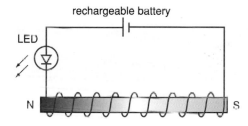

   a) What is a light-emitting diode?
   b) Explain why a diode is used in this circuit.
   c) Explain how the battery is recharged.

2 This question refers to the waveform in Figure 8.3(a). Copy the graph and add additional graphs to show what happens to the waveform as each of these changes is made. Explain your answers.
   a) The coil rotation is reversed.
   b) An extra turn of wire is added.
   c) The coil is rotated twice as quickly.

3 In the diagram below left, the dynamo is connected to a flywheel by a drive belt. The dynamo is operated by winding the handle. When a student turns the handle as fast as she can, the dynamo produces a voltage of 6 V. The graph shows how long the dynamo takes to stop after the student stops winding the handle. The time taken to stop depends on how many bulbs are connected to the dynamo.
   a) Explain the energy changes that occur after the student stops winding the handle:
      i) when the switches S_1, S_2 and S_3 are open (as shown),
      ii) when the switches are closed.
   b) Why does the flywheel take longer to stop when no light bulb is being lit by the dynamo?
   c) Make a copy of the graph. Use your graph to predict how long the flywheel turns when you make it light four bulbs.
   d) The experiment is repeated using bulbs that use a smaller current. They use 0.15 A rather than 0.3 A. Using the same axes, sketch a graph to show how the time taken to stop depends on the number of bulbs, in this second case.

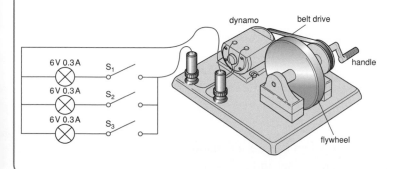

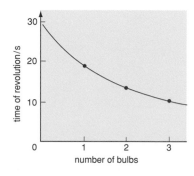

6.9 Transformers

Figure 9.1 is a familiar sight. The electricity is carried at very high voltages – as high as 400 000 V. Why is the electricity transmitted at such high voltages?

Figure 9.1 Pylons carrying electrical transmission lines.

■ Changing fields and changing currents

In Figure 9.2, when the switch is closed in the first circuit, the ammeter in the second circuit kicks to the right. For a moment a current flows through coil 2. When the switch is opened again the ammeter kicks to the left.

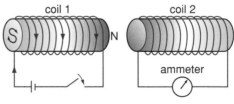

Figure 9.2

Closing the switch makes the current through coil 1 grow quickly. This makes the coil's magnetic field grow quickly. For coil 2 this is like pushing the north pole of a magnet towards it, so a current is induced in coil 2. When the switch is opened the magnetic field near coil 1 falls rapidly. This is like pulling a north pole away from coil 2. Now the induced current flows the other way.

The ammeter reads zero when there is a constant current through coil 1. A current is only induced in the second coil by a changing magnetic field. This happens when the switch is opened and closed.

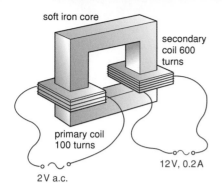

soft iron core

secondary coil 600 turns

primary coil 100 turns

12V, 0.2A

2V a.c.

(a) A step-up transformer

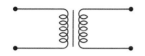

(b) The circuit symbol for a transformer

Figure 9.3

Figure 9.4 A small transformer for use in a laboratory.

■ Transformers

A **transformer** is made by putting two coils of wire onto a soft iron core as shown in Figure 9.3. The primary coil is connected to a 2 V alternating current supply. The alternating current in the primary coil makes a magnetic field, which rises and then falls again. The soft iron core carries this changing magnetic field to the secondary coil and a changing voltage is induced in the secondary coil. In this way, energy can be transferred continuously from the primary circuit to the secondary circuit.

Transformers are useful because they allow you to change the voltage of a supply. For example, model railways have transformers that decrease the mains supply from 230 V to a safe 12 V; these are **step-down transformers**. The transformer in Figure 9.3 steps *up* the voltage from 2 V to 12 V; this is a **step-up transformer**.

To make a step-up transformer the secondary coil must have more turns of wire in it than the primary coil. In a step-down transformer the secondary has fewer turns of wire than the primary coil.

The rule for calculating voltages in a transformer is:

$$\frac{V_s}{V_P} = \frac{N_s}{N_P}$$

V_P = primary voltage; V_s = secondary voltage; N_P = number of turns on the primary coil; N_s = number of turns on the secondary coil.

■ Power in transformers

We use transformers to transfer electrical power from the primary circuit to the secondary circuit. Many transformers do this very efficiently and there is little loss of power in the transformer itself. For a transformer that is 100% efficient we can write:

power supplied by primary circuit = power used in the secondary circuit
$$V_P \times I_P = V_s \times I_s$$

In practice transformers are not 100% efficient. These are the most important reasons for transformers losing energy:

- The windings on the coils have a small resistance. So when a current flows through them they heat up a little.
- The iron core conducts electricity. Therefore the changing magnetic field from the coils can induce currents in the iron. These are called **eddy currents**.
- Energy is lost if some of the magnetic field from the primary coil does not pass through the secondary coil.

■ The National Grid

Figure 9.5 shows how electricity is generated at a power station, and how it is distributed around the country through the National Grid.

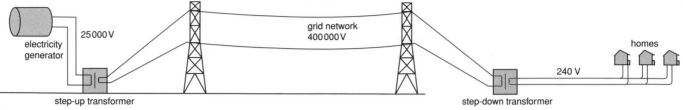

Figure 9.5 How the power gets to your home.

You may have seen a sign at the bottom of an electricity pylon saying 'Danger high voltage'. Power is transmitted around the country at voltages as high as 400 000 V. There is a very good reason for this – it saves a lot of energy. The following calculations explain why.

Figure 9.6 suggests two ways of transmitting 25 MW of power from a Yorkshire power station to the Midlands in the UK:
(a) The 25 000 V supply from the power station could be used to send 1000 A down the power cables.
(b) The voltage could be stepped up to 250 000 V and 100 A could be sent along the cables.

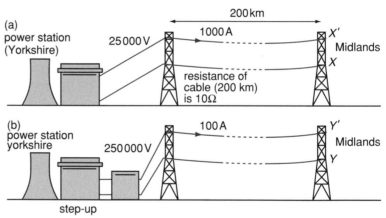

Figure 9.6

How much power would be wasted in heating the cables in each case, given that 200 km of cable has a resistance of 10 Ω?

(a) power lost = voltage drop along cable × current
$$= IR \times I$$
$$= I^2R$$
$$= (1000)^2 \times 10$$
$$= 10\,000\,000 \text{ W or } 10 \text{ MW}$$

(b) power lost $= I^2R$
$$= (100)^2 \times 10$$
$$= 100\,000 \text{ W or } 0.1 \text{ MW}$$

We waste a lot less power in the second case. The power loss is proportional to the square of the current. Transmitting power at high voltages allows smaller currents to flow along our overhead power lines.

Now go through the tutorial *Transformers*.

STUDY QUESTIONS

1 a) In Figure 9.2 when the switch is opened the ammeter kicks to the left. Describe what happens to the ammeter during each of the following:
   i) The switch is closed and left closed so that a current flows through coil 1.
   ii) The coils are pushed towards each other.
   iii) The coils are left close together.
   iv) The coils are pulled apart.
   b) The battery is replaced by an a.c. voltage supply, which has a frequency of 2 Hz. What will the ammeter show when the switch is closed?

2 Explain why a transformer does not work when you plug in the primary coil to a battery. Why do transformers only work with an a.c. supply?

3 The question refers to Figure 9.3.
   a) What power is used in the secondary circuit?
   b) Explain why the smallest current that can be flowing in the primary circuit is 1.2 A.
   c) Why is the primary current likely to be a little larger than 1.2 A?

4 Table 1 below gives some data about four transformers. Copy the table and fill the gaps.

5 Explain why very high voltages are used to transmit electrical power long distances across the country.

6 This is about how a transformer could be used to melt a nail (see the diagram below).

You will need to use the data provided.
   • The nail has a resistance of 0.02 Ω.
   • The melting point of the nail is 1540 °C.
   • The nail needs 10 J to warm it through 1 °C.
   a) Calculate the voltage across the nail.
   b) Calculate the current flowing in:
      i) the secondary circuit
      ii) the primary circuit.
   c) Why must the secondary circuit have thick wires?
   d) Calculate the rate at which power is used in the secondary circuit to heat the nail.
   e) Estimate roughly how long it will take the nail to melt. Mention any assumptions or approximations that you make in this calculation.
   f) Explain how a transformer can be used to produce high currents for welding.

7 The data in Table 2 were obtained using samples of copper, aluminium and steel wires. Each wire was 100 m long and had a diameter of 2 mm. Use these data to explain why our overhead power cables are made out of aluminium with a steel core.

8 Overhead power cables use wires with a cross-sectional area of about 1 cm².
   a) Discuss the advantages and disadvantages of using wires of greater area.
   b) Discuss how engineers decide the optimum diameter of a power cable.

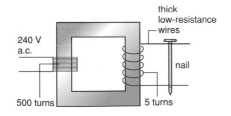

240 V a.c. — 500 turns — thick low-resistance wires — nail — 5 turns

Table 1

Primary turns	Secondary turns	Primary voltage / V	Secondary voltage / V	Step-up or step-down
100	20		3	
400	10 000	10		
	50	240	12	
	5 000	33 000	11 000	

Table 2

Material	Resistance / Ω	Force needed to break wire	Density / kg/m³	Cost of wire
copper	2.2	320 N	8900	€11.20
aluminium	3.2	160 N	2700	€3.20
steel	127	1600 N	9000	€0.28

Summary

 Make sure you can answer all the questions in the *Interactive quiz*.

I am confident that:

✓ I can recall facts and concepts about magnetism

- I know that magnets have a north and south pole.
- I understand that like poles repel and unlike poles attract.
- I understand the term magnetic 'field line'.
- I can draw magnetic field patterns accurately.
- I can describe experiments to plot magnetic field patterns.
- I can describe how to use two bar magnets to produce a uniform magnetic field.
- I understand that magnetism is induced in some materials when they are placed in a magnetic field.
- I can describe the properties of magnetically hard and soft materials.

✓ I can recall facts and concepts about electromagnetism

- I understand that an electric current in a conductor produces a magnetic field around it.
- I understand that a force is exerted on a current-carrying wire in a magnetic field.
- I understand the action of motors and loudspeakers.
- I can use the left-hand rule to predict the direction of the force when a wire carries a current in a magnetic field.

- I can describe the construction of electromagnets.
- I can draw and recognise the magnetic field patterns for a straight wire, a flat coil and a long solenoid when each carries a current.
- I understand that a moving charged particle experiences a force in a magnetic field (unless it moves parallel to the field).

✓ I can explain electromagnetic induction:

- I understand that a voltage is induced in a wire or coil when it moves through a magnetic field, or when the magnetic field changes its strength.
- I understand the factors that affect the size and direction of the induced voltage.
- I can describe the generation of electricity by the rotation of a magnet inside a coil of wire.
- I can describe the construction and action of a transformer.
- I can explain the action and uses of step-up and step-down transformers.
- I know and can use the relationship:

$$\frac{V_S}{V_P} = \frac{N_S}{N_P}$$

- I know and can use the relationship:
$$V_P I_P = V_S I_S$$
for a transformer that is 100% efficient.

Exam-style questions

1 a) Draw accurately the magnetic field pattern close to a bar magnet. [2]

b) Explain how you would use a compass to plot this magnetic field. [2]

c) Explain how you would use two bar magnets to produce a uniform magnetic field. Draw a diagram to illustrate a uniform magnetic field. [2]

2 Draw carefully the shape of a magnetic field close to:

a) a long wire

b) a long solenoid

c) a flat coil

when each is carrying a current. [6]

3 a) Explain what is meant by 'magnetic domain'. [2]

b) What is meant by:

i) a magnetically hard material

ii) a magnetically soft material? [2]

4 When a wire carries an electric current and it is placed in a magnetic field, a force may act on it.

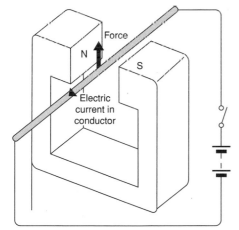

a) State **two** ways in which this force can be made larger. [2]

b) State **two** ways in which this force can be reversed. [2]

c) Under what circumstances will no force act on this wire when it is carrying an electric current and it is placed in a magnetic field? [1]

5 The diagram shows part of a bicycle dynamo, which is in contact with the wheel.

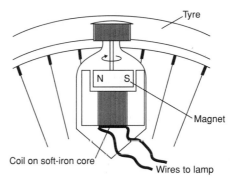

a) Explain fully why a current flows through the lamp when the bicycle wheel turns. [3]

b) Why does the lamp get brighter as the cycle moves faster? [1]

c) Why does the lamp not work when the bicycle is stationary? [1]

6 The diagram shows a transformer that is being used to light a 12 V bulb. The bulb only lights dimly.

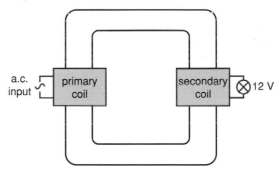

a) Describe **three** ways in which you could make the bulb light more brightly. [3]

b) Explain fully why a transformer only works using an a.c. supply. [3]

c) Electrical energy is distributed across countries using very high voltage networks.

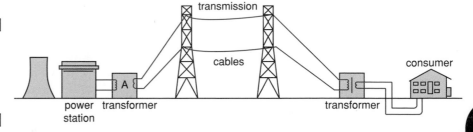

Explain:

i) why very high voltages are used

ii) how transformers are used in the distribution of electrical energy. [4]

d) The power station generates 50 MW of power at 25 kV, to deliver to transformer A, which links the power station to the transmission lines. The transformer has 48000 turns in its 400 kV secondary coil.

i) Calculate the number of turns in the transformer's primary coil.

ii) Calculate the current in the transformer's primary coil.

iii) Calculate the current in the transformer's secondary coil. [6]

7 In the diagram a magnet, which is attached to a spring, is free to vibrate up and down inside a coil of wire.

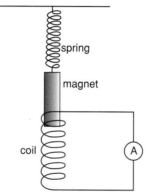

When the magnet is pushed down, the vibrations die away quickly. The magnet is replaced with a piece of iron with exactly the same mass and shape as the magnet. When the iron is displaced from exactly the same position as the magnet had been, the vibrations take much longer to die away.

Explain carefully why the iron bar vibrates for longer than the magnet. [4]

8 a) Copy this diagram. Then draw lines to represent the magnetic field between the two magnets.

[2]

b) The next diagram shows a wire that is at right-angles to the plane of the paper. The current

in the wire flows up out of the paper. Copy the diagram and add lines to represent the magnetic field. ⊙ [2]

c) In the diagram below the wire has been placed between the poles of the magnet. Draw the field lines now. [3]

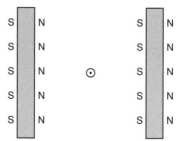

d) Which way will the wire move in part (c)?

e) The diagram below shows a model motor.

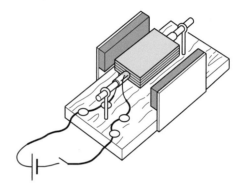

i) Explain why the coil rotates. [2]

ii) Which position is the coil likely to stick in? [1]

iii) State and explain two changes that will make the coil turn faster. [2]

9 The diagram shows a laboratory electromagnet, made from two iron cores and a length of wire. W and X are connected to a d.c. supply.

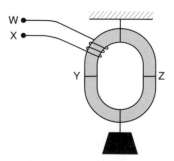

The number of turns of wire on the magnet is varied, and the largest weight that the magnet can support is shown in the table on the next page. For each measurement, the current remains at the same value of 2 A.

Number of turns in coil	5	10	15	20	25	30
Weight supported / N	1.1		3.2	4.0	4.3	4.3

a) What weight do you think can be supported when the magnet has 10 turns? [1]

b) Explain why the same load is supported by 25 or 30 turns. [2]

c) What happens if poor contact is made between the cores at Y and Z? [1]

10 The diagram below shows a coil connected to a sensitive meter. The meter is a 'centre zero' type: the needle is in the centre when no current flows.

A student does two experiments.

First experiment
First the magnet is pushed into the coil. Then the magnet is removed. The metre only reads a current when the magnet is moving.

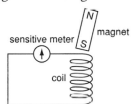

Second experiment
A second coil is brought close to the first. The student switched the current on and off in the second coil. The needle deflects for a brief time each time the current is turned on or off.

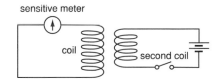

a) In the first experiment:

i) What is happening in the coil while the magnet is moving? [1]

ii) How does the deflection of the needle as the magnet is pushed towards the coil compare with the deflection of the needle as the magnet is pulled away? [1]

iii) State three ways in which the student could increase the deflection on the metre, when the magnet is moved. [3]

b) Use the second experiment to help explain why transformers only work with alternating current. [3]

11 The waves from earthquakes are detected by instruments called seismometers. The diagram shows a simple seismometer.

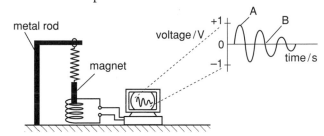

It consists of a bar magnet suspended on a spring. The spring hangs from a metal rod that transmits vibrations from the Earth. When there is an earthquake, the magnet moves in and out of the coil. A computer monitors the voltage across the coil.

a) Explain why a voltage is induced in the coil. [1]

b) Why is the induced voltage alternating? [1]

c) Describe the movement of the magnet when the induced voltage has its greatest value, at the point labelled A. [1]

d) Describe the movement of the magnet when the induced voltage is zero, as at point B [1]

e) Suggest **two** ways in which the seismometer could be made more sensitive, so that it can detect smaller earthquakes. [2]

12 The diagram shows a long wire placed between the poles of a magnet. When a current *I* flows through the wire, a force acts on the wire causing it to move.

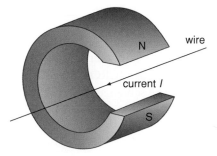

a) Use the left-hand rule to find the direction of the force on the wire.

b) State what happens to the force on the wire when:

   i) the size of the current through the wire is decreased [1]

   ii) a stronger magnet is used [1]

   iii) the direction of the current is reversed. [1]

c) Name **one** practical device that uses this effect. [1]

13 a) A student investigates how a short copper wire can be made to move in a magnetic field. The diagram shows the apparatus.

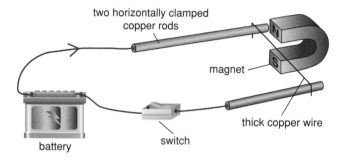

The wire is placed between the poles of the magnet.

   i) Use the information in the diagram to predict the direction of motion of the wire. [1]

   ii) Explain what happens to the motion of the wire when the magnet is turned with the north pole to the left of the wire. [2]

b) The diagram shows a model generator.

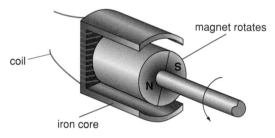

   i) Explain why a voltage is induced across the ends of the coil when the magnet rotates. [2]

   ii) Explain why the voltage is alternating. [1]

c) The ends of the coil are connected to a cathode ray oscilloscope (CRO). The diagram shoes the trace on the screen as the magnet rotates.

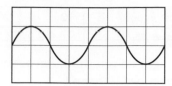

Copy the diagram and draw new traces for each of the following changes using the same scale. The settings of the oscilloscope remain the same.

   i) The magnet rotates at the same speed but in the opposite direction. [1]

   ii) The magnet rotates at the same speed, in the same direction, as the original, but the number of turns of the coil is doubled. [2]

   iii) The magnet rotates at twice the speed, in the same direction, with the original number of turns of the coil. [2]

d) Explain why **iron** is used as the core in the model generator. [1]

14 The diagram shows a step-down transformer in the plug of an electric shaver, which is used in the mains socket in a bathroom.

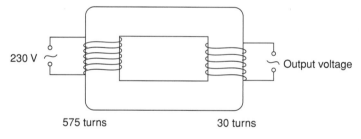

a) Explain why it is a good safety measure to use a step-down transformer for the electric shaver. [2]

b) The manufacturer has written on the shaver that the output voltage of the transformer is 12 V.

Use the information in the diagram to show that the output voltage of the transformer is about 12 V. [3]

c) When the shaver is working normally, the current in it is 0.9 A and the voltage 12 V.

Calculate the input current from the mains, assuming that the transformer is 100% efficient in transferring electrical power from the input (primary) coil to the output (secondary) coil. [3]

d) Explain why some transformers are not 100% efficient. [2]

EXTEND AND CHALLENGE

1 Two students, Rajeeb and Emma, have designed a new ammeter shown below. They have plotted a calibration graph to show the extension of the spring for a particular current.

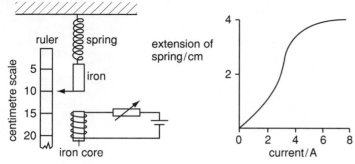

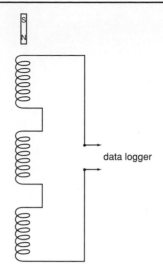

data logger

a) Explain why their device can be used as an ammeter.

b) Explain the shape of the graph in as much detail as you can.

c) Here are some remarks that the students made about their ammeter. Evaluate their comments.

   i) *Rajeeb:* Our ammeter is not really any good for measuring currents above 4 A.
   Emma: It would be better at measuring large currents if we used fewer turns on the solenoid.

   ii) *Rajeeb:* It does not matter which way the current flows, the spring still gets pulled down.
   Emma: That's useful, we can use our ammeter to measure a.c.

2 The diagram on the right shows three coils connected in series to a data logger. A magnet is dropped through the three coils. The graph shows the voltage measured by the data logger as the magnet falls. Explain the shape of the graph.

You should comment on these points

   i)   the height of the peaks on the graph
   ii) the width of the peaks
   iii) the gaps between the peaks
   iv) the direction of the peaks

voltage/mV

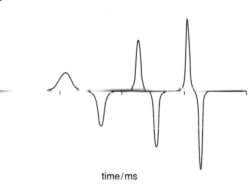

time/ms

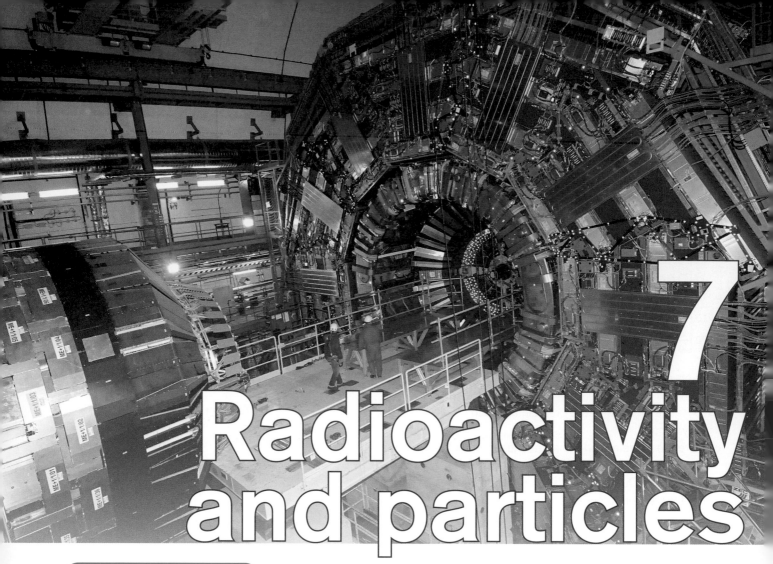

7 Radioactivity and particles

1 In Section 1 you learnt that the braking distance of a car travelling at 30 m/s is about 75 m. If a car could travel at the same speed as protons in the LHC, which of the following distances would you think would be its approximate stopping distance when you apply the brakes:
   a) 7500 m
   b) 7500 km
   c) 7500 light years?

2 Which do you think is the greatest scientific discovery in history – the discovery of the nucleus of an atom, the discovery of DNA or the working out of the periodic table? Or can you think of another more important discovery?

3 A new school costs €25 million, a new hospital €100 million. Can governments justify spending €7.5 billion on looking for a Higgs boson?

The Large Hadron Collider (LHC) at the European Centre for Nuclear Research (CERN) is the most expensive scientific instrument in history, costing a total of about €7.5 billion. It has been funded by several European governments.

The LHC accelerates beams of protons close to the speed of light (99.999 999 1% of the speed of light to be precise). When protons collide with this great energy, many other particles are produced. Nuclear physicists at CERN have discovered quarks, W and Z bosons and the Higgs boson, which is thought to be responsible for giving all particles their mass.

By the end of this section you should:
- be familiar with the structure of an atom
- know the three types of radioactivity, and know the differences between them
- understand what is meant by radioactive decay
- know about nuclear fission and how it is used in nuclear power stations to produce electricity
- be aware of the dangers associated with radiation
- be familiar with the many useful ways in which radioactive materials are used.

7.1 Atomic structure

Figure 1.1 Aerial view of an atomic bomb exploding at a test site in Nevada, USA.

The photograph in Figure 1.1 illustrates the distinctive mushroom cloud that atomic bombs produce. A complete ban on nuclear weapons testing in this manner was implemented in 1996 by the United Nations, after much concern over the increase in incidents of cancer in areas surrounding test sites. This picture shows how research into nuclear physics has led to some destructive ends, alongside more constructive ones. Has the discovery of the nucleus and nuclear energy done more good than harm?

■ Neutrons, protons and electrons

Experiments done at the beginning of the twentieth century led to the nuclear model of the atom. We now understand that an atom has a very small **nucleus**, of diameter approximately 10^{-15} m. Inside the nucleus there are two types of particle, **protons** and **neutrons**. The protons and neutrons have approximately the same mass; a proton has a positive charge whereas the neutron is neutral. Outside the nucleus there are **electrons**, which orbit the nucleus at a distance of approximately 10^{-10} m. Electrons have very little mass, in comparison with neutrons or protons, and they carry a negative charge (see Table 1). Evidence for the structure of the nuclear atom is discussed in Chapter 7.5.

A hydrogen atom has one proton and one electron; it is electrically neutral because the charges of the electron and proton cancel each other. A helium atom has two protons and two neutrons in its nucleus, and two electrons outside that. The helium atom is also neutral because it has the same number of electrons as it has protons; it has four times the mass of a hydrogen atom because it has four particles in the nucleus (see Figure 1.2 and Table 2).

Table 1

Particle	Mass*	Charge*
proton	1	1
neutron	1	0
electron	1/1840	−1

* by comparison with a proton's mass and change

Table 2 Characteristics of the three smallest atoms

Element	Hydrogen, H	Helium, He	Lithium, Li
number of electrons	1	2	3
number of protons	1	2	3
number of neutrons	0	2	4
number of particles in nucleus	1	4	7
mass relative to hydrogen	1	4	7

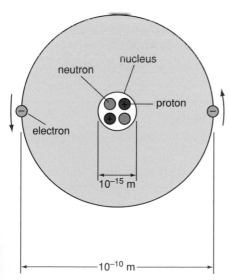

Figure 1.2 The helium atom; this is not drawn to scale – the diameter of the nucleus is about 100 000 times smaller than that of the atom itself.

■ Ions

Atoms are electrically neutral since the number of protons balances exactly the number of electrons. However, it is possible either to add extra electrons to an atom, or to take them away. When an electron is added to an atom a **negative ion** is formed; when an electron is removed a **positive ion** is formed. Ions are made in pairs because an electron that is removed from one atom attracts itself to another atom, so a positive and negative ion pair

EXAM TIP

Remember that nearly all of an atom's mass is in the nucleus.

is formed. Some examples are given in Table 3. The name ion is also used to describe charged molecules. The process of making ions is called **ionisation**.

Table 3 Examples of ions

Element	Number of protons	Number of electrons	Total charge	Ion
helium, He	2	1	+1	He$^+$
magnesium, Mg	12	10	+2	Mg^{2+}
chlorine, Cl	17	18	−1	Cl$^-$

■ Atomic and mass numbers

The number of protons in the nucleus of an atom determines what element it is. Hydrogen atoms have one proton, helium atoms two protons, uranium atoms 92 protons. The number of protons in the nucleus decides the number of electrons surrounding the nucleus. The number of electrons determines the chemical properties of an atom. The number of protons in the nucleus is called the **atomic (or proton) number** of the atom (symbol Z). So the proton number of hydrogen is 1, $Z = 1$.

The mass of an atom is decided by the number of neutrons and protons added together. Scientists call this number the **mass (or nucleon) number** of an atom. The name nucleon refers to either a proton or a neutron.

EXAM TIP

mass number 12
atomic number 6 C

> atomic (or proton) number = number of protons
> mass (or nucleon) number = number of protons and neutrons

For example, an atom of carbon has six protons and six neutrons. So its atomic number is 6, and its mass number is 12. To save time in describing carbon we can write it as $^{12}_{6}C$; the mass number appears on the left and above the symbol C, for carbon, and the atomic number on the left and below.

■ Isotopes

EXAM TIP

The symbols $^{12}_{6}C$ describe only the nucleus of a carbon atom.

Not all the atoms of a particular element have the same mass. For example, two carbon atoms might have mass numbers of 12 and 14. The nucleus of each atom has the same number of protons, six, but one atom has six neutrons and the other eight neutrons. Atoms of the same element (carbon in this case) that have different masses are called **isotopes**. These two isotopes of carbon can be written as carbon-12, $^{12}_{6}C$, and carbon-14, $^{14}_{6}C$.

STUDY QUESTIONS

1 a) An oxygen atom has eight protons, eight neutrons, and eight electrons. What is its:
   i) atomic number?
   ii) mass number?
  b) Why is the oxygen atom electrically neutral?

2 Calculate the number of protons and neutrons in each of the following nuclei:
  a) $^{17}_{8}O$ b) $^{238}_{92}U$
  c) $^{235}_{92}U$ d) $^{40}_{19}K$

3 Write a paragraph to explain and describe the structure of an atom. In your answer, mention atomic number, mass number and electrons.

4 a) Explain the term 'isotope'.
  b) Explain why isotopes are difficult to separate by chemical methods.

5 Lead-209 and Lead-210 are isotopes of lead, and they both have the same atomic number, 82.
  a) What do the numbers 209, 210 and 82 represent?
  b) Explain what these two isotopes of lead have in common.
  c) How are the isotopes different?

7.2 Radioactivity

Henry Becquerel discovered radioactivity in 1896. He placed some uranium salts next to a photographic plate, which had been sealed in a thick black bag to prevent light exposing the plate. When the plate was later developed it had been affected as if it had been exposed to light. Becquerel realised that a new form of energy was being emitted from the uranium salts. In his honour, the activity of a radioactive source is measured in becquerels.

What travelled through the black bag? Where did it come from? What is radioactivity?

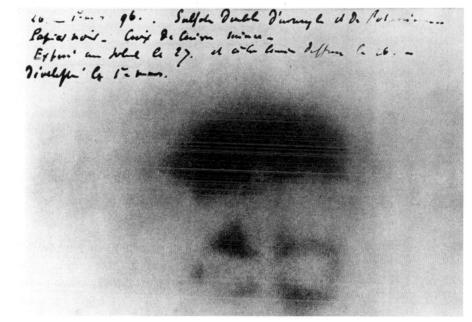

Figure 2.1 Becquerel's film.

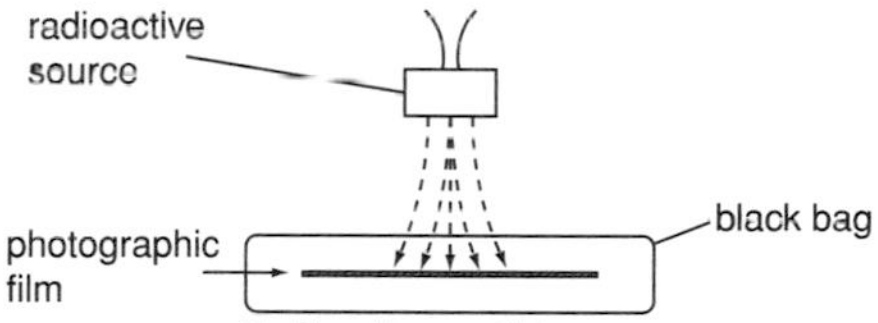

radioactive source

photographic film

black bag

Radioactive particles pass through a lightproof bag to expose a photographic film.

Figure 2.2 How Becquerel discovered radioactivity.

■ Nuclear decay

The nuclei of most atoms are very stable; the atoms that we are made of have been around for thousands of millions of years. Atoms may lose or gain a few electrons during chemical reactions, but the nucleus does not change during such processes.

The activity of a source is equal to the number of particles emitted per second. This is measured in becquerel (Bq).

> 1 becquerel (1 Bq) = an emission of 1 particle/second

However, there are some atoms that have unstable nuclei which throw out particles to make the nucleus more stable. This is a random process that depends only on the nature of the nucleus; the rate at which particles are emitted from a nucleus is not affected by other factors such as temperature or chemical reactions. One element discovered that emits these particles is radium, and the name **radioactivity** is given to this process.

There are three types of radioactive emission:

- **Alpha particles** are the nuclei of helium atoms. The alpha particle is formed from two protons and two neutrons, so it has a mass number of 4 and an atomic number of two. When an alpha particle is emitted from a nucleus it causes the nucleus to change into another nucleus with a mass number 4 less and an atomic number 2 less than the original one. It is usually only very heavy elements that emit alpha particles, for example:

$$\underset{\substack{\text{uranium}\\\text{nucleus}}}{^{238}_{92}\text{U}} \quad \rightarrow \quad \underset{\substack{\text{thorium}\\\text{nucleus}}}{^{234}_{90}\text{Th}} \quad + \quad \underset{\substack{\text{alpha particle}\\\text{(helium nucleus)}}}{^{4}_{2}\text{He}}$$

This is called **alpha decay**.

- **Beta particles** are electrons. In a nucleus there are only protons and neutrons, but a beta particle is made and ejected from a nucleus when a neutron turns into a proton and an electron. Since an electron has a very small mass, when it leaves a nucleus it does not alter the mass number of that nucleus. However, the electron carries away a negative charge so the removal of an electron increases the atomic number of a nucleus by 1. For example, carbon-14 decays into nitrogen by emitting a beta particle:

$$\underset{\text{carbon nucleus}}{^{14}_{6}\text{C}} \quad \rightarrow \quad \underset{\text{nitrogen nucleus}}{^{14}_{7}\text{N}} \quad + \quad \underset{\text{beta particle (electron)}}{^{0}_{-1}\text{e}}$$

This is called **beta decay**.

- When some nuclei decay by sending out an alpha or beta particle, they also give out a **gamma ray**. Gamma rays are electromagnetic waves, like radio waves or light. They carry away from the nucleus a lot of energy, so that the nucleus is left in a more stable state. Gamma rays have no mass or charge, so when one is emitted there is no change to the mass or atomic number of a nucleus (see Table 1).

Table 1 The three types of radioactive emission

	Particle lost from nucleus	Change in mass number	Change in atomic number
alpha (α) decay	helium nucleus $^{4}_{2}\text{He}$	−4	−2
beta (β) decay	electron $^{0}_{-1}\text{e}$	0	+1
gamma (γ) decay	electromagnetic waves	0	0

■ Ionisation

All three types of radiation (alpha, beta and gamma) cause **ionisation** and this is why we must be careful when we handle radioactive materials. The radiation makes ions in our bodies and these ions can then damage our body tissues (see Chapter 7.6).

Your teacher can show the ionising effect of radium by holding some close to a charged gold leaf electroscope (Figure 2.4). The electroscope is initially charged positively so that the gold leaf is repelled from the metal stem. When

EXAM TIP

An alpha particle is formed from two protons and two neutrons.

EXAM TIP

When a β-particle is emitted from a nucleus, a neutron turns into a proton. The mass number of the nucleus increases by 1.

EXAM TIP

Make sure you can write balanced equations for alpha and beta decay.

EXAM TIP

Make sure you know the nature of alpha, beta and gamma radiations.

SAFETY

Students under 16 may not handle radioactive sources.

a radium source is brought close to the electroscope, the leaf falls, showing that the electroscope has been discharged. The reason for this is that the alpha particles from the radium create ions in the air above the electroscope. This is because the charges on the alpha particles pull some electrons out of air molecules (Figure 2.3). Both negative and positive ions are made; the positive ones are repelled from the electroscope, but the negative ones are attracted so that the charge on the electroscope is neutralised. It is important that you understand that it is not the charge of the alpha particles that discharges the electroscope, but the ions that they produce.

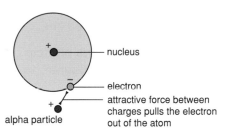

Figure 2.3 Alpha particles cause ionisation.

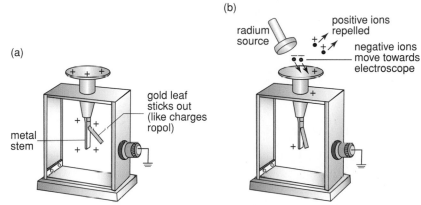

Figure 2.4 (a) Positively charged electroscope. **(b)** Negative ions neutralise the electroscope.

STUDY QUESTIONS

1 Explain what is meant by the word 'radioactivity'.

2 Why did Becquerel conclude that he had discovered a new form of energy?

3 a) What is meant by the word 'ionisation'?
   b) Why are ions always produced in pairs?

4 What are the following:
   a) an alpha particle
   b) a beta particle
   c) a gamma ray?

5 Fill in the gaps in the following radioactive decay equations.
   a) $^{3}_{?}H \rightarrow {}^{?}_{2}He + {}^{0}_{?}e$
   b) $^{229}_{90}Th \rightarrow {}^{?}_{?}Ra + {}^{4}_{2}He$

c) $^{14}_{6}C \rightarrow ? + {}^{0}_{-1}e$

d) $^{209}_{82}Pb \rightarrow {}^{?}_{83}Bi + ?$

e) $^{225}_{89}Ac \rightarrow {}^{?}_{87}Fr + ?$

6 $^{238}_{92}U$ decays by emitting an alpha particle and two beta particles; which element is produced after those three decays?

7 Explain what effect losing a gamma ray has on a nucleus.

8 Explain carefully how a radioactive source which is emitting only alpha particles can discharge a negatively charged electroscope.

7.3 The nature of α, β and γ radiation

Figure 3.1 Cloud chamber tracks, shown in false colour.

In Figure 3.1 the green lines illustrate the straight paths of alpha particles in a cloud chamber. One of the alpha particles, coloured yellow, strikes a nitrogen nucleus and recoils. The nitrogen nucleus travels a short distance forward, and this is shown by the red line.

Use your knowledge of momentum to explain why an alpha particle bounces back when it strikes a nitrogen nucleus. Draw a diagram to show what happens when an alpha particle strikes a proton.

■ Detecting particles

We make use of the ionising properties of alpha, beta and gamma radiations to detect them. This is done using a **Geiger-Müller (GM) tube**. Figure 3.2 shows how such a tube works. A metal tube is filled with argon under low pressure; inside the tube there is a thin wire anode (positive electrode). A voltage of about 450 V is applied between the inside and outside of the tube. When alpha, beta or gamma radiation enters the tube the argon atoms inside are ionised. These ions are then attracted to the electrodes in the tube so a small current flows. This current pulse is then amplified and a counter can be used to count the number of ionising particles entering the tube.

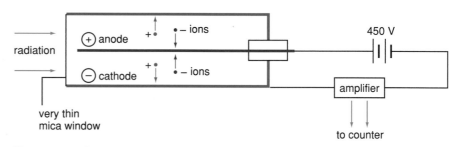

Figure 3.2 A Geiger-Müller tube.

■ Cloud chambers

Another way of detecting radiation is to use a **cloud chamber** (Figure 3.3). The bottom of the cloud chamber is kept cold by placing some solid carbon dioxide ('dry ice') underneath the metal base plate. The inside of the chamber is filled with alcohol vapour. When a radioactive source is placed inside the cloud chamber, tracks are formed in the dense alcohol vapour. The alcohol molecules condense to leave a vapour trail in the region where ions have been produced by the passage of a particle. The tracks can be seen clearly against the black base of the chamber. The tracks left by alpha particles are straight and thick (see Figure 3.1); this is because alpha particles are very strongly ionising. Beta particles and gamma rays do not ionise air so strongly, so it is very difficult to see their tracks.

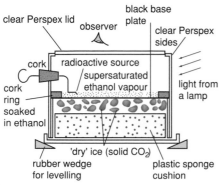

Figure 3.3 A cloud chamber.

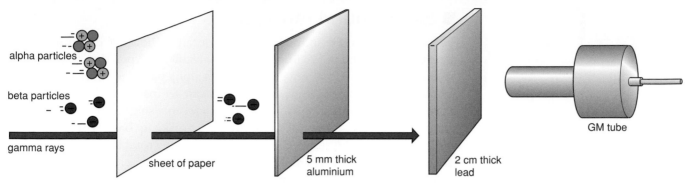

Figure 3.4 Penetration of alpha, beta and gamma radiation.

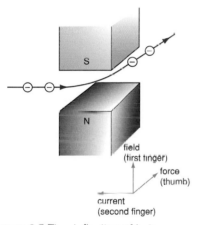

Figure 3.5 The deflection of beta particles by a magnetic field. Note that the deflection is not towards the poles of the magnet, but at right angles to them. The direction of the force on them can be found using the left-hand rule (see Chapter 6.4).

■ Properties of radiation

- Alpha particles travel about 5 cm through air but can be stopped by a sheet of paper (Figure 3.4). They ionise air very strongly. Alpha particles travel at speeds of about 10^7 m/s. This is more slowly than beta or gamma rays travel. They can be deflected by a very strong magnetic field, but the deflection is very small because alpha particles are so massive.
- Beta particles can travel several metres through air and they will be stopped by a sheet of aluminium a few millimetres thick (Figure 3.4). They do not ionise air as strongly as alpha particles. Beta particles travel at speeds just less than the speed of light (3×10^8 m/s). Beta particles can be deflected quite easily by a magnetic field, because they are such light particles (Figure 3.5).
- Gamma rays can only effectively be stopped by a very thick piece of lead (Figure 3.4). They are electromagnetic waves, so they travel at the speed of light. Gamma rays only ionise air very weakly, and they cannot be deflected by a magnetic field because they carry no charge.

Alpha particles will cause the most damage to your bodies if they get inside you; this could happen if you were to breathe in a radioactive gas. An alpha source in school is less dangerous because the source will not enter your body. You must keep well away from gamma sources since these rays can get right into the middle of your body and cause damage there. In all cases you will see your teacher take great care with sources, and handle them with tongs or special holders.

Table 1 A summary of radiation properties

Radiation	Nature	Speed	Ionising power	Penetrating power	Deflection by magnetic field
alpha α	helium nucleus	10^7 m/s	very strong	stopped by paper	very small
beta β	electron	just less than 3×10^8 m/s	medium	stopped by aluminium	large
gamma γ	electro-magnetic waves	3×10^8 m/s	weak	stopped by thick lead	none

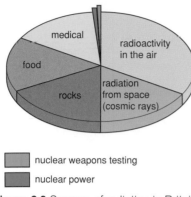

Figure 3.6 Sources of radiation in Britain.

Legend:
- nuclear weapons testing
- nuclear power

Pie chart labels: medical, radioactivity in the air, food, rocks, radiation from space (cosmic rays)

■ Background radiation

There are a lot of rocks in the Earth that contain radioactive uranium, thorium, radon and potassium, and so we are always exposed to some ionising particles. Radon is a gas that emits alpha particles. Since we can inhale this gas it is dangerous, as radiation can get inside our lungs. In addition the Sun emits lots of protons, which can also create ions in our atmosphere. These are two of the sources that make up **background radiation**. Figure 3.6 shows the contribution to the total background radiation from all sources in Britain. Fortunately the level of background radiation is quite low and in most places it does not cause a serious health risk.

In some jobs, people are at a greater risk. X-rays used in hospitals also cause ionisation. Radiographers make sure that their exposure to X-rays is as small as possible. In nuclear power stations neutrons are produced in **nuclear reactors**. The damage caused by neutrons is a source of danger for workers in that industry.

STUDY QUESTIONS

1 a) Explain what is meant by the term 'background radiation'.

Without the Earth's protective atmosphere this astronaut was exposed to greater background radiation from cosmic rays.

   b) What is a cosmic ray?
   c) Discuss whether nuclear power stations pose a significant risk to health. Although nuclear power stations contribute only a small fraction of the total background radiation, some people are worried by nuclear power. Why?

2 A radioactive source is placed 2 cm from a GM tube and an activity of 120 Bq is measured. When a piece of paper is put between the source and the GM tube the activity reduces to 75 Bq. A 5 mm thick piece of aluminium between the source and tube reduces the measured activity to zero.
   Explain what this tells you about the source.

3 a) Radon gas is a product of radioactive decay in granite rocks. Radon is also radioactive and emits alpha particles. Explain why radon might be a hazard to mining engineers working underground in granite rocks.
   b) Explain why a strong gamma source left in a laboratory might be dangerous to us.

4 a) Why do gamma rays leave only very faint tracks in cloud chambers?
   b) Why does the nitrogen nucleus leave a thick track in the photograph in Figure 3.1?

5 This question is about testing the thickness of aluminium foil. The foil moves between a β-source and Geiger counter at a speed of 0.2 m/s.
   a) Plot a graph from the data below. Explain why the count rate changes over the first 50 s. Remember that particles are emitted *randomly* from a nucleus.
   b) Explain why the count rate drops and then rises again, after 50 s. What has happened to the thickness of the foil?

Count rate / s⁻¹	75	80	77	73	76	75	63	57	50	55	67	75	77
Time / s	0	10	20	30	40	50	60	70	80	90	100	110	120

7.4 Radioactive decay

Figure 4.1 On average, how many sixes will there be when you roll these dice? Why can you not predict what will be thrown on each occasion?

Table 1 Coin-tossing experiment

Throw	Number of coins left
0	1000
1	500
2	250
3	125
4	62
5	31
6	16
7	8
8	4
9	2
10	1

Table 2 The number of nuclei left in a sample: half-life 1 hour

Time (hour)	Number of nuclei left
0	1000000
1	500000
2	250000
3	125000
4	62500
5	31250
6	15620
7	7810
8	3900
9	1950
10	980

The atoms of some radioactive materials decay by emitting alpha or beta particles from their nuclei. But it is not possible to predict when the nucleus of one particular atom will decay. It could be in the next second, or sometime next week, or not for a million years. Radioactive decay is a random process.

■ Random process

The radioactive decay of an atom is rather like tossing a coin. You cannot say with certainty that the next time you toss a coin it will fall heads up. However, if you throw a lot of coins you can start to predict how many of them will fall heads up. You can use this idea to help you understand how radioactive decay happens. You start off with a thousand coins, if any coin falls heads up then it has 'decayed' and you must take it out of the game. Table 1 shows the likely result (on average). Every time you throw a lot of coins about half of them will turn up heads.

■ Decay

Radioactive materials decay in a similar way. If we start off with a million atoms then after a period of time (for example 1 hour), half of them have decayed. In the next hour we find that half of the remaining atoms have decayed, leaving us with a quarter of the original number (Table 2). The period of time taken for half the number of atoms to decay in a radioactive sample is called the **half-life**, and it is given the symbol $t_{1/2}$. It is important to understand that we have chosen a half-life here of 1 hour to explain the idea. Different radioisotopes have different half-lives.

■ Measurement of half-life

If you look at Table 2 you can see that the number of nuclei that decayed in the first hour was 500000, then in the next hour 250000 and in the third hour 125000. So as time passes not only does the number of nuclei left get smaller but so does the rate at which the nuclei decay. So by measuring the activity of a radioactive sample we can determine its half-life.

Figure 4.2 shows how we can measure the half-life of radon, which is a gas. The gas is produced in a plastic bottle; we can give the bottle a squeeze and

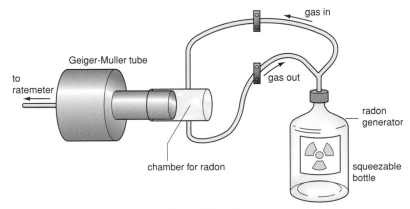

Figure 4.2 Experiment to determine the half-life of radon.

PRACTICAL

Correcting for the background count

When we measure the activity of a weak radiation source we need to make a correction for background radiation before we calculate its half-life. In the experiment to find the half-life of radon we would take a **background count** before pushing radon into the chamber. If the GM tube is left for 2 minutes with no radon in the chamber it will record radioactive decays from background sources. When we begin the experiment we need to remember that some of the count rate is due to background radiation. If the background count is 3 Bq and the activity measured by a counter is 43 Bq, then we know that only 40 Bq is due to the radioactive source.

Figure 4.4 Carbon dating shows us that this piece of wood is 4000 years old.

force some gas into a chamber, which is fixed on to the end of a GM tube. The GM tube is attached to a ratemeter, which tells us the rate at which radon is decaying in the chamber. We measure the rate of decay on the ratemeter every 10 seconds and plot a graph of the count rate against time, Figure 4.3. We can see that the count rate halves every 50 seconds, so that is the half-life of radon.

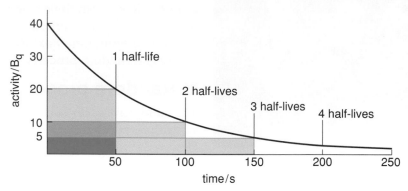

Figure 4.3 Finding the half-life from a decay curve.

■ Dating archaeological remains

Carbon-14, $^{14}_{6}C$, is a radioactive isotope; it decays to nitrogen with a half-life of about 5700 years. All living things (including you) have a lot of carbon in them, and a small fraction of this is carbon-14. When a tree dies, for example, the radioactive carbon decays and after 5700 years the fraction of carbon-14 in the dead tree will be half as much as you would find in a living tree. So by measuring the amount of carbon-14 in ancient relics, scientists can calculate their age (see Study Question 6).

■ Disposal of radioactive waste

Nuclear power stations produce radioactive waste materials, some of which have half-lives of hundreds of years. These waste products are packaged up in concrete and steel containers and are buried deep underground or are dropped to the bottom of the sea. This is a controversial issue; some scientists tell us that radioactive wastes produce only a very low level of radiation, and that the storage containers will remain intact for a very long time. Others worry that these products will contaminate our environment and believe it is wrong to dump radioactive materials that could harm future generations.

■ Half-life and stability

Elements usually have several isotopes – two isotopes of an element have the same atomic (or proton) number but they have a different number of neutrons in the nucleus, so they have different mass (or neutron) numbers. Some isotopes – radioisotopes – are unstable and they undergo radioactive decay. Less stable isotopes decay more quickly, so they have shorter half-lives than the more stable isotopes. Half-lives can be very long: for example uranium-238 decays with a half-life of 4.5 billion years; by contrast other half-lives are measured in fractions of a second. Table 3 lists the half-lives of some radioactive isotopes.

Table 3

Isotope	Half-life
potassium-40	1.3 billion years
carbon-14	5700 years
caesium-137	30 years
iodine-131	8 days
lawrencium-260	3 minutes

Figure 4.5 This geiger counter is being used to determine the activity of radioactive waste which is stored underground.

STUDY QUESTIONS

1 A GM tube is placed near to a radioactive source with a long half-life. In three 10-second periods the following number of counts were recorded: 150, 157, 145. Why were the three counts different?

2 A radioactive material has a half-life of 2 minutes. What does that mean? How much of the material will be left after 8 minutes?

3 The following results for the count rate of a radioactive source were recorded every minute.

Count rate (Bq)	Time (minutes)
1000	0
590	1
340	2
200	3
120	4
70	5

a) A correction was made for background count. What does this mean?

b) Plot a graph of the count rate (y-axis) against time (x-axis), and use the graph to work out the half-life of the source.

4 A radioisotope has a half-life of 8 hours. At 12 noon on 2 March a GM tube measures an activity of 2400 Bq.

a) What will be the activity at 4.00 am on 3 March?

b) At what time will an activity of approximately 75 Bq be measured?

5 Use Table 3 to answers these questions.

a) Choose one of the isotopes for each of these purposes:
   i) determining the age of a rock
   ii) as a radioactive tracer inside the human body
   iii) determining the age of an old human settlement.

b) Caesium-137 is a waste product from nuclear power stations. Explain why nuclear waste needs careful disposal.

c) Lawrencium-260 (Lr) decays by alpha emission to an isotope of mendelevium (Md). Copy and complete the equation for this decay below:

$$^{260}_{?}\text{Lr} \rightarrow \ ^{?}_{101}\text{Md} + \ ^{?}_{?}\text{He}$$

6 a) Archaeologists are analysing ancient bones from a human settlement. They discover that a sample

of bone has one-sixteenth of the carbon-14 of modern human bones. How old is the settlement? (The half-life of carbon-14 is 5700 years.)

b) The limit of carbon dating is about 50 000 years. Explain why.

7 The age of rocks can be estimated by measuring the ratio of the isotopes potassium-40 and argon-40. We assume that when the rock was formed it was molten, and that any argon would have escaped. So, at the rock's formation there was no argon. The half-life of potassium-40 is 1.3×10^9 years, and it decays to argon-40. Analysis of two rocks gives these potassium (K) to argon (A) ratios:

$$\text{Rock A } \frac{K}{A} = \frac{1}{1}; \quad \text{Rock B } \frac{K}{A} = \frac{1}{7}$$

Calculate the ages of the two rocks.

8 The diagram shows a gamma ray unit in a hospital. Box A is a container of the radioactive material cobalt-60 ($^{60}_{27}\text{Co}$). This isotope has a half-life of 5 years.

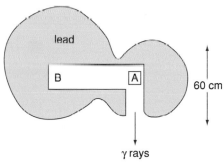

a) Why is the container made mainly from lead?

b) The unit can be made 'safe' by moving the container to position B. Explain why.

c) How many protons, neutrons and electrons are there in one atom of cobalt-60?

d) The activity of the source was 2 million Bq in January 2013. What will it be in January 2023?

e) Suggest **three** safety precautions that someone should take when removing a container of cobalt-60 from the unit.

9 Explain why archaeologists do not use carbon dating to help them find the age of metal objects that they discover.

7.5 Uses of radioactive materials

Radioactive materials have a great number of uses in medicine, industry and agriculture. People who work with radioactive materials must wear radiation badges that record the amount of radiation to which they are exposed.

■ Medicine

Radioactive **tracers** help doctors to examine the insides of our bodies. For example, iodine-131 is used to see if our thyroid glands are working properly. The thyroid is an important gland in the throat that controls the rate at which our bodies function. The thyroid gland absorbs iodine, so a dose of radioactive iodine (the tracer) is given to a patient. Doctors can then detect the radioactivity of the patient's throat, to see how well the patient's thyroid is working. The tracer needs to be an isotope with a short half-life.

Cobalt-60 emits very energetic gamma rays. These rays can damage our body cells, but they can also kill bacteria. Nearly all medical equipment such as syringes, dressings and surgeons' instruments is first packed into sealed plastic bags, and then exposed to intense gamma radiation. In this way all the bacteria are killed and so the equipment is sterilised.

The same material, cobalt-60, is used in the treatment of cancers. Radiographers direct a strong beam of radiation on to the cancerous tissue to kill the cancer cells. This radiotherapy treatment is very unpleasant and can cause serious side-effects, but it is often successful in slowing down the growth or completely curing the cancer.

■ Industry

Radioactive tracers may be used to detect leaks in underground pipes (Figure 5.3). The idea is very simple; the radioactive tracer is fed into the pipe and then a GM tube can be used above ground to detect an increase in radiation levels and hence the leak. This saves time and money because the whole length of the pipe does not have to be dug up to find the leak.

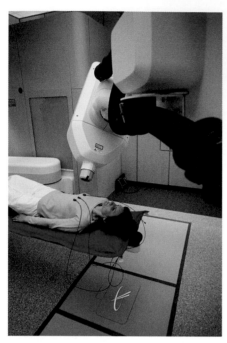

Figure 5.1 Gamma rays can be used to destroy cancer cells. This photograph shows a patient with Hodgkins disease (cancer of the lymph nodes) being treated by radiotherapy. What precautions must the radiographer take when working with radiation?

Figure 5.2 To check the amount of radiation that workers in a nuclear power station are exposed to, they wear special radiation-sensitive badges, like the ones in this photograph. At the end of each month the sensitive film in the badges is developed and examined.

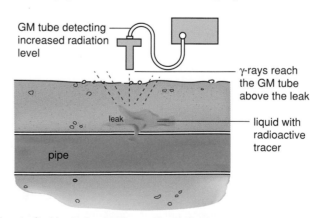

GM tube detecting increased radiation level

γ-rays reach the GM tube above the leak

leak

liquid with radioactive tracer

pipe

Figure 5.3 How to find leaks in pipelines without digging.

A radioisotope of iron is used in industry to estimate the wear on moving parts of machinery. For example, car companies want to know how long their piston rings last for. A piston ring that has radioactive iron in it is put into an engine and run for several days. At the end of the trial, the oil from the engine can be collected, and from the radioactivity of the oil the engineers can calculate how much of the piston ring has worn away.

■ Agriculture

Radioactive tracers are used in agriculture too. Phosphates are vital to the growth of plants and are an important component of fertilisers. Radioactive phosphorous-32 is used as a tracer to show how well plants are absorbing phosphates.

Gamma radiation is used to prolong the shelf-life of food. Gamma rays are very penetrating so this process can be used on pre-packaged or frozen foods. Gamma rays kill the bacteria in the food and so can eliminate the risk of food poisoning. However, the gamma rays will also kill some cells in the food itself and therefore could alter the taste.

Gamma rays are also used to help produce new types of crops. Large doses of gamma rays will kill cells, but smaller doses can cause mutations to the cells, which will change the nature of the crop. The seeds of crops are exposed to gamma radiation to encourage mutations. The new crops may show desirable qualities, such as being stronger or producing a greater yield. These successful mutations can be kept and used in the fields.

> **EXAM TIP**
>
> Make sure you can name and explain at least three uses of radioactive materials.

STUDY QUESTIONS

1 Explain what is meant by the word 'mutation'.
2 a) What is a radioactive tracer?
   b) Do radioactive tracers show any chemical differences from other isotopes of the same element?
3 The table shows information about some radioactive isotopes. You are a medical physicist working in a hospital. Advise the doctors which isotopes are suitable for the following tasks:
   a) Checking for a blockage in a patient's lungs.
   b) Directing a strong dose of radiation deep into a patient to treat cancer.
   Explain in each case what apparatus you would use, explain why you have chosen a particular isotope and what safety precautions you would take to protect the doctors and the patient.
4 A company makes plastic sheeting by rolling it out between rollers. Two problems arise:

   a) They need to check that the sheet is of uniform thickness.
   b) The sheet gets charged and needs to be discharged.
   Choose two isotopes from the table to help solve these problems. Explain your choice and how the problems will be solved. What safety regulations will you enforce?

Isotope	Solid, liquid or gas at 20°C	Type of radiation	Half-life
hydrogen-3	gas	beta	12 years
cobalt-60	solid	gamma	5 years
strontium-90	solid	beta	28 years
xenon-133	gas	gamma	5 days
terbium-160	solid	beta	72 days
actinium-227	solid	alpha	22 years
americium-241	solid	alpha	430 years

7.6 The hazards of radiation

The Fukushima Daiichi nuclear power plant in Japan was devastated by the tsunami produced by the Tohoku earthquake on 11 March, 2011. This was the second biggest nuclear disaster in history, producing at its peak a local activity of about 400 million million Bq. Should countries be allowed to build nuclear reactors in earthquake zones?

Figure 6.1 The Fukushima nuclear power plant disaster.

■ Measuring radiation dose

When scientists try to work out the effect on our bodies of a dose of radiation, they need to know how much energy each part of the body has absorbed. The damage done to us will depend on the amount of energy that each kilogram of body tissue absorbs. The unit used to measure a **radiation dose** is the **gray** (symbol Gy). A dose of 1 Gy means that each kilogram of flesh absorbs 1 joule of energy.

$$1 \text{ Gy} = 1 \text{ J/kg}$$

Some radiations are more damaging than others, so scientists prefer to talk in terms of a **dose equivalent**, which is measured in **sieverts** (symbol Sv).

$$\text{dose equivalent (Sv)} = Q \times \text{dose (Gy)}$$

Q is a number that depends on the radiation, as shown in Table 1. Alpha particles are very strongly ionising and cause far more damage than a dose of beta or gamma radiation that carries the same energy. Usually the amounts of radiation that we are exposed to are very small. Most people receive about 1/1000 sievert each year, this is 1 **millisievert** (1 mSv). However this dose varies according to where you live.

Table 1

Q	Type of radiation
1	beta particles/gamma rays
10	protons and neutrons
20	alpha particles

Figure 6.2 View of the remains of the Chernobyl nuclear power station in the Ukraine. The core of the reactor overheated, resulting in an explosion that sent radioactive material into the atmoshpere. The effects of this, the worst nuclear accident to date, were felt across the whole of northern Europe. The peak activity was about 10 times greater than that of the Fukushima accident.

■ Risk estimates

On 26 April 1986 there was an explosion in the Ukrainian nuclear reactor at Chernobyl, causing a large leakage of radiation. During May 1986 the background count in Britain increased, causing the population to be exposed (on average) to an extra dose equivalent to 0.1 mSv. This is a small dose and no worse than going on holiday to a region where granite rock areas produce low amounts of radiation. However, estimates have been made to suggest that in the 30 years following the Chernobyl disaster, extra people will have developed cancer as a result.

Research suggests that for a population of 1000, about 12 fatal cancers will be caused by a dose equivalent of 1 Sv. In Britain, the population is about 60 million, so the number of deaths expected by a dose of 1 Sv for everybody would be:

$$\frac{12}{1000} \times 60\,000\,000 = 720\,000$$

However, the dose from Chernobyl was only 0.0001 Sv. So the estimated number of deaths from the Chernobyl disaster in Britain in the 30 years following the disaster, is about $720\,000 \times 0.0001 = 72$. This is such a small number in comparison with the annual death rate from cancer, that it would be impossible to prove.

■ How dangerous is radiation?

Radiation affects materials by ionising atoms and molecules. When an atom is ionised, electrons are removed or added to it. This means a chemical change has occurred. In our bodies such a chemical change could cause the production of a strong acid, which will attack and destroy cells.

High doses

High doses of radiation will kill you. There is only a 50 per cent chance of surviving a dose equivalent to 4 Sv. A dose equivalent to 10 Sv would give

Figure 6.3 X-rays are used to identify broken bones. This helps the patient in recovering from a painful accident, but each dose of radiation carries a small risk.

you no chance of survival. Such high doses kill too many cells in the gut and bone marrow for your body to be able to work normally. People died in Hiroshima and Nagasaki as a result of such doses following atomic bombs.

Moderate doses

Moderate doses of radiation below 1 Sv will not kill you. Damage will be done to cells in your body, but not enough to be fatal. The body will be able to replace the dead cells and the chances are that you would then recover totally. However, a study of the survivors from Hiroshima and Nagasaki shows that there is an increased chance of dying from cancer some years after the radiation dose. Even so, you would only have a chance of about 1 in 100 of getting cancer from such levels of radiation.

Low doses

Low doses of radiation, below 10 mSv, are thought to have little effect on us. However, some people think that any exposure to radiation will increase your chances of getting cancer, by causing **mutations** in your cells. A mutation is a change to a cell so that it is abnormal. Some mutations can cause cancer.

There can be no doubt that radiation doses can cause cancer or leukaemia (see Table 2). Uranium miners are exposed to radon gas, and girls who painted luminous watch dials were exposed to radium.

Table 2 The connection between radiation and the increased chance of cancer

Source of radiation	Type of radiation	Number of people studied	Extra number of cancer deaths caused by radiation
uranium miners	alpha	3400	60
radium luminisers	alpha	800	50
medical treatment	alpha	4500	60
medical treatment	X-rays	14000	25
Hiroshima bomb	gamma rays and neutrons	15000	100
Nagasaki bomb	gamma rays	7000	20

When you are in hospital with an injury or illness you might be treated with x-rays. The dose for most x-rays treatment is low – about 0.001 mSv for an x-ray of your hand and about 0.1 mSv for a chest x-ray. Some treatments can produce more. A Computer Tomograph (CT) scan on the body can expose the patient to a dose of about 10 mSv.

STUDY QUESTIONS

1 In Table 1, the value of Q for alpha radiation is 20. Why is it so high?
2 What does a sievert measure?
3 Summarise the effects of high, moderate and low doses of radiation on us.
4 What precautions do radiographers in a hospital take before taking an X-ray photograph of a patient?
5 Many modern watches and clocks do not have luminous dials. Instead they have small lights that turn on at the press of a switch. Explain why lights are safer.

6 Use the data in Table 2 to show that exposure to alpha radiation is more likely to cause cancer than exposure to gamma radiation or X-rays.
7 In a nuclear reactor disaster about 200 workers are exposed to a radiation dose equivalent to 2 Sv. Use the data in the text to estimate the number of them likely to die from cancer some time after the accident.
8 Use the information in the text to work out how many days of background radiation is equivalent to the dose from a chest x-ray.

7.7 Inside the nucleus

Figure 7.1 Greek philosopher Democritus.

Democritus, a Greek philosopher, lived from 460–370BC. He was the first person to suggest the idea of atoms (small particles that cannot be cut or divided). Democritus was very accurate in his suggestion but he had no evidence. Now we talk of atoms and their nuclei. What evidence do we have?

■ Atoms in the nineteenth century

By the end of the nineteenth century scientists understood that matter was made of atoms. Evidence from experiments such as Brownian motion (Chapter 5.8) helped us to think of atoms as hard bouncy balls, with gas atoms or molecules moving quickly, hitting the walls of their containers and exerting a pressure. By this time J.J. Thomson had discovered the electron. He knew that matter was neutral and made up of equal numbers of positive and negative charges. Thomson suggested that atoms were made up of a ball of positive charge dotted with negative electrons. This idea is known as the 'plum pudding' model of the atom – rather like a solid pudding with plums in it.

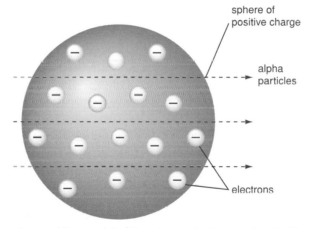

Figure 7.2 The plum pudding model of the atom – electrons embedded in a positive ball. Geiger and Marsden expected fast-moving alpha particles to pass straight through such an atom.

In 1909 Geiger and Marsden discovered a way of exploring the insides of atoms. They directed a beam of alpha particles at a thin sheet of gold foil. Alpha particles were known to be positively charged helium ions, He^{2+}, which were travelling very quickly. They had expected all of these energetic particles to pass straight through the thin foil because they thought the atom was like Professor Thomson's soft plum pudding model. Much to their surprise they discovered that a very small number of them bounced back, although most of them travelled through the foil without any noticeable change of direction.

■ The nuclear model of the atom

Rutherford produced a theory to explain these results; this is illustrated in Figure 7.3. He suggested that the atom is made up of a very small positively charged nucleus, which is surrounded by electrons that are negatively charged. His idea was that the electrons orbit around the nucleus in the

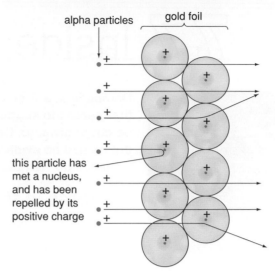

Figure 7.3 Most of the alpha particles pass straight through the gold foil or are deflected slightly. A very small number bounce back; this happens when an alpha particle makes a 'direct hit' on the nucleus.

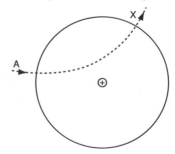

Figure 7.4

same way that planets orbit around the Sun. The gap between the nucleus and electrons is large; the diameter of the atom is about 100 000 times larger than the diameter of the nucleus itself (Figure 7.4).

■ Alpha scattering explained

Because so much of the atom is empty space (Figure 7.4) most of the alpha particles could pass through it without getting close to the nucleus. Some particles passed close to the nucleus and so the positive charges of the alpha particle and the nucleus repelled each other, causing a small deflection. A small number of particles met the nucleus head on; these were turned back the way they came (Figure 7.3). The fact that only a very tiny fraction of the alpha particles bounced backwards tells us that the nucleus is very small indeed. Rutherford proposed that all the mass and positive charge of an atom are contained in the nucleus; the electrons outside the nucleus balance the charge of the protons. Rutherford did not know that there are neutrons in the nucleus; these were not discovered until 1933.

STUDY QUESTIONS

1 Explain why Geiger and Marsden used a vacuum for their alpha particle experiment.
2 Describe the path of an alpha particle that is aimed:
   a) midway between two gold atoms
   b) directly at the nucleus of the gold atom.
3 a) Describe J.J. Thomson's plum pudding model of the atom.
   b) Why did Geiger and Marsden's experiment cause them to reject the plum pudding model?
   c) Explain how Geiger and Marsden's experiment led Rutherford to propose the nuclear model of the atom.
4 The diagram shows the path of an alpha particle being deflected by the charge of a gold nucleus. Make two copies of the diagram.
   a) On one diagram, show the paths of two alpha particles entering along path A when:

   i) one particle is travelling faster
   ii) the second particle is travelling slower than before.

   b) On your second diagram show the paths of two alpha particles entering along path A, travelling at the same speed as before, but now the nucleus has:
   i) a larger charge than a gold nucleus
   ii) a smaller charge than a gold nucleus.

7.8 Nuclear fission

Radioactive zirconium-coated fuel rods produce a blue glow in the water surrounding them. The radiation is caused by high-speed charged particles passing through the water. Why are there traces of zirconium in uranium fuel rods?

Figure 8.1 Nuclear reactor radiation.

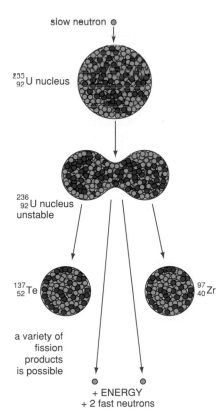

Figure 8.2 The fission of a uranium-235 nucleus.

slow neutron

$^{235}_{92}$U nucleus

$^{236}_{92}$U nucleus unstable

$^{137}_{52}$Te

$^{97}_{40}$Zr

a variety of fission products is possible

+ ENERGY
+ 2 fast neutrons

■ Fission

You read in Chapter 7.2 of this section that the nuclei of some large atoms are unstable and that to become more stable they lose an alpha or a beta particle. Some heavy nuclei, uranium-235 for example, may also increase their stability by **fission**. Figure 8.2 shows how this works. Unlike alpha or beta decay, which happens at random, the fission of a nucleus is usually caused by a neutron hitting it. The ^{235}U nucleus absorbs this neutron and turns into a ^{236}U nucleus, which is so very unstable that it splits into two smaller nuclei. The nuclei that are left are very rarely identical; two or three energetic neutrons are also emitted. The remaining nuclei are usually radioactive and will decay by the emission of beta particles to form more stable nuclei.

■ Nuclear energy

In Figure 8.2, just after fission has been completed, the tellurium-137 ($^{137}_{52}$Te) and the zirconium-97 nucleus ($^{97}_{40}$Zr) are pushed apart by the strong electrostatic repulsion of their nuclear charges. In this way the nuclear energy is transferred to the kinetic energy of the fission fragments. When these fast-moving fragments hit other atoms, this kinetic energy is transferred to heat energy.

283

The fission process releases a tremendous amount of energy. The fission of a nucleus provides about 40 times more energy than the release of an alpha particle from a nucleus. Fission is important because we can control the rate at which it happens, so that we can use the energy released to create electrical energy.

■ Chain reaction

Once a nucleus has divided by fission, the neutrons that are emitted can strike other neighbouring nuclei and cause them to split as well. This **chain reaction** is shown in Figure 8.3. Depending on how we control this process we have two completely different uses for it. In a controlled chain reaction, on average only one neutron from each fission will strike another nucleus and cause it to divide. This is what we want to happen in a power station.

In an uncontrolled chain reaction most of the two or three neutrons from each fission strike other nuclei. This is how nuclear ('atomic') bombs are made. It is a frightening thought that a piece of pure uranium-235 the size of a tennis ball has enough stored energy to flatten a town.

■ Nuclear power stations

Figure 8.4 shows a gas-cooled **nuclear reactor**. The energy released by the fission processes in the uranium fuel rods produces a lot of heat. This heat is carried away by carbon dioxide gas, which is pumped around the reactor. The hot gas then boils water to produce steam, which can be used to work the electrical generators.

- The **fuel rods** are made of uranium-238, 'enriched' with about 3% uranium-235. Uranium-238 is the most common isotope of uranium, but it is only uranium-235 that will produce energy by fission.

Figure 8.3 A chain reaction in uranium-235 (the fission fragments have been omitted for clarity).

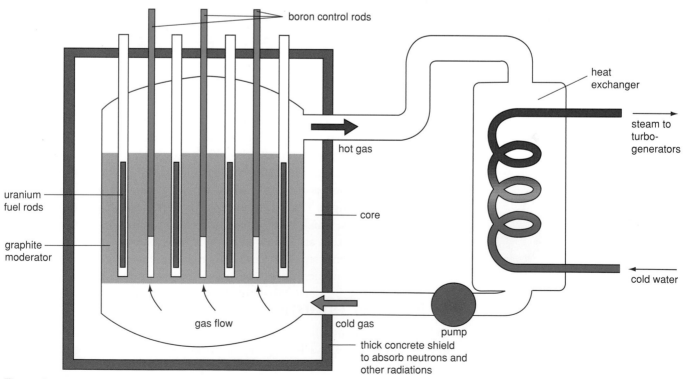

Figure 8.4 A gas-cooled nuclear reactor.

- The fuel rods are embedded in graphite, which is called a **moderator**. The purpose of a moderator is to slow down neutrons that are produced in fission. A nucleus is split more easily by a slow-moving neutron. The fuel rods are long and thin so that neutrons can escape. Neutrons leave one rod and cause another nucleus to split in a neighbouring rod.
- The rate of production of energy in the reactor is carefully regulated by the **boron control rods**. Boron absorbs neutrons very well, so by lowering the control rods into the reactor the reaction can be slowed down. In the event of an emergency the rods are pushed right into the core of the reactor and the chain reaction stops completely.

■ Nuclear equations

Figure 8.2 showed a possible fission of a uranium nucleus. This fission reaction can be described by an equation:

$$^{1}_{0}n + ^{235}_{92}U \rightarrow ^{137}_{52}Te + ^{97}_{40}Zr + 2^{1}_{0}n$$

The mass and atomic numbers on each side balance. However, very accurate measurement shows that the mass on the left-hand side of the equation is slightly more than the mass on the right-hand side. This small reduction in mass is the source of the released nuclear energy.

Now watch the animation *Nuclear fission and fusion.*

STUDY QUESTIONS

1 a) Explain what is meant by nuclear fission?
   b) In what way is fission (i) similar to, (ii) different from radioactive decay?
2 What is a chain reaction? Explain how the chain reaction works in a nuclear bomb and in a nuclear power station.
3 The following questions are about the nuclear reactor shown in Figure 8.4.
   a) What is the purpose of the concrete shield surrounding the reactor?
   b) Why is carbon dioxide gas pumped through the reactor?
   c) Which isotope of uranium produces the energy in the fuel rods?
   d) Will the fuel rods last for ever?
   e) What is the purpose of the graphite moderator?
   f) What would you do if the reactor core suddenly got too hot?
4 This question is about producing energy inside a nuclear reactor core like that shown in Figure 8.4.

This core has 1700 uranium fuel rods. Use the data in the box below to answer the following questions.
   a) How much ^{235}U is there in the core?
   b) What is the total amount of heat energy that this amount of ^{235}U can release?
   c) How long will this amount of nuclear fuel last for, if the core produces power continuously?
   d) How long would the fuel last if the power station is only 33% efficient?

- Mass of one fuel rod is 14 kg.
- 3% of the fuel is ^{235}U.
- Power produced in the reactor core is 2400 MW.
- 1 kg of ^{235}U produces 10^{14} J of heat energy.
- There are 3×10^{7} s in 1 year.

---

5 After absorbing a neutron, uranium-235 can also split into the nuclei barium-141 ($^{141}_{56}Ba$) and krypton-92 ($^{92}_{36}Kr$). Write a balanced symbol equation to show how many neutrons are emitted in this reaction.

7.9 Nuclear power: the future?

Figure 9.1 The Cattenom nuclear power plant in France.

France produces 80% of its electricity using nuclear power. There are about 25 nuclear sites in the country. The Cattenom site accommodates four 1300 MW nuclear reactors. In 2001, over 70% of the nation was in favour of the nuclear programme, but in 2011, after the accident at the Fukushima nuclear plant in Japan, the level of support had dropped to around 50%. Do you think nuclear power should be used in your country?

Chapters 4.8 to 4.10 provide most of the information you need about energy resources and electricity production. This chapter focuses on the debate surrounding nuclear power – do the benefits of electricity generated with low carbon emission outweigh the risks associated with an accident such as the Fukushima disaster of 2011?

■ Nuclear power in France

After an oil supply crisis in 1973, France made the decision to generate most of its electricity using nuclear power. Figure 9.2 shows the progress made, up to the early twenty-first century. Now nearly 80% of the country's electricity is generated in nuclear power stations, which is the highest percentage in the world.

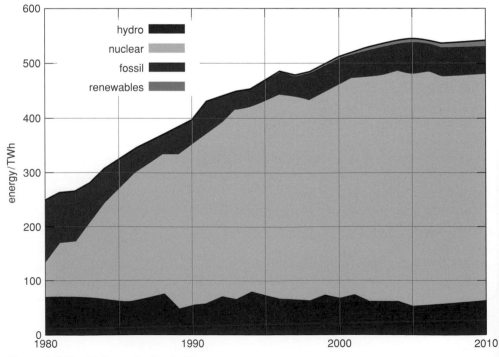

Figure 9.2 Electricity production in France.

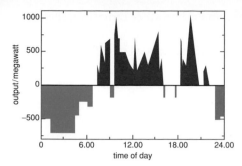

Figure 9.3

Unlike fossil-fuel based power plants, nuclear power plants are quite inflexible. The output from a gas-fired power plant, for example, can be easily adjusted to meet demand. However, the output from a nuclear power plant cannot be changed quickly. France solves this problem in two ways. About 18% of its surplus energy is exported to Italy, the Netherlands, Belgium, Britain and Germany. Also, surplus capacity at night is used to store energy in hydroelectric pumped storage power stations (see Study Question 4 in Chapter 4.8). Figure 9.3 shows how this works. The green area shows power being used to pump water uphill (see also Chapter 10 of Section 4) and the red area illustrates how the pumped storage system can be used to generate power at peak times of the day.

■ Fast-breeder reactors

At present, most nuclear reactors use uranium as fuel, but only 0.7% of the naturally occurring element is the fissionable uranium 235, with most of the element being uranium-238. There are sufficient resources of uranium now, but a **fast-breeder reactor** allows us to produce a new fissionable fuel, **plutonium**.

Plutonium is an element that does not occur naturally, but is produced from uranium-238, as shown in Figure 9.4. A fast-moving neutron (hence the name 'fast reactor') is absorbed by a uranium-238 nucleus to make uranium-239. That nucleus decays by emitting a β-particle to form neptunium-239 (^{239}Np), and a further β emission from the neptunium nucleus produces plutonium-239 (^{239}Pu). Plutonium is fissionable and can be used as a nuclear fuel. By producing plutonium, we could increase our stocks of nuclear fuel.

■ The nuclear debate

Is nuclear power the way forwards? This issue was a matter for debate in France in the 2012 general election. The Union for a Popular Movement party (UMP) were in favour of keeping a high reliance on nuclear power, whereas the Socialist party were in favour of closing France's 24 oldest nuclear reactors by 2025. Listed below are some points that could be made on both sides of the argument.

Views in favour of nuclear power stations

- Fossil fuels are running out, so nuclear power provides a convenient way of producing electricity.
- Nuclear power stations produce a very small level of radiation.
- Coal-fired power stations put out more radiation into the atmosphere than nuclear-power stations, because coal is naturally radioactive. Burning coal also produces acid rain and considerable air pollution.
- Radioactive waste can be safely stored.
- The chances of a large nuclear accident in most countries are very small.

Views against nuclear power stations

- Fossil fuels are running out, so we should be looking to conserve energy. Research should be done to use more of renewable energy sources such as wind and wave power.

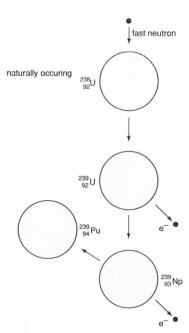

Figure 9.4 Production of plutonium from uranium.

- Coal-fired power stations cause acid rain and produce radiation; they should be closed down as well.
- Nuclear power stations produce dangerous quantities of radioactive waste.
- It is irresponsible to store radioactive wastes with long half-lives; it pollutes the environment for our grandchildren.
- The fact remains that a power station blew up in 1986, and the Fukushima plant was devastated in 2011. We also need to remember that a nuclear plant might be a target for terrorists.

Figure 9.5 A lot of people are worried by the dumping of radioactive waste.

 Now go through the tutorial *Nuclear fission and fusion*.

STUDY QUESTIONS

1 a) State and explain three points in favour of the use of nuclear power in the France to produce electricity.

b) State and explain three points against the use of nuclear power in the France.

c) Evaluate the arguments and decide whether you are for or against the use of nuclear power to produce electricity.

2 a) Why does France export electricity to other countries?

b) Explain how pumped storage power stations are used in France together with nuclear power stations.

3 a) Explain how a fast-breeder reactor could greatly increase the supply of fissionable nuclear fuel.

b) Write nuclear equations to describe the three stages of producing plutonium from uranium shown in Figure 9.4.

4 After the Fukushima disaster, the Japanese Government decided to close all their nuclear power stations. In the UK, the Government plans to start

building new nuclear power stations. Discuss the reasons for these differences in policy.

5 Uranium is the heaviest naturally occurring element, with an atomic number of 92. Elements with higher atomic numbers can be made artificially in nuclear reactors. These are called **transuranic elements**; they are all unstable and undergo radioactive decay. These elements are created by colliding (at high energies) and then fusing together smaller elements. The equation below shows an example of how rutherfordium (Rf) is made.

$$^{238}_{92}U + {}^{26}_{12}Mg \rightarrow {}^{259}_{104}Rf + x{}^{1}_{0}n$$

a) Balance the equation to find the number for x – to show how many neutrons are emitted in this reaction.

b) Rutherfordium-259 emits alpha particles to decay to the element nobelim (No), which emits a further alpha particle to decay to fermium (Fm). Write equations to show the atomic and mass numbers of those two isotopes.

Summary

 Make sure you can answer all the questions in the *Interactive quiz*.

I am confident that:

✓ I can describe the structure of the atom
- The atom is electrically neutral: each proton in the nucleus carries a positive charge, which is balanced by the negative charge on an equal number of electrons.
- The mass of the atom is concentrated in the nucleus: a proton and a neutron have approximately the same mass – an electron has a very small mass by comparison.

✓ I can recall definitions and use symbols correctly
- Atomic (proton) number: the number of protons in the nucleus.
- Mass (nucleon) number: the number of protons and neutrons in the nucleus.
- An ion is formed by either adding or removing an electron from a neutral atom.
- An isotope of an atom is another atom that has the same number of protons, but a different number of neutrons.

✓ I can explain radioactivity
- An alpha particle is a helium nucleus ($^{4}_{2}$He)
- A beta particle is a fast-moving electron ($^{0}_{-1}$e).
- A gamma ray is a short-wavelength electromagnetic wave.
- An alpha particle travels 5 cm through air and is stopped by paper.
- Beta particles travel many metres through air and can be stopped by aluminium sheet a few millimetres thick.
- Gamma rays travel great distances through air and can only be absorbed effectively by very thick lead sheets – several centimetres thick.

✓ I understand nuclear transformation
- On ejecting an α- or a β-particle a nucleus is transformed into another nucleus (a γ-ray makes no change to its nucleus). Two examples are:

α-particle decay	$^{238}_{92}$U $\rightarrow$ $^{234}_{90}$Th + $^{4}_{2}$He
β-particle decay	$^{234}_{90}$Th $\rightarrow$ $^{234}_{91}$Pa + $^{0}_{-1}$e

- β-decay causes the atomic number to increase by 1.

✓ I can calculate radioactive decay
- Radioactive decay is a random process – like throwing a lot of dice or tossing a lot of coins.
- In one half-life, half of the radioactive nuclei will decay. In a further half-life, a further half of what is left will decay.
  - After 1 half-life, ½ the sample is left
  - after 2 half-lifes, ¼ of the sample is left
  - after 3 half-lifes, ⅛ of the sample is left, and so on.

✓ I can discuss hazards of radiation
- Alpha particles, beta particles and gamma rays are ionising radiations. These radiations knock electrons out of atoms thereby making ions.

✓ I understand Rutherford scattering
- When alpha particles are directed towards a thin metal foil (such as gold), most of them pass through with no or only a small deviation. However, a very small number bounce back. This is because the nucleus of the atom is very small, massive and positively charged.

✓ I understand nuclear fission
- A large nucleus can split into two; this is called nuclear fission. This process releases a lot of energy, which can be used to generate electricity in power stations.
- Unlike radioactive decay, fission can be controlled.
- Fission can be triggered by a neutron. The neutrons released in the fission reaction trigger further fissions in other nuclei. This is a chain reaction.

$$^{1}_{0}n + {}^{235}_{92}U \rightarrow {}^{137}_{52}Te + {}^{97}_{40}Zr + 2{}^{1}_{0}n$$

- The fission reaction can be controlled in a nuclear reactor by boron rods.

Exam-style questions

1 a) Copy and complete the table about atomic particles.

Atomic particle	Relative mass	Relative charge
proton		+1
neutron	1	0
electron	negligible	

[2]

b) Read the following passage about sodium.

Sodium is an element with an atomic number of 11.

Its most common isotope is sodium-23, $^{23}_{11}$Na.

Another isotope, sodium-24, is a radioisotope.

i) State the number of protons, neutrons and electrons in sodium-23. [2]

ii) Explain why sodium-24 has a different mass number from sodium-23. [1]

iii) What is meant by a radioisotope? [1]

iv) Atoms of sodium-24 change into atoms of magnesium by beta decay. Write an equation to show the atomic and mass numbers of this isotope of magnesium. [2]

v) Give the name, or symbol, of the element formed when an atom of sodium-24 (proton number = 11) emits gamma radiation. [1]

c) i) Name a suitable detector that could be used to show that sodium-24 gives out radiation. [1]

ii) Name a disease that can be caused by too much exposure to a radioactive substance such as sodium-24. [1]

2 a) The table shows the half-life of some radioactive isotopes.

Radioactive isotope	Half-life
aluminium-29	7 minutes
technetium-99	6 hours
rubidium-83	86 days
cobalt-60	5 years

i) What is meant by the term 'radioactive'? [1]

ii) Which **one** of the isotopes shown in the table is the most suitable for use as a medical tracer? Explain your choice. [2]

iii) Draw a graph to show how the number of radioactive atoms present in the isotope cobalt-60 will change with time. [2]

3 a) Copy and complete the following table for an atom of actinium-225 ($^{225}_{89}$Ac).

mass number	225
number of protons	89
number of neutrons	

[1]

b) Explain what is meant by the terms 'atomic number' and 'mass number'. [2]

c) An atom of actinium-225 ($^{225}_{89}$Ac) decays to form an atom of francium-221 ($^{221}_{87}$Fr).

i) What type of radiation – alpha, beta or gamma – is emitted by actinium-225? [1]

ii) Why does an atom that decays by emitting alpha or beta radiation become an atom of a different element? [1]

4 The radioactive isotope, carbon-14, decays by beta (β) particle emission.

a) Plants absorb carbon-14 from the atmosphere. The graph shows the decay curve for 1 g of modern linen made from a flax plant. The radioactivity is caused by a small fraction of carbon-14 in the linen sample.

Use the graph to find the half-life of carbon-14. [2]

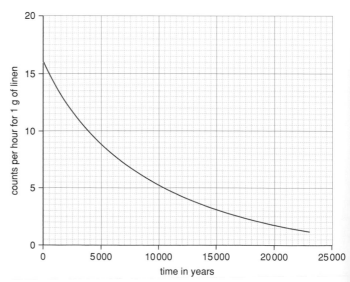

b) Linen has been used to make clothes for thousands of years. It contains radioactive carbon-14, which decays. An old sample of linen has a smaller fraction of carbon-14 than a new sample of linen. A museum has a shirt that may be 2000 years old. The carbon-14 in a 1 g sample of the shirt produces 300 counts in a day.

Is the shirt really 2000 years old? Explain your answer. [3]

c) Suggest why carbon dating is unsuitable for dating samples thought to be:

   i) 100 years old

   ii) 50 000 years old. [2]

5 The table gives information about some of the radioactive substances released into the air by the explosion at the Fukoshima nuclear plant in 2011.

Radioactive substance	Half-life	Type of radiation emitted
iodine-131	8 days	beta and gamma
caesium-134	2 years	beta
caesium-137	30 years	beta

a) How is the structure of a caesium-134 atom different from the structure of a caesium-137 atom? [1]

b) Explain what beta and gamma radiations are. [2]

c) A sample of soil is contaminated with some iodine-131. Its activity is 40 000 Bq. Calculate how long it will take for the activity to drop to 1250 Bq. [2]

d) Which of the three isotopes will be the most dangerous 50 years after the accident? Explain your answer. [2]

6 A radioactive source emits alpha (α), beta (β) and gamma (γ) radiation.

a) Which **two** types of radiation will pass through a sheet of card? [1]

b) Which **two** types of radiation would be deflected by a very strong magnetic field? [2]

c) Which type of radiation has the greatest range in air? [1]

7 Radiation workers wear a special badge to monitor the radiation they receive.

The badge is a lightproof plastic case containing a piece of photographic film. Each worker is given a new badge to wear each month. Part of the film is covered with a thin sheet of aluminium foil.

a) Explain how the badge can show:

   i) how much radiation a worker receives each month [2]

   ii) what type of radiation a worker has received. [2]

b) Why do workers in the nuclear power industry monitor their levels of radiation exposure? [2]

8 A radiation detector and counter are used to measure the background radiation. The background activity is 10 counts per minute. The same detector and counter are then used to measure the radiation from some radioactive gas. The graph shows how the number of counts per minute changes with time.

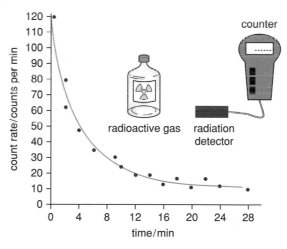

a) Although the readings on the counter are accurately recorded, the points do not exactly fit a smooth curve. Explain why. [2]

b) Explain why the count rate is almost constant after 20 minutes. [2]

c) Use the graph to estimate the half-life of the radioactive gas. [2]

9 The table gives information about some radioactive sources that emit ionising radiation.

Source	Radiation emitted	Half-life
bismuth 213	alpha	45 minutes
iridium-192	beta	74 days
cobalt-60	gamma	5 years
uranium-233	alpha	150 000 years
radon-226	beta	6 minutes
technetium-99	gamma	6 hours

a) What is 'half-life'? [2]

b) i) Explain what is meant by the term 'ionising radiation'. [2]

   ii) Which of the radiations shown in the table is the most ionising? [1]

c) Radiation has many uses in hospitals. Choose a source of radiation from the table for each of the following uses, explaining each of your choices:

   i) to sterilise plastic syringes sealed in a strong plastic bag [3]

   ii) as a medical tracer that is injected into a body and then detected outside the body [3]

   iii) to be used in the form of a wire implant to treat breast cancer (this is called short-range internal radiotherapy) [3]

   iv) to be used in a chemical to treat leukaemia (blood cancer) inside the body (this is called targeted alpha therapy [TAT]). [3]

10 In the early twentieth century scientists thought that atoms were made up of electrons embedded inside a ball of positive charge. They called this the 'plum pudding' model of the atom.

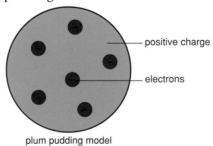

plum pudding model

Geiger and Marsden fired a beam of alpha particles at a thin gold foil. Explain how the results of their experiment led to a new model of the atom. Illustrate your answer with suitable diagrams. [6]

11 a) The diagram shows what can happen when the nucleus of a uranium atom absorbs a neutron.

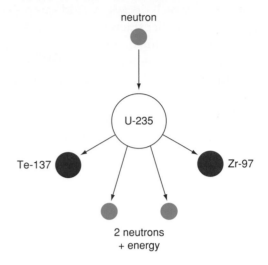

   i) What name is given to the process shown in the diagram? [1]

   ii) Explain how this process could lead to a chain reaction. You may copy and add to the diagram to help your answer. [3]

   iii) How does the mass number of an atom change when its nucleus absorbs a neutron? [1]

b) Uranium-235 is used as a fuel in some nuclear reactors. The reactor core contains control rods used to absorb neutrons. Explain what happens when the control rods are lowered into the reactor. [3]

12 The diagram shows the variation in background radiation in parts of Britain.

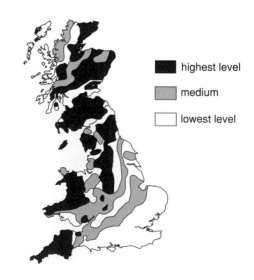

a) The background radiation is calculated by finding the average value of a large number of readings. Suggest why this method is used. [1]

b) The high levels of radiation in some parts of Britain are caused by radon gas escaping from underground rocks such as granite.

Radium-224 ($^{224}_{88}$Ra) decays to form radon-220 ($^{220}_{86}$Rn).

 i) What particle is emitted when radium-224 decays? [1]

 ii) Radon-220 then decays to polonium by emitting an alpha particle. Copy and complete the decay equation for radon-220.

$$^{220}_{86}Rn \rightarrow Po + He$$
[2]

 iii) The half-lives of these isotopes are given in the table.

Isotope	Half-life
radium-224	3.6 days
radon-220	52 seconds

A sample of radium-224 decays at the rate of 360 nuclei per second. The number of radon-220 nuclei is growing at less than 360 per second. Suggest a reason for this. [1]

 iv) Radon-220 has a short half-life and it emits the least penetrative of the three main types of radioactive emissions. Explain why the presence of radon gas in buildings is a health hazard. [2]

13 The diagram shows the piston in the cylinder of a car engine. When the car engine is running, the piston moves up and down inside the cylinder many times each second, which causes the cylinder wall to become worn.

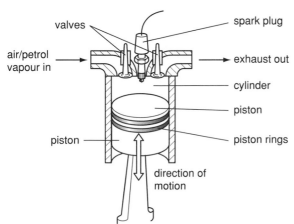

A car manufacturer wants to run tests to measure the wear of the cylinder wall due to the piston movement. A radioactive isotope of chromium with a short half-life is used.

a) Explain what is meant by an isotope. [1]

b) Explain the term 'half-life'. [1]

c) A very thin layer of the radioactive isotope is placed on the inside wall of the cylinder and the car engine run continuously. A detector is placed outside the cylinder to measure the count rate.

 i) Which type of emission from the radioactive isotope would be needed to reach the detector through the metal wall of the cylinder? [1]

 ii) State the name of a detector that could be used to measure the count rate. [1]

d) The half-life of the emitter is 23 hours and the count rate taken at the start of the test was 600 counts/hour.

 i) What would you expect the count rate to be after 46 hours? [2]

 ii) The count rate measured after 46 hours was actually 120 counts/hour. This was explained by assuming that part of the layer of radioactive isotope on the cylinder wall had been worn away. Calculate the fraction that had been worn away. State one assumption you have made in your calculation. [2]

 iii) Explain why the half-life of the radioactive isotope has to be short but not too short. [1]

EXTEND AND CHALLENGE

1 The brain can suffer from a particularly nasty cancer called a glioblastoma. This cancer penetrates the brain and cannot be cured by surgery. Instead the neurosurgeon gives the patient an injection that contains some boron. The boron is absorbed by the glioblastoma. Then the patient is irradiated with neutrons. The following reaction occurs:

$$^{10}_{5}B + ^{1}_{0}n \rightarrow ^{7}_{3}Li + ^{x}_{y}He$$

a) Copy the equation and fill in numbers x and y.
b) The boron nucleus splits up to form lithium and helium. What is this process called? Explain why the lithium and helium nuclei move away from each other very quickly.
c) Explain how this process can kill the glioblastoma.
d) Why is this process dangerous for healthy patients?

2 Plutonium-241 is unstable and it decays by giving out an alpha particle. This is the start of a long decay series. By the emission of more alpha and beta particles, eventually a stable isotope of bismuth is made. The table shows the decay series. For example, $^{241}_{94}Pu$ decays by emitting an α particle to form $^{237}_{92}U$. Copy the table and replace the question marks.

Element	Symbol	Radioactive emission
plutonium	$^{241}_{94}Pu$	α
uranium	$^{237}_{92}U$	β
neptunium	$^{?}_{?}Np$	α
protactinium	$^{?}_{91}Pa$	β
uranium	$^{233}_{?}U$	?
thorium	$^{229}_{90}Th$	α
radium	$^{?}_{?}Ra$	β
actinium	$^{?}_{?}Ac$	?
francium	$^{221}_{87}Fr$	?
astatine	$^{217}_{85}At$	α
bismuth	$^{?}_{?}Bi$	?
polonium	$^{213}_{84}Po$	α
lead	$^{?}_{?}Pb$	β
bismuth	$^{209}_{83}Bi$	stable

3 The diagram shows a method that is used in factories to check the thickness of polythene being produced. In this case a long radioactive source is placed below the whole width of the polythene and a long Geiger-Muller tube is place above it.

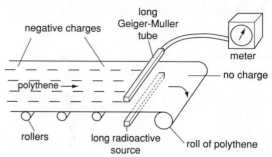

A Geiger-Muller tube is used for detecting radiation. The output pulses of current from the tube may go into a counter, an amplifier connected to a loudspeaker or a meter. In this application, the reading on the meter can then be used as a measure of thickness of the polythene; the thicker the polythene, the lower the meter reading.

When the polythene passes over the rollers, effects of friction cause it to become negatively charged. The presence of the radioactive source enables the polythene to become discharged.

a) It is suggested that because radioactive decay is random this method for checking thickness gives better results when the polythene is going through slowly.
   i) What is meant by *random*?
   ii) Why is the result likely to be more reliable when the polythene is going through slowly?
b) Radiation from the radioactive source ionises the air. This produces many positive and negative ions from atoms in the air. Discuss how these ions are affected by the negative charge on the polythene and hence explain how the polythene becomes discharged.
c) If sources of similar activity giving either α or β radiation were available, which one would be better for:
   i) measuring the thickness of the polythene
   ii) discharging the roll?
   Explain your choice in each case.
d) In view of the presence of the radioactive material, state any **two** suitable precautions that should be observed for the safety of factory workers.
e) A buyer of polythene visits the factory and is alarmed by the use of radioactive sources in the method shown. He is concerned that the polythene may become radioactive.
   i) Why has he no real cause for concern?
   ii) Explain an experimental check that you could make to confirm there is no cause for concern.

Index

Index